The Normative Nature of Social Practices and Ethics in Professional Environments

Marc J. de Vries
Delft University of Technology, The Netherlands

Henk Jochemsen
Wageningen University & Research, The Netherlands

A volume in the Advances in Religious and Cultural Studies (ARCS) Book Series

IGI Global
DISSEMINATOR OF KNOWLEDGE

Published in the United States of America by
IGI Global
Information Science Reference (an imprint of IGI Global)
701 E. Chocolate Avenue
Hershey PA, USA 17033
Tel: 717-533-8845
Fax: 717-533-8661
E-mail: cust@igi-global.com
Web site: http://www.igi-global.com

Library of Congress Cataloging-in-Publication Data

Names: Vries, Marc J. de, 1958- editor. | Jochemsen, H., editor.
Title: The normative nature of social practices and ethics in professional environments / Marc J. de Vries and Henk Jochemsen, editors.
Description: Hershey, PA : Information Science Reference, [2019]
Identifiers: LCCN 2018042411| ISBN 9781522580065 (hardcover) | ISBN 9781522580072 (ebook)
Subjects: LCSH: Business ethics. | Professional ethics.
Classification: LCC HF5387 .N665 2019 | DDC 174/.4--dc23 LC record available at https://lccn.loc.gov/2018042411

This book is published in the IGI Global book series Advances in Religious and Cultural Studies (ARCS) (ISSN: 2475-675X; eISSN: 2475-6768)

British Cataloguing in Publication Data
A Cataloguing in Publication record for this book is available from the British Library.

Advances in Religious and Cultural Studies (ARCS) Book Series

ISSN:2475-675X
EISSN:2475-6768

Editor-in-Chief: Nancy Erbe, California State University-Dominguez Hills, USA

MISSION

In the era of globalization, the diversity of the world and various cultures becomes apparent as cross-cultural interactions turn into a daily occurrence for individuals in all professions. Understanding these differences is necessary in order to promote effective partnerships and interactions between those from different religious and cultural backgrounds.

The **Advances in Religious and Cultural Studies (ARCS)** book series brings together a collection of scholarly publications on topics pertaining to religious beliefs, culture, population studies, and sociology. Books published within this series arc ideal for professionals, theorists, researchers, and students seeking the latest research on collective human behavior in terms of religion, social structure, and cultural identity and practice.

COVERAGE

- Social Stratification and Classes
- Cultural Identity
- Globalization and Culture
- Group Behavior
- Stereotypes and Racism
- Politics and Religion
- Sociology
- Cross-Cultural Interaction
- Cults and Religious Movements
- Impact of Religion on Society

IGI Global is currently accepting manuscripts for publication within this series. To submit a proposal for a volume in this series, please contact our Acquisition Editors at Acquisitions@igi-global.com or visit: http://www.igi-global.com/publish/.

The Advances in Religious and Cultural Studies (ARCS) Book Series (ISSN 2475-675X) is published by IGI Global, 701 E. Chocolate Avenue, Hershey, PA 17033-1240, USA, www.igi-global.com. This series is composed of titles available for purchase individually; each title is edited to be contextually exclusive from any other title within the series. For pricing and ordering information please visit http://www.igi-global.com/book-series/advances-religious-cultural-studies/84269. Postmaster: Send all address changes to above address.

Titles in this Series

For a list of additional titles in this series, please visit:
https://www.igi-global.com/book-series/advances-religious-cultural-studies/84269

Music and Messaging in the African Political Arena
Uche T. Onyebadi (Texas Christian University, USA)
Information Science Reference • ©2019 • 321pp • H/C (ISBN: 9781522572954) • US $175.00

Global Diaspora Politics and Social Movements Emerging Research and Opportunities
Emily B. Stacey (Swansea University, UK)
Information Science Reference • ©2019 • 142pp • H/C (ISBN: 9781522577577) • US $165.00

Conservation, Restoration, and Analysis of Architectural and Archaeological Heritage
Carlo Inglese (Sapienza University of Rome, Italy) and Alfonso Ippolito (Sapienza University of Rome, Italy)
Information Science Reference • ©2019 • 485pp • H/C (ISBN: 9781522575559) • US $195.00

Analysis, Conservation, and Restoration of Tangible and Intangible Cultural Heritage
Carlo Inglese (Sapienza University of Rome, Italy) and Alfonso Ippolito (Sapienza University of Roma, Italy)
Information Science Reference • ©2019 • 491pp • H/C (ISBN: 9781522569367) • US $195.00

Infocommunication Skills as a Rehabilitation and Social Reintegration Tool for Inmates
Lídia Oliveira (University of Aveiro, Portugal) and Daniela Graça (University of Aveiro, Portugal)
Information Science Reference • ©2019 • 326pp • H/C (ISBN: 9781522559757) • US $175.00

Post-Holocaust Studies in a Modern Context
Nitza Davidovitch (Ariel University, Israel) Ronen A. Cohen (Ariel University, Israel) and Eyal Lewin (Ariel University, Israel)
Information Science Reference • ©2019 • 286pp • H/C (ISBN: 9781522562580) • US $185.00

Handbook of Research on Heritage Management and Preservation
Patrick Ngulube (University of South Africa, South Africa)
Information Science Reference • ©2018 • 508pp • H/C (ISBN: 9781522531371) • US $265.00

For an entire list of titles in this series, please visit:
https://www.igi-global.com/book-series/advances-religious-cultural-studies/84269

IGI Global
DISSEMINATOR OF KNOWLEDGE

701 East Chocolate Avenue, Hershey, PA 17033, USA
Tel: 717-533-8845 x100 • Fax: 717-533-8661
E-Mail: cust@igi-global.com • www.igi-global.com

Table of Contents

Detailed Table of Contents

The concept of social practices has received growing attention in interpretative social sciences. This concept is based on a long tradition of hermeneutical, interpretative, action-theoretical, pragmatist, and phenomenological theories in the social sciences, starting with Weber's famous definition of social action. In this chapter, some crucial stepping stones of this tradition are highlighted. In the line of these theories, a new approach of normative practices will be introduced, partially based on core philosophical insights of the Dutch philosopher Herman Dooyeweerd. Central features of this approach are 1) the multi-layered, intrinsically normative structure of social practices (constitutive side) and 2) the importance of regulative convictions, ideals, and attitudes leading the disclosure and development of those practices (regulative side).

Section 2

The 2015 Paris agreement challenges the industry to realize their sustainability goals. The objective of this chapter is to support engineers from R&D departments in the chemical process industry to develop processes and systems that are in agreement with these goals. The authors propose the so-called Triple I model that offers three perspectives to direct the development of sustainable practices. This model encourages engineers to identify all relevant aspects, to integrate the knowledge of different disciplines, and to meet the justified interests of stakeholders. In this chapter, the importance of ideals and basic beliefs is highlighted. First of all, ideals and basic beliefs place the sustainable development of the process industry in a broader perspective. In addition, ideals and basic beliefs motivate people to face the challenges of the 2015 Paris agreement and encourage them to develop sustainable solutions.

Engineering is one of the social practices for which a normative practice approach in analyzing tensions in the practice can be fruitful, particularly when combined with an actor-network analysis. That is illustrated in this chapter by the Zayandehrud river case of water management in Iran. The modernist hydrocracy that was installed appeared to backfire strongly and resulted in serious environmental damage. The normative practice analysis shows how conflicting norms between different sub-practices can explain the problems that emerged. The analysis also suggests an alternative for this modernist hydrocracy.

Modern military operations are characterized by ubiquitous use of technology, in particular the use of information and communication technologies for real-time information sharing. The use of technology on the battlefield is assumed to improve decision making in military practice. By making use of a friendly fire incident in Afghanistan, namely the Sangin incident in 2011, the author highlights why moral decision making could be hampered by technology. This is partly due to the fact that information and communication technologies subtly connect sub-practices that exist within the broader military practice, thus potentially blurring normative structures. Blurring of normative structures can cause problems for moral decision making on the battlefield, because it is suddenly not clear who is responsible for the course of action.

Today's predominant food system on the one hand produces plenty of food, making food relatively cheap for most people in the world. However, for many people, the food they can afford is insufficiently nutritious. Major global health problems like obesity are partly a result of the present food system. Furthermore, the modern industrial way of producing food has negative environmental consequences, consisting among others of a decline in soil fertility and a loss of biodiversity. Another food system is required to obtain sustainable global food and nutrition security. This food system should observe the normativity of the agricultural practices that produce food. The authors' analysis of agricultural practices shows that the farm is economically qualified but that the primary process of care for soil, crops, and animals can best be seen as an ethically qualified supporting practice that steers the "meaningful shaping" of the interventions foundational for agricultural practices.

This chapter explains how and why healthcare might profit from a normative practice approach (NPA). This approach sketches a conceptual and normative framework that helps to locate and identify relevant points of view for clinical practice as well as for policy making in healthcare. The chapter starts in medias res: in the consulting room, in the encounter between clinician and patient. What kinds of relations are relevant for the understanding of what is going in the patient who feels ill and between the patient and the doctor (or nurse)? Are there normative principles and values which guide these relationships? The focus then broadens to the meso- and macro-contexts of current medicine and healthcare. The NPA will be re-introduced. Its relevance is shown for topics like the increase in the administrative burden in medicine, the role of expert knowledge, the hospital and its purposes, and the changing focus of medicine given the rapid changes in the macro-sphere. The chapter ends by saying that the NPA may help in different ways: by taking it as a point of reference; by relating the different normative dimensions to core responsibilities of doctors, other employees, and stakeholders beside medical professionals; and by relating these core responsibilities to the relevant contexts in which these doctors, other employees, and stakeholders are working.

Present discontents and concerns about schooling and learning call for critical reflection about education as a practice. Education is not to be degraded to instrumentalism. The profession is about the formation of pupils in a process of interaction to bring them to "human flourishing." Learning implies mastery and self-responsibility, guided by the "right desire" to do what is ultimately good. This "right desire" in the Aristotelian and Christian tradition precedes the work of any professional or practitioner. The normative practice approach serves as a valuable help for the reflection that is needed. It presents a given set of norms that are appropriate to understand a professional practice. Reflection on the "right desire" in schooling, learning, and teaching helps to redirect education in our time of discontent.

In this chapter, the nature of the management practice is investigated. The scene is sketched by telling a couple of stories from the experience of the author. Then, it is argued that an organizational approach is needed to understand the thinking and behavior of managers. It is shown that practice approaches are very suitable because they take their starting point in the daily activities, do justice to the nature of different activities, and make underlying ideals, values, and basic beliefs explicit. The Triple I model is used to investigate the practice of management in detail. It is shown that practices and management practices are intimately intertwined. The author's conclusion is that management is a supportive practice that is disclosed by the intrinsic values of the specific domain.

In September 2015, it appeared that the Volkswagen Group had circumvented the rules for testing diesel car exhaust gases. Although the organization presents itself as eco-friendly, it used a "default device" for diesel cars to produce less CO2 during test situations. Due to this kind of scandal, corporate communication is often associated with greenwashing and the manipulation of minds. Using the normative practice approach, the authors introduce some basic distinctions that may help to come to a better understanding of what the specific duty and responsibility of communication professionals is. They argue that corporate communication stands or falls with public trust. Building confidence and public legitimation is the main task of communication professionals. Although communication is about the construction of a communal world, that does not mean that framing and strategic reasoning are not important. In order to bring in a legitimate point of view, one has to present this point of view in an impactful way. Communication professionals have to balance between the interests of the organization and the requirements of public legitimation. They also have to make convincingly clear how their personal biography and the narrative of the organization are interrelated.

Preface

This book was written because of a real concern and not just because of a theoretical interest. Professionals in various social domains seem to feel unhappy about the way their work is increasingly influenced by a tendency to dehumanize the practice and focus entirely on formal procedures and quantifiable criteria (like efficiency and economic value). This is related to the tendency to treat professional practices as scientific practices, or applications of science. This view, we will argue in this book, is particularly unhelpful for the way professionals experience their work. We will show that the overestimation of - in itself abstract - scientific knowledge, including technological knowledge, has been a source of many tensions in practices. This concern was the reason for developing a philosophical perspective on social practices that would put practices in a different perspective. This so-called Normative Practice Approach was originally developed by, Jan Hoogland, Henk Jochemsen and Gerrit Glas. Later others joined them and applied the approach for different practices. In this book the concept of normative practices is presented and applied to a variety of practices by a team of authors all of whom are involved in normative practice research. In this Preface we will briefly inform the readers how the concept was born and how this book is structured to guide the reader through the Normative Practice Approach and its applications.

In the beginning of the Nineties of last century the Health department of the Dutch government was seeking ways to contain the rising costs of health care. Against that background the Lindeboom Institute for medical ethics, directed at that time by Henk Jochemsen, received a subsidy of the Health department to perform a study to advice the ministry with respect to measures to control the increasing expenses of publicly funded health care. Health care insurance constitutes a significant part of social security and the government wants to prevent social security costs taking too large a share of the national income. It was diagnosed that most expenses in health care flow from the pen of physicians as they prescribe indicated health care provisions, including specialist care and institutionalization in care facilities of psychiatric care, nursing care and others. For the functioning of physicians their *professional autonomy* is considered crucial as it gives the guarantee that the physician can provide the care to patients that is medically indicated, independent of pressure from others, e.g. insurance companies. As will be explained in Chapter 1 characteristic of professions is their liberty to define and control the quality of performance of their profession. But precisely this discretionary freedom of physicians is part of the background of the rising health care expenses. In light of this analysis the government felt the need to have an ethical reflection on the concept of professional autonomy as a requirement for the quality of care and the right of patients to receive care that is medically indicated.

The Lindeboom Institute, with a research team consisting of Jan Hoogland (philosopher), Johan Polder (health economist), Sytse Strijbos (philosopher) and Henk Jochemsen (ethicist, project leader), approached this issue from the perspective of professions, in this case the medical profession. Different understandings of this concept have been defended; in those years the emancipation approach of Freidson was dominant. In this approach professionals were seen as groups of people who tried to use their expertise to improve their social and economic status. Instead of this sociological approach we took a normative approach, emphasizing that professions exist and are respected in a society because they are oriented towards the realization of a certain value that society appreciates. The definition of profession of Alisdair MacIntyre in his 'After virtue' inspired us in this approach. But instead of using MacIntyre's distinction between internal and external goods, we analyzed the concept of practice with the use of philosophical insights of the Amsterdam philosopher Herman Dooyeweerd. We want to point out here that in the curse of this project we developed a first version of the normative practice approach. This enabled us to advice the Health department on the issue of professional autonomy in relation to health policy measures to contain health care expenses. We argued that professional autonomy as the discretionary power of the physician to act primarily on view of the health interests of the patient in the individual treatment relation, is a 'right of the patient', lest financial interests of third parties become to dominate individual treatment decisions. However, the profession should take into account the financial aspect of health care provisions as one of the aspects of quality of care and the profession should monitor the quality of the work of its members and intervene if necessary. Decisions on the provisions in the basic insurance packet should be taken at the level of the government, in consultation with the relevant professions. It should be noted that although the practice approach concentrated on the work of individual professionals (physicians) the approach was developed and applied in view of the position of professionals in larger social political and economic structures. This will come back in several of the contributions to this book. The normative view at the background of discussions of professions in broader structures is that those broader structures should respect as much a possible the intrinsic normativity of the professional practices.

This book is structured as follows. In Section 1 we present the basics of the Normative Practice Approach. Chapter 1 by Glas first elaborates on what we have indicated in this Preface briefly as the need for this approach, namely increasing tensions in professional practices. Chapter 2 provides the philosophical background of the approach, namely the work by Dutch philosopher Herman Dooyeweerd. This philosophy was developed from a Christian perspective. Readers may not share this perspective, but we believe the consequences that are drawn for a philosophical view on reality, in humans, on knowledge and on values will be recognized as valuable also by people who hold different worldviews. In Chapter 3, Hoogland shows how the Normative Practice Approach fits in a broader movement in social philosophy in which the concept of practices is central and relates the NPA to other views on social practices. He also provides a general description of the NPA. This chapter is useful to recognize that sometimes a similar terminology can have different meanings in different perspectives and therefore the chapter helps to see in what respects the normative practice approach is unique as compared to other approaches that sometimes use the same terms. For those who are less interested in the philosophical background of the Normative Practice Approach, Chapters 2 and 3 can initially be skipped when reading this book. There will be references to these texts in later chapters and it is always possible to go back to Chapters 2 and 3 when these references give reason for that.

Section 2 of the book applies the Normative Practice Approach to a variety of professional practices that directly serve a social purpose, like caring for people or educating people. The practices discussed in this section are: industry (Chapter 4), engineering (Chapter 5), military operations (Chapter 6), food (Chapter 7), health (Chapter 8), and education (Chapter 9). Section 3 contains practices that indirectly serve social purposes because they exist to support the sort of practices that are described in Section 2. Management is an example of that, because it supports practices like medical practices or engineering practices. This section begins with two practices that in their organizational realization are mostly embedded in the organizations that represent the practices of Section 2: management (Chapter 10) and communication (Chapter 11). Management is mostly part of another social practices at a higher organization level, like the medical practices (a hospital that has a management department) or the engineering practice (an engineering agency that has a management department). This embedding is not a necessity, though, because a business company can also hire an independent communication bureau to develop a marketing strategy. The remaining two ‘supportive’ practices in Section 3 are, however, mostly independent: international cooperation for development (Chapter 12) and security networks (Chapter 13) are practices in which independent organizations feature to support the sort of type of practices that feature in Section 2. The police, for instance, is not part of a hospital. But it is part of a security network. Exceptions are possible here, too, as a business corporation can have its own security department. That means the boundaries between the first and the latter two supportive practices in Section 3 are not absolute in terms of organizational structures, but they do refer to a difference in the majority of instances.

The book closes with a Conclusion in which we ty together the insights that have been presented over the various chapters. Some common themes that run through the chapters are identified and we present once more what our main concern was in writing this book.

We hope this book will inspire professionals to reflect on their practices and find hope and inspiration for working with pleasure and satisfaction in their respective domains. We as editors and authors believe that the Normative Practice Approach has a value for that and we will certainly keep working on its further elaboration and application.

Marc J. de Vries
Delft University of Technology, The Netherlands

Henk Jochemsen
Wageningen University & Research, The Netherlands

Delft/Wageningen, January 2019

Section 1

Chapter 1
The Crisis in Professionalism and the Need for a Normative Approach

Gerrit Glas
Vrije Universiteit, The Netherlands

ABSTRACT

This chapter analyzes the crisis in professionalism from a historical and conceptual point of view. It describes the development of professional practices as part of the process of modernization (i.e., the rationalization of working processes and the increasing division and specialization of labor). This process was successful, but has also been accompanied by tendencies to bureaucracy, alienation, meaninglessness, and dehumanization. The chapter describes a set of desiderata for a conceptual framework that successfully avoids these pitfalls and sketches how a so-called normative practice approach could provide a conceptual and normative framework that enables professionals to disentangle and remedy the tensions and ambivalences within their professional practices.

INTRODUCTION

This chapter focuses on the concept of professionalism. It gives an analysis of the crisis in professionalism and argues for a normative approach.[1] It provides a conceptual framework to understand professionalism and analyses what is needed to solve critical issues in the current debate about professions. It describes how the development of professional practices should be understood as part of the process of modernization, i.e., the rationalization of working processes and the increasing

DOI: 10.4018/978-1-5225-8006-5.ch001

division and specialization of labor. Critical elements in this process are alienation of laborers from their labor; dehumanizing tendencies in the provision of services; and risk of a decline towards bureaucracy, anonymity and meaninglessness.

The chapter proceeds with a description of what is needed for a professionalism that is able to withstand these tendencies. It ends with a summary of the argument that will be developed in this and the next introductory chapters.

THE CRISIS OF PROFESSIONALISM

Professionalism

Most definitions of professionalism mention expert knowledge and skills as one of its core features, together with certain jurisdictions or privileges of the professional. These jurisdictions and privileges are granted by society and/or patients based on the professional's commitment, accountability, and competence. Among these privileges (and their related requirements) are self-regulation with respect to standards of excellence, membership in the professional subgroup, training requirements, and criteria for licensing and quality control. Rueschemeyer describes the traditional (functionalist) conception of professionals as follows:

Individually and, in association, collectively, the professions 'strike a bargain with society' in which they exchange competence and integrity against the trust of client and community, relative freedom from lay supervision and interference, protection against unqualified competition as well as substantial remuneration and higher social status.(Rueschemeyer, 1983, p. 41)

He also emphasizes that the way we think about expert occupations transcends the confines of occupational sociology and comes close to a central theme in classical sociology: the emergence of modern society and culture as such.

How expert knowledge is deployed in different institutional forms, how it is controlled, how it is used as a resource of power and a basis of privilege, and how in turn different institutional forms of deployment, social control as well as individual and collective advantage, are affected by other and wider social structures and processes—inquiries into these questions tell us much about the structure and the dynamics of society as a whole. (Rueschemeyer, 1983, p. 38)

Moore gives a practical overview and defines the professional as having a full-time occupation, which sets his or her efforts apart from amateurism. The professional has a commitment to a calling; the fulfilment of the profession's requirements is a response to a set of normative and behavioral expectations. Professions are set apart from other forms of occupation by various signs and symbols and are identified by their peers via membership in formalized organizations. Usually the possession of skills and knowledge requires intensive and prolonged training. Professionals need to exhibit an orientation to service; they proceed by their own judgment and authority and are, therefore, professionally autonomous (Moore 1970, 5–6). Freidson's more recent account enumerates similar criteria. He states that professionals have:

1. *Specialized work in the officially recognized economy that is believed to be grounded in a body of theoretically based, discretionary knowledge and skill and that is accordingly given special status in the labor force;*
2. *Exclusive jurisdiction in a particular division of labor created and controlled by occupational negotiation;*
3. *A sheltered position in both external and internal labor markets that is based on qualifying credentials created by the occupation;*
4. *A formal training program lying outside the labor market that produces the qualifying credentials, which is controlled by the occupation and associated with higher education; and*
5. *An ideology that asserts greater commitment to doing good work than to economic gain and to the quality rather than the economic efficiency of work.* (Freidson 2001, 127)

In short, being a professional consists of a unique combination of roles, excellence, and commitment, which includes personal dedication to the welfare of others, mastery at a high level of skills and knowledge, sensitivity to the art of the profession, and a wide range of other commitments. Note that in the quotation, these commitments are positioned as the "basis" for the social contract. It is not unusual to see the social contract described as legitimizing the exertion of certain skills and to see commitments narrowed down to the duty to keep the contract (i.e., to use these skills appropriately).

The Crisis in Professionalism

Professionalism is a big topic in sociology. The history of the concept is complicated, a fact partially reflected by the lack of a single definition of it. It is nevertheless not uncommon to see the sociology of professions described as having gone through at least three stages (Evetts 2003; Kanes 2010; Sciulli 2005). In order to see that professionalism is more than an ability to use a set of skills, we need this broader background.

The first *functionalist* or *structural-functionalist* phase started in the 1930s. The early studies give descriptions of the development of the professions and give a rationale for their emergence. Professionalism is generally seen as representing an outspoken, institutionalized form of division of labor. The term "division of labor" was not new at that time. It was, for instance, an important topic in the works of both Karl Marx and Max Weber, although obviously for different reasons. Marx considered the division of labor as an evil because it lies at the basis of class differences and of man's alienation from the products of his hands. Max Weber, on the other hand, saw the division as the inevitable counterpart of the processes of modernization and rationalization of Western society. These processes are characterized by the institutionalization of goal-rational economic and administrative activities. These activities crystallize in two broad domains: the market (the capitalist enterprise) and the bureaucracy (public administration). Examples of bureaucratic control are activities of supervisory bodies, of authorities that are occupied with the enforcement of legislation, and of institutes that control whether certain standards are met. Characteristic for both domains are the functional and specific relations between providers and consumers and between representatives of the bureaucracy and those who make use of its services. Other resemblances are the existence of a restricted domain of competence and/or power and the application of universalistic, impersonal standards.

This first phase in the development of professions is usually seen as the expression of another form of rational and functional division of labor, with traits of a bureaucracy. Leading sociologists like Talcott Parsons (1964) emphasize not only the rationality of this process but also its integrating function and uplifting potential. Professions have an integrative function because their members are not only experts but bound to certain norms and codes of conduct. These norms and codes embody goods that never would have been realized when professional–client relationships would have been defined in terms of the market. Freidson suggests in his later work that the professional–client relationship conforms to a "third logic" (Freidson 2001), apart from the logic of the market (consumerism) *and* of the bureaucracy (managerialism). Most significant for professions is that they are permitted to regulate and control their own practices. Professions would lose all resemblance to their current manifestations if they became on the one hand "mere casual labor in a spot market controlled by consumers" or on the other "mere job-holders in firms controlled by managers" (Freidson 2001, 7; see also Chapter 8). The third logic consists therefore in the specific form of giving-and-taking within the social contract that underlies the professions.

The second, critical (or revisionist, ideological, or post-modern) phase in the sociological analysis of the professions puts emphasis on the negative effects of professionalism. The way these negative effects are described sometimes seems a far cry from Karl Marx's objections against the division of labor. The professional is now seen as someone who exploits his or her position of power to sustain a privileged, self-interested monopoly (Evetts 2005). Larson, for instance, one of the major voices in the critical camp, states about the medical profession in the US that it has not shown enough integrity to safeguard its public mandate. Doctors have been more interested in their own private interests than in pursuing the collective value of health. She deplores the lack of benefit the medical profession has yielded for the public good (Larson 1977; 2003, 460; cited in Kanes 2010). Illich (1976) goes one step further in his influential book *Limits to Medicine* by suggesting that the system of healthcare produces its own illness (iatrogenesis). Modern medicine disempowers people and expropriates their health. Such criticisms are not restricted to the medical field, however.

Freidson mentions three general issues in what he calls the "assault on professionalism": criticism on the monopoly of professions, on social closure, and on credentialism. These three issues are related. The monopoly concerns the privileged position of professions in the market (i.e., their jurisdiction and exclusive command about how expert knowledge and technical means are used). Social closure refers to the claim that professions have the right to determine their own criteria for membership. And credentialism denotes the profession's right to establish its own "credentials" (i.e., its standards of excellence and systems of accreditation).

Focusing specifically on medicine, Marmor and Gordon (2014) discuss several themes in the critical literature. Critics complain that the inherent inequality in terms of knowledge and skills has turned into misplaced superiority and display of authority (paternalism). Another issue is self-regulation. This has become a protective shield, instead of a way to strike a balance among the competing priorities of self-interest, service to the public good, and striving for the appropriate level of competence. This is the mild version of Larson's criticism. Another issue is the traditional disdain of doctors for any form of competition and competitive commercialism. This disdain has sometimes turned into detrimental indifference to medical costs and the problem of controlling them. Finally, the individual patient–doctor relationship has become so central that it has led to a relative neglect of medicine's role with respect to larger societal problems and public health concerns.

Such criticisms have brought some scholars to predict the decline and even the end of professions (Broadbent et al. 1997; see also Tallis 2004). For example, according to Kaul (1986), professional elites are becoming "proletarian," and this will dramatically change the profession. For a while, the term "proletarianism" enjoyed some popularity as a way to describe the process of de-professionalization. The idea is that, as the proletarian has been alienated from his labor, so the professional is being alienated from his work. Krause (1996) states that professions behave like guilds and that, because they keep doing so, they will die out. However, with the exception of some radical proponents of the free market, like Milton Friedman (1962), few scholars really believe that people can independently gain all the relevant information and use it in their own interests. The information that is available in the media and on the Internet is often incomplete or distorted by the framing of interest groups. The "transaction costs" of deprofessionalization will moreover be enormous. Inexperienced service users need to reach the point at which they can assess the risks and benefits of the different options in a sufficiently realistic and adequate way. Many users will never reach this position or will simply not be willing to deliver the amount of effort that is needed (Freidson 2001, 205).

The third phase in the sociological study of the professions began in the late 1980s and early 1990s. This phase is characterized by a cautious reappraisal of the role of professions and by a search for balance and a more empirical orientation (Irvine 2001). Abbott (1988), for instance, puts more emphasis on the internal dynamics within and between professions. Professions are not only interacting with governments and other bureaucratic agencies and financial partners but also with each other; there are constant negotiations between professions about their jurisdictions. Abbott also draws attention to the relationship between kinds of professional work and the way the respective professions safeguard their credibility, accountability, and level of expertise. Different types of work require different credentials and different forms of education, quality control, and organization.

Other studies point to the different ways of organizing work and how this has led to a plurality of professional styles, also in medicine. Castellani and Hafferty (2006) mention seven of these styles for medicine: nostalgic, unreflective, academic, entrepreneurial, empirical, lifestyle, and activist. Bloom et al. (2008) see this plurality in the creation of new partnerships between states, market players, and civil society organizations. Given the larger role of formal and informal markets in the system of healthcare, the information asymmetry between experts and clients has become increasingly important. This asymmetry requires additional regulatory arrangements to protect vulnerable consumers against exploitation, misinformation, and insufficient care. These new arrangements require new and targeted negotiations on specific aspects of the social contract. Today, these negotiations are more than ever mediated by non-market institutions, such as public health bureaucracies, non-profit organizations, advocacy groups, and regulatory bodies.

TOWARD AN ALTERNATIVE VIEW

Desiderata for a Normative Approach to Professional Practice

Is there a remedy for the tensions and ambiguities in the development of professions? How can trust in the professions be restored? How can the professions regain and maintain their societal legitimacy?

What is needed is a coherent view on professions; on their societal legitimacy; on the responsibilities of individual professionals compared the responsibilities of other stakeholders; on the role of (scientific) knowledge and technology. Ideally, this account should provide a perspective on how micro-, meso-, and macro-contexts of professionalism intersect. It should provide an organizing idea, a principle, or set of principles or ideas to get a grasp on the bewildering multitude of insights, points of view, contexts, and normative issues with respect to the professions. Expertise should, ideally, no longer be one-sidedly defined in terms of outcome and performance but instead be conceived of as an expression of inner conviction and dedication (Hafferty 2006; Sullivan 2004; Levinson et al. 2014, chapter 5; Brint 2015).

In this book we will refer to this approach as 'normative practice approach' (NPA). The NPA is *normative*, or norm-responsive, because it defines the norms and principles that hold for professional practices, and because it sketches how these norms and principles cohere and interact. The NPA is an approach that focuses on *practices*, because it sees professions as practices that are inherently norm-responsive.

The NPA, central in this book, should in short:

- Give a comprehensive account of all the norms, duties, and responsibilities that are relevant for and shape professional practices;
- Do justice to the differences and the coherence between these norms;
- Properly locate and define the role of expert knowledge and skills amidst the many different roles and responsibilities of professionals and consumers/ service users;
- Avoid both scientistic absolutizing and critical relativizing of professional knowledge;
- Give a plausible outline of norms, duties, and responsibilities other than the epistemic ones;
- Give a social and moral justification of the professional role;
- Offer an account of the meso- and macro-contexts of professionalism;
- Provide a convincing approach to solve the "legitimacy crisis", i.e., the public's distrust of professionalism.

Outline of the NPA

Figure 1 gives an outline of the most essential components of the NPA that will developed and discussed in later chapters of this book (see also Hoogland et al. 1995; Jochemsen & Glas 1997; Hoogland & Jochemsen 2000; Jochemsen 2006; Verkerk et al. 2016; Glas 2017; Glas accepted). The model is meant to serve as a heuristic conceptual framework and not as a blueprint. It invites the reader to adopt the point of view the model proposes; and to investigate how and to what extent it elucidates and solves the problems that were discussed so far.

The diagram contains two boxes: one listing different types of rules/principles and one indicating a regulative dimension. What stands out initially is the distinction between these two boxes, the constitutive rules/principles and the regulative direction. In this subsection, I discuss this distinction; the next subsection is then devoted to how they interrelate.

Constitutive are those aspects or dimensions of professional practices without which there cannot be such a thing as a professional practice. Constitutive rules or principles define a profession as the practice it is. The principles and rules I aim at in this context, form the basis of a practice and serve at the same time as integrating normative ideals or maxims that guide that practice. The principle of beneficence is a well-known example in medicine: It is the both the basis and the aim of the doctor-patient relationships. It functions as an ideal, as a norm with an integrating potential that guides physicians when they are dealing with difficult situations.

When we look closer at these constitutive norms, there appear to be at least three kinds of norms/principles/rules:

- Those that hold for the expert role per se; these norms/principles/rules are *'foundational'*; they form the basis without which there would be no professionalism;
- Those that pertain to the purpose (destination, telos) of a practice; these norms/principles/rules are *'qualifying'*, they qualify the practice as the ultimate aim of the practice;
- Those that serve as facilitators or principles that shape the conditions for performing the practice (*conditioning* norms/principles).

So far, the constitutive part of professional practices. The right side of the diagram refers to the so-called regulative dimension of professions. "Regulative" means in this context that practices are determined by their inner, intrinsic directedness, which—ideally—is reflected by the commitment, motivation, and dedication of those who sustain and shape such practices. Regulative ideals provide a general idea about the destination of a practice. These ideals are embodied in the motivation

Figure 1. Professions as normative practices

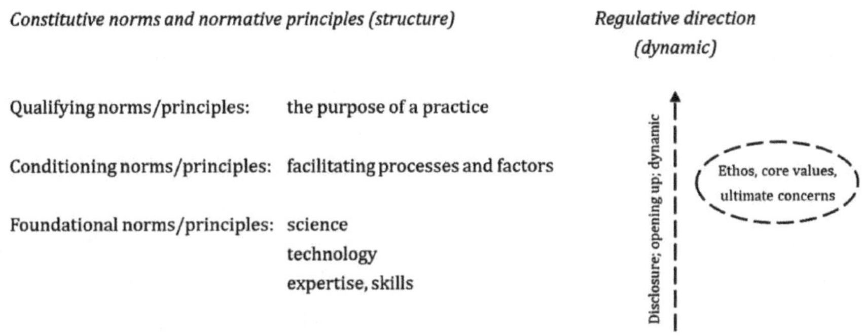

and dedication of practitioners. These can be conceptualized in terms of ultimate concerns, core values, or meaningfulness.

The regulative ideal or purpose of a practice is in other words not some distant or abstract goal that stands apart from that practice. It is, instead, the perfect (ideal) realization (or excellence) of that practice. The regulative dimension of a normative practice embodies the attitudes, motivations, and ideals in virtue of which the practice becomes the practice it is meant to be. In other words, the purposiveness of a practice become manifest in the practice itself, as a fundamental motivation, commitment, or ethos that helps professionals and other stakeholders fulfil their proper roles.

The NPA depicts how professional practices ideally work, i.e., when the constitutive and regulative sides of professional practices are attuned and collaborate. Neither side can exist without the other, and thus the schematic presentation in Figure 1 is somewhat off the mark because it seems to lock the two sides into two separate boxes. In reality, however, the constitutive side is opened up under the guidance of regulative notions (ideas and overarching values), whereas the regulative side can only be brought to life via the existence and holding of different sorts of constitutive principles and norms.

In this book the interplay between the constitutive and the regulative side of a practice will sometimes be indicated as an intertwinement between the "structure" and the "direction" of that practice. Structure refers to the constitutive side, direction to the regulative dimension of practices. To understand this interplay of a practice one may, for instance, focus on the historical development of a practice. Practices evolve over time and develop into a direction that corresponds with or deviates from their purpose. Practices may flourish or fall into decay. Their directedness may be conceived of as a kind of dynamic that pervades their development. This dynamic is fundamental, in the sense that it gives perspective and meaning to one's practice, not as a mission statement or ideology, but in an embodied, embedded, and enacted form. What precedes is a set of attitudes, aspirations, and ideals that function as a motivating force operating from within.

Contexts play an important role in the way this dynamic unfolds. It is in the interplay between contexts and practices that certain aspects of a practice become more important than others. Small-scale practices are often part of larger networks with their own dynamic. One of the advantages of the term "dynamic" is that it allows us to see practices as subject to heterogeneous dynamic forces. This corresponds with the experience that many professional practices are usually somewhat mixed and that participation in them often leads to a certain measure of ambivalence. It is not uncommon for professional practices to fall under the influence of more than one dynamic. Different motives guide them in different directions, and this may lead to ambivalence, alienation, and conflict.

An example. Earlier in this chapter, several such ambivalences and conflicts were analyzed. We saw, how professions are burdened by managerialism, i.e., by the urge to bring professional practices under control, not only economically, but also in terms of efficiency, accountability, and transparency. Lack of professional self-regulation and uncontrollable economic and technological growth appeared to lie at the basis of this managerialism. We interpreted it as the societal response to distrust of the public about whether professionals really put all their efforts into the service of others instead of into their own interests. However, overemphasis on bureaucratic control leads to the ironic consequence of diminishment of control. Both in medicine and in education, the massive increase of control—administrative, economic, and in terms of accountability, safety, and access —has paradoxically led to an increase in discomfort and distrust, both among (service) users, who are confronted with an increasingly complex system of care/education, and among professionals, who feel more and more alienated from their proper role.

With the help of the NPA, we can now understand these tensions as the product of a role reversal between conditioning and qualifying norms. The conditioning, economic norm of efficiency is dealt with as if it were a qualifying norm. This role reversal leads to a different definition of professionalism. In healthcare systems in which efficiency norms prevail above values related to care, a good doctor is an efficient doctor, not primarily a caring doctor. Efficiency, instead of beneficence, becomes the overarching and qualifying norm for a sound and sustainable practice. Of course, advocates of efficiency in medicine claim that there need be no contradiction between efficiency and caring for suffering people. They will argue that these aims are complementary. But that is not the issue. The issue is the specific role that is ascribed to the norm of efficiency and the place it takes in the hierarchy of values of medical practice. Efficiency is no longer an auxiliary quality, together with the other necessary conditions. It becomes the most defining (or qualifying) characteristic of good practice. In the end, this distorted view on the structure of medical practice will have an eroding effect on the ethos of doctors (Tallis 2004).

Structure and directedness always interact and cannot be analyzed apart from one another. In one's analysis, one can begin at either side. One can start with an analysis of the structure of a practice and argue toward underlying tensions in the direction. Or one can begin with the identification of underlying ambivalences and tensions in professional cultures and then reconstruct how these tensions affect the development of a certain practice, more specifically, the ordering and relative importance of the various constitutive norms/principles/rules.

CONCLUSION

This chapter analyzed the crisis in professionalism from a historical and conceptual point of view and described the development of professional practices as part of a process of modernization, i.e., as an expression of the rationalization of working processes and an increasing division and specialization of labor. This process has led to tendencies to bureaucracy, alienation, meaninglessness, and dehumanization. The chapter describes a set of desiderata for a normative framework that avoids these pitfalls. It briefly sketches a so-called normative practice approach, which consists of a framework of interacting constitutive norms (qualifying, foundational, and conditioning/facilitating) driven by regulative ideals and values. It sketches how this framework could enable professionals to disentangle and remedy the tensions and ambivalences within their professional practices.

REFERENCES

Abbott, A. D. (1988). *The System of Professions: An Essay on the Division of Expert Labor*. Chicago: University of Chicago Press. doi:10.7208/chicago/9780226189666.001.0001

Bloom, G., Standing, H., & Lloyd, R. (2008). Markets, information asymmetry and health care: Towards new social contracts. *Social Science & Medicine*, *66*(10), 2076–2087. doi:10.1016/j.socscimed.2008.01.034 PMID:18316147

Brint, S. (2015). Professional Responsibility in an Age of Experts and Large Organizations. In D. E. Mitchell & R. K. Ream (Eds.), *Professional Responsibility. The Fundamental Issue in Education and Health Care Reform* (Vol. 4, pp. 89–107). New York: Springer. doi:10.1007/978-3-319-02603-9_6

Broadbent, J., Dietrich, M., & Roberts, J. (Eds.). (1997). *The End of the Professions? The Restructuring of Professional Work*. London: Routledge.

Castellani, B., & Hafferty, F. W. (2006). The Complexities of Medical Professionalism: A Preliminary Investigation. In D. Wear & J. M. Aultman (Eds.), *Professionalism in Medicine. Critical Perspectives* (pp. 3–24). New York: Springer. doi:10.1007/0-387-32727-4_1

Evetts, J. (2003). The Sociological Analysis of Professionalism. Occupational Change in the Modern World. *International Sociology*, *18*(2), 395–415. doi:10.1177/0268580903018002005

Freidson, E. (2001). *Professionalism. The Third Logic*. Chicago: University of Chicago Press.

Friedman, M. (1962). *Capitalism and Freedom*. Chicago: The University of Chicago Press.

Glas, G. (2017). Public and Institutional Aspects of Professional Responsibility in Medicine and Psychiatry. *Philosophia Reformata*, *82*(2), 146–166. doi:10.1163/23528230-08202005

Glas, G. (accepted). Psychiatry as normative practice. *Philosophy, Psychiatry, & Psychology*.

Hafferty, F. W. (2006b). Professionalism—The Next Wave. *The New England Journal of Medicine*, *355*(20), 2151–2152. doi:10.1056/NEJMe068217 PMID:17065632

Hoogland, J., & Jochemsen, H. (2000). Professional autonomy and the normative structure of medical practise. *Theoretical Medicine and Bioethics*, *21*(5), 457–475. doi:10.1023/A:1009925423036 PMID:11142442

Hoogland, J., Jochemsen, H., Polder, J. J., & Strijbos, S. (1995). *Professioneel beheerst— Professionele autonomie van de arts in relatie tot instrumenten voor beheersing van kosten en kwaliteit van de gezondheidszorg. Rapport van het Prof. dr. G.A. Lindeboom Instituut (no.12)*. Ede: Lindeboom Instituut.

Irvine, D. (2001). Doctors in the UK: Their new professionalism and its regulatory framework. *Lancet*, *38*(9295), 1807–1810. doi:10.1016/S0140-6736(01)06800-3 PMID:11734261

Irvine, D. (2003). *The Doctors' Tale. Professionalism and Public Trust*. Abingdon, UK: Radcliffe Medical Press.

Jochemsen, H. (2006). Normative practices as an intermediate between theoretical ethics and morality. *Philosophia Reformata*, *71*(1), 96–112. doi:10.1163/22116117-90000377

Jochemsen, H., & Glas, G. (1997). *Verantwoord medisch handelen. Proeve van een christelijke medische ethiek*. Amsterdam: Buijten & Schipperheijn.

Kanes, C. (2010). Challenging professionalism. In C. Kanes (Ed.), *Elaborating Professionalism, Studies in Practice and Theory 5* (pp. 1–16). Dordrecht: Springer.

Kaul, A. J. (1986). The proletarian journalist: A critique on professionalism. *Journal of Mass Media Ethics*, *1*(2), 47–55. doi:10.1080/08900528609358266

Krause, E. A. (1996). *Death of the Guilds: Professions, States and the Advance of Capitalism, 1930 to the Present*. New Haven, CT: Yale University Press.

Larson, M. (2003). Professionalism: The third logic. *Perspectives in Biology and Medicine*, *46*(3), 458–462. doi:10.1353/pbm.2003.0037

Larson, M. S. (2013). The Rise of Professionalism. Monopolies of Competence and Sheltered Markets. New Brunswick, NJ: Transaction Publishers. (Originally published 1977)

Levinson, W., Ginsburg, S., Hafferty, F. W., & Lucey, C. R. (2014). *Understanding Medical Professionalism*. New York: McGraw Hill.

Marmor, T. R., & Gordon, R. W. (2014). Commercial Pressures on Professionalism in American Medical Care: From Medicare to the Affordable Care Act. *The Journal of Law, Medicine & Ethics*, *42*(4), 412–419. doi:10.1111/jlme.12164 PMID:25565609

Moore, W. E. (1970). *The Professions: Roles and Rules*. New York: The Russell Sage Foundation.

Parsons, T. (1964). The Professions and Social Structure. In T. Parsons (Ed.), Essays in Sociological Theory (rev. ed.; pp. 34-49). New York: Free Press. (Originally published 1939)

Rueschemeyer, D. (1983). Professional Autonomy and the Social Control of Expertise. In R. Dingwall & P. Lewis (Eds.), *The Sociology of the Professions: Lawyers, Doctors and Others* (pp. 38–53). London: Macmillan. doi:10.1007/978-1-349-16979-5_3

Sciulli, D. (2005). Continental Sociology of Professions Today: Conceptual Contributions. *Current Sociology*, *53*(6), 915–942. doi:10.1177/0011392105057155

Sullivan, W. M. (2004). Can professionalism still be a viable ethic? *The Good Society - PEGS*, *13*(1), 15–20. doi:10.1353/gso.2004.0032

Tallis, R. (2004). *Hippocratic Oaths. Medicine and its Discontents*. London: Atlantic Books.

Verkerk, M., Hoogland, J., Van der Stoep, J., & De Vries, M. J. (2016). *Philosophy of Technology. An Introduction for Technology and Business Students*. London: Routledge.

ENDNOTE

1 Parts of this text were published in G. Glas (2017). The current text has been shortened, adapted and improved and discusses professionalism in general.

Chapter 2
Roots of the Normative Practice Approach:
The Philosophy of Herman Dooyeweerd

Gerrit Glas
Vrije Universiteit, The Netherlands

ABSTRACT

This chapter focuses on the philosophy of Dutch philosopher Herman Dooyeweerd (1894-1977), whose systematic philosophy has informed and inspired the initial formulations of the normative practice approach. Central concepts like mode, aspect, entity, meaning, heart, and ground motive will be discussed. The relevance of these concepts for the normative practice approach will be pointed out.

INTRODUCTION

This chapter provides the philosophical background of the Normative Practice Approach (NPA) and, more particularly, its roots in the systematic philosophy of the Dutch philosopher Herman Dooyeweerd.[1] His work is not well-known and needs a more extensive introduction, since it has been important for the initial formulations of the NPA. This chapter will especially draw on Dooyeweerd's idea that norms are intrinsic, i.e., 'structurally given', and the idea that all human activity is ultimately rooted in existential, ultimate concerns. The chapter will highlight the connections between Dooyeweerd's philosophy and early formulations of the NPA (for similar attempts, cf. Mouw & Griffioen 1993; Verkerk 2004; Chaplin 2011; Verkerk et al. 2016). In the next chapter Jan Hoogland will focus on other philosophical and sociological sources for the NPA and give a general description of this approach.

DOI: 10.4018/978-1-5225-8006-5.ch002

HERMAN DOOYEWEERD

Who was Dooyeweerd and what were his most important ideas? Herman Dooyeweerd (1894-1977) was one of the founders of what has become known as reformational (or 'neo-Calvinist') philosophy. He developed his philosophy in the interbellum, in an intellectual climate which was characterized by uncertainty, deep divides between philosophical traditions, and the presentiment of decline of Western culture. Dooyeweerd studied law and philosophy. He had a brief career in public administration before he became secretary of the Abraham Kuyper Foundation, a precursor of the scientific institute of one of the Christian political parties in the Netherlands before World War II. From 1926 until his retirement in 1965 he was professor of philosophy and history of law at the Vrije Universiteit in Amsterdam.

He wrote extensively and had an almost encyclopedic knowledge not only of philosophy and the history of philosophy (especially Neo-Kantianism and ancient philosophy), but also of the sciences of his time, esp. mathematics, physics, biology, law, and social and political sciences. Most of his ideas in systematic philosophy were developed and refined in the interaction with the sciences (Dooyeweerd 1953-1958).

For the understanding of Dooyeweerd's philosophy it is useful to keep in mind that it is built up around two main themes: (1) the distinction between different modal aspects (or ways of functioning); and (2) the idea that all human activity is rooted in what he calls the 'heart' and which he denotes as 'concentration point' within our existence out of which our ultimate concerns originate.

In the following sections, we discuss first the theory of modal aspects, then the theory of entities or 'individuality structures' (which informed the development of the NPA), subsequently the concepts of law and cosmic order, next the idea of heart and, finally, what Dooyeweerd saw as the fundamental flaw of Western philosophy and science: its absolutization of the theoretical attitude of thought.

MODAL ASPECTS

Dooyeweerd tells in an interview that idea of modal diversity came as a flash during a walk in the dunes somewhere around 1921 when he was overwhelmed by the astonishing diversity and the incredible coherence in the way things exist and are functioning (van Dunné et al. 1977, 37). Everything exists in different ways, ways that are both distinguishable and interconnected in our ordinary experience of the world. A flower, for instance, exists in a spatial, in a physical and in a biotic way: it occupies a certain space, it has physical properties (such as mass), and it functions as a biotic entity, because it grows, blossoms, and reproduces. Flowers may also exist in other spheres or aspects, for instance in the economic or the aesthetic aspect.

They then function as economic or aesthetic object, respectively: they are bought (economic) or be valued because of their beauty (aesthetic).

All these different ways of functioning are weaved together in a seemingly self-evident and natural way in our everyday experience. We don't even notice the differences. However, we can become aware of them in certain contexts in which a particular feature stands out or when we step back and reflect on the differences. A flower seller, for instance, is especially aware of the economic qualities of plants and flowers, their consumer value on the market. Consumers on the other hand may be more interested in how flowers smell, feel, and look like, i.e., in their aesthetic qualities. Dooyeweerd calls the most general ways (or: kinds) of existing or functioning: aspects, or modal aspects, or functions, or modal functions, or (more technically) law spheres. The term 'modal' does not refer to logic (modal logic), but to the Latin term 'modus', which means: way of existing or functioning. Everything functions in a number of 'spheres', not one sphere at a time, diachronically, but all spheres synchronically, in an orderly way and in close conjunction. (For an overview of the 15 aspects and their meaning kernel, see Table 1).

Things function in these aspects in basically two ways, as subject or as object. Flowers exist (function) within the numerical, geometrical (spatial), physical and biotic sphere, as we saw. This means that, flowers manifest discreteness (numerical),

Table 1. The fifteen modal aspects as distinguished in Dooyeweerdian philosophy

Aspect	Meaning Kernel
1. Quantitative	discrete quantity
2. Spatial	continuous extension
3. Kinematic	uniform movement, flow
4. Physical	energy, matter
5. Biotic/Organic	life functions, self-maintenance
6. Sensitive/Psychic	feeling and response
7. Analytical	distinction, conceptualization
8. Formative	formative power, achievement, technology, technique
9. Lingual	symbolic communication
10. Social	social interaction
11. Economic	frugal use of resources
12. Aesthetic	harmony, surprise, imaginativity
13. Juridical	retribution (rights, responsibility)
14. Ethical	self-giving love
15. Pistic	faith, vision, commitment, belief

spatial continuity (geometrical), physical qualities (mass, energy) and capacities to reproduce and to maintain a metabolic equilibrium (biotic). In these four spheres flowers function as subject, i.e., they manifest these qualities themselves, actively. Flowers also function in other spheres, i.e., as object; for instance, as object of scientific analysis (logical), as products that can be bought or sold (economic), or as objects with aesthetic qualities (aesthetic). In all these other spheres flowers function as objects, passively. From a practical point of view, things begin to function as objects as a result of their interaction with human beings (or animals or plants).

It is safe to say that modal aspects refer to kinds of properties instead of properties per se. The term property is usually understood as referring to an instantiation of a more general category. When I say: "This car is black", then 'black' is a property of the car. It is an instantiation of the general category of blackness, namely, the instantiation of the general category of blackness in this car. Modes or modal aspects refer to these general categories, i.e., in fact, to very general kinds of properties, not to concrete and individual instantiations. The distinctness of these kinds has something to do with the distinctness (or: 'sovereignty') of laws and/or lawful principles, according to Dooyeweerd. More precisely, the distinctness of kinds of properties should be considered as a reflection of the irreducible distinctness of types of laws. This distinctness is reflected in the way they determine what exists and occurs.

This idea of distinctness of (types of) laws is in a certain way an extension of thoughts that were originally formulated by the thinker who inspired Dooyeweerd probably most: Abraham Kuyper; theologian, philosopher, statesman, and prolific writer. Kuyper had developed the idea of 'sphere sovereignty' to understand how different social spheres can overlap and at the same time retain a relative independence. The activities of the church and of the state overlap, but they are at the same time 'sovereign in their own sphere'. This is because both obey to their own normative principles. These normative principles are ultimately not man-made, but intrinsic to our social existence and 'given' (though, of course, influenced by culture and local circumstances). Dooyeweerd applied this 'sociological' principle of sphere sovereignty to all kinds of laws. The cosmos we inhabit manifests an order with a multiplicity of laws. Each of these laws belongs to a particular type and these types represent distinct modal 'spheres' (aspects).

Dooyeweerd devoted an entire volume of his opus magnum to the analysis of and distinction between these modal aspects (Dooyeweerd 1953-1958, Vol. II). He distinguished not three or four but as many as fourteen (later: fifteen) modal aspects (see Table1), each with their own typical character or meaning. It is important to notice that the aspects are not layers, components, ontic cross-sections, or whatever other form of substantial existence in an entity. They are ways of functioning or existing, not parts of substances. Modal aspects indicate how things function, not what they are. In the next section, we will discuss what Dooyeweerd has to say about the what, i.e. about entities and their structure.

In Dooyeweerd's systematic philosophy, the analysis of modal spheres is more fundamental than the analysis of entities. Dooyeweerd is, of course, aware of the fact that most scientists are primarily occupied with entities, i.e., with part-whole relationships and with the interactions and relations between particular types or properties of things. He, nevertheless, maintains that the study of these interactions, relations and properties always (implicitly) starts by selecting a particular modal point of view. Scientists don't study relations, interactions and properties as such, but spatial relations, or physical interactions, or psychological properties. It is only after having gone through "the gate of modal analysis" that the scientist studies the relationships, interactions and properties of and between things. This modal point of view can be any modal aspect; it does not have to be similar to the modal aspect that qualifies the thing in question. Physics became a science, not by adopting a physical point of view, but by applying mathematical principles to physical phenomena.

THE DIFFERENCE BETWEEN MODES AND ENTITIES

Not recognizing the relevance of the distinction between modes and entities is the cause of much trouble in the sciences, according to Dooyeweerd. Mental phenomena, for instance, are often conceived as expressions of a mental part (an ontic layer or component) within the organism. In other cases they are seen as products that are causally brought about by some mechanism in the brain. This mechanism is usually considered to be non-mental. Both ways of conceptualizing mental phenomena are problematic in the Dooyeweerdian view.

The implicit assumption of the first position (mental phenomena as expression of the existence of a mental 'layer' or 'part') is that if mental properties and functions require some mental 'stuff' as bearer of these properties and functions, this inevitably leads to a form of mind-body dualism, which is very unattractive for most scientists and philosophers today (and for Dooyeweerd too). From a Dooyeweerdian point of view the argument is based on a *non-sequitur*, namely a confusion between the modal and the entitary point of view. Mental properties and functions are not 'just mental', the phenomena they are referring to are always *also*, synchronously, biological, social and moral, to mention only a few of the most obvious other candidate spheres. The term mental is already a bit confusing because it refers to so many kinds of psychological activities and experiences. But all these psychological kinds of functioning presuppose entities (processes) that realize them and these entities have also other qualifications: they involve the working of certain brain circuits (biotic), they presuppose molecular and metabolic processes in these circuits (physical) and they have a developmental history with social, cultural and moral characteristics. In short, mental phenomena are 'entities' (activities, processes, actions) that function in all modal spheres, either as subject or as object. To see them as immaterial expressions of an immaterial 'part' within the organism is mixing the modal point of view (their modal qualification) with the entitary point of view: the psychological *aspect* of the thing (thought, feeling) is held to be a proof of the existence of a psychic *thing* (entity) in us. Dooyeweerd would, for this reason, be very hesitant to speak of levels or layers as ontic realities. Such layers often don't exist in reality and are, in fact, the product of the ontologizing of a modal point of view. We can distinguish biological, psychological, social and moral aspects in our functioning as human beings. But that doesn't offer us a ticket for the conclusion that we are composites that are built up of biological, psychological, social and moral components (layers; levels; parts).

The implicit assumption of the second, more popular, position (mental phenomena as 'products', or 'by-products', of an underlying mechanism or [brain] process) is also based on confusion between the modal and the entitary point of view, but differently. The point is here that mental phenomena are first isolated and secondarily conceptualized as products of the preceding operations of another entity, 'the brain'. The problem becomes, then, how to conceive the transition from matter to mind: How can immaterial mental phenomena be the output of material biotic processes? It is again a conceptual confusion that lies at the basis of this question, i.e., the confusion between modes and entities. Psychological qualities of someone's behavior are first implicitly reified to manifestations of a mental reality, or mind stuff. This is because the relationship between brain processes and mental phenomena is conceived as a causal relationship. Causal relationships are typically relationships between things, not between properties or kinds of things. The conflation of the modal and entitary point of view leads to an artificial separation between production process and product and to a reification of mental processes as product of processes in the brain. In most contemporary conceptualizations, the idea that there exists a mental substance or a bearer for these mental processes evaporates. Instead of 'products' mental phenomena become mysterious 'by-products' of the brain.

The picture of the brain as an organ that produces mental phenomena is as old as the sciences of psychology and psychiatry. For Dooyeweerd, it is problematic, because it construes causal relationships between processes which, in fact, logically and factually imply one another. Psychological phenomena are always mediated by brain processes and cannot be separated from these processes. Mental processes are embodied; their existence can never be seen apart from a context of embodiment and embeddedness. Brain functioning is always embedded in the functioning of the nervous system as a whole (i.e., central and peripheral) and the nervous system as a whole can only function in its interlacements with the body. The body in turn functions in its interlacements with all other aspects of who we are; persons who are interacting with their physical and social environment. This relatedness and these interactions are not secondary but constitutive for what it is to be a brain and to function as a person with a brain and a bunch of psychological capacities. The production metaphor is therefore wrong. It suggests that mental processes and brain processes are separated in time and that they belong to a different order, logically and factually. Mental (psychological) properties indeed fundamentally differ from physical or biotic properties, but these modal differences as such don't prove entitary distinctness.

DOOYEWEERD ON LAWS, ORDER, AND TRANSCENDENTAL IDEAS

Let us return to the relationship between modal aspects and laws. The distinctness of kinds of properties, it was said, is a reflection of the irreducible distinctness between types of laws. What is meant with this statement?

Dooyeweerd is a (kind of) realist with respect to laws and, consequently, of order. He holds, more precisely, a transcendental version of them. In the transcendental view laws do exist as conditions without which the things for which they hold, would not exist. The term 'transcendental' refers, in other words, to fundamental concepts and/or conditions which need to be presupposed in order to conceive certain states of affairs in the world as real and existing. This necessity is not only logical, as in the Kantian, idealistic version of transcendental philosophy, but also ontological, or cosmological, as Dooyeweerd prefers to say. Without these transcendental (cosmological) conditions, not only logical thinking would be impossible, but also our everyday experience, and, even, existence itself. The existence of flowers, for instance, requires (=necessarily presupposes) laws or lawful regularities in the spatial, physical, and biotic sphere. We have a pretheoretical understanding of plants as living things. This intuition of what it is 'to live' or 'to be living' is translated in biological, i.e., theoretical terms. But this theoretical approach of what it is, for a plant, to live, falls short. We have numerous theoretical concepts (physiological, biochemical, molecular) referring to what it is to live or to be living, but none of them fully grasps the meaning of 'living'. In order to do justice to the pretheoretical intuition that the biotic aspect is fundamentally distinct from the physical and spatial aspects of the flower, we need a notion of modal distinctness that neither reduces biotic distinctness to cultural and/or subjective habits (like in constructivist epistemologies) nor identifies it with things in the world that can be objectified and conceptually grasped (like in rationalistic or scientistic ontologies). The proper meaning of being biotic cannot theoretically be deduced nor scientifically be defined. The meaning of what it is 'to live' transcends, so to say, the logical conception of it.

An analogy with beauty might be helpful in this respect: beauty as a real-life phenomenon entails more than what is meant with the (theoretical; logical) concept of beauty. What it is for a piece of music or poem to be beautiful cannot be defined in a scientific way, in the form of a certain concept of beauty. This is because scientific concepts only highlight the logically graspable aspects of things. Concepts are therefore logical artefacts. Beauty is more than its concept, which is a logical derivative. What beauty is, can hardly be expressed, even in ordinary language. Beauty must be experienced, it emanates as an enigmatic quality of our experience. It is there, undeniable; we can approach it in different ways, by undergoing the experience, by scientific study of all sorts, by practicing the relevant form of art, and by learning from what others say about their experiences. But in all these instances we never grasp a fixed conceptual structure, behind or within the phenomenon itself. We intuit that there is something special and distinct in the phenomenon of beauty, but we cannot grasp and define it.

Let us now, for the sake of the argument, presume that beauty is the essential feature of the aesthetical aspect. Then, Dooyeweerd would say something like this: just as the essential feature (or: 'meaning kernel', as Dooyeweerd would call it) of the aesthetic aspect cannot be grasped conceptually/theoretically/ scientifically, so too the essential feature of the biotic aspect cannot conceptually/theoretically/ scientifically be defined. This also would hold for all the other aspects: they have essential features that 'transcend' their scientific/theoretical conceptualization. These features should rather be conceived as presupposed (i.e., as being always already there) than as products of theoretical/philosophical reflection. This is what Dooyeweerd has in mind when he speaks about the irreducible nature of the modal aspects.

In the above, we have connected Dooyeweerd's conception of law with his ideas about modal aspects, especially their irreducibility, logical as well as cosmological. We can now see why this connection can be made. The lawful order is not a logical, but a transcendental order; it is an order that we should presuppose as being necessarily there, in how things behave and are, according to Dooyeweerd. Laws hold, which means that they determine how things exist.

Transcendental conditions are special in the sense that they refer to realities of which we have a pre-theoretical intuition but to which we have no immediate epistemic access. Our pre-theoretical intuitions can be deepened and explicated into theoretical, philosophical intuitions. But these intuitions remain fallible. They do not form a firm conceptual, logical foundation for any possible science. They function more as invitations to let thinking and interpreting never stop. Behind these considerations looms the old (Kantian) distinction between concept and idea. Concepts can be grasped by pure (=theoretical; scientific) reason; i.e., they can accurately be defined. Transcendental ideas cannot accurately be defined; they are a kind of intuitions, more like Kantian 'ideas', they are, so to say, invitations to view reality under a certain overarching perspective. They give a clue about what transcends theoretical understanding and what nevertheless should be presupposed as true and existing within theoretical understanding, a.o., the irrevocable distinctness between the different modes of functioning.

It will be clear that Dooyeweerd's conception of law differs from what scientists use to call law (or: principle) or lawful regularity/pattern. Scientific laws are interpretations, or approximations, of a lawful order. They are not the order itself. Dooyeweerd's notions of law and of a lawful order are (transcendental) boundary concepts for theoretical thinking. Scientists and philosophers need to presuppose the existence of a lawful order in order to make sense of the regularities and causally relevant relations they discover in their sciences, Dooyeweerd suggests. It is on basis of the (transcendental) presupposition that there is such order, that they are able and entitled to discern the more mundane laws of their respective branches of science, he says. The laws that the sciences discover are interpretations, fallible attempts to grasp the order of reality.

Let us now take one final step with respect to this notion of transcendental order. We have strong pre-theoretical intuitions, Dooyeweerd says, about the fundamental *diversity* of reality, a diversity which finds its origins in a cosmic order that transcends our logical/theoretical mode of knowing and of which we also have no empirical proof. In a similar fashion Dooyeweerd also speaks of other important (transcendental) features of our knowledge, experience and existence; especially, of the *coherence*, *unity* and *origin* of the cosmic order we inhabit. The fundamental *diversity* in our experience of reality reflects the fundamental distinctness of laws and of how they hold. There is, however, also and at the same time a fundamental connectedness between the things in the world and between us and the world. This experience of connectedness is a reflection of what theoretically is expressed with the term *coherence*, as transcendental idea. Coherence and diversity belong together; they are two sides of the same coin and indicate the first transcendental idea. The experience of meaning – the fact that things refer to one another, together with the suggestion that their connectedness reflects a deeper wholeness and unity – is the pretheoretical precursor of the transcendental idea of *unity*, which is Dooyeweerd's second transcendental idea. This sense of unity and wholeness requires in turn a notion of *origin of meaning*. This is expressed in the third transcendental idea: the idea of an origin of meaning. Diversity (in conjunction with coherence), unity, and origin are the three most fundamental ideas or transcendental presuppositions of our experience of reality – and of reality itself, Dooyeweerd would add.

DO WE STILL NEED THIS PHILOSOPHY?

I am aware that many readers will have difficulty with swallowing these statements. The question arises whether we really need this difficult and unpopular transcendental conception of law and of an underlying lawful order. What are Dooyeweerd arguments? Isn't it sufficient to maintain a much more pragmatic notion of law, for instance the notion of laws as models for the lawful regularities we notice in the object under study; or laws in the sense of the regularities (equations, statistical probabilities), constants and definitions scientists are working with in their everyday practices?

Let me give two responses to these doubts, one more pragmatic, the other more fundamental. The pragmatic response runs as follows. Maybe we don't need Dooyeweerd's strict notion of law in the everyday practice of laboratory research, or while digesting large amounts of data, as in genetic or epidemiological research. But some of Dooyeweerd's core concerns are always on the table, especially his concerns about diversity, coherence and wholeness (unity). Ultimately scientists must face the question of how their findings should be interpreted and fit into a larger picture of the world. Old, well-known questions will then recur. What does this hypothesis or theory mean with respect the object under study? What does it say in a larger context? Are the reductions valid and to what extent? Coherence and wholeness are in other words always on the agenda, not only in science itself, but also in its applications, implicitly, but nevertheless inescapable. References to these broader notions will always emerge when scientists tell their stories about what they have been doing to colleagues or the broader public. Pointing out what we know about the brain, the origin of the universe, our genes or artificial intelligence, inevitably brings the scientist to a point where his implicit assumptions can no longer be held private. Ultimate questions about coherence, wholeness and meaning can never completely be evaded, particularly not outside the laboratory or other research settings.

For Dooyeweerd there is also a more fundamental, philosophical reason for his difficult, transcendental route. The argument for cosmic order and for the (modal) distinctness of laws is indirect and in fact a philosophical conjecture, he would say; a conjecture that is defensible given the unattractiveness of some of the alternatives. Trying to account for what we know without presupposing the ideas of order and law, sooner or later leads to inconsistency, he suggests. More precisely, without the presupposition of a (transcendental) cosmic order our philosophical position would easily slip either toward a nominalistic or toward a rationalistic position. Nominalists traditionally say that laws only exist in our minds. Rationalists think that the order of reality is intelligible and that laws can be accessed and known by (theoretical) reason.

Both positions are unattractive for Dooyeweerd. He rejects nominalism because it removes the point of contact between the sciences and everyday experience. For Dooyeweerd pretheoretical intuitions are important, not because they are always true, but because they give a clue of the different forms of distinctness (and coherence) in the cosmic order; a distinctness (and sense of coherence) that is lost as soon as the scientific attitude is adopted. From a more practical perspective nominalism is also unattractive because it is so much in contrast with the common-sense realism of most scientists. Their hypotheses are conjectures about what they think really exists. Nominalism with respect to laws would in other words introduce a contradiction in the heart of the empirical sciences.

Dooyeweerd's resistance against rationalism is mainly based on and, in fact, coincides with his objections against classical realism (Aristotle; the scholastics). Classical realism supposes that we can grasp the order of reality with our intellectual faculties. The capabilities of our intellect, in other words, comply with the intelligibility of reality. Dooyeweerd rejects this position because it – ultimately – absolutizes theoretical reason, or, more precisely, the theoretical attitude of thought. For Dooyeweerd theoretical reasoning is always a derivative of our everyday understanding of the world. What is lost in the theoretical attitude is the 'indissoluble interrelation' among the modal aspects which present themselves as completely interwoven within our everyday experience (NC I, 3). This everyday understanding is of course less precise and more subject to error than scientific knowing, but it is characterized by a holism as well as a sense of diversity that is very characteristic for our understanding of the world and that fades away as soon as the scientific attitude is adopted. The experience of coherence and diversity is so fundamental that we cannot go behind it, neither by reasoning, nor by experience; and even not by a scientific reconstruction of the phenomenological properties of our experience.

These phrases will still raise many questions. Dooyeweerd's position seems to thrive on what some would call a certain mysterianism, i.e., on pretheoretical intuitions that only partially can be made explicit in the form transcendental ideas. For readers with a primary empirical scientific interest, philosophical details about the status of transcendental conceptions are less relevant. It is much more important to understand the idea that something is lost by adopting the scientific attitude, most fundamentally our pretheoretical sense of diversity, coherence, and wholeness, than to understand and grasp the transcendental framework in which these ideas are caught and expressed. The discussion about this framework is for philosophers and has no immediate bearing on the discussion about absolutization and reification, which are crucial for the evaluation of what goes on in science.

In our world the scientific image of the world has merged in many respects with our pretheoretical understandings. It is very much in line with Dooyeweerd's philosophy to see this as a challenge, as the inevitable counterpart of the differentiation of our culture and not as something which in itself is wrong or deplorable. Today, it is important to recognize such mergers and to investigate what they imply and mean, and to evaluate them in terms of their benefits and of disadvantages.

DOOYEWEERD ON THE 'HEART'

Let us now turn to Dooyeweerd's other core idea, which concerns our functioning as humans, individually and collectively. It is Dooyeweerd's deep conviction that all human functioning is ultimately rooted in what he calls the 'heart'. The heart is the concentration point of our existence. The term refers to the idea that we humans are driven by fundamental concerns, motivations, commitments, and convictions. These commitments and convictions are not only individual psychological realities, they have an existential and moral/spiritual core and typically aim at what is beyond the horizon of our knowledge and experience (something 'greater than us'). The heart itself is not something that can be studied with empirical means, it is presupposed, and it expresses itself in all human functioning, most clearly and explicitly in the life- and worldview of a person.

Dooyeweerd's Christian, Neo-Calvinist inspiration is definitely important in this idea of rootedness in the 'heart' and of striving beyond the horizon of our knowledge and experience. However, Dooyeweerd goes at length to make plausible that the idea of the heart as origin of an existential/religious dynamic refers to a reality which is structurally given and not a philosophical translation of insights taken from a religious tradition. All human beings have an inclination to transcendence, so to speak, independent of their ethnicity or religion. This inclination is ingrained and structurally given. Philosophy cannot answer the question what (or who) the existential dynamic is aiming at. It can only argue that the deepest and most central human commitments are aiming at an ultimate meaning of which the source cannot be grasped or explained or immediately experienced. Dooyeweerd calls this source 'origin' or 'origin of meaning'. This source of meaning lies, in other words, beyond the horizon of experience and reflection.

The difficulty with conceptualizing the notion of the heart is that it cannot be equated with functioning in one or another modal aspect or be identified with a part of our biopsychosocial existence. It is not the same as aesthetic feeling, or moral sensitivity, or spiritual openness, or value-sensitivity, though all of these may represent what is 'in' our hearts. We could call the functioning of the heart a 'dynamic'; a dynamic which itself is not bound to one modal aspect, and which resonates with a person's character, morality, ethos, and worldview. If the modal aspects are plotted on the Y-axis, then the activity of the heart could be plotted on the X-axis. Followers of Dooyeweerd have described this as a relation between 'structure' and 'direction'. Structure refers then to modal functioning (Y-axis) and direction to the existential, moral, and/or religious dynamic within the person or group or culture (X-axis).

DOOYEWEERD ON ABSOLUTIZATION

From the above it is no big step to understand where for Dooyeweerd things go wrong in philosophy and in the sciences. This occurs when philosophers or scientists ignore the transcendence of the notion of order and the transcendental nature of the ideas of diversity/coherence, unity, and origin. This ignorance inevitably leads to identification of some aspect of reality with what these transcendental notions stand for and represent. This identification means that something within reality (say, elementary particles and the laws they are subjected to) is held to be the ultimate foundation (origin), the most unifying element (unity), and/or ultimate binding principle (coherence) of reality. Dooyeweerd calls this unjustified identification of an aspect of reality with these principles of coherence, unity and origin: absolutization (from the Latin 'absolvere', to loosen and to set apart). This part or aspect is set apart and dealt with as if it is self-sustaining (as substance), has a meaning by itself and is the ultimate source (origin) of the world. This absolutizing is reflected in what earlier in this chapter was called reification.

Absolutizations are characteristic for what Dooyeweerd calls 'immanence' philosophies; philosophies which take one element or aspect of the world we inhabit as the basic 'material' and/or most fundamental explanatory principle for all that exists. The –ism's in the sciences are good examples of such absolutizations (physicalism, biologism, psychologism, and so on). Other examples are less bound to one modal aspect and related to major themes in cosmology, epistemology or anthropology: the absolutization of individual freedom, for instance; or the exclusive reliance on reason and scientific thinking; or utopian ideas about the malleability of the social and cultural world.

It is one of the main thrusts of Dooyeweerd's philosophy to unmask these absolutizations. It is his philosophical bet that the absolutization of an aspect (or part) of reality always leads to inner contradictions in one's overall conception of reality. This is because absolutization by itself is already a form of reality distortion. Distortions resulting from absolutization inevitably lead to tensions in one's overall picture of reality and, therefore, to what Dooyeweerd calls inner antinomies. One-sided emphasis on scientific and/or technological control causes, for instance, problems in one's concept of freedom. One-sided emphasis on human freedom is incompatible with the idea that we are in many ways determined by our biology and culture. This also holds for the analysis of the Western culture. Long before Adorno and Horkheimer published their landmark study *Dialektik der Aufklärung (Dialectic of the Enlightenment)* (1947) Dooyeweerd had already pointed out that a fundamental tension exists between technocratic control and individual freedom; or: between 'the ideal of science' and the 'ideal of personhood' (being a free person). This tension or polarity is irresolvable without a fundamental critique on the presumed autonomy of scientific reason. In this context Dooyeweerd speaks of an irresolvable dialectic in the ground-motive of our culture. The root of this dialectic is a dogmatic adherence to the idea of autonomy of (scientific) reason. A real critical philosophy will adopt a reflective attitude toward its own biases, including the bias of a one-sided scientistic look at reality.

Dooyeweerd entertained an extensive dialogue with scientists and philosophers of his days – Neo-Kantians, positivists, and phenomenologists alike – to show the inner antinomies in their thinking. His most important target was the absolutization of theoretical thought itself, especially in the Neo-Kantian tradition. It is the presumed autonomy of theoretical reasoning that lies at the heart of the crisis in philosophy and the culture of his days, he says. Scientism can be seen as a variant of this absolutization. Scientism is the view that science and science alone gives us access to true knowledge of what exists. Philosophers and scientists who accept and proclaim this idea, tend to think that their work is critical, independent, and objective. Dooyeweerd's thesis would instead be that their work is not critical enough. The presumption of the supremacy of the theoretical view on the world is biased, because it forgets that all human activity, theoretical thinking included, is always rooted in attitudes that embody a broader conception of reality. Adherents of scientism insufficiently recognize that the scientifically abstracted aspects of reality they are studying (elementary particles, molecules, cells, and the relations between them) are not identical with reality itself and that knowledge about other aspects of reality always remains insufficient and inadequate (albeit probably more precise, in certain respects) if caught in terms of these particles, molecules, cells and their relations. The reductive physicalism that feeds current variants of scientism has transformed legitimate reduction into illegitimate reductionism. This transformation is what Dooyeweerd meant with 'absolutization'.

DOOYEWEERD ON ENTITIES (THINGS, PROCESSES, SOCIAL INSTITUTIONS)

After highlighting two main strands in Dooyeweerd's philosophy – the idea of modal distinctness and the idea of the 'heart' as core of human existence – and their background in a cosmology that emphasizes diversity, coherence and unity, the next step is to apply these insights to 'entities', i.e., to things (like chairs, cars, rocks), to processes (physical, biotic, psychic, logical, social, and so on) and to social and societal structures like institutions (the state, the family) and practices (professional practices). Typically, the identity of an entity cannot completely be defined. This is because of its individuality. Identity has an individual side (this particular thing) and a more universal side (this kind of thing). It is the individuality of things which escapes from theoretical reasoning and, in fact, any attempt to define it. With respect to the universal side of things, their 'kindness', Dooyeweerd introduces the term qualifying function: things like rocks or plants are qualified by the fact that they function as and are determined by their existence as physical, respectively biotic entities. In other words, these things find their internal purpose, or destination, in their functioning in these spheres. With respect to human-made artefacts like chairs and traffic signs Dooyeweerd not only distinguishes a qualifying, but also a foundational function. They are based on a process of construction (which Dooyeweerd describes as a 'historical' foundation) and they are qualified by their functioning as facilitator of our activities (chairs) and as regulators of human traffic (traffic signs). The distinction between functioning as subject and as object becomes important here. These artefacts derive their specific role (and, therefore, their qualifying function) from their use as objects in interaction with humans. In other words, the qualifying function of chairs and traffic signs is determined by their role as social and signifying objects, respectively, in different types of social and public interaction. Something similar holds for social institutions like the family, the state, the company, and the church. They are based on foundational functions (biotic for the family, historical for the other three) whereas their qualifying function is derived from their internal destination as moral, economic, juridical, and religious institution, respectively.

REFERENCES

Adorno, Th. W., & Horkheimer, M. (1947). *Dialektik der Aufklärung*. Amsterdam: Querido.

Chaplin, J. (2011). *Herman Dooyeweerd: Christian Philosopher of State and Civil Society*. Notre Dame, IN: Notre Dame University Press.

Dooyeweerd, H. (1953–1958). *A New Critique of Theoretical Thought, Vol. I–IV*. Amsterdam: Presbyterian and Reformed Publishing Company.

Glas, G. (2017). Public and Institutional Aspects of Professional Responsibility in Medicine and Psychiatry. *Philosophia Reformata*, *82*(2), 146–166. doi:10.1163/23528230-08202005

Glas, G. (2019). Person-centered care in psychiatry. self-relational, normative, and contextual perspectives. London: Routledge.

Glas, G., & de Ridder, J. (Eds.). (2018). The Future of Creation Order: Vol. I. *Philosophical, scientific, and religious perspectives on order and creation*. Dordrecht: Springer.

Hoogland, J., & Jochemsen, H. (2000). Professional autonomy and the normative structure of medical practice. *Theoretical Medicine and Bioethics*, *21*(5), 457–475. doi:10.1023/A:1009925423036 PMID:11142442

Hoogland, J., Polder, J. J., Strijbos, S., & Jochemsen, H. (1995). *Professioneel beheerst. Professionele autonomie van de arts in relatie tot instrumenten voor beheersing van kosten en kwaliteit van de gezondheidszorg (rapport no.12)*. Ede: Prof. Dr. G.A. Lindeboom Instituut.

Jochemsen, H. (2006). Normative practices as an intermediate between theoretical ethics and morality. *Philosophia Reformata*, *71*(1), 96–112. doi:10.1163/22116117-90000377

Jochemsen, H., & Glas, G. (1997). *Verantwoord medisch handelen. Proeve van een christelijke medische ethiek*. Amsterdam: Buijten & Schipperheijn.

Mouw, R. J., & Griffioen, S. (1993). *Pluralisms and Horizons: An Essay in Christian Public Philosophy*. Grand Rapids, MI: W.B. Eerdmans Publ. Comp.

Van Dunné, J. M., Boeles, P., & Heerma van Voss, A. J. (1977). *Acht civilisten in burger*. Zwolle: Tjeerd Willink.

Verkerk, M. (2004). *Trust and Power on the Shop Floor. An Ethnographical, Ethical, and Philosophical Study on Responsible Behavior in Industrial Organisations* (Dissertation). Delft: Eburon Academic Publishers.

Verkerk, M., Hoogland, J., van der Stoep, J., & de Vries, J. (2016). *Philosophy of Technology: An Introduction for Technology and Business Students*. London: Routledge.

Wolters, A. (1984). *Creation regained*. Grand Rapids, MI: Eerdmans.

Chapter 3
Positioning the Normative Practice Approach

Jan Hoogland
University of Twente, The Netherlands & VU University Amsterdam, The Netherlands

ABSTRACT

The concept of social practices has received growing attention in interpretative social sciences. This concept is based on a long tradition of hermeneutical, interpretative, action-theoretical, pragmatist, and phenomenological theories in the social sciences, starting with Weber's famous definition of social action. In this chapter, some crucial stepping stones of this tradition are highlighted. In the line of these theories, a new approach of normative practices will be introduced, partially based on core philosophical insights of the Dutch philosopher Herman Dooyeweerd. Central features of this approach are 1) the multi-layered, intrinsically normative structure of social practices (constitutive side) and 2) the importance of regulative convictions, ideals, and attitudes leading the disclosure and development of those practices (regulative side).

INTRODUCTION

In the former chapter we saw that professionalism is going through a crisis. A key characteristic of professions as understood here is that their members are highly educated and skilled in a certain field of knowledge and practice. That specialist knowledge is a requirement for a competent performance of the practice. However, this observation does not yet determine how that knowledge is actually used in the performance of the practice. How does (abstract) scientific knowledge guide human

DOI: 10.4018/978-1-5225-8006-5.ch003

action? In social sciences and philosophy this question gets a more general form: How can one explain and understand human actions, including the use of language, and their consequences in a scientific way? This question has always guided the development of the humanities and social sciences. How come?

The scientific development since the Enlightenment has come about as a result of the enormous progression in the study of physical reality. In other words: science has been concerned with describing and explaining what happens in the objective reality outside the researcher. It has attempted to explain physical reality as accurately as possible. But what if the scientific interest extends to human reality, culture and society itself and human beings and their behavior will become 'the object of research'? This step raises many questions for the simple reason that then the human being is simultaneously the subject (researcher) and the object (researched phenomenon) of that kind of research.

Anthony Giddens calls this the problem of 'double hermeneutics'. The natural scientist has to deal with a single hermeneutical question, namely the question about the meaning of the scientific discourse he or she produces about reality. However, the researcher in the humanities and social sciences has to deal with a double hermeneutical question. Namely not only the meaning of the discourse on the object of research, but also the meaning that plays a role in the people that are the object of research: after all, people themselves make sense to the things that happen to them and act on the basis of those insights. In his own words: "The sociologist has as a field of study phenomena which are already constituted as meaningful. The condition of 'entry' to this field is getting to know what actors already know, and have to know, to 'go on' in the daily activities of social life. The concepts that sociological observers invent are 'second-order' concepts in so far as they presume certain conceptual capabilities on the part of the actors to whose conduct they refer. But it is in the nature of social science that these can become 'first-order' concepts by being appropriated within social life itself. What is 'hermeneutic' about the double hermeneutic? The appropriateness of the term derives from the double process of translation or interpretation which is involved. Sociological descriptions have the task of mediating the frames of meaning within which actors orient their conduct. But such descriptions are interpretative categories which also demand an effort of translation in and out of the frames of meaning involved in sociological theories" (Giddens 1984, 284).

One of the ways in which this problem is solved is by introducing a kind of dichotomy between two approaches in humanities and social sciences, namely one in which the social is studied purely from an outsider perspective and another one in which attention is also paid to the inner perspective of the actors and their actions. One could reflect on this distinction by talking about behavioral sciences versus sciences of action. From the outsider perspective, human reality is mainly studied on the basis of empirically observable behavior. From the inside perspective, questions are always asked about the meaning that people themselves give to their own actions. This not only regards the visible behavior, but also the underlying motives, reasons and the like.

An important attempt to keep both perspectives together was made by the classical sociologist Max Weber who proposed the following definition of sociology (as one of the founding human sciences): "Sociology (…) is a science concerning itself with the interpretive understanding of social action and thereby with a causal explanation of its course and consequences. We shall speak of 'action' insofar as the acting individual attaches a subjective meaning to his behavior – be it overt or covert, omission or acquiescence. Action is 'social' insofar as its subjective meaning takes account of the behavior of others and is thereby oriented in its course" (Weber 1978, 3-4).

In this definition two important perspectives on the humanities and the social sciences are brought together: that of explaining (*Erklären*) and that of understanding (*Verstehen*). In the first type of science, social reality is looked at in terms of causes and consequences, independent and dependent variables that in one way or another are empirically connected. The second type of sciences also looks at reasons, motives that make the behavior of people understandable from their own (subjective) perspective.

Even after Weber the discussion continues on questions such as: which of the two types of science is the 'most scientific'? Or about the question of how to make 'objective, universally valid' statements about sense and meaning? One could also say: the first type of humanities and social sciences leads to far-reaching objectified knowledge about the social, but without being able to do justice to the intrinsic meaning and normativity of social phenomena. The second type of science can do much more justice to that intrinsic meaning and normativity, but it is much more difficult to show that the knowledge it produces can actually meet the criteria of objective independent science. This debate is ongoing and participants take many different positions.

Discussing this debate in depth is beyond this treatise. It can be concluded that one of the ways in which the social sciences give shape to the second type of social science is in line with central insights of the philosopher Wittgenstein. In this discourse the concept of 'social practice' became an important theoretical concept.

THE RISE OF THE CONCEPT OF 'SOCIAL PRACTICE'

Wittgenstein

Wittgenstein is an author who exercised considerable influence on the questions posed above without having the explicit intention to contribute to this discussion. In his philosophy he is mainly concerned with the function and meaning of language. Particularly in his later philosophy (especially in the *Philosophical Investigations*, published after his death, Wittgenstein shows insights that have decisively influenced the discussion about the role of meaning in science.

Central concepts in the philosophy of (the late) Wittgenstein are 'language-game' and 'life-form'. These concepts are important to understand how language actually functions. In contrast to his early philosophy, according to the late Wittgenstein the function of language is not situated in the 'representation of reality', but in playing a role in human action. In fact, according to Wittgenstein, using language is an act. And the meaning of words is not primarily located in their referral relation to reality, but in the role they play in a situation of human action. Wittgenstein's famous formulation for this is: "the meaning of a word is its use in the language" (Wittgenstein 1968, 43). According to him we can understand the whole process of using words in a specific context "as one of those games by which children learn their native language. I will call these games 'language-games' and will sometimes speak of a primitive language as a language-game" (Wittgenstein 1968, 7). So, the meaning of words is determined by the rules that apply to the specific language-game in which they function.

The use of the term language-game makes clear that using language is always part of a practice: "the term 'language-game' is meant to bring into prominence the fact that the speaking of language is part of an activity or of a form of life" (Wittgenstein 1968, 23). With this term 'form of life' Wittgenstein expresses the linkage between the meaning of words ("its use in the language") and the human actions around it: using words is always a part of a practice in which words and deeds go together. Put differently, using words, speaking and writing is a form of human action, which is part of chains of mental and bodily actions within the coherence of a specific life-form (or what we later will appoint to as social practices).

Characteristic of language-games and life-forms is that one can only grasp their meaning by participating in it. And active participation is only possible if one masters the rules of the game. Within language-games and life-forms one needs a competence, the ability to act according to the rules. A characteristic of a rule is that it forms the criterion for the question whether an action is appropriate or inappropriate within the context of the language-game and associated life-form. In the game of football the ball may not be touched with the hands with exception of the keeper. If someone does, it is immediately corrected by the referee or the teammates: the act of picking up the ball or touch it with the hands is not appropriate within the rules of the game. A rule, therefore, only exists when people can correct each other for following them. In other words: a rule is a mentally shared reality, even in those cases where people cannot even formulate the rule explicitly but 'feel' whether something is going according to the rules or not.

Based on this line of thinking, one could indicate the difference between the two views of the humanities and the social sciences indicated above, namely between studying observable behavior on the one hand and meaningful action on the other. *In order to be able to study meaningful actions, it is essential that the researcher actively understands and manages the rules that underlie the studied actions.*

It was Peter Winch who introduced the philosophy of Wittgenstein into the field of the social sciences and the discussion about their philosophical and epistemological backgrounds. In his *The idea of a social science and its relation to philosophy* (1958) he emphasizes the importance of the Wittgensteinian concept of 'shared rule following' for understanding the specific epistemology of the social sciences.

In following this line of thought of Wittgenstein and Winch, the leading terms are 'language-game', 'life-form', 'rules' and 'grammar' (as the coherent package of rules applying to a certain language-game or a certain form of life). Wittgenstein does not use words like 'praxis' or 'practice' in this context. For the background of this concept we need to take our philosophical investigation some steps further.

One of the connecting philosophical tracks is that of the critical theory of Jürgen Habermas, which gives our analysis a specific and rich follow-up. A second track is that of moral philosophy, in particular that of Charles Taylor and Alisdair MacIntyre, with its concept of 'social practice'.

We will briefly discuss these two lines of thought to arrive at a paradigm, in which many of the lines indicated so far appear to converge, that of the 'social practice theory'.

Habermas

Although 'social practice' is not a key concept in the work of Jürgen Habermas and there are fundamental differences between Habermas' intersubjectivism and practice theory (Reckwitz 2002), for us it is one of the steps towards our Normative Practices approach. The reason is that his theory of communicative action explains what it means to be responsible for your actions and how actors can account for their own actions.

Habermas tries to expand the ideas of Wittgenstein to a theory of communicative action. He distinguishes between three different forms of action. The first one is built on the Weberian category of 'goal-oriented action' ('zweckrationales Handeln'): instrumental action. Next to this category Habermas distinguishes two forms of social action ('soziales Handeln'): strategic and communicative action. The distinguishing perspectives are the orientation of action (oriented to success or result vs. oriented to reaching mutual understanding) and the action situation (social vs. not social) (Table 1).

Habermas' theory of communicative action builds further on Wittgenstein's ideas and the expansion of them in the work of Austin, Searle and Winch. Habermas has doubts about Wittgenstein's statement that it is impossible to formulate a scientific theory about language-games and forms of life. Habermas also has objections to the relativistic consequences of Wittgenstein's view, in which every language-game and form of life forms its own horizon of understanding. One can only understand the meaning of a specific language-game and life-form from within, by participating in it, without any reference to a more encompassing theory about language-games or forms of life in general. These hesitations form one of the reasons why Habermas comes to the formulation of his theory of communicative action in which Wittgenstein's notions are expanded to a broader theory about human action and the role of speech-acts in it.

According to Wittgenstein the ability to understand language and human action presupposes the participation in the language-game and form of life which the speech-acts and actions belong to. This means that understanding normative structures presupposes that one takes a stand towards the implicit normative claims that are at stake in a certain social practice.

According to Habermas these normative claims should be understood as universal claims in three different domains: the objective world, the social world and the subjective world of one's inner feelings and experiences. Claims concerning the objective world are truth claims about empirical (observable) reality, which can be explicated in propositions. Claims concerning the social world are expressed in an illocution of a speech-act as one of its constituent parts. It expresses the will of the

Table 1.

Action Situation	**Action Orientation**	
	Oriented to Success	**Oriented to Reaching Understanding**
Not social	Instrumental action	-
Social	Strategic action	Communicative action

From: Habermas, J. 1984, vol. I 285

actor and the purpose for executing it. Claims concerning the subjective world are related to the correspondence between the real identity and motives of the actor and the meaning of what he or she says: is the actor authentic, sincere in his or her speech-acts.

Especially interesting in Habermas' theory is that he presents communicative action as a process of reciprocal alignment, coordination and accountability, based on the pursuit of mutual agreement or consensus about the situation of action. Often this process of alignment proceeds very implicitly. But in situations of more or less serious differences in opinion about the definition of the situation of action, it may be necessary to continue this process in a more explicit way by making clear which of the validity claims of the actors involved is controversial. In those cases, communicative action can be continued in a different mode, in which the differences in opinion can be discussed explicitly in different discourses. (Namely a theoretical discourse in the case of differences in opinion about truth-claims, a practical or ethical discourse in the case of moral claims; in the case of the authenticity-claim there is no specific type of discourse available according to Habermas.)

For the argument in this article it is important to stress that Habermas enhances the 'therapeutical' notes of Wittgenstein to a full-blown theory of communicative action. He presents this theory mainly as a view on the way in which human beings are able to strive for mutual understanding and to show accountability for their actions by their willingness to explicate the underlying validity-claims.

Taylor and MacIntyre

MacIntyre and Taylor in a sense also build on the insights of Wittgenstein. However, the emphasis is different, namely the moral side of social actions of people. Furthermore, these authors make use of the concept of 'practice'. According to them the concept of 'social practice' is at the heart of human social life. According to Taylor, the very nature of social sciences lies in that "there is always a pre-theoretical understanding of what is going on among the members of a society, which is formulated in the descriptions of self and other which are involved in the institutions and practices of that society. A society is among other things a set of institutions and practices, and these cannot exist and be carried on without certain self-understandings" (Taylor 1985, 93).

What both philosophers add to the reflections so far is the strong sense of 'hermeneutical presuppositions' that are always present in social practices (Heidegger and Gadamer), which Taylor, in the quotation above, indicates with 'pre-theoretical understanding'. MacIntyre mainly focuses on the moral side of practices. Think of his much cited definition: "By a 'practice' I am going to mean any coherent and complex form of socially established cooperative human activity through which goods internal to that form of activity are realized in the course of trying to achieve those standards of excellence which are appropriate to, and partially definitive of, that form of activity, with the result that human powers to achieve excellence, and human conceptions of the ends and goods involved, are systematically extended" (MacIntyre 2007, 187).

MacIntyre actually develops the concept of 'practice' in his *After Virtue* relatively casually. The main assumption of that book is that the concept of 'virtues', strongly emphasized by Aristotle, may be helpful in breaking the 'modern crisis in ethics'. According to the analysis of MacIntyre, in modern times ethics is more and more stripped down into a procedure by means of which we can make decisions based on widely divergent moral preferences of individuals. MacIntyre speaks of 'emotivism' here: "Emotivism is the doctrine that all evaluative judgments and more specifically all moral judgments are *nothing but* expressions of preference, expressions of attitude or feeling, insofar as they are moral or evaluative in character" (MacIntyre 2007, 11-12). Instead of looking at moral decision-making in a context of moral plurality in a purely procedural way based on a variety of different individual moral preferences, it may be more rewarding to re-focus on the moral qualities of individuals. In this case we are not primarily concerned with the question whether certain actions do receive our approval or not, but whether people have a good character and are qualified by a morally good disposition. After all, the question of whether someone is characterized by qualities such as honesty, justice and courage says a lot about that person. It is easy to acknowledge that such a person is virtuous.

For MacIntyre 'social practices' are particularly important as the institutional contexts in which virtues are 'practiced'. Social practices like care or education get their shape in social institutions like hospitals and schools. These institutions are the contexts in which human beings practice their moral attitude towards each other. Nobody is virtuous by nature. Virtues are not innate. One can only become virtuous through effort. Virtues can be seen as dispositions, as patterns of action that have become character traits and characterize a person. And a certain pattern of action can only be a sustainable property of a person by becoming a basic attitude of that person.

In MacIntyre's definition of 'social practices' the link with the concept of virtue is not immediately visible. The (Greek) word that Aristotle uses for virtue is 'aretè', which can best be translated as 'excellent'. That word 'excellent' is also present in the above-mentioned definition of 'social practices'. According to that definition, "practices" contribute to the trend "that human powers to achieve excellence (...) are systematically extended".

According to MacIntyre, the pursuit of the realization of the internal goods of social practices is highly dependent on the degree to which the actors are virtuous people. The formation of a virtuous person ('a good character') is therefore important in order to enable them to contribute to the realization of the internal goods of a practice.

The distinction between 'internal' and 'external goods' is also important here. MacIntyre defines 'internal goods' in terms of the concept of Praxis in Aristotle: actions that are not aimed at a certain goal outside the action, but activities which have "their ends and objectives within themselves" (Eikeland 2006, 23). Take for example 'good football' or 'beautifully playing the flute'. These are activities which are only undertaken because of the value of the activity itself.

The realization of external goods is much more related to actions that are instrumentally needed to realize an external goal. For example, if one uses his or her ability to play football or the flute to earn a living by means of that activity. MacIntyre distinguishes sharply between internal and external goods, suggesting that external goods can be disturbing for the realization of internal goods. The reason for that is that external goods feed forms of competition between actors: what is in favor for one actor is disadvantageous for the other. To quote MacIntyre: "We are now in a position to notice an important difference between what I have called internal and what I have called external goods. It is characteristic of what I have called external goods that when achieved they are always some individual's property and possession. Moreover, characteristically they are such that the more someone has of them, the less there is for other people. This is sometimes necessarily the case, as with power and fame, and sometimes the case by reason of contingent circumstance as with money. External goods are therefore characteristically objects of competition in which there must be losers as well as winners. Internal goods are indeed the outcome of competition to excel, but it is characteristic of them that their achievement is a good for the whole community who participate in the practice" (MacIntyre 2007, 190-191).

In *After Virtue* the terms 'praxis' and 'practice' come close together. Each 'social practice' is characterized by a praxis, a form of activity which has its own internal good. It is a condition for the ability to realize that internal good, that the actor is virtuous. Because only a virtuous person is able to dedicate himself in such a way to the internal good of a practice that it meets the standards of excellence.

Social Practice Theory

Above we have stipulated some of the highlights of one line of thinking within the view that the humanities have a fundamentally different status and methodology from the social sciences. Another line that provided elements for social practice theory is that of hermeneutics and phenomenology with authors such as Dilthey, Heidegger, Gadamer and Ricoeur. Yet another line of thinking is that of pragmatism: Peirce, James and Dewey. These various lines offer their own perspectives on the way in which social practices as the building blocks of society and social life can be analyzed and understood. These different perspectives come together in the work of several more recent authors who work on 'social practice theory', for example Schatzki (2008) and Nicolini (2012).

In his article 'Toward a Theory of Social Practices' Reckwitz, who strongly borrows from Schatzki, presents 'social practice theory' as a specific approach in the social sciences, associated with the tradition of 'cultural theories'. According to him, 'cultural theories' oppose two dominant lines in the classical social sciences, one of which starts with the *homo economicus* and the other with the *homo sociologicus* as their elementary view on the functioning of human beings: "Cultural theories, including practice theory, are founded upon a different form of explaining and understanding action, namely by having recourse to symbolic structures of meaning" (Reckwitz 2002, 244).

Reckwitz argues that there are three fundamentally different paradigms for explaining actions and social order in the tradition of social theory: 1) the purpose-rational ('purpose-oriented') model of explaining human actions; 2) the value-rational ('norm-oriented') model; 3) the culturalist model that developed in the course of the 20th century (following the 'interpretative turn' of the 1970s: Reckwitz 2002, 243).

What is unique about the culturalist model and hence also about the theory of social practices is "their way of grasping the conditions of human action and social order." "In contrast, the newness of the cultural theory consists in explaining and understanding actions by reconstructing the symbolic structures of knowledge that enable and constrain the agents of the world according to certain forms, and to behave in corresponding ways. Social order then does not appear as a product of compliance or mutual normative expectations, but is embedded in collective cognitive and symbolic structures, in a 'shared knowledge' which enables a socially shared way of ascribing meaning to the world."

According to Reckwitz, a 'social practice' consists of various elements that are an integral part of it: 'mind', 'things', 'knowledge', 'discourse / language', 'structure / process' and 'agent / individual'. 'Practice theory' thus appears to be primarily an integrative theory: all matters that play a role in the social life of people are included in this concept, because it all plays a role in the meaningful coherence that forms our daily social world.

Reckwitz derives his view for an important part from Theodore R. Schatzki. The latter came in 1996 with a more detailed elaboration of the concept in his *Social Practices. A Wittgensteinian approach to Human Activity and the Social*. In this book he tries to give an integral theory of the social. This means, among other things, that 'social practices' must be seen as including both mental and material components. That is not surprising, since both - body and mind - come together in the actions of people. It is the body that acts, but in its actions it is guided by processes of interpretation and sense-giving.

According to Schatzki, most authors who deal with this subject regard 'social practices' as the 'fundamental social phenomenon'. In addition, they share "the idea that the practices are the site where understanding is structured and intelligibility (...) articulated (...)" (Schatzki 2008, 12). Those who want to study 'the social' cannot ignore the term 'practice'. This concept lies according to these thinkers in the heart of their theories about the social: "By virtue of the understandings and intelligibilities they carry, practices are where the realms of sociality and individual mentality/activity are at once organized and linked. Both social order and individuality (…) result from practices" (Schatzki 2008, 13). It is all about 'human coexistence' and therefore also about 'Zusammenhang', 'a state of held-togetherness' (Schatzki 2008, 14).

The concept of social practice has many definitions. Schatzki (2001, p. 2) defines it as "embodied, materially mediated arrays of human activity centrally organized around shared practical understanding". He distinguishes 'at least three notions' around the concept of 'practice': 1) "practicing is learning how to improve one's ability to do something by working and carrying it out"; 2) "practice as a temporally unfolding and spatially dispersed nexus or donations and sayings." "To say that doings and sayings are a matter of fact, that they are linked in certain ways. Three major avenues of linkage are involved: i) through understanding, for example, or what to say and do; ii) through explicit rules, principles, precepts, and instructions; and iii) through what I want to call 'teleoaffective' structures embracing ends, projects, tasks, purposes, beliefs, emotions and moods "; 3) 'practice' as 'performing an action or carrying out a practice of the second sort'. "It is this notion of practice that the Western philosophical tradition has often been opposed to theory: theory versus practice, contemplation and reflection versus doing" (Schatzki 2008, 90-91).

Schatzki distinguishes different types of 'practices': 'dispersed' and 'integrative practices'. "The dispersed practice of X-ing is a set of doings and sayings linked primarily, usually exclusively, by the understanding of X-ing. This understanding, in turn, normally has three components: 1) the ability to carry out acts of X-ing (e.g., describing, ordering, questioning), 2) the ability to identify and attribute X-ings, in both one's own and other's cases, and 3) the ability to prompt or respond to X-ings. Another expression for 'the ability to' in this context is 'knowing how to' "(Schatzki 2008, 91). According to Schatzki, this third component is not an omnipresent feature of dispersed practices. It is present when established ways of prompting or responding to a given sort of action exist.

What is generally lacking in what Schatzki refers to as 'dispersed practices' is that they are rarely interconnected by "rules and teleoaffective structures" (91): "The dispersion of practice actually requires the absence of the teleoaffective component of practice organization. If the doings and sayings that make up such practices as describing, explaining, and questioning were tied to particular arrays of ends, purposes, emotions, and the like, the practices could not appear in more or less all walks of life and in a wide variety of situations "(92). In other words, the 'dispersed practices are the building blocks of more complex practices.

This brings us to the second type of 'practices', the integrative practices: "By 'integrative practices' I mean the more complex practices found in and constitutive of particular domains or social life." "Like dispersed practices, integrative ones are collections of linked doings and sayings. The doings and sayings involved are joined by: 1) understandings of Q-ing and R-ing (etc.), along with 'sensitized' understandings or X-ing and Y-ing (etc.), the latter carried by the transfigured forms that the dispersed practices of X-ing and Y-ing adopt within integrative practices; 2) explicit rules, principles, precepts, and instructions; and 3) teleoaffective structures comprising hierarchies or ends, tasks, projects, beliefs, emotions, moods, and the like. I will henceforth refer to the understandings, rules, and teleoaffective structure that link integrative practice's doings and sayings as the 'organization' of the practice" (Schatzki 2008, 98-99).

With these 'integrative practices' we come close to MacIntyre's definition of practice again. In his definition it was particularly striking that this was 'coherent and complex form or socially established cooperative human activity', aimed at the realization of 'goods internal to that form of activity'. In the 'teleoaffective structure' of Schatzki you can hear those 'internal goods' return.

For Schatzki, the 'teleoaffective structure' of 'practices' is associated with a more Heideggerian view of action. "The notion of signifying (*bedeuten*) hails from Heidegger. On his analysis, what a person does is structured by *Verstehen* (understanding) and *Befindlichkeit* (attunement). Understanding houses the teleological component of the structuring of action, while attunement is the locus of its affective component. Together, they lay out why, at a given moment in a particular situation, an actor performs a particular action" (Schatzki 2008, 122).

The 'Normative Practice Approach' presented in this book is closely aligned with this concept of 'integrative practices'. We could say that in the 'Normative Practice Approach' a theoretical framework is offered which makes it possible to analyze 'integrative practices' in more detail.

THE NORMATIVE PRACTICE APPROACH

Roots in Dooyeweerdian Philosophy

Partly within and partly alongside the aforementioned lines of philosophical reflection of Wittgenstein, Habermas, Taylor and MacIntyre that led to an elaborated concept of social practices a number of Dutch philosophers have developed their own approach, the Normative Practice Approach. This approach is not only based on the ideas of the just-mentioned authors, but also on some key insights of the Dutch philosopher Herman Dooyeweerd (for a short, general introduction into the philosophy of Herman Dooyeweerd, from which the following section borrows heavily; see Chapter 2). Of this philosophy we single out four core elements that we need for an understanding of the NPA.

1. For Dooyeweerd, 'meaning' is not attributed to reality by people's 'sense-giving' but belongs to the very nature of reality itself. In other words, it is a dimension of reality. As Dooyeweerd succinctly stated 'meaning is the being of all that has been created' (Dooyeweerd 1953-1957, vol. 1,4). This meaning is 'naturally' given in daily experience. We experience reality in our daily lives as a given meaningful coherence, which according to Dooyeweerd refers to a totality (cf. section above Wittgenstein). This does not necessarily mean that everything we experience is meaningful to us. Often the meaning of things or appearances is unclear to us or even disturbed by destructive forces. But we normally experience the world in which we live our daily life as a meaningful coherence where everything has its own, 'natural' place.
2. Since science is based on abstraction, scientific research will break up the meaning of being in a variety of different meaning perspectives which are part of a totality but are irreducible to each other (the modal aspects) (Dooyeweerd 1953-1957, Vol 1, 22f.) This does not mean that meaning vanishes, but that it is discounted during doing research. Here we encounter his teaching about the modal aspects (or functions) that, according to Dooyeweerd can be distinguished in reality. (The term 'modal' does not refer to logic (modal logic), but to the Latin term 'modus', which means: way of existing or functioning.)

He distinguishes fifteen of these aspects or modalities. All those aspects have their own meaning-kernel expressing the specific aspect of meaning characteristic for it. In addition, those aspects are mutually irreducible. All things (entities) function in all these different aspects and all those ways of functioning are weaved together in a seemingly self-evident and natural way in our everyday experience.

The meaning kernel of these perspectives cannot be grasped in a theoretical concept but only be explicated as a pre-theoretical idea. In the following tablet the set of modal aspects is presented with a concise description of their kernel. In the act of scientific research, depending on the specific discipline of that research, one of these aspects of meaning will be isolated from the integral coherence of daily life to enable its study from a logical point of view.

3. Everything that exists in our reality (things, artefacts, happenings, processes, relations, etc.) functions in all the different aspects of meaning. Here we encounter Dooyeweerd's theory of the structures of individuality of temporal things' (Dooyeweerd 1953-1957, Vol 3, 53f.) By 'individual, temporal things' he understands not only material things (stones, plants, trees) or artefacts (chairs, tables, tools), but also events, processes and social relations, like social practices. All those things are temporal in their very nature. That means that they are continually changing. This raises the question of their identity: what is lasting in their changeability. In this theory we apply Dooyeweerd's theory of the 'modal aspects' as a framework for the analysis of the general structure of 'individual, temporal things'. Scientific analysis does not lead to an understanding of the individual thing, as science always is aiming at the elucidation of general structural features that can be formulated in laws that apply to a type or class of things, like horses, or social practices. In other words, although science can study individual practice performance from the angle of the structural features that can be identified in it, the full individual performance is not open for scientific analysis. This means that to understand and explain individual performance we need to observe all the modal perspectives in which the practice functions.

Entities function simultaneously in all modal aspects. But not all modal aspects have the same function in an entity. The first special function which Dooyeweerd discerns is the *qualifying* function. This is the modal aspect which is capable of qualifying a certain thing as structural whole. The qualifying function of entities, whether they are material objects of social structures, is determined by the aspects that gives that entity its specific character. A tree is qualified by the biotic aspect and a chair by the social aspect. Social practices are qualified by the aspect that indicates its reason of existence, e.g. government by the juridical aspect with justice as its meaning kernel, that we also call normative principle. In addition to the qualifying aspect we distinguish the foundational aspect and conditioning aspects. This will be further explained in the presentation of the normative practice approach.

4. The idea that all human activity is rooted in what Dooyeweerd calls the 'heart' and which he denotes as 'concentration point' within our existence out of which our ultimate concerns originate.

The term 'heart' refers to the idea that we humans are driven by fundamental concerns, motivations, commitments, and convictions. These commitments and convictions are not only individual psychological realities, they have an existential and moral/spiritual core and typically aim at what is beyond the horizon of our knowledge and experience (something 'greater than us').

The heart itself is not something that can be studied with empirical means, it is presupposed, and it expresses itself in all human functioning, most clearly and explicitly in the life- and worldview of a person.

The difficulty with conceptualizing the notion of the heart is that it cannot be equated with functioning in one or another modal aspect or be identified with a part of our biopsychosocial existence. It is not the same as aesthetic feeling, or moral sensitivity, or spiritual openness, or value-sensitivity, though all of these may represent what is 'in' our hearts. If the modal aspects are plotted on the Y-axis, then the activity of the heart could be plotted on the X-axis. Followers of Dooyeweerd have described this as a relation between 'structure' and 'direction' a distinction that is also used in the normative practice approach. S*tructure* refers to the *constitutive* side of practices—i.e., to aspects that refer to the foundation or basis of a certain practice. Without compliance to norms that constitute a practice, practices cannot be qualified as the practices they are: medical practice, economic practice, educational practice, and so on. The term 'direction', sometimes called the regulative side, refers to this religious dynamic, rooted in the heart, that brings individuality structures, like practices, to their destination. In other words, 'direction' aims at the *regulative* dimension—i.e., to the moral, spiritual, and religious values and spirit that guide practices.

In Hoogland et al. (1995), Hoogland & Jochemsen (2000), and in Jochemsen and Glas (1997), additional distinctions were proposed with respect to the constitutive side (of medical practice, in their case). Like Dooyeweerd, these authors discerned *qualifying* as well as *foundational* principles (or: structures). But they also introduced the term *conditioning* (or: conditions-enabling) principles (or structures) to indicate the relevance and complexity of current healthcare practices; and its dependence on non-foundational, non-qualifying, but nevertheless crucially enabling conditions (agreements, codes, social conditions, economic conditions, juridical conditions). Jochemsen and Glas (1997) associated the regulative dimension of medical practice with the *ethos*—the ensemble of core values and ultimate concerns—of the medical profession and began to write about the existential core of professionalism (Glas, 2019). Other authors began to emphasize the role of *contexts* in the definition of the certain practices, for instance Mouw and Griffioen (1993) in their discussion of the structure of the family and of societal institutions; Verkerk et al. (2016) in their analysis of the role of technology in organizations; Glas (2017; accepted), again, in the context of healthcare.

In most of its initial formulations (Hoogland et al. [1995] is an exception, especially section 4.4 and chapter 10), the NPA aimed primarily at the individual professional–client relation. In this book, the perspective will be broadened by focusing on other actors, operating at meso- and macrolevels (e.g., institutions, policy making bodies, advisory committees and government).

The Main Characteristics of the Normative Practice Approach

Our proposal now is to analyze social practices as distinguished by various (social) philosophers and sociologists from Dooyeweerd's philosophy as structures of individuality.

In any case, it is clear from the definitions given above that practices are characterized by the interrelationship of human actions, in which people act interactively according to certain rules that are constitutive for the practice in question.

According to MacIntyre those practices are characterized by their own, internal good. In terms of Schatzki, integrative social practices are characterized by their own 'teleo-affective structure'. Boutellier describes it as the 'core function' of social practices (Boutellier 2013, 151). These are terms to indicate that a practice does not simply exist, as a factual phenomenon, but is a dynamic reality which continually is shaped by human action and is focused on a certain 'telos' or goal or has its own intention or destination. Seen from the perspective of Dooyeweerd's theory about of the structures of individuality it must be possible to determine which modal aspect is qualifying for this core function of a specific social practice and therefore is leading in the development of that practice.

But whereas MacIntyre speaks in terms of a dichotomy of an 'internal good' and 'external goods' and Schatzky uses the general term of 'teleoaffective structure', Dooyeweerdian philosophy makes it possible to analyze social practices in a more differentiated and detailed way by stressing that a practice functions in all fifteen modal aspects. Below we will present the main lines of such an analysis will work.

The Constitutive Side of Normative Practices (Structure)

The Normative Practice Approach (NPA) begins by asking for the qualifying function of a practice. In other words: what is the modal aspect that is qualifying the 'internal good' of the 'core function' of the practice in question. Which of the fifteen aspects can be seen as typical for the 'finality' of that practice? According to

Dooyeweerd the qualifying modal aspect can be seen as the function of that practice which determines the unity (coherence) of it in its daily functioning. The remaining aspects of that practice have a serving function towards this qualifying function.

Take for example the medical practice. Assuming that 'caring for and – if possible – curing sick, wounded or handicapped people' is the 'internal good' or 'core function' of this practice, the NPA speaks of the 'ethical aspect' as the qualifying function of this practice. However, a hospital can only give shape to this 'finality' properly if, among other things, it has a sustainable financial basis. The economic aspect of the hospital is, therefore, of great importance too. We could see this economic function as a necessary condition for its functioning as a hospital. All those functions which are necessary conditions for the functioning of a specific social practice in the NPA are referred to as the 'conditioning 'or 'facilitating functions' of this practice.

Furthermore, next to the 'qualifying function' and the different 'conditioning functions' of a specific social practice it is important to identify its 'foundational function'. Because all social practices are existing as forms of 'socially established cooperative human activity' (MacIntyre) they must be seen as founded in the 'formative aspect' which is typical for the formative power of human action. So, the foundational aspect of all social practices as established by human activity is the 'formative aspect'. It means that in all social practices historical and technical phenomena are involved: documents, techniques, computers, ICT-networks, methods of working and functioning, task descriptions or annual reports. All those artefacts, referring to human action, its instruments and its results, are integral part of the social practice in question and belong to its structural features.

We see that by the NPA a highly differentiated analysis of social practices is made possible. First of all, it is possible to distinguish different categories (species) of social practices which are qualified by the same 'qualifying function'. Think of all social practices which are qualified by the economic aspect: companies, industries, farms; or social practices qualified by the 'ethical aspect': cure and care, welfare; or social practices qualified by the aesthetic aspect': art, music, theatre, museums, concert halls. Furthermore, within each species one can also distinguish different types: practices aimed at short-term cure or at long-term care, practices aimed at 'restoring normal daily life' (e.g. addiction care) or practices aimed at supporting people to live as independently as possible (e.g. 'assisted living').

Secondly, the NPA helps to demonstrate how the various modal aspects of social practices can be of service to the 'qualifying function' which is typical for the 'internal good' or 'core function' of the practice concerned. In the NPA this is called the 'simultaneous realization of norms'. This means that a good practice always requires a balanced attention for the diversity of normative rules that are relevant within it, without threatening the realization of its 'internal good' or 'core function'.

Maybe, this last remark sounds rather normative and therefore less 'scientific' (objective) as one would like. However, from the NPA point of view this is inevitable: social practices are intrinsically normative. They exist by the grace of the rules that make them possible. These normative structures are constitutive for these social practices. Without them they won't exist. So, our ability to discern social practices, to participate in them and to evaluate their performance, is constituted by these normative structures. So, for example, the game of chess would not exist without the rules constitutive for it. The existence of chess is therefore much more than the material existence of the 'chessboard' and the 'pieces' with which it is played. In fact, the game of chess can possibly be played even without these pieces. The chess game exists because of its constitutive rules and the actualization of the game by human beings practicing it by applying the rules of the game every time it is played.

Within the NPA the 1) foundational, 2) conditioning or facilitating and 3) qualifying aspects are called the constitutive side of a practice. By analyzing a practice with the help of these categories it is possible to get more insight into the normative structure of specific social practices. However, by this explanation little or nothing has been said about the concrete interpretations, ideas and ideals of the actors who are acting in that peculiar practice. Take for example two chess players who meet each other in a match. They both have their own motivation, drive, style of play, preferences and allergies. They both have their own stand in life, their own trusts and distrusts and their own ethos (moral attitude). All these things are important factors in the way in which each of them plays his part in the match in which they meet each other. All these factors are part of what above we have called the regulative side of social practices.

The Regulative Side of Normative Practices (Direction)

People's actions generally take place within a variety of social practices, sometimes even simultaneously. People apply the rules that are valid for the specific social practices in which they are active at the moment of their participation. At the same time, everyone can imagine that people's concern with those practices goes deeper than only following the rules applying to that specific practice. All human action roots in the 'heart'. This means humans are responsible for their actions and, as a consequence, for their participation in those practices. So, the willingness to participate in a specific practice also means taking responsibility for the internal good of that practice in particular and of the rules which are used to be applied in that practice. This responsibility is essential and, among others, means that people can never simply hide behind the rules they follow in their actions. Responsibility goes beyond blindly following rules. In the NPA this responsibility for one's own participation within a practice and for consenting to the rules which apply to that practice, is referred to with the concept of 'accountability' (more about this later). All those personal factors, rooted in the professionals' heart', belong to what in the NPA is called the regulative side. This notion of regulative side also has a background in social (language) philosophy which will be briefly explained.

At first sight the distinction between the constitutive and regulative side of social practices seems to refer to the distinction between constitutive and regulative rules in the work of Searle: "Regulating rules regulate an already existing activity. The existence of this activity is logically independent of the rules. Constituting rules constitute an activity whose existence logically depends on rules, which this activity also regulate" (Searle 1969, 45).

Duintjer describes Searle's distinction as follows: "Some make a distinction between rules that create, found and enable a new practice (for example rules for chess, football, arithmetic; syntactic and semantic language rules) on the one hand, and rules that further modify behavior that already exists and is identifiable independently of these rules on the other hand (for example moral rules, etiquette rules, rules for the way we eat, sleep, converse, etc." (Duintjer 1977, 45; translation from Dutch by JH). A little further he specifies this a bit more: "Constitutive rules (...) define a practice and do not allow alternatives without going beyond this practice (...). Continued violation of constitutive rules means that one no longer participates in that particular practice (...)" (Duintjer 1977, 46; translation by JH). In his case, too, the regulative - or in his terms: modifying - rules appear as relatively second-class.

Within the NPA, however, the sphere of the regulative side of social practices has a much more prominent role. This is prompted by an important point concerning practices that hitherto has not been addressed.

What we have shown is that practices are constituted by rules which determine what can be considered as appropriate action within these practices. In order to participate in a particular practice, the actor must be a 'competent performer' according to those rules.

Although social practices are constituted by rules, the actions within them are far from fixed. Actors make their own choices. They can make several independent choices in the way they would like to give shape to the practice in which they participate. Duintjer shows that constitutive rules have both an enabling and a restricting function (Shwayder): "making room for possible behavior and limiting boundaries of possible behavior" (Duintjer 1977, 47). Perhaps the example of chess can clarify this again: the rules that are constitutive for this game lay down both which moves are allowed and which are not. By determining the permitted moves, those constitutive rules allow for a certain course of play that can lead to a draw or to the victory of one of the two players.

However, this does not mean anything about the actual course that an individual game of chess shows. Because this depends on many more factors than just the restrictive and enabling rules of the game itself. Factors that do influence the course of the game, but do not determine the game called 'chess'. Moreover, the constitutive rules of a practice are not fixed forever, but can change in the course of history. Social practices are constantly in a process of development, further development and - hopefully - into the right direction, so that change is also an improvement. The course of this development process is also open and undetermined, dependent of human choices.

This observation opens a new space, the dimension which Duintjer has indicated as a dimension 'around rules' or as 'the inexhaustible': "rules are those under the guidance of which we can determine whether or not behavior (...) is justified, well-founded, (...), but which itself contains no ground or justification for itself. For 'rule' means (...) 'criterion for criticism (...) of behavior'; and the rule itself is, by negative definition, not behavior'. The conclusion Duintjer draws from this is that rules are not 'self-founding, self-justifying, self-evident' (Duintjer 1977, 72; translation from JH). In other words, there is no practice of founding practices. Above we have expressed this by saying that the meaning of practices is given by the existence of those practices themselves.

This space 'around rules', the 'inexhaustible', makes visible that human responsibility extends beyond following the rules. The question of whether or not a person wants to participate in certain practices and agrees with their rules is also part of human responsibility.

We choose to refer to all those factors that play a role in this space 'around rules' as the regulative side of social practices. In doing so, we deviate from Searle's distinction between constitutive and regulatory (or: regulative?) rules. For us, the regulative side of social practices relates to the notions, ideas and considerations that play a role in the space around the rules and gives direction to human action within these practices. With this distinction we are more in keeping with the distinction Kant makes between 'constitutive rules' of human knowledge and the 'regulatory ideas' of the practical reason.

So, the regulative side of social practices includes all those factors that, given peoples involvement in practices, determine their attitude towards them: their motivation, their inspiration, or as Glas puts it: their "ethos, core values and ultimate concerns" (see chapter 1 of this book). This ethos, core values, and ultimate concerns root in the 'heart' as it functions in the philosophy of Dooyeweerd (see above). On the basis of this attitude they contribute to the continuation and further development of those practices in daily life. Talking about the regulative side of social practices means paying attention to what the actors within a practice understand as a good way of acting within that practice. Take again the example of chess: a game of chess that unfolds according to the rules that are constitutive for chess not necessarily is a good, let alone sparkling, match at all. The concept of the regulative side of practices deals with the factors that can make that difference, for example the difference between a match according to the rules and a sparkling and challenging match.

In brief: the constitutive side of social practices determines what makes a practice to be that specific practice (what makes a game a game of chess?); the regulatory side determines what makes that the actions within a practice satisfy the standards of good quality (or 'excellence' in the words of MacIntyre) and contribute to improvement of that practice in its continuous development.

Accountability and Moral Capital

Notions which can be used in NPA to give more clarity about this regulative side of social practices are the notion of accountability at the individual level and the notions of ethos and moral capital at the community level.

The concept of accountability can be defined as the personal attitude by which an actor responds to the normative appeal of a social practice. This attitude can be understood to mean: 1) the ownership demonstrated by the actor in response to that appeal; 2) the extent to which the actor takes responsibility (agency); 3) the extent to which the actor shows a virtuous character, which in MacIntyre terms determines her/his ability to satisfy the standards of excellence belonging to that practice, i.e. the ability to excel.

The concept of ethos can be understood as the more collective counterpart of the concept of accountability. A group or community can be characterized by a specific ethos. It is about the virtues, values and moral standards which are respected or even revered within a specific group or community closely associated with a certain social practice. (Take for example the community of nurses within health care.) The concept of ethos refers to social attitudes and processes within a group which can strengthen and improve the accountability of its members, their positive attitude towards the normative appeals and responsibilities they experience. Another meaningful term in this context with roughly the same meaning as ethos, is 'moral capital'. All these terms are suited to express certain elements which we consider as part of the regulative side of practices.

The Environment of Social Practices (Context)

In addition to the constitutive and regulative side of normative practices something must be said about their environment, their context. Social practices are always part of a broader context of a plurality of other practices, societies, cultures and nations. This context also has its influence on the way in which social practices function. For example large differences exist between health care practices in an individualized and wealthy society as the United States or the Netherlands and similar practices in large parts of African and Asian societies. Those differences have nothing to do with the constitutive rules of this practice or with its 'internal good' or 'core function'. To a high extent they are determined by the specific features of the context in which these practices are functioning. In other words, the specific context in which a social practice is developing itself can have an enormous influence on the way in which a social practice gets its unique, individual shape within local and regional circumstances.

This context of social practices partly consists of other social practices. Sometimes there are mutual relations between those practices (interlinkages) and they interact with each other in a more or less intensive way. Sometimes there are cases in which social practices cooperate or are strongly interlinked with other practices by using the same sources or by working together on goals that are of interest for both. In all these cases it is important to look carefully to the common features of the context, but also to the differences between these practices and their functioning within this context. In particular it is important to do justice to the different 'internal goods' these different practices stand for and the differences in the qualifying aspect of those internal goods.

CONCLUSION

The Normative Practice Approach provides a framework to study social practices from a spectrum of meaning perspectives in which they function. It does this by doing justice to the fact that the meaning of practices cannot be *reconstructed* theoretically, wherefore it is necessary to respect this inherent meaning in the way in which these practices are theoretically *reflected* upon.

Human existence is primarily an active life. The contemplation at the level of reflection on social practices can only prove its relevance to the extent to which it contributes to a further opening up and improvement of practical implementation. In the various contributions in this book we want to show how the theory presented in this introductory chapter can provide more insight into the diversity of meaning in which social practices function and how the various aspects of them relate to each other and can be kept in balance. Especially for social practices in which scientific knowledge and professional work play an important role, this form of reflection can be helpful in keeping theory and practice in balance.

But the most important feature of the Normative Practice Approach is that the regulative side of normative practices is as much part of its structure as the constitutive side is. Participating within normative practices is not only knowing how to act within those practices by following its rules. It always is also: being personal responsible for your own actions within these rule-led practices. As a professional, one cannot hide oneself behind the prevailing constitutive rules of a practice, because you are personally responsible for your own normative position within the practices in which you participate. This idea of personal responsibility is emphasized by acknowledging the crucial role of the regulative side of social practices.

REFERENCES

Boutellier, H. (2013). *The improvising society – Social order in a boundless world.* The Hague: Eleven International Publishers.

Dooyeweerd, H. (1953-1957). *A New Critique of Theoretical Thought* (3 Vols.). Philadelphia: The Presbyterian and Reformed Publishing Company.

Duintjer, O. D. (1977). *Rondom regels: Wijsgerige gedachten omtrent regel-geleid gedrag [Around Rules – Philosophical Thoughts about Rule-following Behavior].* Boom.

Eikeland, O. (2006). Phrónêsis, Aristotle, and action research. *International Journal of Action Research, 2*(1), 5–53.

Giddens, A. (1984). *The Constitution of Society. Outline of the Theory of Structuration.* Berkeley, CA: University of California Press.

Glas, G. (2017). Public and institutional aspects of professional responsibility in medicine and psychiatry. *Philosophia Reformata, 82*(2), 146–166.

Glas, G. (2019forthcoming). *Person-centered care in psychiatry: Self-relational, normative, and contextual perspectives.* London: Routledge.

Habermas, J. (1984). The Theory of Communicative Action. (2 Vols.; T. A. MacCarthy, Trans.). Boston: Beacon.

Hoogland, J., & Jochemsen, H. (2000). Professional autonomy and the normative structure of medical practice. *Theoretical Medicine and Bioethics, 21*(5), 457–475. doi:10.1023/A:1009925423036

Hoogland, J., Polder, J.J., Jochemsen, H., & Strijbos, S. (1995). *Professioneel beheerst - Professionele autonomie van de arts in relatie tot instrumenten voor beheersing van kosten en kwaliteit van de gezondheidszorg* [Professional autonomy of the physician in relation to instruments for controlling costs and quality of health care]. Ede, The Netherlands: Prof. dr. G.A. Lindeboom Instituut.

Jochemsen, H., & Glas, G. (1997). *Verantwoord medisch handelen: Proeve van een christelijke medische ethiek* [Responsible Medical Action. A Preliminary Draft of Christian Medical Ethics]. Amsterdam: Buijten & Schipperheijn.

MacIntyre, A. (2007). *After virtue: A study in moral theory* (3rd ed.). Notre Dame, IN: University of Notre Dame Press.

Mouw, R., & Griffioen, S. (1993). *Pluralisms and horizons: An essay in christian public philosophy*. Grand Rapids, MI: W.B. Eerdmans.

Nicolini, D. (2012). *Practice Theory, Work, and Organization – An Introduction*. Oxford, UK: Oxford University Press.

Reckwitz, A. (2002). Toward a Theory of Social Practices. A Development in Culturalist Theorizing. *European Journal of Social Theory*, *5*(2), 243–263. doi:10.1177/13684310222225432

Schatzki, T. R. (2008). Social Practices – A Wittgensteinian Approach to Human Activity and Social Practices. Cambridge, UK: Cambridge University Press. (Originally published 1996)

Schatzki, T. R., Knorr Cetina, K., & von Savigny, E. (Eds.). (2001). *The Practice Turn in Contemporary Theory*. London: Routledge.

Searle, J. (1969). *Speech acts: An essay in the philosophy of language*. Cambridge, UK: Cambridge University Press. doi:10.1017/CBO9781139173438

Taylor, C. (1985). *Philosophical papers. Philosophy and the Human Sciences* (Vol. 2). Cambridge, UK: Cambridge University Press. doi:10.1017/CBO9781139173490

Verkerk, M. J., Hoogland, J., van der Stoep, J., & de Vries, M. J. (2016). *Philosophy of technology: An introduction for technology and business students*. Routledge.

Weber, M. (1978). *Economy and Society*. Berkeley, CA: University of Calefornia Press.

Winch, P. (1958). *The idea of a social science and its relation to philosophy (Studies in philosophical psychology)*. London: Routledge & Kegan Paul.

Wittgenstein, L. (1968). *Philosophical investigations*. Oxford, UK: Basil Blackwell.

Section 2

Chapter 4
Industrial Practices, Sustainable Development and Circular Economy:
Mitigation of Reductionism and Silo Mentality in the Industry

Maarten J. Verkerk
Maastricht University, The Netherlands

Frans Visscher
SABIC, The Netherlands

ABSTRACT

The 2015 Paris agreement challenges the industry to realize their sustainability goals. The objective of this chapter is to support engineers from R&D departments in the chemical process industry to develop processes and systems that are in agreement with these goals. The authors propose the so-called Triple I model that offers three perspectives to direct the development of sustainable practices. This model encourages engineers to identify all relevant aspects, to integrate the knowledge of different disciplines, and to meet the justified interests of stakeholders. In this chapter, the importance of ideals and basic beliefs is highlighted. First of all, ideals and basic beliefs place the sustainable development of the process industry in a broader perspective. In addition, ideals and basic beliefs motivate people to face the challenges of the 2015 Paris agreement and encourage them to develop sustainable solutions.

DOI: 10.4018/978-1-5225-8006-5.ch004

INTRODUCTION

Since the 2015 Paris climate agreement, the idea of a sustainable future has acquired solid ground in global and national politics. It is widely believed that the idea of a sustainable future refers not only to ecological values but also to social and economic values. The United Nations defined the Sustainable Development Goals under the title 'Transforming our World: the 2030 Agenda for Sustainable Development'. It is a collection of 17 global goals with subsequent targets (UN, 2015).

The development goals cover the following social, economic and ecological development issues: poverty, hunger and food, health and well-being, education, gender equality, water and sanitation, sustainable energy, sustainable energy and work for all, sustainable industrialization, reduction inequality, urbanization, sustainable consumption and production, climate change, sustainable use of oceans and seas, sustainable use of ecosystems, peaceful and just societies, and global partnership for sustainable development.

Recently, Kate Raworth (2017) has argued that the limits of a sustainable future are determined by two factors: a social-economic minimum and an ecological maximum. She argues that a stable societal order only can develop when all countries and all population groups in these countries have reached this social-economic minimum. She proposes the following topics to constitute such a minimum: food, health, education, income & work, peace & justice, political voice, social equity, gender equality, housing, networks, and energy. Additionally, she claims that a stable ecological order requires all countries to limit their environmental load to the capacity of our planet. It goes within saying that social-economic minimum is undercut by many countries and by many population groups in rich countries. At the same time, our ecological maximum is already exceeded globally.

The industrial sector is challenged to contribute to a sustainable future. In this chapter we focus on the chemical process industry. The chemical process industry has joined forces to accelerate a sustainable development. European policy makers have launched innovation programs like Sustainable Process Industry through Resource and Energy Efficiency (SPIRE). Also, they have proposed an ambitious Circular Economy package that covers the whole cycle of materials (EC, 2017). This type of programs and packages are a mixture of visions, values, targets and concrete projects.

One of the main challenges in industry is to mitigate the phenomena of reductionism and silo thinking. Reductionism refers to the idea that the challenges of a sustainable future are completely described in terms of technology and economy. With that, the social, moral and spiritual aspects of sustainability are ignored. Silo thinking refers to the idea that actors think and act too much from their own perspective and overlook the perspective of others.

This inhibits effective communication between different disciplines, and as a consequence, increases the likelihood of invalid assumptions due to insufficient mutual understanding. Silo thinking may occur both within and outside the company. Reductionism and silo thinking result not only in 'reduced' and 'narrowed' analysis but also in 'reduced' and 'narrowed' solutions.

Engineers in Research & Development (R&D) play a key role in transforming the chemical process industry. After all, they have to develop processes and systems that meet the requirements for a sustainable future. This brings us to the research question of this chapter: How to support engineers in R&D to mitigate the phenomena of reductionism and silo thinking?

Positively formulated: How to support engineers in R&D to analyze the relevant aspects, to integrate the knowledge of different disciplines, and to meet the justified interests of stakeholders, in order to transform the chemical process industry into a sustainable sector? This research question falls apart in three sub-questions:

1. What type of approach is required?
2. How to analyze the relevant aspects, to integrate the knowledge of all disciplines, and to do justice to the justified interests of stakeholders?
3. How to motivate engineers to find creative solutions and to effectuate change?

This chapter has the following outline. In section 2 we explore the chemical process industry. In section 3 we present some cases and policy reports as sources for ideas, visions and values. In section 4 we argue that the practice approach is very suitable to answer the research question. We present a first exploration of practices in the chemical process industry based on the so-called Triple I model and make it plausible that this model supports engineers to overcome reductionism and silo thinking. In section 5 we apply this model to a case: the process intensification of chlorine. In section 6 we address the question of motivation to change and to shape change. We close this chapter with some conclusions.

BACKGROUND: EXPLORING THE CHEMICAL PROCESS INDUSTRY

Large scale production of chemicals is known since ancient times, with earliest examples being gold extraction from gold ore, making glass, and the production of gun powder. The 16th century book *De re metallica* (1556) illustrates the process where gold is obtained from gold ore (Stankiewicz and Moulijn, 2000). With the industrial revolution, chemical industry grew with the commissioning of sulphuric acid plants (1740, Richmond, UK), soda production (1793, near Paris, France), and the production of fertilizers (1843, Hertfordshire, UK) (Aftalion, 1991).

The variety of sectors served by chemical process industries increased ever since. Nowadays, the global sales of chemicals consist of petrochemicals (25.9%), specialty chemicals (27.2%) polymers (21.6%), consumer chemicals (13.6%) and basic inorganics (11.7%). The global chemicals turnover was valued at €3.360 billion in 2016.

The sales of the European chemical industry increased by more than 50% in last twenty years (CEFIC, 2017). In the period 1990-2015 the energy consumption of the process industry (energy consumption per unit of production) was reduced with 26% (CEFIC 2017).

The reverse side of the growth of the chemical industry is that the impact of incidents in chemical plants increased with production scale, with well-known examples being the Bhopal disaster (1984), the Seveso release (1976), and the Grande Paroisse Fertilizer Plant Explosion (2001). These disasters clearly showed that safety has to be top priority and that safety considerations have to play a dominant role in the design phase of new chemical plants and processes.

Despite the efforts to embed safety as a core priority in work processes and daily practices, the reputation of the chemical process industry might vary. Public opinions and political parties often promote a 'Not in My Backyard' point of view (NIMBY), which has enforced the centralization of chemical industry in industrial sites and networks. This phenomenon, however, is of all times. One of the largest chemical industrial sites in Europe is Chemelot (>800 ha). At founding of this industrial site in 1908 the city council of Geleen protested to the Dutch national government against the possible location of a state mine because to potential 'moral' and 'material' degradation of the community (Chemelot). This site employs now more than 8.000 employees of more than 100 nationalities (Chemelot).

CASE STUDIES AND POLICY REPORTS

In this section we present some case studies and policy reports to explore the scene of a sustainable process industry. The objective is to identify visions and values that drive innovations in this field. We hope that these case studies and policy reports inspire R&D engineers to develop their own visions and values for their own work.

Process Intensification

Generations of chemical engineers are taught that overall cost-benefits will increase when production of base chemicals is scaled-up. As a result, there has been a tendency to produce chemicals on a large scale at centralized locations from where the chemicals are transported to customers. One way to overcome transportation of (dangerous) chemicals would be to produce on-demand and on-location. Such a downscale of production is known as 'process intensification'.

Process intensification has been described as 'Any chemical engineering development that leads to a substantially smaller, cleaner, safer, and more energy efficient technology' (Stankiewicz & Moulijn, 2000). This definition clearly highlights some aspects of sustainability: 'cleaner' and 'more energy efficient'. From a historical perspective, process intensification is an approach to process and plant designs that breaks with the trend of scaling-up and focuses on a miniaturization of process equipment. Process intensification implies a reduction in plant size by at least a factor 100.

It is believed that process intensification will lay a new basis for the chemical industry of the future as indicated by Stankiewicz & Moulijn (2000), Harmsen (2010), European Roadmap PI, and Action Plan PI.

Additionally, several institutions and networks have been initiated to facilitate and enhance the further deployment like the Dutch Process Intensification Network, the Chemical Process Intensification Chair (Eindhoven, The Netherlands), and Fraunhofer Institute for Microengineering and Microsystems (Mainz, Germany). The phenomena are globally recognized, as can be derived from the deployment of the activities in the near east, far-east and the USA, e.g. the Rapid Advancement in Process Intensification Deployment Manufacturing Institute that was established in 2016.

The first international conference on process intensification was held in 1995. A challenge for process intensification is that the lower economy of scale is balanced by lower operating costs or by other economic, logistic, safety or environmental considerations.

Stankiewicz & Moulijn (2000) envisioned the field as two distinct areas. The first area focuses on process-intensifying equipment, e.g. novel reactor types that enable intensive mixing, heat-transfer and mass-transfer. The second area concentrates on process-intensifying methods, e.g. new or hybrid separations, reaction-separation integration, and techniques using alternative energy forms like light or ultrasound.

Harmsen (2010) reviewed the experiences with process intensification from the perspective of drivers and hurdles for innovation. The four most important drivers for innovation in this field are: feedstock cost savings, capital cost reduction, energy saving, and inherently safe and healthy process. The four most important hurdles for innovation are: high risk of failure by a combination of novel elements, lacking of scale-up knowledge, low or unknown equipment reliability, and higher risk of Safety, Health or Environment compared to conventional technologies. In section 5, we will elaborate the process intensification of chlorine.

In summary, initiatives of process intensification are driven by values and visions like:

- EFFICIENT use of materials;
- Energy efficient processes;
- Reduction of costs and investments;
- Reduction in transport of dangerous materials;
- Reduction of environmental load;
- And increase in safety.

Plastic and Plastic Recycling

Plastic is one of the great achievements of our industrialized society. It is a highly useful material for packaging, automotive industry, building and construction, electrical applications, furniture and houseware, and so on.

Applications are rising as new types are developed to meet specific demands, chemical or mechanical resistance. However, the increased use and production of plastic in western, developing and emerging countries is of particular concern. The most important are decomposition in micro-plastics, the non-renewable nature of mixed composites, the toxicity of entrained additives, and accumulation in underdeveloped areas. A specific thread is the decomposition of plastics (size larger than 20 mm) in micro-plastics (1 μm to 5 mm). Recently, it was shown that weathering of plastic even can produce nanoscale particles, which could potentially be easily absorbed by phytoplankton and zooplankton (Andrady, 2011). The case of plastics and plastic recycling clearly shows the need of redesign of the whole plastics cycle in view of littering of environmental issues and recycling or reuse of expensive raw materials.

The European Strategy for Plastics in a Circular Economy is an example of a policy report that aims to transform the design, production, use and recycling of plastics in the EU (EC, 2018). The significance of this strategy comes from a European plastic demand of 49 million tons in 2015 (15% of the global demand in 2015).

In Europe about 26 million tons of plastic waste is generated on an annual base: 30% thereof is collected for recycling. 31% is used as landfilling, and 39% is incinerated. This policy explicitly addresses the environmental issues of the littering of plastics. For example, in the EU, 150.000 to 500.000 tons of plastic waste enter the oceans every year.

The environmental effects of recycling are enormous: from the perspective of CO_2 benefits, the recycling of one million tons of plastic is equivalent to one million cars off the road (EC, 2018)! The European Commission formulates the following vision for Europe's new plastics economy: 'A smart, innovative and sustainable plastics industry, where design and production fully respects the needs of reuse, repair, and recycling, brings growth and jobs to Europe and helps cut EU's greenhouse gas emissions and dependence on imported fossil fuels' and 'In Europe, citizens, government and industry support more sustainable and safer consumption and production patterns for plastics' (EC, 2018).

Several methods exist for the recycling of plastics, being re-extrusion, mechanical treatment, chemical treatment and energy recovery (Al-Salem, 2009). It has to be remarked that there are large differences between household plastics waste with undefined composition and industrial plastics waste with a defined composition. Generally, each types of recycling starts with the separation of plastic waste from the initial waste streams. For re-extrusion (plastic-to-plastic) a plastic waste stream needs to be transported to a plastic waste recycler, which will sort this stream into separate streams per plastics-type, and shredder, wash, dry and granulate it into a usable plastic stream.

Local, national and international governments have aimed to influence this process at various points in time. Examples of such regulatory aims are the taxation of household waste-collection, container deposit legislation, the subsidization of research regarding plastic recycling, and the limitations to use recycled plastic for the packing of food, medicine and other uses.

A typical example of energy recovery (plastics-to-fuel) is exploited by the company Bin2Barrel, which is located in the port of Amsterdam (The Netherlands). They aim to obtain a plastic waste-stream from an existing waste-collecting agent, and to produce the fuel for marine-purposes. Their business plan is to turn 35.000 metric tons of non-recyclable plastic into 30 million liters of clean fuel annually, preventing the emission of 57.000 metric tons of CO_2 every year. Additionally, resources for the production of new plastics are gained (Bin2Barrel). It has to be remarked that the methods of plastic recycling and energy recovery are still in its infancy. An estimate of its future energy and feedstock efficiency cannot yet be made.

In conclusion, the case of plastic and plastic recycling is driven by values and visions like:

- Care for the natural environment (air, land, cities, oceans). Thus the aim to avoid littering, sediments in oceans, toxic chemicals in plastics, micro-plastics, and reduction of greenhouse gases;
- Care for animals: toxic chemicals in plastics, micro-plastics in food chain, entanglement;
- Care for humans: toxic chemicals in plastics, micro-plastics in food chain;
- Care for natural resources: prevention of use of plastics, design for recyclability;

- Care for the economy: prevention economic losses by litter, development of an innovative plastics industry, development of 'compostable' and/or 'biodegradable' plastics, development of a market for recycled plastics, new jobs for citizens, less dependence on imported fossil fuels, transformation of the plastics value chain to a circular model.

Climate-Neutral Chemelot

In 2015 the United Nations Climate Change Conference was held in Paris. There the potential limits of global warming of the earth's atmosphere were discussed. Measurements have shown that in the post-industrialization era the global warming became more pronounced, which often is linked to enhanced levels of greenhouse gases like carbon dioxide (CO_2) and methane.

Researchers have measured the concentration of CO_2 in air bubble's that have been entrained in the arctic ice. Based on their measurement and the estimated age of ice-layers this allowed them to measure the concentration of CO_2 over time.

Based on that study CO_2 concentrations have historically been below 300 parts-per-million (PPM, or mg/m^3). However, as of the 1950s, the concentration is higher than 300 PPM and has not been below that value. More, the concentration passed the 400 PPM in 2013 for first time in recorded history (Petit, 1999). Once trapped in the atmosphere at elevated concentration, CO_2 is known to trap heat: it is a so-called greenhouse gas. Possible sources of CO_2 are: burning fossil fuels (coal, natural gas, oil), burning trees and wood products, and also a result of certain chemical reactions (like the manufacturing of cement). Chemical industries are often energy intensive: they require continuous consumption of energy / fuel to provide heat or power. Other greenhouse gases are CH_4 and N_2O that have a 28 and 256 times larger effect than CO_2.

This is also the case for many industrial sites, like the Dutch site Chemelot referred to earlier. By heating naphtha long molecules are broken into smaller molecules (monomers) that in their turn are suited for production of plastics (polymers). The production of naphtha in refineries and the intense heating of naphtha in crackers is energy intensive and contributes to the CO_2 emissions.

This can also be quantified: the estimated energy need of the overall chemical industry in the Netherlands sums up to 360 petajoules per year. This is about 10% of the total Dutch energy consumption. The industrial site Chemelot requires about 70 petajoules per year which makes Chemelot a non-negligible contributor (DSM).

The industrial park Chemelot has issued their multiyear vision in which they announced the aim to half their CO_2 emissions by 2030 and, ultimately to be climate neutral in 2050. The reduction of CO_2 emissions would be achieved based on five parallel paths:

1. Switching to electrification of (green) energy.
2. Utilizing sustainable feedstocks for natural gas and naphtha
3. Working with more circular processes
4. Process improvement & optimization
5. Carbon Capture Sequestration and Carbon Capture Utilization.

An example of a more circular process is the re-vitalized feasibility study that aims to transport CO_2 via an existing 60 kilometers long pipeline that was owned and used formerly by NATO, to greenhouses near the Dutch city of Venlo. CO_2 is an undesired by-product from the production of fertilizers. Chemelot produces 4.7 million tons of CO_2 per year. In greenhouses the CO_2 is used to enhance growth of crops and/or flowers. Currently three to four truck a day transport this feed stream from Chemelot to the greenhouses. With the re-vitalization of the pipeline this would be more sustainable, safer and less expensive (Hortinext, 2018).

Another example that shows the utilization of sustainable feedstocks, would be the development of pyrolis oil (originating from recycled plastics) as feedstock for naphtha crackers. With the output of the naphtha crackers renewed polymer can be produced. SABIC is preparing for a pilot plant with this purpose with the intention to scale-up this program, which recycles from mixed plastic waste to the original polymer (SABIC). The Chemelot case is very instructive. It shows that ambitious goals challenge organizations to realize circular material streams, to reduce waste and pollution, and to changeover to renewable energy sources. It also expresses visions and values:

- Sharing concerns about the future of our communities and the environment.
- Inspire, Engage, Create and Deliver to a sustainable future.
- Use natural resources to their best advantage by innovating, educating and using the latest technology.

Policy Reports

Finally, policy reports are sources of inspiration for R&D engineers. Chemical process industry has joint forces to accelerate a sustainable development. European policy makers have launched innovation programs like Sustainable Process Industry through Resource and Energy Efficiency (SPIRE, 2018). SPIRE targets a 30% reduction in use of fossil fuels for energy, a 20% decrease in use of non-renewable primary raw materials, and a 40% reduction in CO_2 equivalent footprint by 2030 (SPIRE, 2018).

It is important to understand the approach of SPIRE. The SPIRE roadmap for sustainable development 'represents a coordinated and integrated framework from research to business following a staged approach with short-term, medium-term and long-term objectives and benefits. It allows therefore a strategic and time-framed basis for driving and investing in specific innovation areas that are concretely and practically contributing to achieving the sustainable growth objectives.' This framework distinguishes six key components: feed, process, applications, waste2resource, horizontal & outreach (SPIRE).

In addition, the European Commission has proposed an ambitious Circular Economy package that covers the whole cycle: production, consumption, waste management and secondary raw materials (EC, 2017). In this package sustainability plays a key role. Six spearheads are defined:

1. Catalysis to eliminate pollutants and to convert CO_2;
2. Industrial biotechnology to improve chemical processes and to recycle carbon;
3. Sustainable process industry (SPIRE program);
4. Improvement of waste and resource management by re-manufacturing, reusing and recycling;
5. Closed-loop manufacturing systems to minimizer waste and pollution;
6. New water systems and services, reuse of reclaimed water and recovery of valuable resources from treated water.

All these roadmaps, programs and initiatives present building blocks for the transformation of the process industry. These building blocks are a mixture of values, visions, motivations, and targets. Especially, we will focus on values. We have four reasons for that. To start, values form the core of the vision. They define what is important for the future. They specify what qualities have to be realized by the transformation. Next, the different actors often share the same values with respect to sustainability while they have different motivations to thrive the transformation. Furthermore, values precede targets. That means that values define what kind of targets have to be realized and what the standard for every target is. Lastly, values form an important entrance gate to design. More specifically, they are key to the various value-based design approaches.

Evaluation

The case studies and the policy reports teach us a lot about the chemical process industry, sustainability, and circular economics. First, many of the processes in the chemical industry go back decades or even centuries. In the course of the time, a complex and interwoven set of supply and demand chains has been developed. Often, the plants of large multinationals and the manufacturing and transport operations of smaller retail companies are located in each other's vicinity. The transformation of the chemical process industry does not only imply a transformation of chemical processes but also a transformation of the whole network of suppliers and customers.

Second, they show us that there are general visions, values and possible solutions that describe how the industry can contribute to a sustainable future. These visions, values and solutions challenge us to reflect on the future, stimulate us to be creative, motivate us to learn from others, support us to set priorities, and urge us to take action.

Finally, the case studies and policy reports teach us every process, product and plant needs a customized approach. Specific knowhow about the feedstock, waste, process conditions, product characteristic, possibilities for re-use and recycling, and so on is required. In addition, every process, product, and plant has its own set of stakeholders with their justified interests. As a consequence, general visions have to be translated into dedicated visions, and possible solutions have to be translated into concrete proposals.

PRACTICE APPROACH

How to translate general visions in dedicated views and possible solutions in concrete proposals? This question leads us to the research question of this study: How to support R&D engineers to develop processes and systems that meet the requirements for a sustainable future?

In our view, practice approaches support engineers to mitigate reductionism and silo thinking in the development of dedicated views and making concrete proposals by analyzing all relevant aspects, by integrating the knowledge of different disciplines, and by taking into consideration the justified interests of stakeholders.

Some Key Ideas

In the chapters 1 to 3 of this book the idea of professional practices has been outlined. In this section we will discuss some key ideas that are relevant in view of our research question.

MacIntyre (1984) highlights that professional practices are not an invention of our times but are developed and shaped in a historical process. He emphasizes that these practices do not develop themselves on their own strength but are embedded in the community and are co-shaped by society.

He also stresses that professional practices operate to certain standard of quality – 'standards of excellence'. The perspective of MacIntyre fits to the process industry. This industry has a long tradition, is well embedded in society, and has defined standards of quality.

Jochemsen, Glas and Hoogland (Jochemsen & Glas, 1997; Hoogland & Jochemsen, 2000; Jochemsen, 2006) have developed the so-called normative practice approach for understanding professional practices in healthcare.

Later on, it was elaborated for technology and sustainability (Verkerk et al., 2016; Verkerk et al., 2018). The normative practice approach offers three perspectives to understand the nature of practices: structure, context, and direction. This approach appears to be fruitful for the chemical process industry as it unravels the complexity of professional practices, identifies the normative aspect of these practices and highlights the influence of ideals and basic beliefs.

Finally, Nicolini (2012) emphasizes the transformative power of practice approaches. In his view, these approaches are so important because they are inherently relational, bring the critical role of material things to the fore, leave space for initiative and creativity, and put emphasis on the importance of power, conflict and politics. He stresses that practice approaches are so fruitful because they offer 'radically new ways of understanding and explaining social and organizational phenomena'. Especially, because they focus on actions, on what is said and what is done. The perspective of Nicolini seems to be relevant because the transformation to a sustainable process industry requires 'radically new ways of understanding' and 'radically new ways of acting'. Such a transformation never will be realized when we continue to think as we thought and to act as we have acted.

The Triple I Model

Verkerk (2014) has developed – in close cooperation with engineers – the so-called Triple I model that is based on the ideas of McIntyre, Jochemsen, Glas, Hoogland and others. Verkerk argues that we only can understand what happens in practices, when we consider that practices are embedded in organizations, that organizations function in networks, and that every organization interacts with its stakeholders. With that, he recognizes the interactions of practices with other organizations (Freeman, 2001) and the importance of power, conflict and politics (Nicolini, 2012; Verkerk, 2004).

The Triple I approach offers three perspectives to understand professional practices: 'identity and intrinsic values', 'interests of stakeholders', 'ideals and basic beliefs' (Figure 1).

The first 'I' refers to the 'identity and intrinsic values' of a practice. For example, the identity of a chemical plant is characterized by 'controlled production'. All activities in this practice have to be focused on the control of the manufacturing process. The intrinsic values of the manufacturing process are values like process control, efficiency, effectivity, and safety. The relationship between identity and intrinsic values is a reciprocal one. On the one hand, values concretize the identity of the practice, and on the other hand, values constitute the identity.

Figure 1. Graphical representation of the triple-I model for professional practices

The second 'I' refers to the 'interests of stakeholders' of a practice'. Industrial practices have their own specific network of stakeholders. Important stakeholders are the customers, suppliers, shareholders, banks, and authorities. Every stakeholder has its own justified interests. For example, the justified interest of customers is the delivery of chemical products with a good quality and at a reasonable price. And the justified interests of the local authorities are safety, environmental concerns and employment opportunities.

The third 'I' refers to the 'ideals and basic beliefs' that are embedded in the professional practice (past), that influence the professional practice (present), and that will change the professional practice (future). Ideals and basic beliefs co-shape protocols and guidelines, habits and attitudes of the employees, and managerial relationships. At this moment ideals and basic beliefs like sustainability and circular economy are 'in the air' and will change professional practices substantially.

The Triple model can be used in two different ways. Firstly, it can be used in descriptive way to analyze an existing practice. In that case, this model offers three perspectives or three pairs of glasses to analyze the status quo. Secondly, it can be used in a prescriptive way to guide the development of an existing practice.

Then, this model offers three perspectives or three pair of glasses to define the future status. We would like to emphasize that the three 'I's' are not 'sold separately' but form an integral part of a specific practice. It also has to be noted that the Triple I model doesn't offer tools for quantitative risk assessments, root cause analysis studies, process control and so on.

Different Practices: Beyond Silo Thinking

In the chemical process industry three different departments play a key role: R&D, Operations (OPS) and Marketing & Sales (M&S). These departments have different cultures. In the words of Nicolini (2012): they have different 'patterns of doing and saying'. In our view, there are three different practices. Especially, this comes to the fore in analyzing the first I of these departments.

The objective of R&D is to develop new or to improve present processes, products, and services. These activities require an innovative and creative attitude. The nature of these activities is technological. Intrinsic values are creativity, need of customers, safety, compliance with standards and regulations, and controlled development process.

The objective of OPS is to produce existing products in an efficient way. This activity requires a conservative attitude: operations is a repetitive activity. The nature of these activities is also technological. Intrinsic values are efficiency, controlled processes, safety, and compliance with standards and regulations.

The objective of M&S is to sell products of the company at a profitable price. Also, it has to investigate the future needs and wishes of customers. This activity requires a commercial attitude. The nature of these activities is economic. Intrinsic values are making profit, satisfying existing customers, and understanding needs and wishes of (new) customers.

Our conclusion is that R&D, OPS, and M&S are different practices. Easily, these practices establish themselves too independently resulting in a 'silo thinking' that hampers communication and cooperation between these different practices. It is a challenge for the R&D engineer to integrate the knowledge and the experience of PD and M&S is their new designs.

Multiple Interests: Beyond Reductionism

The second I focuses on stakeholders. R&D, OPS, and M&S have each an own set of stakeholders. They will be partly the same and partly different. A philosophical analysis shows that these stakeholders have different interests. An extensive analysis of their interests mitigates reductionism. For example, the interests of governments are mainly juridical: they make and maintain laws. The interests of commercial customers are economic: they also want to make a profit. The interests of an action group are moral: they care for nature and human beings.

The interests of the local community are social and economic: the local community is a social group that earns a living. And so on. This analysis shows that R&D engineers have to take into account not only technical and economic considerations, but also for example juridical, moral and social considerations, as shown by an analysis of the interests of stakeholders. Table 1 gives an overview of stakeholders and their primary interests.

An analysis of the third I, ideals and basic beliefs, highlights the spiritual aspects that R&D engineers also have to take into account. It has to be noted that spiritual aspects can have a religious and a non-religious source. Especially, spiritual aspects come to the fore in dialogues with churches, mosques and other religious or ideological organizations. Table 1 gives an overview of stakeholders and their primary interests. As will be illustrated in section 5.3., the primary interests of the stakeholders reflect the justified interests.

Customer Practices

The case study 'Plastic recycling' clearly shows that we have to understand the world of customers to search for alternatives, to minimize the use of raw materials, to promote reuse and recycling, and to prevent any environment pollution.

It goes without saying that co- creation is a condition sine qua non to realize a sustainable and circular plastics industry. In our opinion, this observation can be generalized. We need to know our customers in-depth in order to work on a sustainable

Table 1. Overview of stakeholders and their primary interests

Stakeholder	Primary Interests
Employees	Economic, social
Government (local, national)	Juridical, economic
Shareholders	Economic
Banks	Economic
Suppliers	Economic
Commercial customers	Economic
Local community	Economic, social, ecological
Local environment	Social, economic, ecological
Action groups	Moral, Ideological
Universities	Technical
Professional associations	Technical
Labor unions	Social, economic, moral
Hospitals and long term homes	Moral
Religious and secular employees	Spiritual
Churches, mosques and other religious or ideological organizations	Spiritual

and circular society. The Triple I model also can be used as a tool to understand the 'sayings' and 'doings' (Nicolini) of our customers. See Figure 2.

CASE STUDY: TRANSFORMATION BY PROCESS INTENSIFICATION

The objective of this section is to show that the Triple I model offers a methodology for R&D engineers to analyze relevant aspects, disciplines, and stakeholders for the development of sustainable processes. We illustrate this methodology by analyzing process intensification of chlorine.

The Production of Chlorine

A specific example of process intensification is the production of chlorine from the chlor-alkali process. This process is an electrochemical process producing chlorine, sodium hydroxide and hydrogen. It is regarded a capital and energy intensive process. Several day-to-day products require chlorine as a feedstock in their production process, like PVC, Teflon and disinfectants. In Europe, on an annual base, more than 12.000 kiloton of chlorine is produced, of which 847 kiloton is produced in The Netherlands (EuroChlor, 2016).

The production of chlorine requires 2500 kWh per ton of chlorine produced by the membrane process (COVESTRO) and 3700 kWh for the mercury process.

Figure 2. Graphical representation of the Triple-I model for customer practices

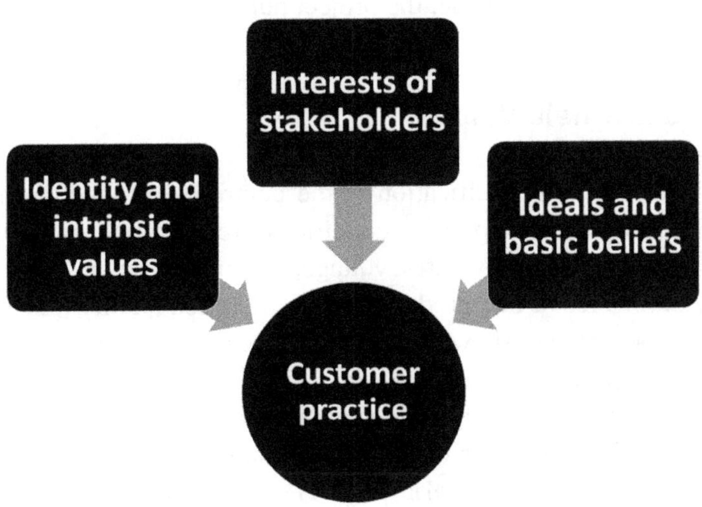

The production units have to be made from specific metal-alloys (like Hastelloy) due to the excessive reactivity of chemical species involved. Chlorine production often involves other chemicals as well, like caustic soda and hydrogen. For large consumers, the transportation of chlorine can be executed by pipeline. For smaller consumers, however, transportation by rail is used, raising significant concerns from residents nearby the transportation route (NRC, 2006). One way to overcome transportation would be to produce chlorine on-demand and on-location. This is only possible if transportable production units are used, which would require intensified (reactor) technologies in order to achieve a higher productivity in smaller volumes (Granados-Mendoza, 2016).

Akzo Nobel is a producer that openly aimed to apply novel process technologies, amongst others by producing chlorine with small scale chemical reactors. Currently, AkzoNobel produces chlorine with the latest electrolyzer technology. This technology is capital and energy intensive and is reaching its limits. New processes are required to reduce the amount of electrical energy needed and to reduce the costs per ton of chlorine. As an example, AkzoNobel made their effort public in 2015 to study the possibility of chlorine production in so-called Spinning Disc Reactors (FLOWID).

This is a certain branch of rotating chemical reactors of which an earlier version was described in the very first works of Process Intensification, aiming specifically for decentralization of the production. The start-up company FLOWID initiated the construction of a related small-scale plant at the Chemelot campus – requiring an investment of 1.7 million euros (FLOWID)

Chemical process industry utilizes often a specific chain of activities to develop a new technology as shown in Figure 3. Typically formal stage-gating sessions are held as the project moves through the project development process. With each phase a next level of detail is achieved. For example in the phase in which a cost-estimate of the total project has to be made, the project duration has to be assessed and the interests of stakeholders have to be analyzed.

Identity and Intrinsic Values

The identity of process intensification is the controlled production of chlorine. 'Controlled' implies that all process conditions are specified in conditions like temperature, pressure, feed flow rates, voltage, current and so on. Additionally, the specified conditions result in a product with the required quality (purity). In other words, all activities that are shown in Figure 3 have to be focused on the control of the manufacturing process of chlorine.

A core intrinsic value is safety. Safety is a moral value that focuses at the health of employees and the well-being of the surrounding environment. Safety has both a technical as well as a behavioral aspect. The technical aspect implies that the

Figure 3. Typical phases of an R&D project in the chemical industry

designed process is robust from a safety point of view. The behavioral aspect involves that the designed process facilitates operators to run the equipment in a safe way.

Further, the whole system of checks and balances has to be designed in such a way that the whole crew (operators, technicians, engineers, management) understands that safety is the first priority. Another important intrinsic value is efficiency. Efficiency is an economic value that focuses on maximizing the product yield and minimizing the use of energy, the amount of waste, the depreciation costs, and so on. As a rule of thumb, efficient processes also involve the efficient use of feedstock. One more intrinsic value is the protection of the environment. The exhaust of waste gases and waste water has to be minimized.

We have described the identity of the chlorine process as 'controlled production'. We have identified three key intrinsic values: safety, efficiency, and protection of the environment. It goes without saying that a controlled process that is safe, efficient, and that protects the environment is a key condition for a sustainable process. However, in our view 'sustainability' also has to be defined as a key intrinsic value.

It challenges R&D engineers to design processes and equipment from a broader perspective. In every phase of the project, see Figure 3, the identity and the intrinsic values have to (re-)evaluated. For learning purposes this examination needs to be completed after the project closure as well. Only by doing so knowledge gained can be shared to future generations of engineers which are on-boarding to transform the chemical process industry into a sustainable sector.

Last but not least, we would like to emphasize the human aspect of technology. Technology is designed by humans and is operated by humans. A controlled, safe, efficient, environmental-friendly, and sustainable production is only possible when operators, technicians, engineers and managers have internalized the identity and intrinsic values. Generally, it requires a high level of integrity to pursue this identity and to maintain these values in view of (unjustified) pressures of internal or external stakeholders.

Interests of Stakeholders Related to Intensified Chlorine Production

For the case intensification of chlorine production, a stakeholder can be defined as an individual, a group or an organization that has a 'stake' or interest in the production of chlorine by means of process intensification. Generally, it is useful to make a distinction between internal and external stakeholders. Internal stakeholders are all departments, disciplines and managers that have to be involved in decisions about process intensification of chlorine. External stakeholders are all external parties that have an interest in process intensification of chlorine.

The analysis of the second 'I' consists out of two phases. The first phase is the identification of (relevant) stakeholders and the second one the exploration of their (justified) interests. The identification of the (relevant) stakeholders can be obtained by answering questions like:

- Who would be interested in this intensified technology and what is their role?
  - Customers who demand to receive safely chlorine at a specified quality;
  - Engineers from the side of R&D, Project Executing & Management, or Manufacturing who want this technology in their own plant;
  - Authorities who issue a permit and monitor environmental requirements;
  - Action groups that oppose transport of chlorine;
- Who are the potential beneficiaries?
  - Chlorine customers requiring in-frequent chlorine delivery;
  - Chlorine producers being able to open-up a new market segments;
  - Citizens living close-by production and transportation routes;
  - Universities aiming for valorization of their technology;
- Who could have constraints about the initiative?
  - Safety authorities;
  - Engineers involved;
  - Company board due to project time-line & required Total Project Costs;
- Who has the power to influence?
  - Governmental bodies that make legislation and/or subsidies;
  - Action groups and local citizens that can block chlorine transport;
  - Company board of management.

The most important internal stakeholders are: research & development, manufacturing, marketing & sales, and supply chain. The most important external stakeholders are: customers, authorities, competitors, industrial site, contractors, action groups, and natural environment.

The second phase is to explore the (justified) interests of stakeholders. In the first phases of the project this analysis will be done on a more general level. In the course of the project the analysis will become more specific and more detailed. For example, in the research phase a desk study may be sufficient, but in the later phases intensive dialogues with the different stakeholders are required.

Table 1 gives an overview of stakeholders and their primary interests. This overview guides both the desk study as well as the dialogues with stakeholders. It should be remarked that the primary interests reflect the justified interests.

For example, justified interests of shareholders are the share price and the dividend payment. So, the company has to take into account these interests in decision making about process intensification of chlorine. Another example, the justified interests of the local community have a social, economic and ecological nature. So, the R&D engineers have to understand the interests of the community in-depth to do justice to their interests.

At first sight, the interests of shareholders and the local community often will conflict. After all, shareholders focus 'only' on economic values and the local community also on social and ecological values. At second sight, however, may show that such a conflict is 'superficial'. For example, shareholders have to realize themselves that an inadequate reaction to safety issues with respect to transport of chlorine may affect their economic interests negatively, e.g. action groups inducing a breakdown in production or safety measures that will endanger the chlorine transport leading to dangerous situations and an increase of costs.

At the same time, the local community has to realize itself that on the long term the business has to stay profitable. That means that the economic consequences of process intensification have to be discussed. The idea of 'justified interests' requires that the management has to weight and to balance the different interests of their stakeholders. It is their challenge to develop solutions that serve the interests of all stakeholders. In practice, however, ideal solutions are not always possible.

Regularly, there are conflicting interests that cannot be solved easily. Then it comes down to an honest consideration of the different interests of stakeholders. Such a consideration requires a high level if integrity.

There are a number of methods to analyze the desires and needs of stakeholders in a systematic way. For example:

- Stakeholders can be ordered with respect to their level of involvement in the innovation. In a decreasing order: Responsible, Accountable, Supportive, Consulting, and Inform (RASCI). The stakeholders can be plotted in concentric circles: in the inner circle stakeholders that are responsible, accountable and supportive, in the next ring stakeholders that must be consulted, and in the outer ring stakeholders that need to be informed.

- Stakeholders also can be positioned in a power-interest matrix. On the vertical axis a low or a high level of power and on the horizontal axis a low of high level of interest. This analysis results in four quadrants and four policies. High level of power and high level of interest: manage closely. High level of power and low level of interest: keep satisfied. Low level of power and low level of interest: monitor. Low level of power and high level of interest: keep informed.
- The Salience Model of stakeholder classification identifies the prominence of stakeholders by classifying them according to three attributes: power or influence, legitimacy, and urgency. The Salience Model can be graphically depicted as a Venn diagram, in this case of three partially overlapping circles. The three circles represent Power, Legitimacy and Urgency. There are eight regions in this diagram each representing interactions with different types of stakeholders.

Ideals and Basic Beliefs Related to Intensified Chlorine Production

Once the identity and intrinsic values have been established (first I), and the interests of stakeholders are identified (second I), then it is the right time to understand the ideals and basic beliefs that have to underlay our new designs (third I).

Ideals and basic beliefs that typical occur in chemical process industry are:

- The idea that technology is the key-parameter that will enable future growth of the chemical industry;
- The idea that technology is the key-parameter that will solve present sustainability problems;
- The idea of closed chemical cycles from 'feedstock to feedstock' and 'feedstock to product';
- The use of only sustainable energy;
- Humans are the weakest link in a technology-dominated environment;
- Documented processes and procedures will lead to safe operations;

It goes without saying that these 'typical' ideals and basic beliefs are of utmost importance for the development of intensified chlorine production. It is a challenge for R&D engineers to 'translate' these ideals and basic beliefs in processes and equipment. We would like to emphasize the importance of investigating ideals and basic beliefs explicit. We have three reasons for that.

First, the investments in new chemical factories are high and the depreciation periods are long. So, new facilities have not only to meet the requirements of today but also the requirements of tomorrow and the day after tomorrow. The implications for intensified chlorine production are two-fold. On the one hand, it challenges R&D engineers and business managers to reflect not only on the challenges of 'today and tomorrow' but also on the challenges of 'the day after tomorrow'. On the other hand, intensified production of chlorine facilitates lower investments and supports shorter depreciation periods. On the long term, the operating costs also have to be lower.

Secondly, the chemical process industry is inherently conservative, especially, because the investments for new processes are very high. An old adage is 'never change a well-running and well-controlled process'. The 'typical' ideals and basic beliefs of the current chemical process industry challenge the old adage. The same holds for the idea of intensified production of chlorine.

So far so good. In view of the present challenges, however, it cannot be taken for granted that the chemical process industry will continue to grow and that all sustainability problems can be solved by technological interventions.

For example, intensified production of chlorine also has to face economic and/or political scenarios in which the economy does not grow or in which the production of materials that need chlorine as feedstock have to be decreased due to sustainability considerations.

In addition, the ideas that 'humans are the weakest link in a technology-dominated environment' and that 'documented processes and procedures will lead to safe operations' are good guidelines for R&D engineers to design safe equipment and to develop safe procedures. However, an unwanted side effect of these ideals can be that we 'forget' to invest in human resources. High-tech environments need also highly educated, highly motivated, highly trustworthy employees.

Thirdly, nothing is as difficult as predicting the future. It always appears again that our society is too complex and our models are too simple to do a reliable forecast. In our opinion, future scenarios of (intensified) chlorine production need not only be fed by economic, technological and political considerations but also by 'deep' ideals and 'deep' basic beliefs. We consciously use the word 'deep'.

Firstly, it is a wink to the philosopher Arne Naess who introduced the word 'deep ecology' to plea for radical changes to keep our planet liveable. Secondly, it is an invitation to stay away from the issues of the day, to recognize valuable approaches, and to reflect on the future from a more fundamental perspective.

For example, the Sustainable Development Goals of the United Nations and the ideas of the socio-economic minimums of Kate Raworth are not 'just' some goals or some ideas, but they are current wordings of deep human values like 'human responsibility' and 'justice' that are – from a historical point of view – intrinsically interwoven with the development of western society.

We do not believe that addressing deep ideals and deep basic beliefs will result in easy answers about the intensification of chlorine. We believe that dialogues about Sustainable Development Goals and socio-economic minimums places intensified chlorine production in a broader perspective.

The importance of the reflection on ideals and basic beliefs cannot be underestimated. We would like to emphasize the importance of this reflection for the whole design and decision process. May be, it is the most important contribution of the Triple I model to prevent reductionism and to overcome silo thinking.

MOTIVATION FOR CHANGE

Why do so many people deny the need for a fundamental change? Why is it so difficult to face reality? Why is it so difficult to change the chemical process industry? And why is it so difficult to change the economic order of our society? These questions belong to the core of the problem. They have to be addressed at every level of the chemical process industry: from the individual engineer to the CEO of the company. They also have to be addressed at every level of our society: from the individual citizen to the global organizations.

The questions are too big to answer in one book, let alone a chapter or a short section. We would like to emphasize only one aspect: the importance of ideals and basic beliefs. Change management literature teaches that the energy to realize far-reaching changes and the courage to make radical choices can only be utilized if alignment is reached between ideals and basic beliefs of individuals and groups on the one hand and the vision and objectives of a sustainable chemical process industry on the other hand (McAllister et al., 2010).

In industry, dialogues about ideals and basic beliefs are almost absent. It is believed that such dialogues are a waste of time because they do not contribute to the development of the business. However, change management shows that such dialogues are not a waste of time but are a deep motivator for change.

In other words, the transformation of the chemical process industry needs not only engineers that are well-trained in their discipline but also engineers that are well-motivated to face change and that have the courage to make sustainable choices.

These observations shows that the Triple I model not only offers an heuristics to analyze relevant aspects, to integrate the knowledge of different disciplines, and to do justice to justified interests of stakeholders, but also offers a tool to bring ideals and basic beliefs into discussion to facilitate change.

CONCLUSION

The chemical process industry has joined forces to accelerate a sustainable development. On European level innovation programs have been launched to facilitate the transformation to a sustainable sector. The execution of these programs is hampered by the phenomena of reductionism and silo thinking that result not only in 'reduced' and 'narrowed' analysis but also in 'reduced' and 'narrowed' solutions.

The research question of this chapter was: How to support engineers in R&D to analyze all relevant aspects, to integrate the knowledge of different disciplines, and to do justice to the justified interests of stakeholders, to transform the chemical process industry into a sustainable sector? The first sub question was: What type of approach is required? We have shown that the practice approach, as outlined in section 4, is very suitable to answer the research question.

Especially, because practice approaches take their starting point in the daily life of professionals and focus on what is 'said' and what is 'done'. It is also made plausible that this type of approaches has a high transformative power. One of the practice approaches is the so-called Triple I model. This model is developed in close cooperation with engineers and offers three perspectives to understand professional practices: Identity and intrinsic values, Interests of stakeholders, and Ideals and basic beliefs. This model can be used to analyses a professional practice and to develop a professional practice.

The second sub question was: How to analyze relevant aspects, to integrate the knowledge of all disciplines, and to do justice to the justified interests of stakeholders? We have shown that thee Triple I model offers an heuristics to answer this question. As a case study we have used the process intensification of chlorine. The first I, identity and intrinsic values, focuses on the world of the engineer. It forces engineers to address the identity of their processes and to make the intrinsic values explicit. The second I, interests of stakeholders, explore focuses on the stakeholders of professional practices. We have offered a methodology to identify and to rank stakeholders. Also, we have shown that the nature of the justified interests differ from stakeholder to stakeholder. The third I, ideals and basic beliefs, shows that an exploration of 'deep' ideals and 'deep' basic beliefs is of utmost importance to address the transformation of the process industry into a sustainable sector.

The third and last sub question of this study was: How to motivate engineers to find creative solutions and to effectuate change? A key insight in change management is that the energy to realize far-reaching changes and the courage to make radical choices only can be tapped into when there is an alignment between ideals and basic beliefs of the key actors and the vision and objectives of a sustainable process. It is argued that dialogues about ideals and basic beliefs are not a waste of time but motivate for change.

These observations shows that the Triple I model not only offers an heuristics to analyze all relevant aspects, to integrate the knowledge of different disciplines, and to do justice to justified interests of stakeholders, but also offers a tool to bring ideals and basic beliefs into discussion to facilitate change.

ACKNOWLEDGMENT

We would like to thank Jan Harmsen for the stimulating discussions and Ger van der Horst for his comments on an earlier version of the manuscript.

REFERENCES

Action plan Process Intensification. (n.d.). Retrieved August 31 2018 from https://www.rvo.nl/sites/default/files/bijlagen/Action_Plan_Process_Intensification.pdf

Aftalion, F. (1991). *History of the International Chemical Industry: From the Early Days to 2000*. Philadelphia: University of Pennsylvania Press.

Agricola, G. (1556). *De re metallica*. Basil: Hieronymus Froben & Nicolaus Episcopius.

Al-Salem, S. M., Lettieri, P., & Baeyens, J. (2009). Recycling and recovery routes of plastic solid waste (PSW): A review. *Waste Management (New York, N.Y.)*, *29*(10), 2625–2643. doi:10.1016/j.wasman.2009.06.004 PMID:19577459

Andrady, A. L. (2011). Microplastics in the marine environment. *Marine Pollution Bulletin*, *62*(8), 1596–1605. doi:10.1016/j.marpolbul.2011.05.030 PMID:21742351

Bin2Barrel. (n.d.). Retrieved August 6 2018 from Http://bin2barrel.com/

CEFIC. (2018). *Facts & Figures 2017 of the European chemical industry*. Retrieved August 6 2018 from Http://www.cefic.org/Facts-and-Figures/

Chemelot. (n.d.a). *Staatsmijn Maurits: kolen (1926-1967).* Retrieved May 24 2018 from https://www.chemelot.nl/chemelot/historie/staatsmijn-maurits

Chemelot. (n.d.b). *See the synergy, feel the energy.* Retrieved August 24 2018 from https://www.chemelot.nl/chemelot/feiten-cijfers

Dooyeweerd, H. (1969). *A new critique of theoretical thought*. Philadelphia: The Presbyterian and Reformed Publishing Company.

DSM. (n.d.). Vision Chemelot, 2025. *DSM*.

EC (European Commission). (2011). *'Plastic Waste: Ecological and Human Health Impacts', Science for Environment Policy, In-depth Reports*. EC.

EC (European Commission). (2017). *Circular Economy research and innovation - Connecting economic & environmental gains*. Retrieved October 31 2018 from Https://ec.europa.eu/programmes/horizon2020/sites/horizon2020/files/ce_booklet.pdf

EC (European Commission). (2018). *A European Strategy for Plastics in a Circular Economy*. Retrieved October 31 2018 from Http://ec.europa.eu/environment/circular-economy/pdf/plastics-strategy-brochure.pdf

EFCE. (n.d.). *European Roadmap for Process identification*. Retrieved August 31 2018 from http://efce.info/efce_media/Downloads/wppi/European_Roadmap_PI.pdf

Euro Chlor. (2016). Retrieved October 31 2018 from Http://www.eurochlor.org/media/110998/capacities_1-1-2016-for_information_sheet.pdf

FLOWID. (2016). Retrieved October 31 2018 from https://www.flowid.nl/akzonobel-making-a-big-effort-on-breakthrough-technology/

Freeman, R. E. (2001). The Stakeholder Theory of the Modern Corporation. In Ethical Theory and Business (6th ed.; pp. 56-65). Prentice Hall.

Granados-Mendoza, P. (2016). *Intensification of the chlor-alkali process using a rotor-stator spinning disc membrane electrochemical reactor* (PhD thesis). Eindhoven University of Technology.

NRC Handelsblad. (2006). *Laatste chloortrein Akzo is vertrokken* [Last chlorine train Akzo has left]. Author.

Harmsen, J. (2010). Process intensification in the petrochemicals industry: Drivers and hurdles for commercial implementation. *Chemical Engineering and Processing*, *49*(1), 70–73.

Hoogland, J., & Jochemsen, H. (2000). Professional autonomy and the normative structure of medical practice. *Theoretical Medicine and Bioethics*, *21*(5), 457–475. doi:10.1023/A:1009925423036 PMID:11142442

Hortinext. (2018). *Haalbaarheid CO2-transport Limburg via NAVO-pijpleiding opnieuw onder de loep*. Retrieved August 24 2018 from https://hortinext.nl/haalbaarheid-co2-transport-limburg/

Jochemsen, H. (2006). Normative practices as an intermediate between theoretical ethics and morality. *Philosophia Reformata*, *71*(1), 96–112. doi:10.1163/22116117-90000377

Jochemsen, H., & Glas, G. (1997). *Verantwoord medisch handelen*. Amsterdam: Buijten & Schipperheijn.

MacIntyre, A. (1984). *After Virtue. A Study in Moral Theory* (2nd ed.). Notre Dame, IN: University of Notre Dame Press.

McAllister, J., van Praag, E., & van Soest, J. P. (2010). *Earth Fever. Living consciously with climate change*. New York: Cosmo Books.

Nicolini, D. (2012). *Practice Theory, Work, & Organisation, An Introduction*. Oxford, UK: Oxford University Press.

Petit, J. R., Jouzel, J., Raynaud, D., Barkov, N. I., Barnola, J.-M., Basile, I., ... Stievenard, M. (1999). Climate and atmospheric history of the past 420,000 years from the Vostok ice core, Antarctica. *Nature*, *399*(6735), 429–436. doi:10.1038/20859

Raworth, K. (2017). *Doughnut Economics. Seven Ways to Think Like a 21st-Century Economist*. New York: Random House Business Books.

SABIC. (2018). *SABIC demonstrates commitment to sustainable development*. Retrieved August 24 2018 from https://www.sabic.com/en/news/10040-sabic-demonstrates-commitment-to-sustainable-development-at-wef-with-iconic-structure-icehouse

SPIRE. (n.d.). *SPIRE roadmap, A-spire*. Retrieved May 24 2018 via https://www.spire2030.eu/sites/default/files/pressoffice/spire-roadmap.pdf

Stankiewicz, A., & Moulijn, J. (2000). Process intensification transforming chemical engineering. *Chemical Engineering Progress*, *96*(1), 22–34.

TNO. (n.d.). *TNO roadmap 'Sustainable chemical industry: reducing cost & time to market'*. Retrieved May 24 2018 via https://www.tno.nl/en/focus-areas/industry/roadmaps/sustainable-chemical-industry/

UN. (2015). *Sustainable Development Knowledge Platform*. Retrieved August 24 2018 from Https://sustainabledevelopment.un.org/topics/sustainabledevelopmentgoals

Verkerk, Ribeiro, Basden, & Hoogland. (2018). An Explorative Philosophical Study of Envisaging the Electrical Energy Infrastructure of the Future. *Philosophia reformata*, *83*, 90-110.

Verkerk, M. J. (2004). *Trust and Power on the Shop Floor* (Thesis). University Maastricht.

Verkerk, M.J. (2014). A philosophy-based "toolbox" for designing technology: The conceptual power of Dooyeweerdian philosophy. *Koers – Bulletin for Christian Scholarship, 79*(3), 1-7.

Verkerk, M. J. (2015). A practitioner's reflections on moral leadership: Towards a philosophical foundation. In P. Nullens & S. van de Heuvel (Eds.), *Challenges of Moral Leadership* (pp. 47–72). Leuven: Peeters.

Verkerk, M. J., Holtkamp, F. C., Wouters, E. J. M., & Van Hoof, J. (2017). Professional Practices and User Practices: An Explorative Study in Health Care. *Philosophia Reformata, 82*(2), 167–191. doi:10.1163/23528230-08202001

Verkerk, M. J., Hoogland, J., van der Stoep, J., & de Vries, M. (2016). *Philosophy of technology. An introduction for technology and business students*. Oxon, UK: Routledge.

WCED (World Commission on Environment and Development). (1987). *Our Common Future*. United Nations. Retrieved October 31 2018 via http://www.un-documents.net/our-common-future.pdf

Chapter 5
Engineering:
The Zayandehrud River Case

Mehdi F. Harandi
Delft University of Technology, The Netherlands

ABSTRACT

Engineering is one of the social practices for which a normative practice approach in analyzing tensions in the practice can be fruitful, particularly when combined with an actor-network analysis. That is illustrated in this chapter by the Zayandehrud river case of water management in Iran. The modernist hydrocracy that was installed appeared to backfire strongly and resulted in serious environmental damage. The normative practice analysis shows how conflicting norms between different sub-practices can explain the problems that emerged. The analysis also suggests an alternative for this modernist hydrocracy.

INTRODUCTION

In the early 1970s in Iran a large dam was built in the Zayandehrud river to arrange availability of water for industries and reclamation projects as well as irrigation in the fields surrounding the touristic historical city of Isfahan and for local industries, to supply electricity for that city, and also to protect it against flooding by the river. The river is one of the largest in Iran and had always served as the lifeline of Iran's Central Plateau. The reservoir created by the dam has a capacity of 1250 million m^3 and the surface of the lake behind the dam is 54,000 m^2. The building of the dam was part of the White Revolution of 1962, defined by the Iranian government and elaborated in the Land Reforms plan in 1968. Heavy machinery was imported for drainage and in the process the existing natural water wells, or Qanats, were

DOI: 10.4018/978-1-5225-8006-5.ch005

largely destroyed. Before the construction of the dam, the Zayandehrud river had been an impressive stream in the city of Isfahan. The name of the river means: 'procreator river' and this name had been most appropriate for many ages. Today the bed of the river is mostly dry. The famous Khaju bridge across the river now seems complete obsolete as the river can just as well be crossed through the dry bed. A sad view for the citizens of Isfahan who had known the river in its earlier glory. The explanation for this dramatic effect of the dam, in combination with the water management governance system that had been developed after its construction, is it was based on a modernist way of thinking in terms of command and efficiency and control rather than in terms of care for nature and humans. The case is a paradigmatic example of an engineering practice that got caught in an approach in which engineering was seen as 'conquering nature' and a 'utopian dream of mastering nature' (Molle 2008). According to Molle, the new governance system mode was as based on the Hydraulic Mission, 'a strong conviction that every drop of water flowing to the ocean is a waste and that the state should develop hydraulic infrastructure to capture as much water as possible for human uses' (Wester 2008). The carrier of the mission is the 'hydrocracy' ((Swyngedouw 1999; Molle et al. 2009) which, based on a high-modernist world-view, sets out to control nature and 'conquer the desert' by 'developing' water resources for the sake of 'progress and development' (Harandi et al. 2015 from Molle 2008). Clearly, many engineers were involved in this movement. The Zayandeh Rud river case is not a stand-alone case. Many contemporary developments in engineering are supported by utopian rhetoric. Society expects engineers to create a perfect world in which all diseases have been banned, information is available in an 'unlimited' way (mark the many advertisements that have that word: unlimited Internet, unlimited data; people can connect with whomever and whenever they want and more of those promises).

As the philosopher of technology Albert Borgmann has noted, the dominant role of devices in our society and the commodities they provide, cause us to skip the question: what is real progress? We take for granted that more information is progress, that living longer is always progress, that more communication is progress, etcetera. We are not even aware that our ideas about what is progress shift in the course of time and are different for different cultures. There was a time in which it was believed that artificial products were better than natural products. In artificial products, it was knowns exactly what was in it, but in natural product one was never sure. Now we value natural products above artificial products and favor eco-products over 'less natural' products. In our Western culture for the beauty of women we see getting slimmer as progress, but in other cultures getting thicker is beauty progress for women. We enjoy a landscape with a meandering river, but in 1789 a German engineer, Johan Gottfried Tulla decided that the river Rhine had to be controlled and 'corrected' by straightening it with canals and dikes (the example is from David

Blackbourn and cited in Jan Boersema's farewell lecture at the Vrije Universiteit Amsterdam in 2012). Mastering nature again as the aim of engineering.

For engineers making trade-offs is a natural element in their work. More perhaps than anyone else in technological developments, they are aware of the impossibility to create a perfect world. Trade-offs are a necessary part of engineering and it makes much more sense to seek optimal trade-offs than to try and create a perfect solution. Thus engineers are in a constant dilemma. On the one hand, the rhetoric requires them to seek the perfect solution, and on the other hand their professional knowledge tells them that they have to look for sensible trade-offs. It is this tension that begs for analysis in terms of a normative practice approach. This need is enhanced by the fact that engineering is also a matter of many actors being involved. In the Zayandeh Rud case, the sad outcome of the new water management was the outcome of a process in which not only engineers, but also national and local governments were involved, as well as farmers and other water users, and not in the least the new Mirab company that had been set up to be in charge of the water division. In the ethics of technology this issues is addressed as the 'problem of the many hands'; because so many actors are involved in the process, it is very difficult to identify the role of individual actors in the decisions that resulted in the sometimes disastrous outcomes (Van de Poel, Fahlquist, Doorn, Zwart & Royakkers, 2012). A case that illustrates this and is often used in engineering ethics courses, is the explosion of the Challenger space shuttle in 1986. The committee that was appointed to analyses how this could have happened, chaired by the famous physicist Richard Feynman, had great difficulties disentangling the complicated decision making process that had led to the ultimate decision to launch the shuttle in spite of the low air temperature and the risks for failure of the O-rings that separated the fuel tanks. The Zayandeh Rud river and the Challenger case together show that engineering practices must somehow deal with conflicting norms and a variety of actors. It is this combination that makes the normative practice approach so useful to analyses how such practices can go wrong and how this can be prevented by more explicit discussions about what values are pursued and how responsibilities are divided over the actors.

NORMATIVITY IN THE NATURE OF ENGINEERING

Before moving on to the more elaborate analysis of the Zayandehrud river case, it is useful to see how according to the philosophy of technology, normativity is deeply inherent to the very nature of engineering. Engineering is by definition involved not in the world as it is, but in the world as we would like it to become. Engineers have an opinion on the world, unlike natural scientists, who aim at describing the world, not judging it. Engineers talk about well-functioning drilling machines or broken engines. Natural scientists do not talk about malfunctioning electrons. A particle that does not behave the way an electron does, is not a malfunctioning electron, but it is a different particle. Of course natural scientists do have normativity in their practice. There are norms for when a theory will be accepted in the current canon of the scientific discipline. But there is no normativity in the content of the knowledge. That is the case is engineering, as well as in other practices that aim at changing the world rather than primarily observing it. Engineering is not unique in that respect, because the same can be said of medical practices. Those are, however, the focus of Chapter 7 in this book.

Carl Mitcham in his 'classic' book *Thinking Through Technology* sketches a survey of the philosophy of technology and engineering by using four ways of looking at technology. In the first place, technology can be seen as the vast collection of technical artefacts that we can see around us. This is how the word 'technology' is often used: by 'the technology around us', one refers to the artefacts around us. When children are asked to tell what they think of when the word 'technology' is mentioned, they immediately start listing artefacts, like computers, robots, lasers and the like. A second way of reflecting on technology is by seeing it as a knowledge domain. Technology is something one can study, for instance at a university of technology. An intuitive notion many people hold here, is that this knowledge domain mainly contains knowledge that can be derived from natural sciences. As we will see this can only be part of the story, as otherwise normativity would not feature in technological knowledge. In the third place, technology can be seen as a collection of processes and activities. Three of such processes stand out: designing, making and using. The latter also comprises maintenance, repair and assessment. Fourthly and finally, there is technology as an expression of human volition, human will. In this perspective, normativity stands out quite prominently. For a long time it was the primary focus of philosophy of technology. Particularly philosophers in the Continental tradition (like Heidegger, Marx, Ellul, just to mention a few), reflected on technology as it is related to our human nature, human values, and to culture and society. To investigate the role of normativity in these four domains, we will enter through Mitcham's knowledge perspective. We will do this because the content of the knowledge domain is always in some way related to either artefacts, processes or human values. For that reason, it makes little sense to deal with the knowledge perspective separately from the other three perspectives. A more fruitful approach is to use the knowledge domain as a bridge that connects the other three.

In the Dual Nature of Technical Artefacts approach to understanding technical artefacts, as it was developed at Delft University of Technology, the Netherlands, technical artefacts have two types of properties: structural and functional properties (Kroes & Meijers, 2006). The first type of properties is related to those aspects in which the artefact can be both a subject and an object: the numerical, spatial, motion, physical, and biotic aspect. Examples of such properties are: size and shape, number of parts, material properties (both physical and chemical), and bio-related properties (like growth rate). These properties particularly relate to the artefact as a subject (it takes space, it moves, it exerts forces, it lives, etcetera). The second type of properties refer to aspects in which the artefact can only be an object. Such properties are: its purpose or function, its price, its aesthetic qualities, its role in legislation (e.g. in a law about permitted and forbidden materials), and the trust it raises (or the lack of that). It is clear that the term 'function' is taken broadly here and not just as the 'technical' function of the artefact. For these properties the artefact must be the object of human activity and judgment. Normativity features obviously in the second type of properties. This can be seen immediately when we consider the meaning of the concept of 'function' in the narrower sense. Function then does not mean what the artefact actually does, but what it ought to do or enable. The function of a car is to bring from A to B and that still holds when the car is in the garage for repair and is not even able to bring from A to B. Function is inherently a normative notion. Therefore knowledge of functions – part and parcel of 'what engineers know' – has normativity in its content. Functions are ascribed to artefacts. The first people to do so are the designers, who started the process of developing the artefact mostly with a desired function. Thus they translated into a desired behavior of the artefact and that behavior was in turn translated into a structure that would show that behavior when put into use. Users often start at the other end. They see the structure and evaluate what functions could be realized with that. When seeing a screwdriver, they may recognize that it has a long solid stick that could serve as lever and therefore could be used to open a tin can. Or they could recognize that it has mass, and therefore weight, and for that reason could be used as a paperweight. Of course they may also listen to the designer's voice and use it for what it was designer for, namely to drive screws. This may suggest that the normativity in the function is totally up to the user and that the normativity is totally relational. That this is not the case can easily be seen when a user decides to ascribe the function of flying machine to the screwdriver, takes it up to the top of a building, sits on it and jumps . . . Then it becomes clear that function ascriptions have another normativity layer: they can be appropriate or inappropriate. This has to do with the relation between structure and function: the structure may lack qualities that are needed for realizing a certain ascribed function and it that case the function ascription is inappropriate. That is why we distinguish between 'proper' functions (the ones for which the artefact was designed), 'accidental' functions (alternative, but still appropriate functions that are supported by the structure) and 'inappropriate' functions (or 'abuse') for which the structure is unsuitable. Another layer of normativity is in the level at which norms are: they can be at token level ("this is a good screwdriver"), at type level ("this brand of screwdrivers is good") or artefact level "Screwdrivers are good for driving screws"). So normativity is all over the place when it comes to the functional nature of artefacts. How about the structural nature? Here, too, normativity can be present. Based on functional considerations, norms can be defined for structural properties of the artefact-in-design: "it needs to be rectangular in shape, two meters high and five meters wide". It is clear that this normativity is dependent on the functional normativity. There is nothing inherently 'good' in an object being rectangular and two by five meters. It's 'goodness' is in the context of the function that the artefact is expected to fulfil.

Normativity is also present in knowledge of engineering processes. There are generally established 'good' and 'wrong' ways of doing things in engineering. Designing an artefact without a decent analysis of the underlying need is generally not seen as 'good' practice. Hammering a piece of nail into a piece of wood without a small piece of the other end of the nail coming out of the wood is generally seen as 'good' practice. Being able to operate a CNC-machine properly is also 'good' practice. Making a totally errant assessment of the safety of a drilling machine is 'bad' practice. And so on, and so on. In knowledge of processes we can distinguish between three types of knowledge each of which has normativity in it: propositional knowledge, knowing-how and experiential knowledge. Propositional knowledge of a process is knowledge that is expressed in propositions. This is the type of knowledge we see in manuals, handbooks for practitioners, guidelines for designers, etcetera. In a sequence of sentences that describe procedural steps, the whole process is laid down. There is evidently normativity in most of these propositions. They have the purpose of informing how something ought to be done. This expression of knowledge in propositions is, however, not always possible. Whoever can say "I know how to hammer a nail properly into a piece of wood" and tries to turn this knowledge into propositions, will find out that somehow part of that knowledge fails to make it into the propositions. It is a pity that mostly those are the most crucial bits and pieces of the expert's (tacit) knowledge that cannot be 'codified'. This example can be multiplied by many others: ride a bike, tie a bow tie, lay tiles, etcetera. This knowledge of how to perform a process that cannot be turned into propositions (at least, not complete) is often called 'knowing-how'. The example of "knowing how to hammer a nail properly into a piece of wood" indicates that normativity can be present in this type of knowledge. A third type of knowledge is experiential knowledge. That is the knowledge that can say: "I know what it is to build a cabinet". This, too, cannot be expressed, or at best incompletely, in propositions, neither does it refer to a skill one masters. Maybe the cabinet was a disaster, but the experience of building it has resulted in knowledge one would not have without having that experience. It can also refer to persons, such as a master-carpenter one admires and that one has met ("I know him"). The example of the master-carpenter one 'knows' immediately shows that there can be normativity also in that knowledge: one has gotten to know him as a master, that is, as an example of a very good carpenter.

The fact that some people have knowledge of engineering processes and other people do not have that knowledge, can be expressed in diplomas and certificates. They entitle people to perform certain acts that others without that diploma or certificate are not entitle to do. These diplomas and certificates express another normativity, other than the normativity that is in the knowledge itself. It is an 'extrinsic' normativity that deals with the extent to which one has that knowledge. This normativity is mostly generated by the social practice in which the knower functions. Later we will come back to this role of normativity in engineering practices.

As we have seen, knowledge of engineering processes also has normative content, as has knowledge of technical artefacts. Now we will turn to Mitcham's fourth perspective, that is, technology as an expression of human will.

Engineering is all about changing our environment as an expression of our human will. We have practical needs and desires and seek to realize them through technology. We create artefacts that can protect us against cold, rain, storms and the like, that enable us to move from one place to a remote other, that enable us to communicate over great distances, that provide energy, food, clean water, safety and health. What we want, our ideals, can be expressed in a powerful way in our views on an ideal world. Utopian thinking has become popular since Enlightenment and still features in lot of rhetoric surrounding technological environments. Utopias are normative in nature. They express a world that meets the norms of our human will in optima forma. Therefore the study of utopias in technological developments is very informative if we want to see our own will reflected. An interesting way of expressing utopias is in science fiction, both as a literary genre as in movies. Sometimes the utopia is expressed in the form of its opposite, the dystopia. Dystopias are particularly popular in science fiction movies. By expressing what we fear, however, we also express what we hope for.

In the 1970s and 1980s, Star Trek was a popular science fiction television series. It was produced by Gene Roddenberry, who was a humanist and convinced that if human would live out their goodness in technology, we would reach a world without diseases, without wars, and with unlimited travelling and communicating. The Original Series was shocking to the American audience originally, as it had on one bridge of a spaceship a white male American captain (which was, of course, very much OK), but also a Chinese and a Russian officer (while the series was broadcasted in the middle of the Cold War!), a dark skin colored communications officer (in a time when the country still struggled with the aftermath of the abolition of slavery) and an alien second commander, representing whatever other race the producers might have overlooked. All these people were peacefully kept together in their technological artefact. Whatever problem occurred, their technology was there to fix it. But not without each individual sticking to certain moral values. Normativity was all over the place in this television series. It was discontinued after three seasons, but started up again in The Next Generation, which lasted seven seasons and was in turn was followed by Deep Space Nine (also seven seasons). Then followed Voyager (seven season, too) and Enterprise, the series that, like to original one, was discontinued already after three seasons. The norms for what was morally good and wrong were represented in an almost caricatured way in the consecutive captains. James Kirk (The Original Series) was almost the caricature of a 'good man' and thus represented a strict virtue ethics approach to (moral) normativity. Jean-Luc Picard was a strict duty ethics representative, always keen to work according to the book. Benjamin Cisko becomes more and more religious In his ethics during the seasons. An outspoken utilitarian is Mr. Spock, one of the aliens in The Original Series. The main reason for being rather extensive on this television series is that it can still serve as a model of imaging a practice in which normativity was very important and explicitly pictured in the characters as well as in the rules and responsibility by which they functioned. The message of the series was quite overt: thanks to good morality and clear rules about tasks and responsibilities, the starship practice, so much dominated by engineering and its outcomes, flourished abundantly, in spite of all the dangers and threats.

Two current examples of utopian ideals in engineering are the long-term promises of nanotechnology, particularly its use for medical purposes, and robotics. The ideal of nanotechnology is mastery of matter at the very basic level of atoms and molecules. This would enable us to make a material with any kind of desired property. It would allow the development of extremely small devices that can be brought into organisms and do repair work there. By repositioning molecules in the brain and thus repairing brain tissue brain death could be postponed ad libitum. With lab-on-chip a complete DNA analysis can be produced in a family doctor's practice, using just a drop of the patient's blood. These are just some of the extreme promises of nanotechnology gurus. For robotics the extreme promises deal with creating robots that almost become like humans. Expectations are that robots will display even emotions and free will. Robot Sophia was already given the rights of a civilian in Saudi-Arabia because of her human-likeliness.

NORMATIVITY IN ENGINEERING AS A SOCIAL PRACTICE

We have seen how normativity plays an integral role in the practice of engineering and technological developments. How does that play out in the norms for this practice? Let us go through the different types of norms as they have been introduced in the first chapters of this book.

The structure of the practice is related to three types of constitutive norms, the qualifying, foundational and contextual norms. The qualifying norms are related to the aspect that is qualifying for the practice. For engineering that is the developmental aspect. Engineering is there to bring about new artefacts. These artefacts serve a higher goal. They may enhance social contacts, bring about a sense of beauty, serve justice or support religious acts. But those goals are not realized within the engineering practice, although the engineers need to consider carefully what the goal of the users will be and what values they will hold. What they can do is bring about products and processes and inform intended users about the function they had in mind when developing the artefact. They can do so, for instance, by adding a manual or by giving the artefact a name that suggests its function (screw-driver, bottle-opener). Once the artefact is in the hands of the user, they will determine the qualifying function, although they will be limited, of course, by the structural properties of the artefact that allow for some, but not all accidental functions. What the engineers are entitled to do is to define the 'proper' function of the artefact.

Foundational norms refer to the foundational aspect of the practice. That, too, is the developmental aspect. Now we have to look at the norms in the activities that are executed in the engineering practice. We have seen that here are norms for good practices that are established within the engineering practice. Mastery of those good practices, often expressed in diplomas, determine who is entitled to work with what equipment, or who is entitled to do a certain part of the design work. Technological developments are mostly a matter of 'many hands' and the norms in the practice determine the roles of the various 'hands'. It is known from many cases in engineering ethics that the so-called 'many hands problem', that is the difficulty to identify who is responsible for an accident or bad consequence, is often difficult because norms have not been well defined and distributed over people.

Contextual norms are related to the social economic and legal aspects of the practice. For engineering such norms concern different social cultures (e.g., with respect to hierarchy) in a country, economic conditions under which engineers have to operate, or legal constraints with respect to materials that may or may not be used for sustainability, health or safety reasons. These norms determine what engineers are entitled to do and what not. They will often be laid down in manuals, handbooks and the like.

Finally there are the norms that are related to the direction of the practice. The direction is related to the deeper values that are held in the engineering practice. These can be values like: care for the safety of the future user of an artefact, loyalty to the company the engineers work for, or care for the natural environment as it will be affected by the production and use of the artefact. Such values forms the regulative norms for an engineering practice.

As for all practices, in engineering practices also the norms have to be internally consistent. When the regulative norm is environmental care is claimed to be held, but in the constitutive norms there is no person or department who has environmental care as his/her/its responsibility, something is wrong with this practice. If loyalty to the company is claimed to be held, but nothing in the constitutive norms rewards loyalty, again there is something wrong and the practice will not perform as intended.

Furthermore, there can be clashes between the engineering practice norms and external norms. Technological developments always involve different practices. Besides the engineering practice, there is the government practice, the consumers practice (although one can question if this can be called a practice because there are hardly any norms defined for it, unless the consumers are organized in a certain market), and other social partners such as environmental groups (like Greenpeace). Such clashes between norms can have destructive effects on technological developments. One of the examples of that is the Aramis public transport system that is described by Bruno Latour (Latour, 1996). The system was crushed between the interests of the various social actors that were involved in the development. Now we turn to the main case study in this chapter: the water management system in the Iran's central river, Zayandeh Rud.

CASE STUDY: THE ZAYANDEHRUD RIVER WATER MANAGEMENT

Iran is blessed with an abundance of earth and sun but cursed with a scarcity of life's most fundamental need, water. The Zayandehrud river is the main source of verdure and fertility of Iran's central and the Isfahan metropolitan area. Throughout history the area's progress has been prompted by and depended on the river. Like in many other civilizations, the history of the Zayandehrud has shown how people with different interests, beliefs and norms can come together around a river (Hossaini 2006). For more than six decades, greed to grow has been the engine of irreversible development (Harandi et al. 2015) in Iran. 'This craving for modernity and gigantism (depicted projects like in Sefidrud 1962, Dez 1963, Chadegan 1969 reservoirs etc.) was accompanied, or fuelled, by a vibrant ideology of domination of nature which has its roots in the enlightenment and in 19th century scientism, and blossomed during the 1930–70 period' (Molle 2008). For that reason the Zayandehrud has increasingly faced changing and inconsistent policies challenging the water rights and allocation. The creation of a joint electricity-irrigation scheme was the absolute consequence and focal symbol of the modernization of Iran. The abstraction of and supply to the gigantic steel factories, refinery and power plants, as well as projects for trans-basin water conveyance and flooding newly reclaimed areas with new canals, have all been developed under such beliefs. The idea then was (and evidence suggests still is) that the waters flowing to sea (for Iran for example, the Persian Gulf) are wasted and should be dammed so they can be used more proficiently than what the ancient flourish governance system fulfilled. The agents of such an idea maintain that infrastructures should be laid out on rivers and valleys to capture as much water as possible.

Disruptive policies stemming from this belief were fueled by quite a few policy considerations. First, from the 1980s onwards, in Iran there was an era of food security and self-sufficiency policies. The new agri-business and industrial communities 'ran' on the river. Secondly, the inter-basin water transfers were planned to or from the Zayandehrud from or to the remote areas by means of the 'technology'. However, each of them has only slightly solved the (man-made) water scarcities as demands have been increasing in parallel with added water supply. The first anxiety of the water scarcity was sounded early in the 1990s, when the water rights of the basin's terminal wetland (Gavkhuni Salt Lake) were pared down. Arid conditions have continued since, leaving the main reservoir at record lows where the downstream users (albeit not the industries) have been announcing severe limits on usage for several years. Their 'Hobson's choice' was to rush into aquifers. The river has been witnessing an unprecedented pressure on the resource ending up with a dried river. In the race between supply and use of this 'common-pool resource' (Hardin 1968), there are routine terms that researchers have recently used to argue about such as conflagration, 'socio-ecological breakdown' (Molle and Mamanpoush 2012) and 'vulnerability and damage' (Safaei et al. 2013). Billib et al. (2009) note the complexity of our case study to reason why such a deplorable situation has happened: 'the Zayandehrud River Basin is an example of a complicated watershed system where the lack of complete knowledge about all the interacting sub-systems has led to (the governance) failure (Harandi 2016) of the policy makers in addressing the water shortage in the basin'.

In the grip of an extreme ongoing drought that began in 2000, it is further beset by human-made perils. The farmers of central Iran's Zayandehrud had no advance warning about this water shortage. As the drought continues, decision-makers have stressed the need for continued conservation, but projects for supplying industries and far-off cities with water from the Zayandehrud have nevertheless proceeded. Upstream (in the tributaries that feed the river), others took advantage of their bargaining power to obtain Zayandehrud water (Molle and Mamanpoush, 2012). The river's water rights-holders (mostly downstream farmers and Isfahan City) only realized this when their share gradually started to go down. That was 2009, when the farmers concluded that the (water governance) system places all its structural inefficiency and bureaucracy on their shoulders, misleadingly. Despite numerous restoration schemes, the river and modern canals dried up; the farmers were unemployed, their livestock and equipment were sold, acres of lands were left uncultivated, and the pressure in the Isfahan water network has been shrinking day by day. The groundwater conditions, if not worse, were no better than the river. For years, criminals had been stealing groundwater, which intensified the aquifers' depletion, and the punitive policies of the government did not affect those who circumvent the law.

Apart from technical aspects, the case is also of importance from a socio-technical point of view. The events outlined above show how complex and intractable the Zayandehrud problem is. As with many other shared rivers, in the Zayandehrud case policy-makers also see the use of water as a means to help the state achieve its political goals. That is why societal, natural and political problems are juxtaposed amid the sublime beauty that surrounds the river. It is a classic and well-known example: most of the people, demand and infrastructure are in one and the water resources are in another jurisdiction. It is now suffering from growing flagrant and deleterious types of inter-sectoral conflicts, tensions concerning the river rights between provinces, farmers and cities, and so forth.

The tensions coupled with many factors have led to over-regulation, over-allocation, tapered groundwater recharging and climbing unemployment, all exacerbated by the irresponsible use of economic tools and engineering approaches. We see the engineers use the technology-as-knowledge to concur the nature, rerouting the surface water and extracting underground water from the river basin.

Aridity aside, the lack of comprehensive knowledge (recall technology as knowledge mentioned in the earlier section) about interlocking water cycles, norms and goals were and are hitherto immensely important parts of the issue. We in fact interpret a lack of knowledge about the actors' norms and interests that are inconsistent with each other and a knowledge that links actors to solutions (Hermans, 2005:2) to learn how to be free of friction.

For the aforementioned purposes of this chapter, this quick exploration only serves to give a glimpse of how complex the conflict of the Zayandehrud is. On the one hand this chapter is a sort of painting to show all the various actors and on the other hand it shows how the norms of these actors conflict:

- The case description starts with a bird's eye view on the actors and moves onto the inside of the case study to show where the values conflict. It will review describe what the actors look like in terms of values and norms, their different roles, tasks and responsibilities.
- In the next section, we will analyse the actors, to show who are the most influential ones. Using the actor analysis (as our primary stage analysis) we can show where the ropes for pulling and pushing of the different actors are.

There are different sorts of terms in multi-actor system contexts with different definitions to label the parties' roles in a system. For example, stakeholders are people or groups who hold the power to affect the straightforward (future of a) system (Jones and Wicks, 1999) and the loss of that implies powerless stakeholders. However for now we will present actors as a group of people – a beneficial or relevant party, regardless of having palpable power

- Moving on to the main analysis, we will perform the second analysis by means of the framework of normative practice, to compare different norms in the different actors that are conflicting. Normative practice theory also illustrates how a hydrosystem is influenced by the actors as well as technology over time, externally. Two feats that were missing notably, and had not been seen before in the engineering problem-solving approaches linked to social practices.
- In the conclusion we will argue that such frictions (rising from values conflict) are one of the causes that ultimately coalesce to sink (any) solution over managing (water) conflicts. And we make it clear that conflicts in the norms happen not due to the fact that actors hold different values, but inconsistent direction are linked to different (directional) norms.

The Zayandehrud, Gripped by Actor-Made Perils

Again we stress that the analysis is primarily used here to explore the links between the actors. Using that we will have a basic understanding of the problem and networks, because it is often unclear 'which actors need to be involved in (and/or are responsible for) a water management effort' (Islam and Susskind, 2013: 93). The complex nature of the Zayandehrud conflict, as an issue played out by many 'hands' (Figure 1), meant it was difficult at times to access the central actors. We believe the readability of the chapter could be improved if the number of the actors that are involved in the analysis section is reduced. Therefore we selected the most influential ones for further analysis. We focus on two of the actors, as we think in such complicated cases the fewest actors can explain this water business clearer. In the conclusion we interpret about those actors that can arguably benefit the conflict resolution. Here we rest our case. Henceforth we will slightly move into our main discussion, the actors: those who are playing (in)directly with this water beside the norms in which they are conflicting over or looking for.

Figure 1. Hierarchical system of the Zayandehrud showing the actors

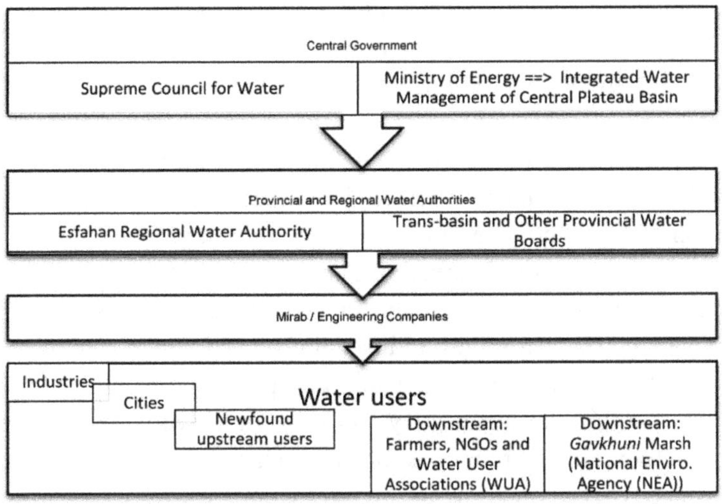

The Actors Involved in Zayandehrud

The Government (Water Authorities and Governors)

As the main river course, main actors and a large part of the river basin are located in the Isfahan Province and most of the river's water comes from Chaharmahal-va-Bakhtiari Province, this has led to some jurisdictional misunderstandings and a lack of agreement over historical rights is far from being resolved. There are reports that upstream users are knowingly using more than their allotment, if any exists (Eslami 2010). Moreover, periodic and country-wide droughts escalate dramatically in sub-national conflicts, as well as Zayandehrud. The severity of such socio-ecological conditions has influenced the decisions to make some so-called 'stepwise, decisive and practical' decisions translated into Integrated Water Resources Management; however the downstream users (mostly farmers) have realized that it has disgraced their 500-year water-rights. For example, the Ministry of Energy has frequently curtailed the downstream users' water by declining the released discharge from the Chadegan reservoir as the upstream users (in Chaharmahal-va-Bakhtiari Province) are constantly pumping and using water for (highland) orchards and remote cities. It is not long since these uppermost lands were vested (directly by the former populist President) and vague and non-peer-reviewed land-water licenses were created. That by itself is still causing chaos in the river rights and is also one of the reasons why others have violated these water rights. These licenses override the pre-existing rights that are hundreds of years old of a huge population in the downstream from a water coming from hundreds of kilometers away. This issue of overriding the rights is not confined to the former presidents; the President presently in office has promised the uphill province to build a tunnel that has been proposed by engineers and a dam (though the volume is low) which has caused an extra load on the river to afford drinking water for another remote city.

Remarkably the large industries in Esfahan and Yazd Province have also been grappling with this provincial conflict. As for Chaharmahal-va-Bakhtiari Province, many of the employees in these industries have migrated from there and are now Esfahan city dwellers, which is creating extra demands for everything as well as water. Yazd Province is another trans-basin user; its neighbors see it as a user that is carelessly wasting the water with industrial uses.

Such interlocking and networked actors and perceptions have been the causes of tumults between these provinces. By focusing exclusively on dividing the water flow, the government and its related actors are engaged in blame games or spin and not yet in a sincere effort to come to an agreement. Such policies have not taken into account how all of the actors are likely to be affected. Cooperation seems less expected in the actors, however, and there is a real confusion because the governance patterns do not create a community of interest over the actors' communalities and has left actors with numerous concerns and unresolved issues. As shown in Figure 1, the policy making is tightly ruled, made and implemented by a top-down administrative process. At the top are the Ministry of Energy and the representatives are at the provincial levels, some of whose responsibilities have been taken over by the Supreme Council for Water.

The question about all of these (governmental) actors could be: why have disputes grown and the pace of progress has slowed by the gridlock created by the deluge of (inter)provincial and national policies? We shall argue, as our account here shows, that it is because the actors and over-centralized policies are mostly obsessive to the tribal- and geographical-oriented interests rather than responsive to the norms and responsibilities for sharing the river.

The Industries

Back to the early 1930s, the idea of having a city like Manchester in Iran turned Esfahan into the home city of the country's textile factories (Atabaki, 2013). It is not so long ago that industries around the Zayandehrud were developing based on two different ideologies of development. The first one was rooted in the coordination of provincial agencies at the river-basin level for planning and management (Molle, 2008). This idea in Iran came in and placed agriculture as the backbone of industries' development in the 1950s (after Balali 2011) that is on-going, accordingly. The second ideology was related to the 1980s that placed industries as much as possible in the center of Iran due to safety and (food) security concerns. The grouping of these two over the years turned Esfahan into Iran's industrial hub. Surely, the Zayandehrud river water played a significant role amongst this centrality. The industries are mostly 'linked to government subsidies for livelihoods' (Harandi et al., 2015). Therefore water deliveries have turned out in a way to be managed not just for industries but also for the purposes that would help those industries. The refineries here produce and supply one quarter of the country's petrol demands, however the petrochemical industry has turned parts of its production into oil to elude the sanctions and consequently the water supply must not be cut. These are the examples leading to additional (re)use of the river and the waters that is not 'theirs'. The rights-holders are complaining that these industries can get water easily. The government has recently banned the use of drinking water for industries. They have to use waste water, this is a costly and long-lasting task.

The Mirab (Company)

Conventionally, governing surface and ground water in the semi-arid areas such as Iran had intrinsic values (Mahmoudian 1969) as it was a societal-based activity and the management of them was performed through an intricate system, known as the Mirab. Therefore we can describe a Mirab as the head of, for example, a river and a person who apportions water share to the water-right holders. The management of rivers was in the hands of a trustworthy Mirab elected by upright local communities' representatives. Only one of these representatives was appointed by the governor. 'Historically the states and central governments rarely directly influenced river management' (Harandi et al. 2015 from Hossaini 2006). He was wisely selected from the hamlets' communities along the central part of the river, to see the river from a normal viewpoint, not from the high-water perspective of the upstream users or the low-water perspective of the downstream people. The Mirab of Zayandehrud appointed six assistants and quite a few observers who were employed as needed. The wages, services of the channels and sharing facilities were entirely paid for by stakeholders based 'upon one's sharing of water' (Mahmoudian 1969; Hossaini 2006; Eslami 2010; Harandi et al. 2015). To devise the governance patterns in the river, the management system was largely local resource- and knowledge-dependent and was implemented according to precise technical- and societal-tuned mechanisms. Perry (2013) describes the distribution process of Mirabs as follows: 'The infrastructure in all these systems provides the capacity to deliver the service that the other elements – how much water is available, priorities for sharing, rules and management arrangements – combine to define. As well as the channel or diversion structures that deliver the water, the infrastructure may also include water-dividing structures, reflecting different shares. Nearly identical structures are found in Nepal, dividing hill streams to serve farmer groups.' An eloquent socio-technical rationality for the Zayandehrud water apportionment came in the compilation of a guidebook (a Tumar) that was the work of Sheikh-Bahai, a sixteenth-century Iranian polymath, to allot the river water into 33 portions for 6 districts (Harandi et al., 2015).

The auto-regulating socio-spatial mechanism embraced the whole range of users as well as e-flow of the Gavkhuni swampland (which is registered by the Ramsar Convention), where the river terminates (Beaumont 1974). The Tumar included each hamlet's share of the river in terms of volume and time, allocating the available natural inflow, which influenced the extent of the cultivation accordingly.

The cities and industries gained a priority. This has gradually thwarted the rights and the lasting water distribution algorithms of the Tumar. The 'fuzzy allocation' scenarios of the earlier orders and 'its attendant social organization and local knowledge' (Molle and Mamanpoush 2012) were thus overridden and replaced by a new but unreliable and amorphous governance pattern.

Perry (2013) has called attention to water resources privatization that has delegated the 'state functions to private and non-sate actors'. He has also pointed out the problem of 're-scaling of state responsibilities' by shifting authorities toward up- and downward sectors and/or levels (e.g. from international, to provincial, to enterprise levels). The idea that favors private rather than state operators (not NGOs) has allowed former staff from ERWA to found 'their own companies and to perform the same service, albeit at a higher cost and private benefit to themselves, and with no increase in accountability ' (Molle and Mamanpoush, 2012; said also tacitly by Harandi et al., 2015). Accordingly, the Mirab Company was founded in 1993 and the government fully changed the old Mirab system into a state-based agency involved in operation, maintenance and remedial measures. Hossaini (2006) has criticized the management in the Zayandehrud and holds as a 'chronic illness', as well as the Mirab Company.

Engineers

Engineering projects often come up with new ideas typically because of a desire identified by their customers. Like many other river basins, in the Zayandehrud the basin development has been fostered by utilitarian engineers (Harandi and De Vries, 2014) to serve — most probably subconsciously, three criteria of development engineering artefacts: needs, requirements and specifications' for 'testing, evaluation and readjustment of different design solutions' (Björnberg, 2013). With few exceptions, engineers as companies (consultants and contractors) and as advisors are forceful drivers of any planned development as they see a river basin as an artefact that could be shaped by 'engineering'. There are countless signposts to show that the engineers' values have seduced the other values to play out their roles.

The companies in the fields of water have gradually and unconsciously fueled the disputes by proposing such proposals. Molle and Mamanpoush (2012) have aptly described another case as a series of cascade projects to argue about; the generation of a critical situation of unpredictable, invisible and ignored actors that has been created by the manipulation of the hydrologic cycle of the Zayandehrud:

'To increase the value and usefulness of the Khamiran dam (a dam located in the lateral valleys of the Zayandehrud) and extend the benefits of the Chadegan reservoir to other valleys, a plan was drawn to pump water from the latter over the mountain ridge into the former (…). In 1991, the Karvan pump station was constructed for that purpose but it faced severe technical problems [authors' italics] and its operation was discontinued after 3 or 4 years.'

The International Federation of Consulting Engineers (FIDIC) recognizes the work of the consulting engineering as 'critical to the achievement of sustainable development of society and the environment' (FIDIC, 2014). Explicitly, engineering obligation is crushed if others interfere with such obligations and the abovementioned three components are compromised. Yet although gigantism (Harandi et al., 2015) fervor has waned, drought itself remains a source of legitimacy for projecting the river. The account showed that we can liberate ourselves from the notion of 'just drought caused this chaos' when looking at what is being proposed by engineers to manufacture more water. However, Zhang (2012) holds that 'although technical experts were invited to contribute to the decision-making, they only played the role of "experts offering suggestions". Government officials made the final decision and the influence of engineers remained relatively weak'.

The Farmers

The last key actor we wish to touch upon in this section deserves more space because as the main and the oldest share/right holders, the river was and is the mainstay of the farmers. As the downstream farmers (D-farmers) own more than half of the shares of the river, according to the edict, and the fact that in recent years, we have too often seen a ceaseless sequence of issues between D-farmers and Esfahan Regional Water Authority (ERWA), therefore we wish to focus on them in this subsection. Since 2000, the river has faced continual and drastic water shortages although the D-farmers were not informed adequately in advance. As the dry conditions have continued officials have kept on supplying more water to the industries, cities and released the remainder to the farmers – recently biannually, and often grudgingly. This is because generally there is a sense that agriculture is drinking up the river and the abnormally dry conditions are exacerbating this. Despite numerous attempts to restore water due to a lack of water, the D-farmers are unemployed, their trees have died and been used as firewood, their livestock and equipment have been sold and acres of their lands have been left uncultivated. Scholarly articles aside, dozens of domestic and international news stories about the Zayandehrud situation have continued to come out. There are lots of news stories about this conflict in the media streams and perhaps the best way to present the deterioration in the condition of this patient is by quoting them: 'Farmers who worked the fertile lands around Isfahan have had to find a new way to make a living since the river at the heart of this Iranian city ran dry. Instead of raising and selling crops irrigated by the Zayandehrud, they are now paid to keep its parched riverbed clean and litter-free' (Bozorgmehr, 2014). The farmers in [Iran's] central Isfahan province have for years complained against unfair apportionment and diversion of their shares of the Zayandehrud River to supply others. It is leaving their farms dry and threatening their livelihoods. These downstream water shareholders of the Zayandehrud River struck out toward the government building, but this time riding on their otherwise redundant tractors.

On the other hand, although other water seekers of the Zayandehrud River have been presented with opportunities by their bargaining power (Molle and Mamanpoush, 2012), the D-farmers have realized their shares are gradually being reduced. They had (have) their convincing argumentations:

Firstly, Isfahan City, in the middle reaches of the river, owing to technology, industrialization and greed for growing, has become a metropolitan of millions of citizens. Nearly half of the Chadegan Reservoir capacity is taken by the city and other small nearby cities and hamlets, as they are the non-removable consumers of the river's water these days although they did not yet exist in the recent past.

The second reason is rooted in the new-found upstream users' abstractions vested by the then president. In Chaharmahal-va-Bakhtiari Province, recent on-site and heterogenic (ad hoc) decisions taken by government allies have caused the development of orchards upon the hills of the Chadegan Reservoir and have complicated the conflict between the up and downstream parts of the river. In this occasion, the D-farmers requested their right-of-river by writing letters to the officials and holding sit-ins. Yet, they welcomed credible commitment from any party to deal with the overlooked rights from the river. Whilst U-users have been trying to use political circles, others think that it is a superficial reason for abstracting water.

Thirdly, the trans-basin projects, where the projects have been biased toward politicians . The water that must be allocated solely for drinking is now also being tapped by (unknown) industries in the Yazd province.

The same situation is happening in the whole dispute of the Zayandehrud as some deals were actually set out in reasonable terms, such as Beheshtabad's trans-basin project where Isfahan, Yazd and Kerman own the plan and Chaharmahal-va-Bakhtiari and Khuzestan provinces do not cooperate there. The project has faced unforeseen political challenges at the national and local level rather than technical issues. The previous client (ERWA) has been recently changed due to such conflicts and it has now been replaced by one of the wealthiest governmental companies – the Iran Water and Power Company. However some industries have allegedly bought this water in advance. Such a good wholesale deal has reassured the downstream rights-holders (farmers) of the basin that will receive no reliable water instead of the rights. The situation was very similar to what Hu et al. (2014) depicted about a Chinese case; 'the market-based instruments widely adopted by the government to achieve an efficient allocation of water resources in arid regions have not provided sufficient incentives for farmers to improve irrigation management.' However there is some talk by farmers and others about legal action against the ERWA and its contractor-led companies and there are persistent anti-trust rumors that may cause society some real 'headaches'.

Nothing nowadays could be diverted from the river as it has fully dried up —from downstream of the node where the river is flooding the industries. The groundwater is also in the process of drying up. As mentioned before, the water rights have dwindled and as a result their incomes, social side effect of the policies (growing number of conflicts) have appeared: after leaving their hamlets years ago, underemployed farmers found themselves in a series of low-paying, often back-breaking jobs. An example of such jobs is the loading of trucks to take fertilizer for some of out-of-the-basin destinations that have already been allotted the river water. Those who could (particularly the youth) have fled to the neighboring cities to find a (decent) job.

To change, they found themselves sitting on the tractors covered with banners proclaiming 'neglected rights ought to be mooted', 'traditional water rights come from our ancestors' heritage', and 'do revive the Zayandehrud'. The farmers tried to draw sympathy by having religious sayings respecting their rights albeit consistent with the basics of the religion of Islam and the revolution. Concurrently, the opening ceremony for the construction of the world's tallest concrete dam was taking place as an engineering feat. Sad scenes were seen, where the trans-basin water conveyance pipeline of Yazd city was smashed by irate drought-stricken people. The water scarcity was acute enough to hold talks with officials even though the farmers' sit-ins continued. The farmers had agreed with the government that they would receive compensation for drought damage (subject to the Law for Fair Distribution of Water). The governor made many other promises such as a moratorium on the repayment of the loans. All this was not to say that we embrace the whole range of the farmers' actions, because they had already agreed to be paid to allow the pipeline ditch to cross over their farmlands.

The Other Actors

Molle and Mamanpoush (2012) analyses the Zayandehrud case study to show how fiat measures have led actors into controversies and 'not surprisingly, those most commonly affected [...] the downstream users, the next generations and the environment, in decreasing order of bargaining power'. Quite often, the environment is the only voice in the decision-makers' room that is not 'right' and does not have rights. The policies have not left any room for maneuvering in extreme events and the environment is the first victim of such water curtailment scenarios. The environment is not an actor solely because it does not have intentions. But of course it is an important user that has its own responsibilities/actor, (Iran's) Department(s) of the Environment (IDE). Therefore, the IDE has umbrella norms, to deserve and care for the environment. The importance of the environment totally and entirely depends on who takes care of it, because it is this actor, the IDE; who decides what is the relevance of the environment? Some actors hold this norm and some actors do not. Like the economy, some actors hold money high as a value while some others may say they do not care about it because they do not depend on it economically. The IDE plays a passive role in the governmental sectors as do the Chamber of Commerce, the City Council and some farmers' NGOs, and they are also less influential actors in the non-governmental sectors too.

Amongst the overlooked actors in this controversial situation who are not only the farmers and the environment, we also see the next generation. The next generation, which is another loser, is trying to sort out its values linked to those actors who are putting them at the top of priorities. The point is that both the next generation as well as the other actors such as the NGOs have their own values and they can choose not to cooperate and can frustrate the procedures of development.

The actor analysis of the Zayandehrud; an invisible hand versus many hands

This might be a repeated introduction for this chapter but we are looking at water as a resource that has interchangeable and straight parameters influenced by climate change and therefore as an example of a situation in which the problem of many hands seems to occur (Van de Poel et al.

2012). Van de Poel et al. (2012) attribute capacity, causality, knowledge, freedom and wrong-doing as five conditions that actors and norms intersect. The problem of many hands may lead us to narrow down the number of the actors for the analysis.

Figure 2 elucidates how the actors are related; in fact in the analysis of the actors is a set of black boxes. They do not look into what they are doing and remain closed. But in order to realize answers to the questions: What are these actors really capable of? What are they entitled to do, forbidden to do and what powers do they have, we will present a secondary analysis to open up the boxes and then inside we will see the 'practices'. However, it eventually is very much dependent on what the chapter's messages are. If our message was to show the relevance of actor(s), network(s) and issue(s) then we needed a complete and figurative picture of all the actors because it is necessary to show which power is trying to pull or push (other) actors into different directions. Against this, if we want to show something theoretically about friction points between actors — a theoretical model that explains what the problem is that has caused conflict and what is central to the cause of the problems — then, a carefully handpicked number of actors and another analysis is preferred.

Secondary Analysis

The development of large hydraulic units and the liability of having the whole responsibility of water resources for a group of actors could be 'a fix that can backfire' (Gohari et al., 2013). Any technological development is something in which all actors are interrelated so there is always a chance of tensions between the different practices. We see that development plans in the Zayandehrud have endlessly changed the norms of the actors; therefore in a way we are talking about a technologically networked river in which the practices have to take or implement decisions on the same phenomena with different norms. However it is not a technology that directly connects them although we claim that in a way, of course, they are norms accompanied by the technology. That is how in this case technology (recall the dam and trans-basin water conveyance projects) creates a connection between practices.

The government reasoning for certain norms tries to push them onto another actor and this has probably led to an impasse. And in fact, then tension arises between the structural norms of the actors when these new values are being pushed by another actor. The same thing happens here because the government pushes certain values upon the farmers in the Zayandehrud. That is why the farmers resist. Especially when one tries to influence the other then that can cause tensions internally and that is only

Figure 2. Actor-network of the Zayandehrud river case

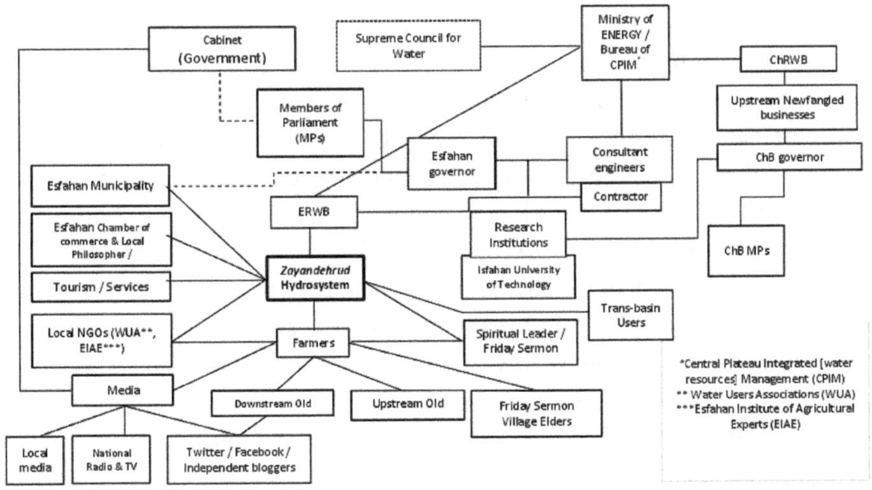

the result of trying to force an unnatural practice. For example, for many years the government and engineers have been encouraging farmers to change their cropping patterns and to flood their crops to make them consistent with the national market values or/and import-export policies. It is not the others' responsibility because for instance the government's responsibility is to foster justice, in order to enrich laws. As the government has thoroughly different accountabilities, the whole issue has become mixed and that is why tensions can arise.

The reluctance of farmers to agree with government values may not be the cause of the current conflicts, but only an expression of the inappropriateness of the values that are being pushed because theirs are truly different from other actors. Such changes could be performed in association with some NGOs, if we assume they can engage in. The government, Mirab or engineers might not have the (indigenous) knowledge nor the responsibility that a farmer does. They are trying to force themselves into the farmer's normative practice. The farmer himself is also overruled in this area even though he has responsibility to conserve water through participatory processes, but the government has overridden the farmers' responsibility in this part as well.

The research has reiterated that structural norms are things that are organized and not to be interfered with by others. In the government there are departments, all of which have tasks and responsibilities that are structural. However they have certain higher-ordered values such as sustainability or holding power etc., which is what we call directional norms. The problem is not only in the higher-order value level (refer to directional norms such as autonomy, welfare, transparency, frugality etc.) but it can also cause a conflict with tasks and responsibilities in the lower level.

What are the main differences between the government and the farmers in terms of value and interests? From the normative practice idea we understand that if they all work with a proper structure and they fit in the direction - they work together in a normal situation, then everything should be alright. A conflict does not necessarily emerge when different actors have different directions, because it is essential to move forward in each society. The problem emerges when there are tensions between different actors that somehow should have the same direction or the same structure for certain purposes, and then it does not work anymore. As long as decision-makers keep practices as they are then there will always be conflict. This is because there is inherently conflict and something in either one or both practices has to change to make them fit well together. The government is there to protect justice and the environment, and farmers have more economic and to some extent environmental interests. If one makes changes there that do not fit with the direction then something really has to go wrong. If the government decides not to go for justice and instead goes for making money, for instance that is a very important shift, of course because they are taking a totally different responsibility. If there had been a set of contextual rules then the change might have been less dramatic. It was routine to find consultant engineering companies to design projects linked directly to the Energy Ministry which itself is mixing engineering and government practices in the case of structural and directional norms, particularly where designing the major projects was fully in the hands of such public-private companies.

In the face of all this, the conflicts are also in structures when for example the government has a target for taking over the responsibilities of the farmers. It is immature when other actors give the government credit for a new (structural) value because it is not what they should do. For the government we would expect justice to be an important value. If they started taking the economy for example as the most important value something hilarious would happen because of the change in direction. It can also go wrong on the farmers' side. Their primary concern should be to survive economically, we suppose. The generous subsidies have encouraged farmers to overflow the yields with water without a thought to their value or to conservation (Nair 2014). A rotation of norms, the farmers had a tacit tendency to take compensation - however although that was legal, to allow the government to cross their land for new projects, in fact it was another push-pull dichotomy in this conflict. Nonetheless, they primarily bowed on the trans-basin conveyance projects - by getting money, but such changes in the values have led them to rework their practices.

The conclusion of this story is that there is no easy answer to the question of how best to balance all the competing water uses priorities of the conflicts. However, analyzing water conflicts in terms of conflicting values generates insights that other analyses cannot offer. The Zayandehrud case showed how an intense tussle over the water can be shaped due to redefining the higher level and jeopardizing lower level norms (tasks and responsibilities). Over the last several decades, utilitarian gigantism (Heidegger 1954) in the Zayandehrud hydrosystem has produced such mega-actors (giant cities, industries and extended farmlands) that traditional systems would no longer meet all their needs. The agents and both public and private sectors have gradually undertaken the responsibility for water, and their ambitions have been replaced with others' norms. This part of the research sorts through the argumentation that conflicts around the water resources development can be not only the matter of higher other-values but it can also be the case that parties reasoning for certain values try to push these values on another actor. However, a conflict can arise with tasks and responsibilities at the lower level.

To a large extent, the Zayandehrud case nicely represents the trends of the practices and conflicts - within socio-technical systems - that have been drawn by the technologies proportionally to the projects aimed to call more water for/from distant regions. The weakness of this strategy is that in general it cannot predict (if it does not overlook or ignore) the role of society and nature, in fact the norms.

We have demonstrated the theory of normative practice to contribute to what Berkes (2002 and 2010) acknowledges about 'cross-scale institutional linkage', 'effects of higher level institutions on local institutions' and devolution of resources governance which nowadays is strictly needed to reappraise in every conflict resolution mechanism, as well as within hydrosystems. Normative practice analysis could be practiced as a part of the decision-making process rules. The NP analysis showed that if one starts interfering in the other(s), new tensions will arise because of a mixture of different structures, although conceivably all the responsibilities could remain the same. Especially when directions and structures get mixed between actors, e.g. when the government starts doing things that actor-farmers should have a say about, real tension can arise. 'This emphasis fit[s] broadly with a role for governments as 'setting the rules' rather than actively managing decisions, and it [is] aligned with the shift in emphasis from 'government to governance' in environmental discourse' (Schmidt, 2014 from Head 2004).

Drawing on Minoia (2012), the current 'water institutional abandonment' has become contradictory to the current setting of the hydrosystems' governance. His reasoning is laid with this argumentation: 'water-saving and demand management [which] are embraced by policy-makers as solutions to the current crisis are misplaced if current water management policies 'do not consider the agricultural, environmental and social restructuring that have reshaped the area'. We need differently-minded decision-makers to realize that the 'problems cannot be solved within the mindset that created them' (Brelet 2004).

In that sense, (good) governance cannot be created by command-and-control rules, only influenced - governance just 'is' (Wegerich et al. 2014). Nevertheless, 'if one sector is favored, then this is a failure to deliver an ethical policy' (Brelet 2004). The water supply industry should consider to whom it is accountable and whether its data is accessible and how it allows stakeholders to participate in its management decisions.

What it has done in this portion of the thesis - which in fact is new to previous considerations not only in this case of water management but in STS studies, is that a combination of actor network studies and normative practice has been used and that seems to be a fruitful and strong collaboration. The actor analysis is an invaluable ally for NP because it allowed us to select and cherry-pick the highly influential actors, while otherwise in the NP analysis we have to deal with too many of them. We suggest that a combination is used in other fields, as well. This chapter has also contributed to the work already shown in the books by de Vries et al., (2012) and Christensen et al. (2012). They have shown most specifically that the roles of norms and values are very important.

We have also addressed the actor-engineer as an example to show how they fuel conflicts. Geels (2004) has blamed such lopsided views that can make engineers 'blind to developments outside their focus[es]'. These contemporary engineering practices produce technological, ecological, and social risks (Christensen et al., 2012). There are no easy solutions to this dilemma, but it seems engineers, hydrologists and socio-technical analysts are largely at fault because due to greed the engineering companies are failing to properly plan the most effective use of all the water resources in an area, country or region where water must be shared. Indeed the actor-the-engineer needs to deal with water through its value. In fact engineering normative practice must be consistent with societal and environmental norms to seek a balance between ethical responsibility and pluralism, to coordinate tasks and plans (Christensen et al., 2012). As negotiating, trading off different competing requirements, customer needs and design specifications are central 'in the engineering design process, there is a need to investigate what normative criteria the goals should meet to be successful: What is a good (i.e. functional or rational) engineering goal' (Björnberg 2013)? This process enables us to rapidly identify and address the inconsistencies. One would hope that such views expressed in this chapter would lead to improvement. However, that is not going to happen in the near future, where 'the challenge is to reconcile our roles as agents within nature and as stewards of nature' (Floridi 2014).

CONCLUSION

Zayandehrud right holders are increasingly at the forefront of water conflicts as their rights have been under pressure from stressors including the intensification of the re resource extraction by up and midstream cities and industries of Isfahan and Chaharmahal provinces.

Critics argue that challenging water rights requires attention to water's social context and the dynamics of its problems, and to reposition Zayandehrud as inherently political.

While UrmiaLake isn't exempt from the pressure of Iran's devastating drought and mismanagement, it's being somehow mediated the pressure and balancing political desires differently. Zayandehrud hasn't been able to cope with the different social and economic problems.

Iran's water governance modes can't micro-manage the water crisis of the country. Water policies are not only obsolete rather work like as an inspector sitting on the shoulder of the local experts as they decide individual cases. It should put efforts on removing hydrocracy.

In this chapter we have shown how a combination of the Normative Practice approach and an analysis of the interplay between the actors involved helps to understand the complexity of socio-technological developments and how modernist and utopian expectations can cause such developments can have disastrous effects on the environment. We have also shown how engineers struggle with their role in the complex interaction between the 'many hands' and in the tensions between the modernist expectations posed by other actors and their own professional awareness of the limitations of technology and engineering. The Zayandehrud case underlines the need to analyses the structural and directional norms within the practices of the various actors involved (including the responsibilities awarded to the various actors) and to identify conflicts between norms in order to seen revision of norms to solve the conflicts. This discussion can bring back to the forefront the question of true progression and the values that we want to pursue in socio-technological developments such as the Zayandehrud water management. This will help engineers to find a proper position in the midst of the many hands that together determine the way technology evolves.

REFERENCES

Atabaki, T. (2013). The Comintern, the Soviet Union and labour militancy in interwar Iran. In Iranian-Russian Encounters: Empires and Revolutions Since 1800 (Vol. 14). Routledge.

Balali, M. R., Keulartz, J., & Korthals, M. (2011). Reflexive land and water management in Iran: Linking Technology, Governance and Culture, Part 1: Land and Water Management Paradigms. *Iranian Journal of Water research in Agriculture, 24*(2), 73–97.

Beaumont, P. (1974). Water resource development in Iran. *The Geographical Journal, 140*(3), 418–431. doi:10.2307/1796535

Billib, M., Bardowicks, K., & Arumí, J. L. (2009). Integrated water resources management for sustainable irrigation at the basin scale. *Chilean Journal of Agricultural Research, 69*(Suppl 1), 69–80.

Björnberg, K. E. (2013). Rational Goals in Engineering Design: The Venice Dams. In *Norms in Technology, Philosophy of Engineering and Technology* (pp. 83–99). Springer Netherlands. doi:10.1007/978-94-007-5243-6_6

Blackbourn, D. (2006). *The Conquest of Nature. Water, Landscape and the Making of Modern Germany*. London: Jonathan Cape.

Borgmann, A. (1984). *Technology and the Character of Contemporary Life*. Chicago: University of Chicago Press.

Bozorgmehr, N. (2014). *Iran: Dried out*. Retrieved from http://www.ft.com/cms/s/0/5a5579c6-0205-11e4-ab5b-00144feab7de.html#ixzz3HjOF1vfm

Brelet, C. (2004). *Some examples of best ethical practice in water use*. Retrieved from http://portal.unesco.org/shs/fr/files/4382/10796934191water_use.pdf/water_use.pdf

Christensen, S. H., Mitcham, C., Li, B., & An, Y. (2012). *Engineering, development and philosophy: American, Chinese and European perspectives* (Vol. 11). Berlin: Springer. doi:10.1007/978-94-007-5282-5

De Vries, M. J., Hansson, S. O., & Meijers, A. W. (2012). *Norms in technology* (Vol. 9). Springer Science & Business Media.

Eslami, M. (2010). *Zayandehrud, the Past, Now and Future*. Paper presented at the A conference on reviewing crisis of the Zayandehrud River, Isfahan, Iran. Retrieved from http://www.isfahan.ir/Dorsapax/userfiles/file/shora/pazhuhesh/zayanderood.pdf. (in Persian)

FIDIC (International Federation of Consulting Engineers). (2014). *Code of Ethics*. Retrieved from http//fidic.org/about-fidic/fidic-code-ethics#sthash.GUfmvN9W.dpuf

Floridi, L. (2014). *The Fourth Revolution: How the Infosphere is Reshaping Human Reality*. Oxford University Press.

Geels, F. W. (2004). From sectoral systems of innovation to socio-technical systems: Insights about dynamics and change from sociology and institutional theory. *Research Policy*, *33*(6), 897–920. doi:10.1016/j.respol.2004.01.015

Gohari, A., Eslamian, S., Mirchi, A., Abedi-Koupaei, J., Massah Bavani, A., & Madani, K. (2013). Water transfer as a solution to water shortage: A fix that can Backfire. *Journal of Hydrology (Amsterdam)*, *491*, 23–39. doi:10.1016/j.jhydrol.2013.03.021

Harandi, M. F., & De Vries, M. J. (2014). An Appraisal of Qualifying Role of Hydraulic Heritage Systems; A Case Study of Qanat in the Central Iran. Journal of Water Science and Technology: *IWA Water Science and Technology. Water Supply Journal*, *14*(6), 1124–1132. doi:10.2166/ws.2014.074

Harandi, M. F., Nia, M. G., & De Vries, M. J. (2015). Water Management: Sacrificing Normative Practice Subverting the Traditions of Water Apportionment—'Whose Justice? Which Rationality?'. *Science and Engineering Ethics*, *21*(5), 1241–1269. doi:10.100711948-014-9593-1 PMID:25300408

Harandi, M. F., Yarahmadian, S., Sepehrifar, M., & Van Gelder, P. (2014). The dichotomous Markov process with nonparametric test application; a decision support method in long-term river behavioural analysis: the *Zayandehrud* River; a case study from central Iran. *Stochastic Environmental Research and Risk Assessment, 28*(7), 1889-1896. doi:10.100700477-014-0854-y

Head, B. W. (2009). From government to governance: explaining and assessing new approaches to NRM. In Contested country: local and regional natural resources management in Australia. Academic Press.

Heidegger, M. (1954). The question concerning technology and Other Essays. In C. Hanks (Ed.), *Technology and values: Essential readings* (pp. 99–113). Singapore: John Wiley & Sons.

Hermans, L. (2005). *Actor analysis for water resources management: putting the promise into practice* (PhD thesis). Delft University of Technology, Delft, The Netherlands.

Hermans, L. M., Naber, A. C., & Enserink, B. (2012). An approach to design long-term monitoring and evaluation frameworks in multi-actor systems--a case in water management. *Evaluation and Program Planning*, *35*(4), 427–438. doi:10.1016/j.evalprogplan.2012.01.006 PMID:22391616

Hossaini, S. (2006). Water use and social organisation in the desert border of Iran. In *Environment agriculture and poverty in developing countries* (pp. 17–32). New Delhi, India: Concept Publishing Company.

Hu, X. J., Xiong, Y. C., Li, Y. J., Wang, J. X., Li, F. M., Wang, H. Y., & Li, L. L. (2014). Integrated water resources management and water users' associations in the arid region of northwest China: A case study of farmers' perceptions. *Journal of Environmental Management*, *145*, 162–169. doi:10.1016/j.jenvman.2014.06.018 PMID:25026372

Jensen, K. M. (2013). Viewpoint–swimming against the Current: Questioning development policy and practice. *Water Alternatives*, *6*(2), 276–283.

Jones, T. M., & Wicks, A. C. (1999). Convergent stakeholder theory. *Academy of Management Review*, *24*(2), 206–221. doi:10.5465/amr.1999.1893929

Kroes, P. A., & Meijers, A. W. M. (2006). Introduction. The dual nature of technical artifacts. *Studies in History and Philosophy of Science*, *37*(1), 1–4. doi:10.1016/j.shpsa.2005.12.001 PMID:16473265

Latour, B. (1996). *Aramis or the love of technology*. Cambridge, MA: Harvard University Press.

Mahmoudian, M. (1969). *Zayandehrud of Isfahan*. Isfahan, Iran: Isfahan University press. (in Persian)

Minoia, P. (2012). Mega-Irrigation and Neoliberalism in Postcolonial States: Evolution and Crisis in the Gharb Plain, Morocco. *Geografiska Annaler. Series B, Human Geography*, *94*(3), 269–286. doi:10.1111/j.1468-0467.2012.00414.x

Molle, F. (2008). Why enough is never enough: The societal determinants of river basin closure. *International Journal of Water Resources Development*, *24*(2), 217–226. doi:10.1080/07900620701723646

Molle, F., & Mamanpoush, A. (2012). Scale, governance and the management of river basins: A case study from Central Iran. *Geoforum*, *43*(2), 285–294. doi:10.1016/j.geoforum.2011.08.004

Molle, F., Mollinga, P. P., & Wester, P. (2009). Hydraulic bureaucracies and the hydraulic mission: Flows of water, flows of power. *Water Alternatives*, *2*(3), 328–349.

Nair, C. (2014). *Tackling a Drought in Iran*. Retrieved from http://www.nytimes.com/2014/11/10/opinion/tackling-a-drought-in-iran.html?_r=0

Perry, C. (2013). ABCDE+ F: A framework for thinking about water resources management. *Water International*, *38*(1), 95–107. doi:10.1080/02508060.2013.754618

Safaei, M., Safavi, H. R., Loucks, D. P., Ahmadi, A., & van der Krogt, W. (2013). Integrated river basin planning and management: A case study of the *Zayandehrud* River basin, Iran. *Water International*, *38*(6), 724–743. doi:10.1080/02508060.2013.823815

Schmidt, J. J., & Peppard, C. Z. (2014). Water ethics on a human-dominated planet: Rationality, context and values in global governance. *Wiley Interdisciplinary Reviews: Water*, *1*(6), 533–547. doi:10.1002/wat2.1043

Swyngedouw, E. (1999). Modernity and hybridity-The production of nature: Water and modernisation in Spain. *Annals of the Association of American Geographers*, *89*(3), 443–465. doi:10.1111/0004-5608.00157 van de Poel, I., Fahlquist, J. N., Doorn, N., Zwart, S., & Royakkers, L. (2012). The problem of many hands: Climate change as an example. *Science and Engineering Ethics*, *18*(1), 49–67. doi:10.100711948-011-9276-0 PMID:21533835

Wester, P., Vargas-Velázquez, S., Mollard, E., & Silva-Ochoa, P. (2008). Negotiating surface water allocations to achieve a soft landing in the closed Lerma-Chapala Basin, Mexico. *International Journal of Water Resources Development*, *24*(2), 283–296. doi:10.1080/07900620701723778

Zhang, Z. (2012). Dam Construction Ethics in China. In S. H. Christensen, C. Mitcham, B. Li, & Y. An (Eds.), *Engineering, development and philosophy: American, Chinese and European perspectives* (Vol. 11). Berlin: Springer. doi:10.1007/978-94-007-5282-5_19

Chapter 6
Modern Military Operations:
A Normative Practice Approach to Moral Decision Making

Christine Boshuijzen-van Burken
Eindhoven University of Technology, The Netherlands & Netherlands Defence Academy, The Netherlands

ABSTRACT

Modern military operations are characterized by ubiquitous use of technology, in particular the use of information and communication technologies for real-time information sharing. The use of technology on the battlefield is assumed to improve decision making in military practice. By making use of a friendly fire incident in Afghanistan, namely the Sangin incident in 2011, the author highlights why moral decision making could be hampered by technology. This is partly due to the fact that information and communication technologies subtly connect sub-practices that exist within the broader military practice, thus potentially blurring normative structures. Blurring of normative structures can cause problems for moral decision making on the battlefield, because it is suddenly not clear who is responsible for the course of action.

INTRODUCTION

In the morning of April 6, 2011, at the Sangin river valley in Afghanistan, the pilot of a remotely piloted aircraft[1] called Predator, performed an airstrike that turned out to be a catastrophe, because it had hit his own troops. Below follows a selection of the article in which the incident was later described.

DOI: 10.4018/978-1-5225-8006-5.ch006

At 8:40 a.m., the Predator crew spotted the heat signatures of three people. At 8:41, a burst of muzzle[2] flashes emanated from the group.

A critical question was the direction of the muzzle fire. If the direction was east, toward friendly lines, they were potential insurgents trying to kill U.S. troops. If it was west, away from friendly lines, they might be U.S. personnel or other allies. The Predator crew and the forces in Afghanistan proceeded as if the muzzle fire were coming toward friendly positions. Only minutes earlier, ground forces had reported contact3 with the enemy over the Predator crew's radio link. As the Predator circled over Sangin, its ARC-210 radio4 received transmissions from the ground and fed them into the drone's satellite link, which relayed them to the Predator control station5 in California. Given the situation, the Predator crew was furiously scanning for targets to strike with one or more of the plane's Hellfire missiles6.

At 8:41, the JTAC[7] in Afghanistan sent the "9-line" message containing coordinates for a strike once approved by the ground commander. The analysts at DGS[8] Indiana (DGS-IN) also saw the targets in the video feed. Their leader chimed in with a series of online messages raising questions about their identification as enemy.

If the DGS-IN analysts meant that the figures were too grainy or shadowy to say for sure whether they were U.S. troops, but that the enemy would not be firing in that direction, they were unable to convey this information unambiguously, partly because they did not have a voice link to the Predator crew.

After the strike, a member of the DGS team in Indiana told investigators about his team's reservations about the strike:

At no time, to my knowledge, did any of the crew members feel comfortable firing upon the personnel," according to written testimony from an Air Force staff sergeant stationed in Indiana, whose name was redacted. (Laster & Iannotta, 2012)[9]

In this incident an American marine staff sergeant and navy hospital man were killed by their own troops who operated the aircraft from thousands of miles away. The friendly fire incident was the result of (a number of) moral decisions. In these decisions, technology played a role, such as the thermal camera that provided the images. In the course of Laster & Iannotta's article a solution to prevent friendly fire incidents in the future is suggested:

The investigators recommended that in the future, any intelligence or information that could prevent fratricide or a violation of the Law of Armed Conflict be posted to the crew's main chat room so that the entire crew would see it. However, despite the pilot's comments and their own recommendation, the investigators said they were doubtful that posting the conflicting information would have changed the outcome in Sangin on April 6.

It was "likely that the strike would have occurred anyway due to the ground force's perception of friendly disposition and the source of enemy contact," the investigators said. In a January interview with Air Force Times, Air Force Maj. Gen. Robert Otto said the investigators' conclusion "rang true" about the near-inevitability of the mistake, given the circumstances. "You have to understand, the Sangin Valley is bad-guy territory," Otto said. "If you don't know where the friendlies are, it's pretty difficult for you to know [what] to overturn based on what one of the supporting forces thought". (ibid)

The solution is sought in adding more technology, by equipping the crew with voice communications on top or instead of the chat communications. One of the spokesmen in the article however adds that merely adding more technology may not be a solution for solving moral concerns in decision making on the battlefield:

Switching from listening mode to two-way conversations won't be as simple as flipping a switch. "There are technical and procedural rules that need to be followed. Some of those rules require installation of additional hardware to enable the two-way communications," Otto said. The right balance also will need to be struck on the issue of voice communication procedures, he added. "There's a point when a discussion's over," he said. "And while we always want somebody to have the ability to speak up when they fear a rule-of-engagement violation or wait a minute, there's women and children, you have to balance fighting a war by committee with a ground-force commander who is presumed to have the situational awareness and has the authority to say, we need to strike this target. (ibid)

The selected passages from Laster & Iannotta's article quoted above set the scene for this chapter on normativity in modern military missions in which technology is ubiquitous. Normativity is related to moral decision making in social practices, as this definition of moral decision making suggests: *cognitive acts and judgements associated with norms, or with facts as they relate to norms* (Casebeer & Churchland, 2003). In this chapter I will show how moral decision making is influenced by the normative structure of the military practice and the technology embedded in the practice.

INFORMATION AND COMMUNICATION TECHNOLOGY IN MILITARY PRACTICE

Thinking through the moral dimension of technologies on the battlefield is not totally new. The use of nuclear technology, anti-personnel mines, non-lethal weapons and drones on the battlefield are, or have been, widely discussed. Information and communication technology (ICT) on the battlefield are a distinctive form of military technology, because they have no immediate lethal or harmful capacities, such as mines, nuclear bombs, non-lethal weapons and armed drones. ICT, in a subtle way, has become immersive on the battlefield and underlie many of the other technologies such as drones, AI, and big data applications. These assumed neutral technologies however play a role in moral decision making in military practice.

ICT on the battlefield is widely used to facilitate cooperation and information sharing within and between military organizations and also with non-military agencies. In today's complex and ad-hoc, multinational settings, the ideal is to create a highly connected military organization, which is believed to create a decisive advance (Alberts et al., 2002; Alberts and Hayes, 2006; Alberts, 2007; Smith, 2006; Lambert & Scholz, 2005; Soeters, 2017).

The underlying vision for establishing these complex and ad hoc multinational environments is the linking up of decision-makers via ICT and communication networks in order to enable synchronized and therefore improved decision-making. Military personnel working in these environments face more and more complex and ad hoc tasks. The social requirements of dealing with multi-national parties, the spatial dimension of transferring information over greater distances, the legal implications of exchanging information between allies are only a glimpse of the complex environment in which a military has to work (Essens, 2008, Bezooijen & Kramer, 2015; Soeters, 2017). An example of a modern military mission is the ability to have immediate air support in the case of a patrol coming unexpectedly under fire, as Laster & Ianotta (2012) describe in the Sangin case in the beginning of this chapter. Information about a patrol under attack is available at all levels of command, vertically from own command lines and horizontally from other units. This differs from the traditional hierarchically organized flow of information and coordination. Being better informed, with opportunities of instant organization should enable a more adaptive approach to dynamic operational situations. From the Sangin case it becomes clear that it is not necessarily true that real-time information sharing leads to better military effect. In this incident a marine staff sergeant and a navy hospital man were killed during a mission to sweep a stretch of farmland

and residential compounds along a key road in the Sangin Valley. They were killed by their own forces that were operating from thousands of miles away from where the incident took place. The empirical facts of this incident have been scrutinized in legal and technical reports describing the incident, trying to sort out how this could have happened and who was to blame (see Laster & Iannotta, 2012). But this case has philosophically relevant aspects too, relating to moral decision in modern military operations, which we will discuss below.

Literature on Interrelations in Military Missions

Various scholars have paid attention to the difficulties arising in (postmodern) cooperative network settings. In military literature on this topic, Oliver (1990) provides a good overview of different causes for difficulties in network enabled operations, but he leaves out any 'formal' issues in explaining the problems. D'Souza (2008) puts an emphasis on the importance of encouraging 'unity of effort', and De Nevers (2007) and Byman (2006) ascribe the problems between military alliances to caveats and discrepancies in rules and mandates. Duffey (2000) and Elron et al. (1999) pay attention to culture, thereby recognizing that in multinational peacekeeping operations, there exist 'distinct perspectives on soldiering', and thus what it means to be a good soldier is not universal among allied partners in a military mission. Soeters & Tresch (2010) are especially worth noting because they recognize both the organizational styles and cultural aspects. Later on in this chapter I will argue that this sensitivity to both organizational styles and cultural aspects is necessary for understanding the complexities in modern military missions, but that it is only part of the problem.

Besides the military literature on cooperation between different stakeholders, Koppenjan & Klijn (2004) are also worth mentioning. They pay attention to the organizational and rule side of the network and the perceptions of the actors in these networks. "What we see and what we do not see is highly influenced by our expectations and by what we find to be relevant: our frame of reference" (p. 29). Their understanding of 'frame of reference' has similarities with the concept of a normative practice. The 'rule' side in Koppenjan & Klijn, however, is considered to be regulative for behavior and this is a crucial deviation from the normative practice framework. In the framework of normative practices, the regulative side is not (only) in the rules, but also in what is perceived to be important, which is influenced by underlying values and worldviews.

MORAL DECISION MAKING ON THE BATTLEFIELD

Definition of Moral Decision Making

Decisions about life and death, not uncommon in military operations, are inevitably moral decisions. In the Sangin case there was little doubt that, once the pilot would push the buttons to engage, people were going to be killed. In the Sangin case it was a decision that came with many tensions and complications. Some of these tensions related to uncertainty with regard to the facts (what is the direction of the firing?), some of the tensions related to the norms that hold for the killing of people (is it right to kill people?). Moral questions relate to the norms in the practice, they are about what one *should* do. Many philosophers and professional ethicists disagree over what counts as a moral question, but this question is not discussed here in depth. In order to give some delimitation I quote Casebeer & Churchland:

As moral philosophers would put it, moral reasoning is probably a species of practical reasoning about what we should do or think now, such as whether to negotiate with terrorists, not necessarily about what others have done nor about strictly empirical matters, such as whether there is water on Mars. [...] Broadly speaking, then, moral reasoning deals with cognitive acts and judgements associated with norms, or with facts as they relate to norms. (2003, p. 170-171)

An important element in this definition is the notion of 'norms'. For the purpose of this chapter I use the concept of norms as they refer to the normative practice model. Different norms exist, such as economic norms, functional norms, social norms and they can be made explicit in the normative practices approach. The norms for moral decision making in military operations are moral norms and they are derived from the (sub-)practices in which professionals do their jobs. A sub-practice is, for example, the military pilot practice, the JTAC practice, the military medic practice; military practice is the overarching practice with general rules and norms that hold for any military practitioner and there are specific rules that hold for military sub-practices on top of the general norms and rules for military practice. Moral decision making in networked operations is about the cognitive acts that concern the moral norms that hold for different practices. For example, a decision to strike or not, or the judgment to assign a level of threat (or safety) to a person or an event during a mission is a cognitive act that regards a moral norm in the practice of pilots or JTACS. Also other norms often play a role in moral decision making. There are juridical norms (is it in line with the laws of armed conflict) or economic norms (is it a reasonable expense with regard to the budget). In short, Casebeer & Churchland speak broadly about norms, but not all norms are moral norms, since there are (amongst others) functional norms, economic norms, and social norms. Moral decision making is a cognitive act or judgment in which moral as well as non-moral norms play a role and of which the outcome of the decision has moral significance.[10]

It is worth noting that the definition of moral decision making that is used here is not necessarily the best suited for all situations. For the role of technology on moral decision making in modern military missions it is a suitable concept, because this environment is a decision and act oriented environment. This is captured by the centrality of the 'cognitive act' in the definition. Another relevant aspect is the explicit mentioning of norms, which brings it in close relation to the theory of normative practices.

Philosophical Background

How can we begin to understand moral decision making in modern military missions? Consider the Sangin incident at the start of this chapter again. Many problems could be pointed out and all of them make sense. The problems can be phrased in terms of technology (a voice link should have been in place), in terms of people (the JTAC made a wrong decision), in terms of organization (the rules for handling confusing situations were not in place) or context (it was a "bad-guy territory" anyway). All of these approaches give insights in what went wrong in some way, however, they tend to simplify or reduce the situation to one aspect, thereby not doing justice to the complex reality in which the decision to strike was made. In order to do justice to the complexity, a more in-depth analysis is needed, which the framework of normative practice can offer.

NORMATIVE PRACTICE ANALYSIS

Several philosophers in the tradition of Reformational philosophy have developed a theory of normative practices over the past decade(s). Some of them have contributed in this volume. The idea of a theory of normative practices came from Hoogland, Jochemsen and Glas (1997, chapter 4), who initiated this development by using MacIntyre's theory of a practice (1981) in combination with concepts from Reformational philosophy to show that normativity is inherent in the medical practice (Glas 2009, Hoogland and Jochemsen 2000, and Jochemsen 2006). The theory of normative practices was also used by Verkerk, Hoogland, Van der Stoep and De Vries (2015) to understand the practice of engineering. In this chapter another field of application is analyzed in light of the theory of normative practices, namely military practice. Some work has been done in this field, namely by Toner (2006), who used MacIntyre's concept of a practice to reappraise a virtue ethics for military practice. I will show that the framework of normative practices helps with understanding moral decision making in real life cases of military operations.

From Social Practices to Normative Practices

Jochemsen, Hoogland and Glas (1997) extended MacIntyre's version of a social practice. Their understanding of a practice is that social practices have specific law-spheres of their own and that they are therefore structurally bound by specific rules, norms and principles. The normative structure of a social practice is not only the boundary of the practice, but also has a constitutive function. Some rules and norms and procedures are what makes the practice that specific practice, in the same way as the rules of the game of chess make what chess is as a game. These rules, norms, procedures are called the structural side of a practice. A practice has a directional side too. This is the way in which people who work in the practices 'open up' the structure, in other words, how they interpret the rules and norms that hold for the practice. This is often inspired by a persons' cultural or religious background and is related to worldview, or ethos.

Military Practice as a Normative Practice: Structure and Direction

A practice is a Form of socially established cultural activity, which has an underlying normative structure. The socially established organizational form of the military practice is for example characterized by hierarchy, how and when to use force, and the explicit use of ranks. It has evolved from a societal need for security, and it is therefore rooted in society, but in such a way that it is not completely absorbed in civil society. In a democratic state, the monopoly on the use of force is delegated to the military and therefore one can say that the military practice functions on behalf of civil society. A distinction is made between civilians and militaries with regard to some fundamental issues, for example, there is a monopoly on the use of force, a special set of laws, such as military discipline, under which militaries do their job. For the further analysis of moral decision making in military missions, this distinction is important. Working in a practice means that one is not as free to act as one is when working outside that practice. Private actions are distinct from military actions. Some actions and decisions are appropriate within the practice, but they would be very inappropriate outside the practice ('searching someone's house' is a good example for the military practice). MacIntyre refers to 'internal goods' and 'standards of excellence' to define appropriate actions for the practice. However, these notions are rather loose and are less coherent than in Jochemsen, Hoogland and Glas' version of a practice. They use the term intrinsic normativity, or inner nature of a practice. Intrinsic normativity is about the structural conditions that are given beforehand, or the ties by which the practice is naturally bound. Intrinsic normativity is not only about internal goods, or what is specific about a practice, but also about the guiding principles of a practice.

A distinction can be made between structure and direction of a practice (see Mouw and Griffioen: 1993). This distinction resembles with Searle's distinction between constitutive and regulative rules of a practice. Searle (1969) defines the constitutive rules (such as the rules of chess) as those rules that make institutional actions possible, whereas regulative rules (such as the rules of etiquette) are rules that regulate an activity that can exist independent from the regulative rules. In the normative practice view, intrinsic normativity of a practice is about the structure (constitutive side) and direction (regulative side) of a practice.

Structure

The structure of a practice is often captured in documentations, articles, manuals procedures and they relate to the formal aspects of the practice. They are different for different practices. The internal organization of the engineering practice is different from a medical practice, and different from the military practice. They have their own internal structure. These differences in structure are mainly caused by differences in the primary processes that drive these practices.

Qualifying Function

All practices function in many aspects, although in different ways, which makes the practices distinguishable. For the military practice the distinguishing aspect is the legal aspect. Military practices are constitutionally bound and ultimately act under the supreme authority of a state.[11] The monopoly of (physical) violence lies with the state, and this is an indispensable premise for maintaining a just society (Besselink, 2008, p. 5). Given that the state is constitutionally bound, it automatically follows that the military practice can only use force within the legal framework provided by that state. The military practice is juridically bound and also qualified in the juridical realm. The actions of a soldier are first and foremost bound by legal norms and procedures that are connected to the state. They form the 'constitutive patterns of behavior' and are often actions that respond to situations of (gross) injustice. As a normative practice, within the legal boundaries provided by a *res publica*, the military practice is the only practice that can solve the problems of gross injustice (where the diplomatic means of the state have exhausted). If the use of force is disconnected from its legal boundaries, there is intrinsically no difference between an army (or police which is, like military practice, juridically bound and mandated by the state) and a group of bandits. If interventions to restore situations of gross injustice are left over to companies, it will often not solve the problem of injustice, but solve an economic problem, potentially enhancing or maintaining an unjust situation[12].

Military practices function in all aspects and the qualifying aspect is the legal aspect, with justice as its 'inner value'. In other words, the inner value of the military practice is to protect and advance justice, and its destination lies in the juridical aspect. The juridical aspect is the abstraction of the inner value of justice. Military practices also function in, for example, the economic aspect, but this is not the leading or qualifying aspect of military practice. If there is, for example, a single valuable natural element like oil or diamonds, which is often the case in poor countries, the use of force may be employed by military practice to protect a war economy which is fueled by the trade of natural treasures. In fact, the military practice ceases to exist if it does not realize this inner value of justice (and the practice changes into another practice, for example a company for property protection). This can be true for poor as well as for well-established nations. In view of the above, for the military practice the intrinsic normativity (or inner moral value) is 'justice'. It is a practice that responds to situations with a normative demand that evolve around an intuitive understanding of justice.[13]

In the case of the Sangin river incident, pilots, data analysts, ground soldiers and a tactical air controller operated in the military practice, however each of them was also part of a distinct sub-practice. Some general rules and norms hold for each of the sub-practices in military practice, for example the rules for wearing uniforms when on duty, or the norm to have a buddy or a second-in-command. However, within the military sub-practices, different additional norms and rules exist. For example, there may be differences in 'rules of engagement', depending on the mission one is involved in. Different norms exist for pilots, JTACs and commanders regarding the checks and procedures for an airstrike.

Direction

'Direction' refers to the different basic convictions about good and evil, right and wrong, that drive people to perform their tasks in that practice. In the military practice this can be seen in the different approaches to the use of force, for example the American approach, which tends to focus on technological superiority (for example, the quick invasion during Gulf War I)), which is different from the Dutch approach which is to 'win hearts and minds' of the local people. It also becomes visible in classic writings on how to perform a war in a good manner, for example Clausewitzian approaches to war differ from non-western military models, such as Sun Tzu's Art of War. 'Direction' is about ones deepest understanding of the actions that one performs, for example using force to 'win a war' or to 'bring stability' in a specific region.

One final remark is that one should keep in mind that practices develop and society changes, and therefore the formulation and interpretation of the principles and rules require a constant process of reflection and debate. Practices change gradually through reinterpretation, adaptation or rejection of rules in daily behavior (see also March and Olsen: 1989; Klijn: 1996).

Technology Connects Practices

Technology often plays an important, but strikingly underestimated role in military practice. For example Dekker (2005) refers to the actors in modern military missions as nodes in a network. This terminology reveals a mechanistic view of how military personnel work in military operations. Developers and users of these technologies tend to think that the technologies are neutral. Connecting the different nodes by means of technology is also assumed to be a neutral activity.

From the Sangin case described in the beginning of this chapter it becomes clear that as soon as technology is introduced, not merely nodes in a network are connected. Instead, practices (such as the pilot-practice, the JTAC practice, DGS-IN, the commander-practice, etcetera), that operated more or less separately before the introduction of ICT, are connected. The use of the DGS system, which relays video feed to the ground personnel, intended to support the JTAC, linked the pilot with the ground commander, causing a 'blurring' of the structure of the two separate practices. It is in the structure of the JTAC to go through intensive and ongoing training in the interpretation of maps, aerial photographs and oral communications. The JTAC rules and norms concern assuring that an attack is done in such a way that the least damage is done to infrastructure, friendly parties or local civilians. He is therefore concerned about details of the situation. The commander operates in a different sub-practice and is trained to keep the overall goals of the mission and rules of engagement in mind. The rules and norms for the commander are therefore different from the JTAC and focus on the bigger operational picture in which an attack takes place. The rules and norms of the commander do not focus on the details, whereas the rules and norms of the JTAC are strongly concerned with details, such as guidelines and limitations on distances and deadly impact of the used means. The DGS structure is different from the commander and from the JTAC structure. The DGS service members process, exploit, and disseminate the video feed, providing intelligence to the ground commanders and fighting forces. The structure for the DGS therefore focus on reliability, validation and trustworthiness of information and rules and norms are in place to decide about which information deserves attention and which information can be left out of the picture. It is not in the structure of the JTAC and the commander to acquire and evaluate information, they have had no in depth training on information processing, but have rules and norms in place as to what one's course of action should be given certain information.

In the Sangin case, it looks like the practices had become blurred, as can be learned from this quote in the investigation report:

Fire support enablers (JTACs and JFOs) could have been more effectively integrated and employed on the battlefield to help enhance the commander's understanding of the situation as well as the ability to integrate fires with ground action.(Petraus, 27 July 2011, DoD Memorandum for Record)

There was no clear integral structure for communication between those that were firing from the remote end (the Predator crew) and the ground commander. Otto, quoted at the start of this chapter, said:

There are technical and procedural rules that need to be followed. Some of those rules require installation of additional hardware to enable the two-way communications. (Laster & Iannotta, 2012, p. 36)

What Otto referred to are the technical and procedural rules, rules of engagement and authority structures. They should not be overlooked when trying to solve problems in moral decision making of an individual on the battlefield. Secondly, technology structures and reorganizes societies, organizations, friendships, etcetera. In the Sangin case there were many social structures connected through ICT, such as the DGS-IN, JTAC and Predator crew. Technology influences the way these social structures are arranged and the way individuals in these structures respond to moral questions.

Clearly the blurring of practices caused a number of pitfalls. Particularly misinterpretations of information and subsequent procedural errors can be seen as direct consequences of the blurring of practices. Moral decision making cannot be understood without reference to the specific social context in which the decision is made. The concept of practice enables us to view a soldier not only as a node in the network, a task performer (for example, pushing a button) directed by rules, a goal-driven agent, but also as someone with a conviction about how he or she should perform his or her task in the right way. This conviction relates to the 'rules of the game' within the various practices. A pilot who does a good job does this in a different way than an army engineer in the field. In modern military missions, practices, all with their own set of rules, can be connected to each other, leading to a possible blurring of practices and consequences as mentioned above.

The social setting of the friendly fire case was that multiple partners were involved and that they were geographically dispersed. The crew in California, a DGS in Indiana, a JTAC in Afghanistan all had different roles, tasks and responsibilities. Conceptualizing these different partners as normative practices, which is a specific way of (and not limited to) being socially organized, reveals relevant issues for moral decision making. The predator crew, DGS and JTAC were bound by procedures, norms and rules for acting. From the Sangin case it becomes clear that there are technical and procedural rules that need to be followed with regard to communications. Apart from rules, these partners have a broader vision and a certain 'drive' to perform their tasks, as the 'furiously looking for targets' reveals. This says something about the *ethos* of the members. Or the remark made by Otto: "*there's women and children*" (Laster & Iannotta, 2012), which reveals a worldview in which woman and children are regarded in a different manner than men or combatants. This influences moral decision making.

Additional Aspects of Moral Decision Making

In the previous section, I showed the normative structure of military practice, and pointed out that military decision making does not take place in a void, but that it takes place in a very unique social structure. Below I will show that moral decision making is neither a purely psychological process nor the result of complex technological circumstances alone. Military moral decision making in a technological environment is rather a combination of at least three factors: a social factor, a technological factor and a

psychological factor. I have addressed the social factor in depth before and will briefly point out the technological and psychological factors below by using the Sangin case.

Technological Factor

Several technological assets played a role in the Sangin incident. There was the airplane itself (the Predator) and ICT systems that connected the control stations in California and Indiana. There were radios, satellites, screens, chat interfaces, the World Wide Web, geographic information systems (GIS), maps, buttons and sticks for controlling the plane, missiles, etcetera. These technologies played a role in the moral concerns that were raised. The DGS-IN for example, perceived information on his screen (the direction of muzzle fire) on the basis of which a moral judgment was made: the judgment of who was an enemy that needed to be killed. The technology also allowed for exchanging (moral) concerns, namely by typing these concerns in the chat box. The chat box had a 'built-in' moral option, namely the option for whisper chats, which in potential allowed for withholding important information.

Psychological Factor

In the Sangin incident there are psychological factors that influence moral decision making. In Laster and Iannotta's article which describes the Sangin case, some of these psychological responses are named, be it in the vocabulary of emotions. For example the crew was '*furiously* scanning for targets', others had '*reservations* about the strike'; people may *fear* violating rules, or *see the importance* to say: "*wait a minute, there's women and children*" and they have a certain 'committee', for example with a ground-force commander. These behavioral responses are influenced by technology and affect moral decision making on the battlefield.

CONCLUSION

A critical reader might remark that, in military practice, there has always been a great deal of cooperation between the (sub)practices. That is certainly true. However, the variety of practices within the overarching military practice was traditionally connected via hierarchical structures and means of communication. The more traditional means of communication, such as radio, served to confirm this hierarchical structure, enabling vertical information exchange via lines of command. What is different today is that all these various practices are connected by means of information and communication technologies. These supposedly 'neutral' technologies can cause clashes between the different standards, rules and principles – what is referred to as 'structure' in this book – that are applicable to these various practices. It has suddenly become unclear – or less clear – which rule should prevail and who has which role. Given the hierarchical nature of the military practice, this problem did not previously arise: if clashes did occur, the hierarchy prescribed the solution. With the introduction of information and communication technology, the number of interactions has increased and has become instantaneous and simultaneous. As a result, the likelihood of clashing rules and guidelines increases. The conclusion can therefore be drawn that the technology that linked the ground forces, intelligence personnel and local commander and that was presumed to be neutral, linked up practices that were previously unconnected. And, even if they did interact in the past, it was along clear lines, namely via one commander communicating with another commander.

If we take a closer look at the individual level of the various practices in which soldiers make decisions and act, it can be concluded that information and communication technologies may in fact be partially blamed for the tragedy at the Sangin river. It was assumed that it was clear what the message was and which rule should prevail, while in reality, there was no such clarity. In this chapter I suggested that the theory of normative practices can give clarity on why this decision to strike was made and how technology played a role in the decision.

In order to avoid further incidents, it is essential that military personnel become aware that technology is not merely facilitating communication, but can lead to an imperceptible blurring of practices. It is therefore important for military personnel to identify the potential pitfalls in modern military operations with respect to their own daily practice, including their specific responsibilities and rules.

REFERENCES

Alberts, D. S. (2007). Agility, Focus, and Convergence: The Future of Command and Control. *The International C2 Journal, 1*(1), 1-30.

Alberts, D. S., Garstka, J. J., Hayes, R. E., & Signori, D. A. (2002). *Understanding Information Age Warfare*. Washington, DC: CCRP Publication Series.

Alberts, D. S., & Hayes, R. E. (2006). *Understanding Command and Control, The Future of Command and Control*. Washington, DC: CCRP Publication Series.

Besselink, L. F. M. (2008). Geweldsmonopolie, Grondwet en krijgsmacht. *Publikaties van de Staatsrechtkring*, *26*, 67–124.

Bezooijen, B. V., & Kramer, E.-H. (2015). Mission Command in the Information Age: A Normal Accidents Perspective on Networked Military Operations. *The Journal of Strategic Studies*, *38*(4), 445–466. doi:10.1080/01402390.2013.844127

Byman, D. (2006). Remaking Alliances for the War on Terrorism. *The Journal of Strategic Studies*, *29*(5), 767–811. doi:10.1080/01402390600900887

Casebeer, W. D., & Churchland, P. S. (2003). The Neural Mechanisms of Moral Cognition: A Multiple-Aspect Approach to Moral Judgment and Decision-Making. *Biology & Philosophy*, *18*(1), 169–194. doi:10.1023/A:1023380907603

D'Souza, S. M. (2008). 'Unity of Effort': The Missing Link in the Afghan Counter-Insurgency Campaign. *Strategic Analysis*, *32*(5), 855–878. doi:10.1080/09700160802309225

De Nevers, R. (2007). NATO's International Security Role in the Terrorist Era. *International Security*, *31*(4), 34–66. doi:10.1162/isec.2007.31.4.34

Dekker, A. (2005). A taxonomy of network centric warfare architectures. *Proceedings of the Systems Engineering / Test and Evaluation Conference.*

Dooyeweerd, H. (1953). *A new critique of theoretical thought* (Vol1. 1-5). Amsterdam: The Presbyterian and Reformed Publishing Company.

Duffey, T. (2000). Cultural Issues in Contemporary Peacekeeping. *International Peacekeeping*, *7*(1), 142–168. doi:10.1080/13533310008413823

Elron, E., Shamir, B., & Ben-Ari, E. (1999). Why Don'T they Fight each Other? Cultural Diversity and Operational Unity in Multinational Forces. *Armed Forces and Society*, *26*(1), 73–97. doi:10.1177/0095327X9902600105

Essens, P. (2008). Cultural Challenges in Joint and Combined Command: A Military Leader's Perspective. *Proceedings of the NATO RTO 'Adaptability in Coalition Teamwork.*

Glas, G. (2009). Modellen Van 'Integratie' in De Psychologie En Psychiatrie (II) - Het Normatieve Praktijk Model. *Psyche en Geloof*, *20*(3/4), 165–177.

Hoogland, J., & Jochemsen, H. (2000). Professional Autonomy and the Normative Structure of Medical Practice. *Theoretical Medicine and Bioethics*, *21*(5), 457–475. doi:10.1023/A:1009925423036 PMID:11142442

Jochemsen, H. (2006). Normative Practices and Theoretical Ethics and Morality. *Philosophia Reformata*, *71*(1), 96–112. doi:10.1163/22116117-90000377

Jochemsen, H., & Hoogland, J. (1997). 'De Normatieve Structuur Van De Medische Praktijk. In H. Jochemsen & G. Glas (Eds.), *Verantwoord Medisch Handelen. Proeve Van Een Christelijke Medische Ethiek, Vol.Lindeboomreeks, deel 10* (pp. 64–99). Amsterdam: Buijten and Schipperheijn.

Klein, G. A. (1993). A recognition-primed decision (RPD) model of rapid decision making. In G. A. Kein, J. Orasanu, R. Calderwood, & C. E. Zsambok (Eds.), Decision Making in Action: Models and Methods (Vol. 1, pp. 138–147). Norwood, NJ: Ablex.

Koppenjan, J. F. M., & Klijn, E. (2004). *Managing Uncertainties in Networks a Network Approach to Problem Solving and Decision Making*. London: Routledge.

Lambert, D. A., & Scholz, J. B. (2005). *A Dialectic for Network Centric Warfare.* DSTO.

Laster, J. & Iannotta, B. (2012). Learning from Fratricide-US Deaths in Sangin Valley Bring Long-Sought Tactical Intel Changes. *C4ISR-Journal of Net-Centric Warfare, 11*(2), 24-27.

MacIntyre, A. (1981). *After Virtue: A Study in Moral Theory*. London: Duckworth.

March, J. G., & Olsen, J. P. (1989). *Rediscovering institutions : The organizational basis of politics*. New York: Free Press.

Mouw, R. J., & Griffioen, S. (1993). *Pluralisms and horizons: An essay in Christian public philosophy*. Grand Rapids, MI: WB Eerdmans.

Oliver, C. (1990). Determinants of Interorganizational Relationships: Integration and Future Directions. *Academy of Management Review, 15*(2), 241–265. doi:10.5465/amr.1990.4308156

Petraeus, D. (2011, July 27). *Memorandum for Record - Sangin friendly fire incident*. DoD. Retrieved from https://archive.org/details/295339-new-redacted-roi

Searle, J. R. (1969). *Speech acts: An essay in the philosophy of language*. Cambridge, UK: Cambridge University Press. doi:10.1017/CBO9781139173438

Smith, E. A. (2006). *Complexity, Networking and Effects Based Approaches to Operations*. Washington, DC: CCRP Publication Series. doi:10.21236/ADA457293

Soeters, J. (2017). Information Sharing in Military and Security Operations. In I. Goldenberg, J. Soeters, & W. H. Dean (Eds.), *Information Sharing in Military Operations* (pp. 1–15). Cham: Springer International Publishing; doi:10.1007/978-3-319-42819-2_1

Soeters, J., & Tresch, T. S. (2010). Towards Cultural Integration in Multinational Peace Operations. *Defence Studies, 10*(1), 272–287. doi:10.1080/14702430903155175

Toner, C. (2006). Military Service as a Practice: Integrating the Sword and Shield Approaches to Military Ethics. *Journal of Military Ethics, 5*(3), 183–200. doi:10.1080/15027570600911993

Verkerk, M. J., Hoogland, J., Stoep, J., & Vries, M. J. (2015). *Philosophy of Technology: an introduction for technology and business students*. Abingdon, UK: Routledge. doi:10.4324/9781315696362

ENDNOTES

1 Remotely piloted aircraft (RPA) is the preferred name in the military for airplanes that are also known as unmanned aerial vehicles (UAVs), unmanned aircrafts or drones.

2 Muzzle flash is the visible light at the barrel of a firearm during shooting.

3 Contact with the enemy (or "*troops in contact*" (TIC) in military jargon) *means* that there is an ongoing, active firefight.

4 ARC-210 is the name of a family of radios for military aircraft, enabling communications from the ground to the Predator.

5 The crew of the Predator, including the pilot, was controlling the unmanned aircraft from California.

6 A Hellfire missile is a 100 lb-class air-to-ground precision weapon. It derives its name from its initial design as a missile to be launched from a helicopter (Helicopter Launched, Fire and Forget Missile).

7 JTAC stands for joint tactical air controller. A JTAC guides the pilot from a ground position during an airstrike, to make sure that the right target is hit and no civilians, infrastructure or allied troops are harmed.

8 DGS stands for Distributed Ground System. It monitors real time video feed from unmanned aerial vehicles hovering the skies over any military area of operation. The DGS servicemembers process, exploit, and disseminate the video feed, providing intelligence to the ground commanders and war-fighting forces.

9 Laster & Iannotta gave this account of the Sangin fratricide incident based on transcripts of interviews conducted by Marine Corps investigators and the detailed timeline contained in the report. All times are local Afghanistan time.

10 A moral outcome only means that there is a moral issue at stake. The outcome of a moral decision can be morally right or morally wrong. The basis for the rightness or wrongness of the outcome depends on one's philosophical orientation (deontological, utilitarian, virtue based, value based, rights based, and etcetera).

11 Dooyeweerd directly relates the use of force to the "state": "In whatever way we consider the matter, this foundational function of the genotype "State" can nowhere else be found but in an *internal monopolistic organization of the power of the sword over a particular cultural area within territorial boundaries.* The reader should remember that this typical historical structural function may in no way be naturalistically misinterpreted. According to its *modal* meaning it is a normative structural function implying a *task,* a *vocation* which can be realized in a better or worse way" (1953, Vol III, pp. 413).

12 The Dutch constitution had a law that stated that hiring a mercenary army is forbidden (artikel 100, according to text 1983). The government withdrew the law, motivated by the assumption that it was not relevant anymore for present-day practice (TK 1996-1997, 25, 367 (R 1593), nr 3, p. 2), thereby not foreseeing contemporary developments with companies such as Blackwater and commercial armed personnel on trade vessels on piracy-risk routes.

13 What I have in mind is put into words at the United Nations General Assembly in 1999 by former Secretary-General Kofi Annan. He posed the central question, about how to respond to cases of injustice, starkly and directly: "...*if humanitarian intervention is, indeed, an unacceptable assault on sovereignty, how should we respond to a Rwanda, to a Srebrenica — to gross and systematic violations of human rights that affect every precept of our common humanity?*"

Chapter 7
Food Systems:
How Can the Normative Practice Approach Help Toward a Just and Sustainable Food System?

Henk Jochemsen
Wageningen University & Research, The Netherlands

Corné J. Rademaker
Wageningen University & Research, The Netherlands

ABSTRACT

Today's predominant food system on the one hand produces plenty of food, making food relatively cheap for most people in the world. However, for many people, the food they can afford is insufficiently nutritious. Major global health problems like obesity are partly a result of the present food system. Furthermore, the modern industrial way of producing food has negative environmental consequences, consisting among others of a decline in soil fertility and a loss of biodiversity. Another food system is required to obtain sustainable global food and nutrition security. This food system should observe the normativity of the agricultural practices that produce food. The authors' analysis of agricultural practices shows that the farm is economically qualified but that the primary process of care for soil, crops, and animals can best be seen as an ethically qualified supporting practice that steers the "meaningful shaping" of the interventions foundational for agricultural practices.

DOI: 10.4018/978-1-5225-8006-5.ch007

INTRODUCTION

Loren Cardeli is the Founder and President of 'A Growing Culture' (AGC), an NGO "that works to uphold farmer autonomy and stimulate agro-ecological innovation" (Cardeli, 2017)..[1] Food Think, a think tank for food, had an interview with Cardeli. Here are some fragments of the interview that simultaneously shows Cardeli's inspiration and the problems our current food systems face (Cardeli, 2017):

Food Tank (FT): *What originally inspired you to get involved in your work?*

Loren Cardeli (LC): *While in Belize, I was living on a kind of compound with two local Belizean guys. We would drink from the same sink where we bathed and washed our clothes. We grew most of our own food, but we were horrible at hunting meat. One day I decided to walk the hour and a half to the local logging village to barter with a neighbor for chickens. During this, I heard screaming nearby. I immediately ran over to where I heard the noise and I saw a man about my age today, holding his son. His son had passed away from drinking pesticides on his farm from an unmarked bottle. That experience really messed me up, I was away from my family and I realized that the potential of industrial agriculture and how destructive it is.*

My most important realization, though, was that environmental erosion is the result of culture and knowledge erosions. We dehumanize and devalue the local knowledge and the culture of the grand communities around the world. Once we do that, then we can bring in this agricultural model, that is now a destructive one. It dismantles their communities and cultural cohesion.[....].

FT: *Are those same things what continue to inspire you to be involved in this kind of work, or has that morphed over time?*

LC: *By now I've traveled around the world, to almost 40 countries, and met with thousands of farmers. There are two primary things that keep me focused in this work.*

The first thing is the amazing innovativeness of the world's farmers. Smallholder farmers are on 19 percent of the land, and 19 percent of land produces 70 percent of the world's food supply. That is ingenuity. This is a community that is operating on a fraction of that land that industrial agriculture is operating, yet they are out-producing industrial agriculture. [...]

The second thing is one of the greatest lessons I've learned in this work: that our relationship with the environment reflects our relationships within societies and with each other. Until we can eradicate the barriers of exploitation, oppression, hierarchy, and social stratification that happen within societies, [we] can't hope to foster relationships with the environment that are inclusive and sustainable. If there are individuals that are oppressed in our society, they are going to reflect that oppression wherever they can, and often that is the environment. I really believe that this is a human rights and social justice issue, and we have to look at that at the forefront to drive an environmental response.[...]

About 1.2 billion people go to bed hungry at night and 100 million are severely hungry, 70 percent of them are farmers. We are starving the ones who we depend on for food. Agriculture has a major role to play in mitigating climate change, combating gender inequalities, and strengthening rural communities.

In these interview fragment with a representative of an NGO lobbying for a more sustainable and just agriculture, some serious problems with the present predominant kind of agriculture in industrial countries are mentioned. These problems in the long run imply a threat to the world food and nutrition security. Against this background the Sustainable Development Goal 22 'End hunger, achieve food security and improved nutrition and promote sustainable agriculture' gets a special urgency. Achieving this goal will require more than 50% increase in food production (Rockström et al., 2017, p. 7).

In this chapter we will present and discuss these problems and elucidate their background in certain characteristics of modernity. Subsequently we will present a normative approach to agriculture and the broader food system and argue why following that normativity can contribute to a way out of the blind alley in which the present dominant food system finds itself. Briefly some policy measures will be put forward that could be part of the implementation of our normative view. The aim of this chapter is to contribute to the reflection and practice performance of professionals involved in agriculture and agricultural policy to realize the change required for realizing long term food and nutrition security.

We will begin our argument with a description of predominant industrial agriculture and an identification of its problems.

INDUSTRIALIZATION OF AGRICULTURE

What Happened

Especially in the second half of the 20th century, in the industrial countries agriculture underwent a process of industrialization, strongly promoted by governments. In

Europe this was also motivated by the experience of hunger during the last stage of World War II. The aim was to produce food as efficient as possible so as to make it available in sufficient quantities at a low price. This development obviously has led to an increase in the volumes of agricultural production, especially to an increase of production per farmer and also to the availability of enough food, at least regarding energy content, for those countries at a relatively low price. Right now, in the wealthy Western countries people spent on average around 10% of their income on food (Gray, 2016).

These achievements were obtained by industrializing agriculture in a development characterized by the following processes (Hardeman & Jochemsen, 2012). The first is *mechanization*: the process of replacing human work forces and techniques with machines and technological procedures. The second is *intensification*, in this case meaning the increase in production per hectare or per animal. The third development is *specialization*, where farmers focus only on one type of crop or activity, e.g. dairying, pig-keeping, poultry production, or growing maize. The *leading role of science and technology* is the fourth development to be mentioned. Agronomic research has focused on the increase of productivity per unit of labor through the use of new technologies and capital. Hence industrial agriculture is – among others – based on developments in plant breeding, resistance to disease, artificial insemination and the feed conversion rate. The final development to be mentioned is the *increase in the scale* of farming, which has been vigorously stimulated by governments. All these developments required the education of farmers, strongly promoted by governments. As a result, the predominant form of agriculture in the industrialized world is characterized by a strong focus on commodification[2] of agricultural products as opposed to a primary focus on a full realization of the right to food security for all; by an emphasis on external inputs of chemicals in the form of pesticides and herbicides and artificial fertilizer, instead of building primarily on soil characteristics and biological relationships; by a focus on a rather limited number of strains of seeds and animal races that are controlled by a few companies instead of diverse systems with a large variety of strains and races that are controlled by farmers; and by putting technical models before the responsibilities and aspirations of people.

Consequences

To what situation did this industrialization of agriculture lead? We summarize well-substantiated data and insights from a number of recent publications.

- In the first place about 6 billion people are fed, which is much more than any Malthusian scenario projected (TEEB, 2018, Chapter 2.1).

- Some 800 million people in the world do not have enough food to lead a healthy and active life. That is about one in nine people on earth (TEEB, 2018, Chapter 2.1; WFP, 2018). This figure is about one third lower than the number mentioned by Cardeli. It is unclear what can account for this incongruence; maybe Cardeli also included people who do not get sufficient *nutritious* food.
- Poor nutrition causes nearly half (45%) of deaths in children under five, i.e. 3.1 million children each year (WFP, 2018).
- Meanwhile, one third of all food produced (1.3 billion tons) is being wasted (Rockström et al., 2017, p. 6).

In addition to these problems, industrial agriculture also causes many ecological problems. Humans are the main driver of change in the epoch in which we live, the new geological era some refer to as the Anthropocene. Especially in this epoch, humanity has had a strongly negative impact on the natural world. Agriculture has been a primary driver of this negative impact and the single largest contributor to the increased environmental risks of the Anthropocene (Rockström et al., 2017, p. 6). "Terrestrial vertebrate populations declined by an astonishing 58 per cent between 1970 and 2010. Invertebrate populations show a global decline of about 45 per cent over the past 40 years. Similar declines have been documented for marine species" (TEEB, 2018, Chapter 2.1).

Furthermore, the increasing homogenization of food sources worldwide is narrowing the genetic diversity in animals and plants that is crucial to meet the challenge of food and nutrition security and ecological sustainability (Sukhdev, May, & Müller, 2016). Food systems are now the source of 60% of terrestrial biodiversity loss, 24% of greenhouse-gas emissions, 33% of soil degradation and 61% of the depletion of commercial fish stocks (Sukhdev et al., 2016). This decline must largely be attributed to habitat loss, pollution and over-exploitation associated with food production systems. "Livestock production is the largest source of anthropogenic alteration to global phosphorus and nitrogen cycles. Since the 1950s, surpluses in these nutrients have increased by a factor of four and five, respectively." (REF) Freshwater and marine eutrophication and the emergence of dead zones affecting aquatic life are mainly caused by relatively high concentrations of these nutrients (TEEB, 2018, Chapter 2.1).

Another point that deserves attention in this context is the influence of the way we produce, process, distribute, and consume – and waste - food (that is, how our prevailing food system works) impacts human health and nutritional security. The present food system leads to the availability of cheap, calorie-rich food, but is often not very nutritious in a broader sense, whereas healthy food like vegetables and fruits are relatively expensive and often not easily accessible for poor people. This implies that overweight and obesity are co-determined by the corporate supply of processed food high in saturated fats, sugar, and salt. As a result, 1.9 billion people above 18 years, take in more than 3,000 kilocalories per day and have overweight.[3] Of these over 600 million are obese, and "the number of children under 5 who are overweight is approaching the number who suffer from wasting" (Sukhdev et al., 2016; WHO, 2018). Importantly, obesity and overweight are increasing in countries all over the world, including developing countries (FAO, 2017).

These health effects, in turn influence the availability of 'labor' and of social life. First of all, it can be noted that six of the top eleven risk factors driving the global burden of disease are diet-related and therefore partly related to the food system. Undernutrition, making people more vulnerable for infectious diseases and parasites, causes stunting, wasting, and diet-related non-communicable diseases (NCDs). Malnutrition associated with diets represents the number one risk factor in the global burden of disease. Globally, maternal and child malnutrition represent the leading cause of disability- adjusted life years (DALY) with dietary risks being the second leading cause (TEEB, 2018, Chapter 4.1).

To all these problems with respect to the way the food system is trying to meet the goal of food and nutrition security for all people, there are additional challenges (FAO, 2017; Godfray, Beddington, et al., 2010; Godfray, Crute, et al., 2010). The world population is expected to grow to almost ten billion people in 2050; the biggest growth is likely to occur in both Asia and Africa. The combination of this population growth and increasing urbanization and expected income-growth in low- and middle-income countries is expected to drive dietary change towards higher consumption of meat, fruit, and vegetables relative to cereals. As a consequence, demand for these products is likely to grow. If the expected food demand is to be met in 2050, the world should produce between 50 to 100% more food than in 2012. For SSA and South Asia to be self-sufficient, their agricultural production would have to more than double by 2050. Furthermore, if food production is increased with the current agricultural practices, already food-insecure regions will suffer disproportionally from increased intense competition for natural resources, increased greenhouse gas emissions (especially in the case of meat production), and further deforestation and land degradation. Specific to smallholder farming in SSA, poor soil fertility is considered the major constraint to agricultural production (Vanlauwe & Giller, 2006).

In Sum

Current patterns of crop and livestock production and of processing, transport and consumption are not delivering healthy, safe and nutritious food to all groups of people in society. They are generating large and unacceptable impacts on the environment and on vulnerable populations, in particular the (extremely) poor.

And in a context of scarce and degraded natural resources and advancing climate change, it is not environmentally sustainable. At the same time, the food system can potentially be an enabler of food and nutrition security, livelihood procurement, and environmental sustainability.

In our view, main causes for this state of affairs have to be sought *both* at the level of *practices* and *of institutions and systems*. With respect to institutions and systems we primarily think of what is called the food system – or food systems. In the remainder of this chapter we will elaborate first the concept of food system, and evaluate the functioning of the present predominant food system. We will then elaborate the normative practice approach to agricultural practices as the basis of the food system, emphasizing the role and responsibility of farmers. Subsequently, the normative implications of this view of the food system, and measures to change the food system, will be discussed.

FOOD SYSTEMS

We have started this chapter by focusing on agricultural practices as major means to produce food. In the course of our argument we felt the need to introduce the term food system, implicitly understood as the (inter)actions of the main stakeholders involved in the production, processing, trade and consumption of food. We now want to elaborate this concept further, as understanding what it is and how it functions is essential in view of pursuing global food and nutrition security.

The term *food system* has been coined to denote the broader constellation of interconnected practices, institutions, and processes around food. CIAT defines a food system as "the set of different processes, activities, infrastructures, and institutions that are involved in the production, processing, distribution, and consumption of food." (CIAT, 2017, p. 4; cf. Capone, Bilali, Debs, Cardone, & Driouech, 2014). The food systems approach is a fruitful model to conceptualize how our food is produced and in what context (CIAT, 2017; De Vries, De Hoog, & Dijstelbloem, 2016; Ingram, 2011). The core of the food system is the value chain from agricultural production to consumption of food items. Central concepts in the food system approach are *drivers, activities, actors, and outcomes* (see Figure 1). *Activities* that take place in the value chain lead to *outcomes* in the socio-economic, food and nutritional, and environmental sphere. Those activities can be classified according to the stage in the value chain. For instance, production activities encompass the growing and harvesting of crops while processing activities include transforming and packaging products. *Actors* can be confined to one specific type of activities, e.g. many farmers are confined to production activities, but there are also actors that perform several types of activities such as exporters of fruit and vegetables that also provide agricultural inputs to contracted farmers (so as to ensure product quality standards will be met; see e.g. Minten, Randrianarison & Swinnen (2009)). The latter is called vertical integration.

Finally, activities and outcomes are influenced by a range of 'drivers', while these activities and outcomes shape drivers in turn (see top part of Figure 1). An example is the 'meatification' of diets in emerging countries like Brazil and China, which is both an outcome of a change in the consumption practice – and behind this, increasing incomes and changing social norms – and a driver for increased meat production including more intensive agricultural practices.

Even though depicted in Figure 1 as a (type of) driver, (governmental) *policy* could be conceptualized as an activity *as well*, i.e., policy-making. Something similar applies to agricultural extension[4] (related to the driver 'Technology and Science' in Figure 1). It is important to realize, therefore, that most drivers are not 'just there' but involve an active human component and have a normative character (as we will see later).

Figure 1. The food system

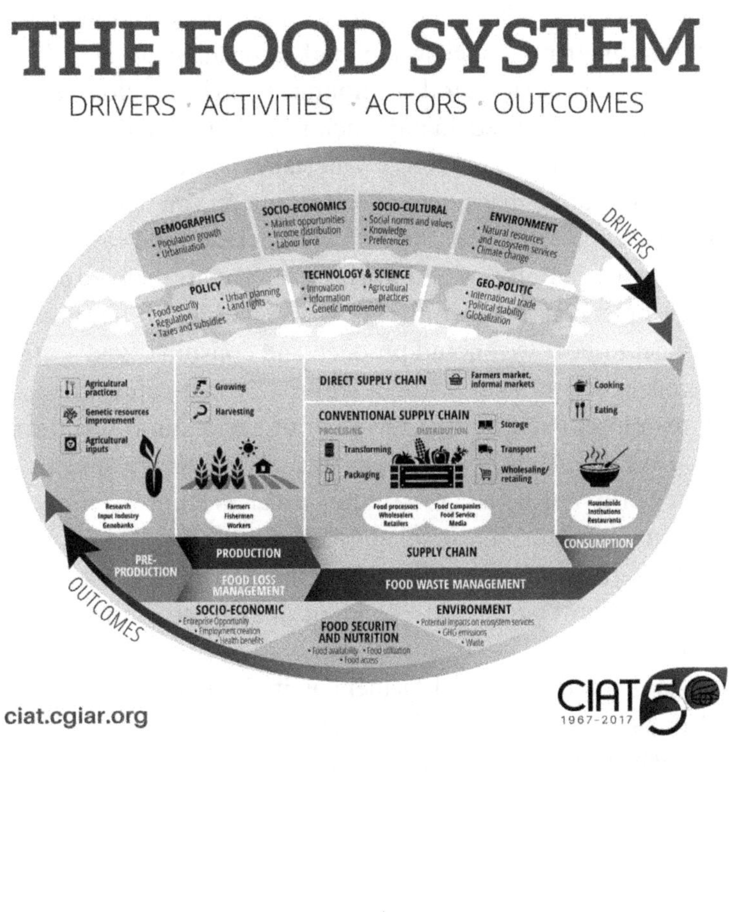

The food system approach not only considers production activities and trade relationships but also other actors and as well as social and ecological *conditions for* and *effects of* these activities (De Vries et al., 2016, p. 82). This raises the question: what are the main characteristics of the present predominant food system and how come it has led to the problematic situation we described above?

In our view, to answer this question, we will have to delve into the worldview and ethos that is dominant in Western thinking and which influences both practices of production and consumption of food, and the institutions and systems that form the food system. The present food system is largely a consequence of the industrialization of agriculture and the commodification of food (see above). The industrialization is closely related to the Enlightenment which built on the cultural movement of modernity of which Descartes (1596-1650) was a prominent philosopher. In Western culture, his influence led to the so-called *Cartesian worldview and related fundamental attitude (ethos) to reality*. Central in this worldview and attitude is the autonomous individual set in an in itself valueless and meaningless reality that employs technology to rearrange that reality, including, we can add, agricultural reality (Jochemsen, 2012, pp. 125–126). Schuurman (2003) has called this the technicist ethos. In other words, the Cartesian worldview has spawned the view in which the individual is the building block of (or for) a society, where interactions among those individuals are seen to be mediated by mechanisms – such as the market mechanism (Hoksbergen, 1986). In the history of Western agricultural development and in development cooperation this Cartesian ethos has inspired an approach in which the natural environment as well as the farmers and others are seen as material to be freely given shape based on a rational design and for an instrumental end (Long & Van der Ploeg, 1989; Scott, 1998), one of these ends being economic growth and material wealth (Goudzwaard & Verweij, 2001, p. 144). Religion and worldview are marginalized to the subjective personal life of people; hence, any truth claims originating in religion and worldview – also with respect to how we should produce and consume food – are considered personal preference and, as such, without legitimacy in a public context.

This view manifests itself both at the level of agricultural practices and at the level of the food system. At the level of agricultural practices, a specific elaboration of the Cartesian worldview is the view of the farmer as *homo economicus*. Farmers are seen as rational maximizers of self-interested utility or profit. Via what later has been called the *agricultural treadmill* (Cochrane, 1979) – note the mechanistic connotation! – this view on human economic being and acting is connected to technological innovations. This treadmill can be described as follows. Farms are seen as (relatively) small firms and farmers as individual decision-makers which all produce the same commodities. Each one is too small to affect the price: they are price-takers who produce as much as they want against the going price (rational choice). Individuals' efforts to improve their income by producing more leads to a constant downward pressure on overall prices (societal outcome of individual choices). Since overall prices are still dictated by the prevailing state of the art, introduction of an innovation allows innovators and early adopters to capture a windfall profit. Soon diffusion leads to over-production and further price squeeze. Adoption becomes necessary to stay in the marketplace. Farmers who cannot keep up drop out. The survivors absorb their resources and capture economies of scale (Röling, 2016; Thompson, 2015). This *agricultural treadmill* has led to overemphasize efficiency in food production, which constitutes an important cause of the problematic development of industrial agriculture as sketched above.

Transnational Corporations

The Cartesian worldview also manifests itself at the level of the food system. Modernization, of which industrialization is a manifestation, forms the ideological background of (economic) globalization. In other words, globalization can be seen as a recent economic expression of modernity (Goudzwaard, VanderVennen, & VanHeemst, 2007). In agriculture, the process of globalization in combination with the neoliberal view on economy has led to concentrations of power in agriculture. In other words, as a consequence of several of the previous processes, an ever-smaller number of corporations control critical parts of value chains ranging from input provision to food distribution (EcoNexus, 2013; Howard, 2016). The so-called transnational corporations (TNCs) largely dominate the prevailing food system. This generally has negative consequences for (unorganized) smallholders because corporations can set prices. Especially in SSA, smallholders that lose out from agriculture contribute to the increasing mass of unemployed people and associated migratory flows. TNCs often have (had?) a narrow focus on (financial) profit and use their power to maximize this profit which comes at the expense of especially smallholder producers (Barrientos & Dolan, 2006; Holt-Giménez & Shattuck, 2011). That is, the primary interest of TNCs does not seem to be providing food to (all) people but rather in making a profit out of agribusiness to which contributing to food provision is rather contingently connected. Because of their power, their behavior largely determines the character of the predominant food system. On the basis of literature we can briefly summarize the dominant role of TNCs in agricultural production as follows.

1. In 1996, the ten biggest seed companies had a market share of less than 30%. In 2015 the three largest control more than 50% of the market. Often seeds become more expensive with fewer varieties available. The three market leaders in seeds are also major pesticide producers. Through genetic modification, the

TNCs can create patented seeds that are resistant to the pesticides they happen to sell as well, thereby increasing the dependency of farmers on their products. Of the global soy production just over 50% is GMO and of corn this is about 30%. The concentration in the input sector will become even stronger by the recent acquisition of Monsanto by Bayer (Varinsky, 2018).

2. The powerful, i.c. the TNCs, largely control the chain. Farmers are pressurized by corporations. The TNCs pay low prices for the farmers' produce such as soya, wheat, and maize, while farmers pay relatively high prices for seeds, pesticides, energy, fertilizers and animal feed (Clapp, 2014; EcoNexus, 2013).
3. The TNCs also increasingly control the value chains of the major food system. In addition to horizontal integration, where one company controls a large share of a particular market segment, corporate strategies aim at vertical integration by processing the product and producing inputs. This is not about distributing business risks across several sectors but about controlling the value chain and having access to cheap raw materials
4. World trade dominates prices. Although 85% of all food is consumed close to where it is produced, global trade actually has a disproportionate influence on prices. On the stock market, batches of the same soya and maize may be traded speculatively several times over, thus increasing price volatility. This has played a major role in the 2007-2008 food crisis (McMichael, 2009; Clapp, 2014)
5. Finally, the TNCs in agribusiness display enormous lobby efforts. Thousands of lobbyists often successfully lobby for corporate interests on food standards, approval of pesticides, GM seeds, trade agreements, or the public research agenda. Although the TNCs officially promote competition in an open market, in fact they try to achieve favorable positions (Howard, 2016).

One study of the neoliberal food system summarizes the situation as follows.

Neoliberalism has produced an unsustainable food system, which might prove inadequate to nourish future generations. Notwithstanding the steady food price increases, natural resources deterioration, loss of resilience of agricultural systems and climate change disturbances, international bodies and national governments continue to propose neoliberal policies. Privatization and deregulation are passed off as bulwarks of liberty and efficiency, while they are consigning the system to corporate power and transnational financial elites. All this is made possible not only through the power of organizations with vested interests, but also through the adamant trust of the majority of academics and bureaucrats in the mainstream economics. (Sodano, 2012, pp. 398–399).

We want to emphasize that these positions concentrate on the predominant food system; there are smaller parallel food systems and food networks that do play a role, like the organic food system that serves a niche market, albeit a substantial niche. And there are local and even regional markets, both in industrial and in developing countries that deliberately aim to operate as much as possible apart from the prevailing global food system, e.g. the *Via Campesina* movement in Latin America. At the same time, those parallel food systems and networks are at constant threat to become coopted by the dominant food system (Howard, 2016). We will argue later that these parallel food systems and networks can be important starting points for a further decentralization and diversification of the major food system.

As stated earlier that the present state of the food system requires changes *both* at the level of *practices* and *of institutions and systems.* At the practical level, we refer to those agricultural techniques and procedures that fit in a normative view on agriculture (see below). At the level of institutions and systems, we think of the positions and roles of all the (main) stakeholders in the system that should lead to a fairer distribution of financial benefits within the food system and particularly for primary producers (Fox & Vorley, 2006).

TOWARDS A NORMATIVE VIEW OF AGRICULTURE

Point of Departure

In our view, we will have to start with observing that the meaning of food systems precisely lies in them being *food* systems. The provision of food therefore provides for the point and purpose of food systems. This is captured in Figure 1 with the outcome of food and nutrition security (FNS). Even though we cannot argue for it at this place, FNS extends to *all people* as a requirement of justice. This has also been expressed in the *right to food* (De Schutter, 2014). FNS for all can only be achieved when all stakeholders involved in the food system take their respective responsibility, where states have the primary responsibility to secure the right to food.. This requires that the actors in the food system acknowledge and respect each other's responsibilities. Those responsibilities are defined by the normativity of the various practices that form part of the system (see above). In other words, actors in the food system should *respect the normativity intrinsic to the respective practices in the food system and in particular those practices in which the primary process of food production takes place, namely (different types of) agricultural practice* (Rademaker & Van den Hee, 2018). Indeed, a key practice in the food system has always been the practice of (different types of) farming. We can view the present state of the food system as the result of a differentiation of specific tasks which originally were performed by farmers, but are now performed by external parties. For instance, whereas in earlier times feed for pigs and poultry was 'produced' on the farm, most pig and poultry farms nowadays rely on feed from external feed manufacturers. In the next paragraph, therefore, we will zoom in on the farming practice. This will give a normative understanding of this practice, but it will also be the beginning of a broader normative view on food systems (see further section *Towards a normative view of food systems*).

Farming as a Normative Practice

The conviction that human acting is inherently directed to norms has been elaborated in the Normative Practice Approach (NPA). The approach has already been introduced in Chapters 1 and 2 in this book, and here we will only briefly recapitulate the main characteristics of the NPA as they apply to agriculture. As a preliminary remark, we note that farming consists of a family of diverse and at the same time mutually related practices. The common thread is that all of them work with living nature in a context of production and consumption. But the practice of an Ethiopian smallholder who cultivates crops on her field and in addition keeps a few goats for milk and meat is totally different from a Dutch pig farmer in intensive husbandry. Yet they both cultivate living nature to produce something that is fulfilling a need or at least is valued by human beings. In the context of this paper that deals with agricultural production in the context of food security, we will concentrate on the practices of cultivating crops and animal husbandry for food and fiber. These practices are characterized by cultivating living nature for the sake of providing prerequisites of human existence, viz. food and clothing. In other words, the direct activities in those practices, i.e. their primary process, pursue the provision of basic human needs by some form of cultivating nature.

Important questions at the beginning of the analysis of a practice are: what is the qualifying aspect and related principle (the telos) of the practice under analysis, and what is the foundational aspect? In the following we will answer these questions and then continue in discussing other relevant aspects of the practice, the conditioning aspects. Together these steps give an elucidation of the structure of the practice. Following another distinction in this philosophy, we will then proceed in dealing with the directional side and the importance of the context. This will give a logical link to discussing the system level in which most farming practices are embedded.

Qualifying Aspect of Farming

The agricultural practice consists of human interventions and activities that are performed in view of bringing forth food and fiber for human use. In agricultural practice, human actions are organized in such a way that resources are transformed into agricultural products that can be harvested. In other words, the reason of its existence is bringing forth those goods in a way that enables people in 'the household' at least to survive and if possible to have a surplus that can be used to generate means for further development of the household. The household in question concerns both the farm household and broader society. Within the farm household, agricultural production can provide for food needs, but also for additional income which can be directed to a range of goods, activities, etc. that enrich human life. Something similar obtains at the macro-level of society (cf. World Bank, 2007). Historically, societies have developed that, on the one hand, secure sufficient and safe food for its members, and on the other hand, enable a rich variety of social structures and cultural achievements. Understanding agricultural practice in this context means that the production process should be realized in an efficient way. In other words, the agricultural practice as a social structure entails the efficient use of a variety of resources, viz. labor, land and other natural and technical means, in view of bringing forth food and fiber. Hence, agricultural practice as a whole is to be seen as an enterprise, commonly indicated as farm (cf. Lagemaat, 1986, p. 59). In Reformational philosophy it is argued that the enterprise is economically qualified (Dooyeweerd, 1984, p. 66; Verkerk & Zijlstra, 2003, p. 115). This also applies to the agricultural enterprise, the farm. A farm also is an enterprise that should give the farmer (and his or her household) a living, as well as contributing to the food and fiber needs of society.

According to Dooyeweerd, the normative principle of the economic aspect is 'frugal administration', or in today's terms 'efficient management of (scarce) resources', in which frugal can be understood as 'avoiding waste' (Basden, n.d.). However, this is a rather negative understanding of the economic. In the economic aspect, we always encounter the notion of *provision*; something is brought forth, or made available through trade. In earlier work the authors of this chapter used Goudzwaard's proposal of coining 'fruitful disposition' as the qualifying principle of the economic aspect (Rademaker, Glas, & Jochemsen, 2017, p. 225), whereas Buijs in this context recently used the term 'careful co-creation' (G.J. Buijs, personal communication, September 7, 2018). We remain somewhat unsatisfied with those two suggestions, however, as efficiency or expediency (Dutch: *doelmatigheid*) remains a central characteristic of economic life. In light of this discussion we see as typical for the economic aspect human activity aiming at providing people (the household) with goods and services through production and trade. Those activities encompass efficient management of resources (the production factors and means of trade). As the core value we propose '*efficient provision*'. The adjective 'efficient' should not be reduced to a short-term and narrow financial efficiency, but should refer to a long-term and broad understanding of the processes that lead to 'provision', understood as providing people with things they value, either by a form of production or trade.

Having said this, the next question here is: how should 'efficient provision' be understood in the farming practice? We saw that in a sense the modern industrial agriculture is very much oriented towards effectiveness and efficiency. Does this mean that this version of agricultural practice responds best to the normative structure of that practice? To obtain an answer to this question we will turn to the foundational aspect of the practice, to discover that, in fact, we should consider various foundational aspects.

Foundational Aspects

What relation to reality is foundational for agricultural practice, that is, characterizes the human actions in which the performance of the practice consists? In agricultural practice the human being works with living nature as 'production factor' in view of the survival and health of human beings. The 'material' for these activities are the soil, plants and animals as they were originally found in nature, but have been increasingly domesticated. Of themselves, plants are biotically qualified, while animals are sensitively qualified. Hence, the biotic aspect is foundational for agricultural practice insofar it deals with crops, while the sensitive aspect is foundational insofar it deals with farm animals. This means that the life and needs of, respectively, crops and farm animals form the precondition for the agricultural practice.

But living nature – including both plants and animals – as such does not characterize the activities in which farming practices consist. In the course of history human beings have tilled the earth, cultivated and bred plants, domesticated and bred animals in view of fulfilling certain human needs. In other words, farming practices consist in techniques and methods by which people intervene in natural processes in order to steer them into the direction of bringing forth the desired food and fiber products. Yet, this implies that the formative aspect should be seen as foundational for the coherent activities in which farming practices consist (Jochemsen, 2012). 'Meaning-oriented shaping' has been suggested as the normative principle of that aspect (Verkerk, Hoogland, Stoep, & Vries, 2015, Chapter 2). This suggests that in *dealing with living nature* in agricultural practices, the *shaping power of human interventions* needs to be oriented towards the *meaning* of the practice: the bringing forth of food and fiber. Two implications follow from this interpretation. First, the search for and use of effective interventions ought to be pursued keeping in view the bringing forth of food and fiber. Effectiveness is not the overriding principle. Second, we now have ended up with two foundational aspects, the biotic (in the case of plant production) or sensitive (in the case of animal production) and the formative. How do those relate to each other?

Supportive Practice

This analysis so far suggests that we can deepen our insight into the agricultural practice if we distinguish two layers in it. In the first layer we meet living nature as 'working material' that nevertheless exhibits its own characteristic ways of being, i.e. biotic and sensitive being in the case of respectively crop and animal production. At the farm level, we note that the telos of the agricultural practice is (primarily) provision in the form of *bringing forth of food and fiber*, the economic aspect (see above). In between these two levels we can identify the foundational aspect of the agricultural practice, namely human (technical) interventions with as core principle 'meaning-oriented shaping'. A guiding rule in the NPA is the 'simultaneous realization of norms'. This means that the interventions in living nature (including the soil which is replete with organisms essential for soil fertility) should follow the normative principles of the biotic (life) and the sensitive (feeling) aspects. In other words, care should be taken to support the health of the soil, microorganisms, and plants (crops), and the sensitive well-functioning of animals as expressed in behavior natural to the species (e.g. pigs wallowing in mud). In our view, this entails at least the following ethical principles for farming practices: maintain biodiversity and foster animal welfare (Jochemsen, 2012; Rademaker et al., 2017). We see that in thinking about how to deal with living nature, the core principle of the ethical aspect, *care*, presents itself (cf. Jochemsen, 2006b). The question therefore rises what the status is of this aspect within the agricultural practice.

Considering this layeredness in farming, our understanding of this practice can become more precise by distinguishing within farming as an economically qualified practice, *an ethically qualified supportive practice consisting of the primary processes like guarding soil quality and weeding fields (in the case of crops) and feeding, watering and prevention and cure of diseases (in the case of animals)* that belong to the formative activities of the practice that the farmer steers towards the telos of farming: bringing forth food and fiber.[5] Distinguishing this supporting practice is motivated by views of reality that in the NPA belong to the regulative side of practices. We will come back to this in the discussion of that side.

Other Normative Principles

In addition to the qualifying normative principle and related norms and the foundational normative principle and their norms, the NPA distinguishes conditioning aspects in the normative structure of practices (Jochemsen, 2006a, p. 105). What does this mean for farming? An agricultural practice is not an isolated unit but embedded in other networks in society on which it depends. Farmers need to buy or rent land, probably provide for infrastructure like barns for animals, they may have to get a loan from a bank, arrange property rights, buy materials like equipment and possibly seeds and chemicals to practice farming, etc. They have to comply with regulations regarding the way animals are kept and the land is cultivated, the chemicals that are allowed and/or obtainable. They have to deal with price regulations or a market that may be unstable, both for the inputs they have to buy and for their products. And they want to sell (part of) their products to have an earning for their living. These activities generally have a primarily economic character (cf. the economic qualification of the practice), but they often are regulated legally and take place in a variety of social interactions. Hence, the primary process not only has to comply with the foundational (formative) and qualifying (economic) principles, but also with the principles related to the other modal aspects of reality, like the lingual (clear information and communication), the social (respecting social relations), the juridical (respecting laws and regulations) and the ethical (dealing with reality in an attitude of respect and care, not just with respect to the soil, plants and animals but also to the food consumers; cf. Rademaker, Glas, and Jochemsen, 2017). All these principles, that together form the *structure* of the practice, should be observed simultaneously. But the way in which this is done by a farmer in the actual performance of his practice will depend on his broader normative view of reality, including his view of the character and meaning of his practice, and on the specific context. This observation brings us to the distinction between structure, direction and context as introduced earlier (cf. chapter 1).

Directional Side

The directional side of social practices refers to the worldview beliefs, fundamental normative attitudes (ethoi, plural of ethos) and images of the good life that people pursue that steer the interpretation and enactment of the normative structure in the concrete situation and therefore the understanding of a competent, or even excellent performance of their practice in that particular situation. This implies that also one's understanding of the virtues required to competently perform practices is influenced by the directional side of the practice (cf. MacIntyre, 1981, pp.185-187).

How does this work out for farming? We have seen that agricultural practice aims at the efficient production of food and fiber by means of both caring and technical interventions in the broadest sense. It is important to emphasize once more that the agricultural practice is not in all respects the same as for example the practice of producing cell phones, even though the two practices have the same general normative structure, namely founded in the formative aspect and qualified by the economic aspect. Agriculture is not a kind of making, producing in the ordinary sense. We do not 'make' a crop or make an animal grow or produce milk or meat. We can only facilitate that natural process. Just like a physician cannot heal the patient, but only take away obstacles to health and promote the natural healing process. That is why above we proposed to distinguish a supportive practice of care for the dealings with soil plants and animals, entailed in the farming practice.

With respect to keeping animals, for which the sensitive aspect is a foundational aspect, De Rooij, De Lauwere, and Van der Ploeg (2010) have investigated the fundamental ethical positions among Dutch dairy farmers and pig breeders, with particular reference to animal welfare (see Rademaker, Glas, and Jochemsen, 2017). They distinguish between three ethoi: an entrepreneurial ethos, a farmers' ethos, and an idealists' ethos. In the first ethos commercial values have priority, animals are seen as means of production. Here animal welfare is considered only where relevant from a commercial perspective and is understood primarily as healthy biological functioning (although unnecessary suffering, pain, and distress is to be reduced), and responsibility for animal welfare is placed with consumers ("If consumers want more animal welfare-friendly production, they need to pay more"). The farmers' ethos is characterized by conceiving of animals in relation to the farmer, seeking for a balance between commercial values and animal welfare on the farm, and more emphasis on freedom from pain and stress for the animals. Finally, the idealists' ethos sees animals as carriers of intrinsic values and needs, privileges animal welfare considerations over commercial values, places the responsibility for animal welfare problems with other (conventional) farmers, and emphasizes respect for the integrity of the animal and the opportunity for animals to display natural behavior.

The entrepreneurial ethos of farmers reflects the modernist, industrial approach to farming described before, whereas the farmer's ethos and the idealist's ethos have different views on the status of animals, animal welfare and the role it should play in their practice. These positions clearly correspond better to the normative structure of farming as presented above. Here we see how elements of the directional side become operative in concrete practice performance. These insights underline the fruitfulness of distinguishing a supportive practice of care within the (economically qualified) farming practice. This distinction calls attention to the way living nature is being treated in the shaping activities directed at production.

It is from an ethos of 'appreciation'[6] of reality (Heschel, 1965), as an element of the directional side of farming, that we realize that our primary responsibility towards nature to 'not-destroy' is the very basis for the production of food which is dependent on the natural capacity of nature, the soil and living organisms to bring forth. We cannot generate natural processes, we can only steer and facilitate them. Good care for the soil and for plants and animals entails the promise of being most effective and efficient in giving harvests in the long-run. Hence, the very nature of the 'material' with which agricultural practice works, brings along the requirement of 'care' in the shaping interventions aiming at production, in order to make the practice sustainable. At the same time, pleading for an attitude of appreciation does not mean that interventions are inherently problematic. Nature is not sacred (which is in fact also a belief of worldview character). Interventions are not just allowed, because of the disorder that is also present in nature, they are desirable to some extent. However, it is important to discover the potencies of nature and align with them rather than 'force' nature by our technical interventions.[7] In other words, the specific character of the primary agricultural practice requires that agronomic techniques are not just production-driven in a quantitative sense but also embody an attitude of care. In the agro-ecological movement – of which Loren Cardeli is a proponent – this is done through building on all kinds of symbioses between bacteria, fungi, crops, animals and humans. For example, symbioses in the soil between the crop and fungi (*mycorrhizae*) can help the crop to absorb nitrogen from the soil, rather than using artificial nitrogen fertilizer that eliminates those fungi from the soil (Visser, 2010, pp. 210–213).

Typology of Agricultural Practices

In addition to the typology of Dutch livestock farmers of De Rooij et al., other authors have developed a typology of global agricultural practices in which agronomic parameters are combined with an institutional characterization (Plumecocq et al., 2018). In this way, this typology combines characteristics of the farming practice itself with the way it relates to the broader institutional context, and therefore with the food system. The agronomic parameters are structured according to the axes 'exogenous inputs' versus 'ecosystem services'. The institutional parameters are structured on the axis 'territorial embeddedness' versus 'globalized commodity-based food systems'. Crossing the two axes gives four quadrants. In addition to conventional farming – the industrial model presented above – (1), they distinguish six other models (Figure 2).

In this typology, conventional farming is at the very end of the quadrant *'Exogenous inputs/ globalized commodity-based food systems (FS)'*. In this same quadrant the authors put specialized crop/livestock systems that represent chemical input-based food systems, e.g. some forms of precision agriculture (2a) and biological input-based food system in globalized commodity-based FS (2b). Another model is 'biological input-based FS in circular economy and globalized food system' (2c), that uses exogenous inputs but is more territorially embedded than 2b. This is located in the quadrant *'Globalized commodity-based FS/ territorial embeddedness'*. It is interesting that the authors locate, among others, agroforestry and conservation agriculture, in the quadrant *'Globalized commodity-based FS'/ecosystem services' (3a)*. In their view these agricultural practices are still integrated in the commodity-based global food system. The two remaining models, 'biodiversity-based FS in alternative food systems and circular economy' (3b) and 'biodiversity-based FS in alternative food

Figure 2. The 7 models of agricultural practices, located in the 4 quadrants as mentioned in the texts. After Plumecocq et al., 2018, 21

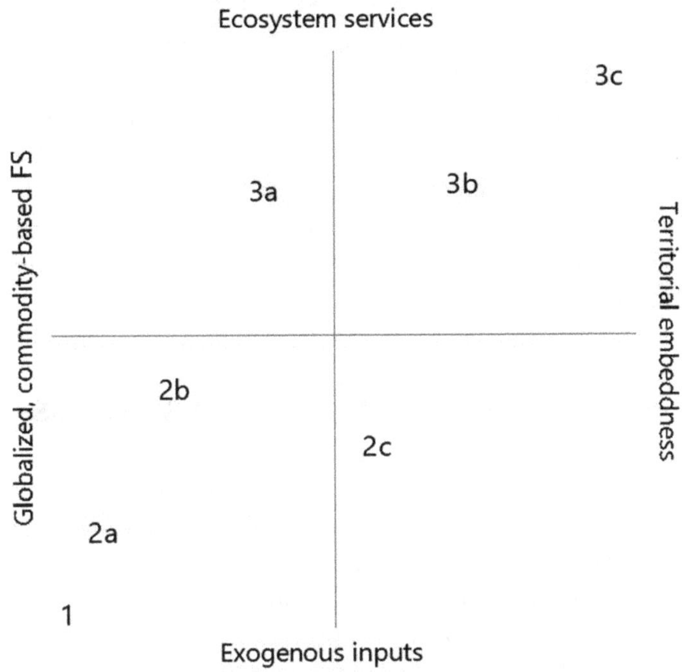

systems and circular economy and collectively managed multiservice landscape' (3c) are located in the middle, respectively, the extreme corner of the quadrant '*Ecosystem services/ territorial embedded*'.

It is beyond the scope of this article to discuss these models in detail and evaluate them in light of the normative view of farming as presented above. We just point out now that evaluating farming practices is not a black and white issue, though some practices clearly correspond better to our normative view than others. To some extent the choice for one or another model will depend, not just on the worldview and ethos of farmers and other value chain actors and government officials, but also on the specific context. For example, for large scale cultivation of cotton, model 2b may do well; it works as much as possible with biological methods, but the production is clearly linked to global markets (though not the food system). We give another example. Keeping cattle for meat for the global market in parts of the Paraguayan Chaco where cultivating crops is very tough, in a way in which nitrogen-binding plants are sown in the grazing fields and few other exogenous inputs are being used (maybe vaccines against certain diseases), may fit model 2c and may well be a rather sustainable way of producing food (Mottet et al., 2017). In agriculture in (western)

Europe we can see a gradual shift from the predominant industrial model 1 to variants of 2 and niches of variants of 3. For large parts of the developing world, especially sub-Saharan Africa and India, we note that dominant actors like TNCs, donor governments and some NGOs support a move from subsistence farming both to 1 and 2a; other stakeholders, mainly farmer organizations, NGOs and social investors, attempt to promote the models 3a and 3b. Considering the disadvantages of model 1 and 2a as summarized earlier (section *Industrialization of agriculture*), we think the former move is anti-normative in light of the desired global food and nutrition security and broader normative concerns like biodiversity and animal welfare.

This leads us finally to consider the level of institutions and systems, that is the level of the food system.

TOWARDS A NORMATIVE VIEW OF FOOD SYSTEMS[8]

In our understanding of reality, trying to formulate a normative view on institutions and systems at the macro-level in society should begin with a normative understanding of the normativity at the level of practices and of the primary processes intertwined in them. That is why above we stated that food systems should *respect the normativity intrinsic [....]to those practices in which the primary process of food production takes place, namely (different types of) farming practice.* If we unpack this we could say that a good food system should have the following characteristics. It must meet social needs and fulfill sustainability criteria that enable food and all other agricultural ecosystem services (i.e., climate stabilization, forms of flood control, support of mental health, nutrition, etc.). This should be done in a way that maintains a stable and resilient Earth system. This will require a sustainable intensification of agriculture in which "yields are increased without adverse environmental impact and without the cultivation of more land." (Rockström et al,, 2017, p.7)

We saw that the farming practice is qualified by the economic aspect, but that the way the interventions are being performed (the foundational formative aspect) should respect the normativity embodied in the supportive practice of care for soil, plants and animals (ethical aspect in relation to the biotic and sensitive). The normative principles of the other, conditioning, aspects should also be observed.

However, in the predominant global food supply systems many actors are involved, arrangements are more complex and often imply less control by producers on price setting. In many complex food systems, both regional and global, the linkages from the food system towards access to nutritious food are often indirect – mediated through incomes, prices, knowledge, and other factors (see Fig 1). They often also involve mainly intensive farming systems with all the disadvantages mentioned above. Larger scale food systems typically carry a wide variety of foods year-round but also sell more highly processed packaged foods that too easily contribute to overweight and obesity.

Food systems should enable the farmer to farm in a sustainable way, that is, to observe the simultaneous realization of all the normative principles and related norms in which the practice functions. In working towards such a situation, we can distinguish between push and pull strategies (LEO, 2015). Of both types we will first mention core principles and subsequently a few strategies.

Push Strategies

Based on the above-given criticisms of the predominant types of agriculture and on our account of the normative structure of agricultural practices we formulate the following core characteristics of good food systems. These characteristics are to govern push strategies that pursue such good food systems:

- It is founded on the profound understanding that all beings are interrelated in the web of life (Peralta, 2017).
- It sees producers and consumers as part of one household;
- It puts farmers – or those who till the land and produce the food, their needs, and their livelihoods at the center;
- It produces a diversity of healthy and nutritious food, medicines, and other products for the sustenance of human communities in accordance with their cultures and norms;
- It nourishes and regenerates soil, water, air, and entire ecosystems upon which the production of food fully depends, recognizing that these are the bases of sustenance not only for current generations but also for future generations of living beings, human and non-human;
- It comprehends that land, water, and air are essentially commons – gifts for the provisioning of all life – and ought not to be privatized or commoditized for narrowly conceived profit;

Push strategies work directly with farmers to enhance agricultural sustainable productivity that meets the constellation of principles and norms of the NPA and/or support their organizational capacity. And they aim at building capacities to engage in markets. In other words, the focus is on the core value chain and role/position of the farmer and other actors in the value chain. This involves, among others, implementing agronomic techniques and methods of organic (or agro-ecological) farming like the application of biological methods of disease and pest management.

Pull Strategies

Pull strategies facilitate the development of market systems and focus on support functions and the rules and governance of a sector in a manner that expands the diversity and quality of opportunities of all those involved to engage more successfully in the economy – be it as a producer, laborer, employee, business owner, etc., or a mixture of these (see also Peralta, 2017). That is, pull strategies "expand the diversity and quality of accessible economic opportunities, to drive more beneficial and sustained inclusion of the extreme poor into market systems through a dynamic process of change" (LEO, 2015, p. 1). Core principles that are to govern pull strategies are:

- They promote just and equitable economic relationships between and among producers, investors, traders, consumers;
- They promote democratic policy-making in food systems with a voice for representatives from all of the different practices that are involved and specifically draw wisdom and learning from indigenous peoples and farming communities that have traditionally lived in close relation with the land;
- They nourish and regenerate soil, water, air, and entire ecosystems upon which the production of food fully depends, recognizing that these are the basis of sustenance not only for current generations but also for future generations of living beings, human and non-human;
- They comprehend that land, water, and air are essentially commons – gifts for the provisioning of all life – that ought not to be privatized or commoditized for narrowly conceived profit (Peralta, 2017).

For agriculture in industrialized countries this involves the development of regional and local value chains for specific food items, e.g. region-typically food items, food produced by organic farming for those who want that type of food. This in many western European countries has led to the establishment of alternative food systems which are, however, relatively small. However, this does not seem to lead to a situation that from a normative point of view is required. The neoliberal position that the market should decide what products will be available and that it is fine when people want to buy the regular cheap food items produced by industrialized agriculture, prevents the necessary change. This view does not take into account that important social and ecological costs are externalized (see section 'Industrialization of agriculture') and that in the long run this system is undermining the global food and nutrition security, as well as other normative considerations like biodiversity and animal welfare. In our view, for agriculture and food the neoliberal approach is destructive in the long run. This means that legislation regarding the way of producing food is necessary, e.g. what substances are allowed in disease and pest management, rules for keeping animals, etc. In several (Western) European countries this is an ongoing process. However, when the free market ideology subsequently forces the acceptance of importation of products from other countries that are cheaper than the national product since those countries lack those cost enhancing legal restrictions, such legislation creates an unfair market and largely misses its purpose. Since the major food systems are global, legislation on agricultural practices should be global or countries should be allowed to protect their own by import taxes for certain food products (cf. Chang, 2008). Within legal constraints, in addition professional and sectorial self-governance may be necessary for proper functioning of the food system.

A detailed elaboration of governmental policies here is beyond the scope of this chapter as well as beyond our competence. A large variety of expertise from different disciplines has to come to together to think this through and formulate feasible policies. It is governmental responsibility to make this happen.

We realize that the situation with respect to global food systems and food security is very complex and there are no one-size-fits-all solutions. At the same time, we are convinced of the urgency of changing the present predominant system in view of the future global food and nutrition security.

REFERENCES

Barrientos, S., & Dolan, C. (Eds.). (2006). *Ethical Sourcing in the Global Food System.* Earthscan.

Basden, A. (n.d.). *The economic aspect*. Retrieved October 11, 2018, from http://dooy.info/economic.html

Capone, R., Bilali, H. E., Debs, P., Cardone, G., & Driouech, N. (2014). Food System Sustainability and Food Security: Connecting the Dots. *Journal of Food Security*, *2*(1), 13–22. doi:10.12691/jfs-2-1-2

Cardeli, L. (2017). *Loren Cardeli: "Agriculture got us here, and agriculture can also save us."* Retrieved from https://foodtank.com/news/2017/09/loren-cardeli-summit-interview/

Chang, H.-J. (2008). *Bad Samaritans: The Guilty Secrets of Rich Nations and the Threat to Global Prosperity*. London: Random House.

CIAT. (2017, June). *CIAT Strategic Initiative on Sustainable Food Systems.* International Center for Tropical Agriculture (CIAT). Retrieved from https://cgspace.cgiar.org/bitstream/handle/10568/79795/SUSTAINABLE_FOOD_SYSTEMS_CIAT_STRATEGY_DOCUMENT.pdf

Clapp, J. (2014). Financialization, distance and global food politics. *The Journal of Peasant Studies*, *41*(5), 797–814. doi:10.1080/03066150.2013.875536

Cochrane, W. (1979). *The Development of American Agriculture: A Historical Analysis*. Minneapolis, MN: University of Minnesota Press.

de Rooij, S. J. G., de Lauwere, C. C., & van der Ploeg, J. D. (2010). Entrapped in Group Solidarity? Animal Welfare, the Ethical Positions of Farmers and the Difficult Search for Alternatives. *Journal of Environmental Policy and Planning*, *12*(4), 341–361. doi:10.1080/1523908X.2010.528882

De Schutter, O. (2014). *Final report: The transformative potential of the right to food. Report of the Special Rapporteur on the right to food, Olivier De Schutter (No. A/HRC/25/57)*. United Nations General Assembly.

De Vries, G., De Hoog, J., & Dijstelbloem, H. (2016). *Towards a Food Policy* (WRR report No. 93). The Hague: The Netherlands Scientific Council for Government Policy (WRR). Retrieved from https://english.wrr.nl/publications/reports/2016/12/13/towards-a-food-policy

Dooyeweerd, H. (1984). A New Critique of Theoretical Thought. The General Theory of the Modal Spheres (3rd ed.; Vol. 2). Jordan Station, Ontario: Paideia Press Ltd.

EcoNexus. (2013). *AGROPOLY - A handful of corporations control world food production*. Berne Declaration (DB) & EcoNexus. Retrieved from http://www.econexus.info/publication/agropoly-handful-corporations-control-world-food-production

FAO. (2017). The future of food and agriculture - Trends and challenges. Rome: FAO (Food and Agriculture Organization of the United Nations).

Fox, T., & Vorley, B. (2006). Small Producers: Constraints and Challenges in the Global Food System. In S. Barrientos & C. Dolan (Eds.), *Ethical Sourcing in the Global Food System* (pp. 163–177). London: Earthscan. Retrieved from http://eureka.sbs.ox.ac.uk/1343/

Godfray, H. C. J., Beddington, J. R., Crute, I. R., Haddad, L., Lawrence, D., Muir, J. F., ... Toulmin, C. (2010). Food Security: The Challenge of Feeding 9 Billion People. *Science*, *327*(5967), 812–818. doi:10.1126cience.1185383 PMID:20110467

Godfray, H. C. J., Crute, I. R., Haddad, L., Lawrence, D., Muir, J. F., Nisbett, N., ... Whiteley, R. (2010). The future of the global food system. *Philosophical Transactions of the Royal Society of London. Series B, Biological Sciences*, *365*(1554), 2769–2777. doi:10.1098/rstb.2010.0180 PMID:20713383

Goudzwaard, B., VanderVennen, M., & VanHeemst, D. (2007). *Hope in troubled times. A new vision for confronting global crises*. Grand Rapids, MI: Baker Academics.

Goudzwaard, B., & Verweij, M. (2001). Kleine autonomie van het ontwikkelingsbegrip. In G. J. Buijs (Ed.), *Als de olifanten vechten... Denken over ontwikkelingssamenwerking vanuit christelijk perspectief* (pp. 138–154). Amsterdam: Buijten & Schipperheijn.

Gray, A. (2016, December 7). *Which countries spend the most on food? This map will show you.* Retrieved October 26, 2018, from https://www.weforum.org/agenda/2016/12/this-map-shows-how-much-each-country-spends-on-food/

Hardeman, E., & Jochemsen, H. (2012). Are There Ideological Aspects to the Modernization of Agriculture? *Journal of Agricultural & Environmental Ethics*, *25*(5), 657–674. doi:10.100710806-011-9331-5

Heschel, A. J. (1965). *Who is Man?* Stanford, CA: Stanford University Press.

Hoksbergen, R. (1986). Approaches to evaluation of development interventions: The importance of world and life views. *World Development*, *14*(2), 283–300. doi:10.1016/0305-750X(86)90060-4

Holt-Giménez, E., & Shattuck, A. (2011). Food crises, food regimes and food movements: Rumblings of reform or tides of transformation? *The Journal of Peasant Studies*, *38*(1), 109–144. doi:10.1080/03066150.2010.538578 PMID:21284237

Howard, P. H. (2016). *Concentration and Power in the Food System: Who Controls What We Eat?* London: Bloomsbury Publishing.

Ingram, J. (2011). A food systems approach to researching food security and its interactions with global environmental change. *Food Security*, *3*(4), 417–431. doi:10.100712571-011-0149-9

Jochemsen, H. (2006a). Normative practices as an intermediate between theoretical ethics and morality. *Philosophia Reformata*, *71*(1), 96–112. doi:10.1163/22116117-90000377

Jochemsen, H. (2006b). Voedselethiek vraagt om landbouwethiek. *DenkWijzer. Studieblad van Het Wetenschappelijk Instituut En de Bestuurdersvereniging van de ChristenUnie. Thema Voedsel.*, *6*(3), 8–11.

Jochemsen, H. (2012). Towards sustainable food production: a normative analysis of agrarian practice. In L. Botes, R. Jongeneel, & S. Strijbos (Eds.), *Reintregrating technology and economy in human life and society* (pp. 121–136). Bloemfontein: IIDE/Rozenberg.

LEO. (2015). *A Framework for a Push/Pull Approach: To Inclusive Market Systems Development*. Washington, DC: United States Agency for International Development (USAID). Retrieved from https://www.marketlinks.org/library/framework-pushpull-approach-inclusive-market-systems-development

Long, N., & Van der Ploeg, J. D. (1989). Demythologizing Planned Intervention: An Actor Perspective. *Sociologia Ruralis*, *29*(3–4), 226–249. doi:10.1111/j.1467-9523.1989.tb00368.x

McMichael, P. (2009). A food regime analysis of the 'world food crisis.'. *Agriculture and Human Values*, *26*(4), 281–295. doi:10.100710460-009-9218-5

Minten, B., Randrianarison, L., & Swinnen, J. F. M. (2009). Global Retail Chains and Poor Farmers: Evidence from Madagascar. *World Development*, *37*(11), 1728–1741. doi:10.1016/j.worlddev.2008.08.024

Mottet, A., de Haan, C., Falcucci, A., Tempio, G., Opio, C., & Gerber, P. (2017). Livestock: On our plates or eating at our table? A new analysis of the feed/food debate. *Global Food Security-Agriculture Policy Economics and Environment*, *14*, 1–8. doi:10.1016/j.gfs.2017.01.001

Peralta, A. (2017). *Food and Finance. Toward Life-Enhancing Agriculture*. Geneva: World Council of Churches Publications.

Plumecocq, G., Debril, T., Duru, M., Magrini, M.-B., Sarthou, J. P., & Therond, O. (2018). The plurality of values in sustainable agriculture models: Diverse lock-in and coevolution patterns. *Ecology and Society*, *23*(1), art21. doi:10.5751/ES-09881-230121

Rademaker, C. J., Glas, G., & Jochemsen, H. (2017). Sustainable livestock farming as normative practice. *Philosophia Reformata*, *82*(2), 216–240. doi:10.1163/23528230-08202002

Rademaker, C. J., & van den Hee, J. (2018). Agribusiness development within the bounds of life-enhancing food systems. In H. Jochemsen (Ed.), *For the twig to blossom... Cooperation in development from a Christian perspective* (Vol. 5, pp. 209–230). Maastricht: Shaker Publishing.

Rockström, J., Williams, J., Daily, G., Noble, A., Matthews, N., Gordon, L., ... Smith, J. (2017). Sustainable intensification of agriculture for human prosperity and global sustainability. *Ambio*, *46*(1), 4–17. doi:10.100713280-016-0793-6 PMID:27405653

Röling, N. (2016). Innovation Systems, Douglas, Douglass and Beyond: Using Cultural Theory to understand Approaches to Smallholder Development in Sub-Saharan Africa. In J. Francis, L. Mytelka, A. van Huis, & N. Röling (Eds.), *Innovation systems: Towards effective strategies in support of smallholder farmers* (pp. 202–238). CTA and Wageningen University and Research Centre. Retrieved from https://cgspace.cgiar.org/handle/10568/79166

Schuurman, E. (2003). *Faith and Hope in Technology*. Toronto: Clements Publishing.

Scott, J. C. (1998). *Seeing Like a State: How Certain Schemes to Improve the Human Condition Have Failed*. New Haven, CT: Yale University Press.

Sodano, V. (2012). Food Policy Beyond Neo-Liberalism. In D. Erasga (Ed.), *Sociological Landscape: Theories, Realities and Trends* (pp. 375–402). InTech. doi:10.5772/37175

Sukhdev, P., May, P., & Müller, A. (2016). Fix food metrics. *NATNews*, *540*(7631), 33. doi:10.1038/540033a PMID:27905460

TEEB. (2018). *The Econonomics of Ecosystems and Biodiversity (TEEB) for Agriculture & Food. Scientific and Economic Foundations Report*. Geneva: UN Environment. Retrieved from http://teebweb.org/agrifood/scientific-and-economic-foundations-report/

Thompson, P. B. (2015). *From Field to Fork: Food Ethics for Everyone*. Oxford, UK: Oxford University Press. doi:10.1093/acprof:oso/9780199391684.001.0001

van de Lagemaat, D. (1986). *Onderwijzen in ondernemen. Een studie betreffende de didactische voorwaarden en uitwerking van de beginselen van de structuurleer en het exemplarisch leren in relatie tot het middelbaar agrarisch onderwijs* (PhD thesis). Landbouwhogeschool Wageningen, Wageningen.

Vanlauwe, B., & Giller, K. E. (2006). Popular myths around soil fertility management in sub-Saharan Africa. *Agriculture, Ecosystems & Environment*, *116*(1), 34–46. doi:10.1016/j.agee.2006.03.016

Varinsky, D. (2018, May 29). *The $66 billion Bayer-Monsanto merger just got a major green light—but farmers are terrified*. Retrieved October 26, 2018, from http://www.businessinsider.com/bayer-monsanto-merger-has-farmers-worried-2018-4

Verkerk, M. J., Hoogland, J., van der Stoep, J., & de Vries, M. J. (2015). *Philosophy of Technology: An Introduction for Technology and Business Students*. Abingdon, UK: Routledge. doi:10.4324/9781315696362

Verkerk, M. J., & Zijlstra, A. (2003). Philosophical analysis of industrial organisations. *Philosophia Reformata*, *68*(2), 101–122. doi:10.1163/22116117-90000286

Visser, J. (2010). *Down to earth. A historical-sociological analysis of the rise and fall of "industrial" agriculture and of the prospects for the re-rooting of agriculture from the factory to the local farmer and ecology*. Wageningen: Wageningen University. Retrieved from http://edepot.wur.nl/135447

WFP. (2018). *Zero Hunger*. Retrieved October 26, 2018, from http://www1.wfp.org/zero-hunger

WHO. (2018, February 16). *Obesity and overweight*. Retrieved October 26, 2018, from http://www.who.int/news-room/fact-sheets/detail/obesity-and-overweight

World Bank. (2007). *World Development Report 2008: Agriculture for Development*. Washington, DC: The World Bank.

ENDNOTES

1 AGC is a nonprofit that works to uphold farmer autonomy and stimulate agro-ecological innovation by supporting farmers' capacity for change, see http://www.agrowingculture.org/#.

2 Commodification is the transformation of goods and services, as well as ideas or other entities that normally may not be considered goods, into a commodity, i.e. something that is assigned just economic value (Wikipedia).

3 Overweight: BMI >25; obese: BMI>30.

4 Agricultural extension or agricultural advisory services are provided by governments, NGOs – including universities – and private actors. It aims at providing farmers with scientific knowledge, insights and experiences so as to improve agriculture, often in terms of productivity but also in terms of sustainability.

5 In more specific philosophical language of Dooyeweerdian philosophy we could say that the primary practice of careful dealings with soil, plants (and animals) is enkaptically intertwined in farming as an economically qualified practice.

6 Appreciation is one pole in Heschel's distinction between two fundamental ways people relate to reality, manipulation being the other pole (Heschel, 1965; cf. Jochemsen, 2012). In 'appreciation' the individual views his surroundings as things to accept, to comprehend, to appreciate or to admire. In the attitude of manipulation, the individual views his surroundings as things to handle, to

control, and to utilize. These two ways are ideal-typically formulated; in real life they do not fully exclude one another.

7 This insight was still prevalent in the beginning of the scientific revolution and found a succinct expression in Francis Bacon's saying: 'Nature to be commanded, must be obeyed'; https://www.brainyquote.com/quotes/francis_bacon_151989.

8 This section extensively uses Rademaker and Van den Hee (2018).

Chapter 8
A Normative Practice Approach to Health Care

Gerrit Glas
Vrije Universiteit, The Netherlands

ABSTRACT

This chapter explains how and why healthcare might profit from a normative practice approach (NPA). This approach sketches a conceptual and normative framework that helps to locate and identify relevant points of view for clinical practice as well as for policy making in healthcare. The chapter starts in medias res: in the consulting room, in the encounter between clinician and patient. What kinds of relations are relevant for the understanding of what is going in the patient who feels ill and between the patient and the doctor (or nurse)? Are there normative principles and values which guide these relationships? The focus then broadens to the meso- and macro-contexts of current medicine and healthcare. The NPA will be re-introduced. Its relevance is shown for topics like the increase in the administrative burden in medicine, the role of expert knowledge, the hospital and its purposes, and the changing focus of medicine given the rapid changes in the macro-sphere. The chapter ends by saying that the NPA may help in different ways: by taking it as a point of reference; by relating the different normative dimensions to core responsibilities of doctors, other employees, and stakeholders beside medical professionals; and by relating these core responsibilities to the relevant contexts in which these doctors, other employees, and stakeholders are working.

DOI: 10.4018/978-1-5225-8006-5.ch008

INTRODUCTION

This chapter highlights and investigates the fundamental potential and the practical use of the Normative Practice Approach (NPA) in healthcare.[1] The NPA offers a conceptual and normative framework that helps to locate and identify relevant points of view for clinical practice as well as for policy making in healthcare. The chapter starts in the consulting room, in the encounter between clinician and patient. What kinds of relations are relevant for the understanding of what is going in the patient who feels ill and between the patient and the doctor (or: nurse)? Are there normative principles and values which guide these relationships? The NPA will be re-introduced. Its relevance is shown for topics like the increase in the administrative burden in medicine, the role of expert knowledge, the function of the hospital, and the changing focus of medicine given the rapid changes in the macro-sphere. The focus then broadens to the meso- and macro-contexts of current medicine and healthcare. The chapter ends by saying that the NPA may help in different ways: by taking it as a point of reference; by relating the different normative dimensions to core responsibilities of doctors, other employees and stakeholders beside medical professionals; and by relating these core responsibilities to the relevant contexts in which these doctors, other employees and stakeholders are working.

NORMATIVE DIMENSIONS OF CLINICAL PRACTICE

The argument will be built-up bottom-up, from clinical practice up to the normative practice approach as general heuristic framework. I will make use of Figures to emphasize the complexity and value-ladenness of the relationships that evolve during the clinical encounter.

The Patient Is More Than Her Illness

Let us start in clinical practice, with patients and doctors (nurses, other healthcare professionals) who are consulted by their patient. The patient has a problem, looks for help, and visits the professional. Figure 1 is a depiction of this initial situation. The professional listens to the story of patient, asks certain questions, performs a physical and/or mental examination, does some testing (blood, X-ray, other diagnostic procedures), comes to a conclusion and shares this conclusion with the patient. All these activities are indicated with arrow 1 in the Figure. Professionals pay attention to more than the illness alone, however. This is indicated by the other arrows. Professionals focus on how patients deal with their illness (Beck et al, 2005), but also on how contextual factors influence the manifestations and the course of

Figure 1.

In his/er professional role, the professional pays attention to different aspects of being-ill [1-5]

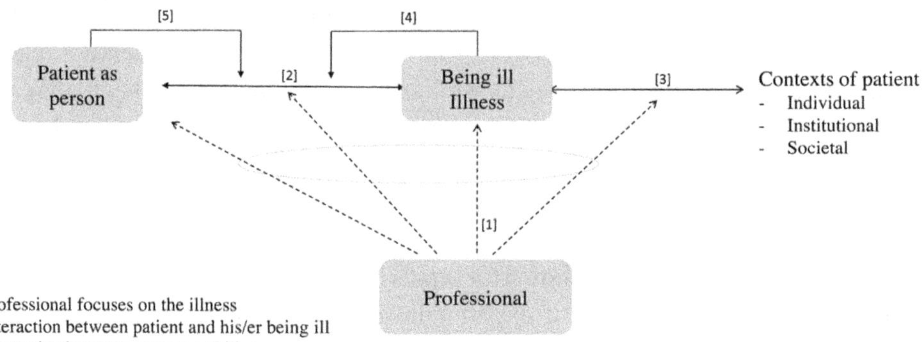

1. Professional focuses on the illness
2. Interaction between patient and his/er being ill
3. Interaction between context and illness
4. Influence of being ill on the way the patient deals with his/er illness
5. Influence of the person on the way the patient deals with his/er illness

the illness (Castellani et al, 2006), on the impact of the illness on how the patient relates to the illness (Frank et al, 1996), and on the role of the patient's personality in relating to the illness (Frank et al, 2005).

I deliberately use the term "illness" (and not "disorder" or "disease") to indicate that the professional focuses at clinical manifestations of disease and not so much on the scientific concepts of disorder that are supposed to exist 'behind' the surface. "Being ill" expresses that the clinical encounter starts with patient's experiences, i.e., with their reports about their symptoms and signs. Disorders do not exist on their own; they are also products of interactions with personal and contextual influences.

All five relationships are norm-responsive and express certain values. This norm-responsivity expresses itself in the way these relationships are shaped and evolve. The norm-responsiveness of relation (Beck et al, 2005) comes to expression when doctors show that it is their aim to gather knowledge, not as an end in itself, but for the benefit of the patient. This benefit can be spelled out in various ways, for instance, as respect for the patient's autonomy, as searching for beneficence, as attention for what the illness means for the patient, and as an attitude that is characterize by honesty and trustworthiness. Relation (Bloom et al, 2008) refers to the way the patient relates to the condition of 'being ill'. The patient may show a responsible, insightful, and/ or courageous stance toward the illness, but she may also neglect what is going on and disregard alarming symptoms. Responsibility, insight, courage and disregard are valued-laden terms that refer to certain standards of proper behavior. It is important to recognize the role of expectations, ideals, and views on life in this context. The patient interprets what is going on and tries to cope with the illness. This occurs against the background of the patient's expectations, ideals, and view on life, which express what the patient finds important in life. These expectations may conflict with those of the clinician. The clinician may, for instance, be inclined to focus on objective forms of dysfunction like diminishing the severity of symptoms or use of medical services, or on possible risk factors, such as poor hygiene, whereas the patient may put emphasis on symptoms with a large impact on self-image and daily functioning. This impact is usually described in terms which refer to what people deem important and consider as valuable. Defining the problem is at the heart of clinical practice and it is highly value laden and often not conflict-free.

Implicit or explicit expectations, ideals and norms are also important in relationship (Castelani et al, 2006). The term context refers to the patient's micro-, meso-, and macro context, i.e., to people (partner, children, family) or circumstances (housing, job) that are important in one's daily environment (micro); to local and regional circumstances, for instance circumstances relevant for delivery of care or the functioning of healthcare related institutions (meso); and to influences at the level of society as whole, for instance, influences related to the role of the government, of insurance companies, and of global financial and social conditions; but also societal issues like safety, social mobility, stigmatization, tolerance, and social cohesion. All these factors and influences are manifestations of underlying values. Social exclusion implies that the lives of certain persons are treated as if they are less valuable and deserve less protection than the lives of 'normal' persons.

Relation (Frank et al, 1996) refers, as we saw, to the impact of the illness on how the patient is dealing with the illness. The very fact of being ill may affect one's value system: what seemed to important, turns out to be of only modest importance; whereas circumstances and interactions that seemed to be self-evident and normal suddenly appear to be crucial for one's well-being and self-esteem. The impact of the illness on one's sense of self implicitly refers to a whole range of values, ideals, and expectations.

Relation (Frank et al, 2005) represents the influence of person-bound factors on the way the illness is dealt with. It is easiest to think here of the personality of the patient (temperament, character). But personal values are important too, like the client's general outlook on life and broader concerns which have roots in the client's biography.

All these different elements together form the patient's story about his or her condition, the illness narrative.

The Professional Is More Than a Bundle of Skills

Figure 2 provides an expanded version of the Figure that we discussed earlier. Its main function is to show that – like patients relate to their illness – professionals

Figure 2.

In his/er professional role the professional relates in different ways to his/er own professional role fulfilment [A-E]

too relate to their professional role in a given context. Being a professional is more than possessing a set of skills.

Relationship [A] concerns the professional role with the spectrum of issues the clinician pays attention to, i.e., issues related to relations A – E (Beck et al, 2005; Bloom et al, 2008; Castellani et al, 2006; Frank et al 1996; Frank et al, 2005).

The previous section highlighted several normative elements in this relationship.

Interaction [B] concerns the relationship between professionals as persons and their professional role. How do professionals as persons relate to their own role fulfilment? Are they capable of monitoring their own behavior? Can they reflect on their role fulfilment? The answer on these questions reveals that there are standards for professionalism

Relation [C] focuses on the interaction between professional behavior and all sorts of contextual influences. Today, these influences are so dominant that they affect and, some would say, threaten professional identity. The institutional settings of medical care have significantly changed in the last twenty years, and the administrative burden has sharply increased in most Western European countries and in North America. The economic context in which professional practices function puts its stamp not only on the agenda of professional organizations but also on how individual professionals organize their practices. Relation [C] invites us to think about the balance between economic, social, moral, and existential values in the encounter with the patient. Should economic value prevail over other values; or should the moral aim of medicine always be put at the center stage? And if so, in which contexts?

At first glance, the meaning of relation [D] may be unclear. This relation is nevertheless important, relevant, and easily recognizable. I am thinking of the young physician, who has recently begun her residency training and, after having been on call the entire night with a succession of problems that were difficult to handle, asks herself: "Is this what I want to do for the rest of my life?" Much of the emotional energy of being in training as a professional must be put into the process of becoming acquainted with one's role. Later in their career, professionals may feel that their self-professional image no longer fits with what their healthcare organization, professional association, or patients require them to do. Professionals may in other words outgrow their roles. Here again, there is a balance between competing values: the value of remaining authentic versus the value of complying with the 'system', the value of doing good to one's patient versus the value of doing well by distributing one's energy and attention such that those with the largest needs profit most.

Relation [E], finally, focuses on the professional as person, on who one is as a professional and who one was and wishes to be. One's learning history is of course of great importance for the development of professional identity. It is the basis on which one's current role fulfilling is built and given shape. Personal values are an important source for the development of one's professional identity.

All these different relationships are highly value-laden and norm-responsive. They depend on views, images, expectations, norms, ambitions, and views professionals, professional organizations, and other stakeholders have with respect to the role the professional needs to play in a certain context. Figure 2 shows that this role depends on a network of relations in which it is embedded. This network ideally helps to constitute, define and support the dual foundation of professionalism, i.e., the presence of *expert skills/knowledge* and the *social contract* that forms the basis for the legitimation of what doctors, nurses and other healthcare workers do. Being a professional consists of a unique combination of roles, excellence, and commitment, which includes personal dedication to the welfare of others, mastery at a high level of certain skills and knowledge, sensitivity to the art of medicine, and a wide range of other commitments. The jurisdictions for the use of these skills and knowledge are defined by the social contract between professionals, the government, insurance companies, and other societal agents. This contract defines the conditions under which the expert role can be executed.

Interestingly, the norm-responsiveness and value-ladenness of the expert role and its underlying basis in the social contract have been recognized in the recent reform of medical specialist's training programs in Canada (and later also other parts of the world). The Canadian Medical Educational Directives for Medical Specialists (or: CanMEDS) describe a framework for competency-based medical specialist's training.[2] These directives mention professionalism as one of the seven core competencies of any physician (Frank et al. 1996). Professionalism is the ability to deal professionally with one's role as a medical specialist. This includes having insight into one's own role, awareness of and ability to deal with role conflicts, and maintenance of professional and ethical boundaries with respect to value-sensitive matters, privacy, and informed consent. Traditional medical virtues return in this conceptualization of professionalism: honesty, altruism, compassion, integrity, trustworthiness, beneficence, accountability, and humanism (Gabbard, Roberts, Crisp-Han et al. 2012). Frank (2005), one of the leading voices in the CanMEDS movements, writes about professionalism:

Physicians have a unique societal role as professionals who are dedicated to the health and caring of others. Their work requires the mastery of a complex body of knowledge and skills, as well as the art of medicine. As such, the Professional Role is guided by codes of ethics and a commitment to clinical competence, the embracing of appropriate attitudes and behaviors, integrity, altruism, personal well-being, and to the promotion of the public good within their domain. These commitments form the basis of a social contract between a physician and society. Society, in return, grants physicians the privilege of profession-led regulation with the understanding that they are accountable to those served. (Frank 2005, p.23)

Note that in the quotation, these commitments are positioned as the basis for and not as the outcome of the social contract. It is not unusual to see the social contract described as legitimizing the exertion of certain skills and to see commitments narrowed down to the duty to keep the contract (i.e., to use these skills appropriately). The CanMEDS framework recognizes a broader embedding of responsibilities and commitments within the professional's role. This is, of course, in line with the Hippocratic oath which requires a similar dedication upon entering the medical profession.

A NORMATIVE PRACTICE APPROACH TO MEDICAL CARE

What emerges from the above is the bewildering number of values, norms, and value-laden ideas that play a role in modern healthcare. There is need for some order in this variety. We believe the normative practice approach (NPA) may offer a framework to identify and locate the various normative dimensions. Let me briefly repeat the core features of this approach as they were sketched in chapter 1 (see also Figure 3).

The NPA offers in the first place a heuristic normative framework, not a blueprint. A distinction was made between *constitutive* norms/rules and *regulative* ideas. Constitutive are those aspects of a professional practice without which there would be such a thing as that practice. Constitutive norms and principles, therefore, define a profession as the practice it is. Regulative ideas indicate the directedness, the overarching purpose and ideal realization of a practice. This directedness and purposiveness is embodied in the motivation, dedication and ethos of practitioners.

We discerned three types of constitutive norms and rules: qualifying norms, conditioning (enabling) norms, and foundational norms and rules. *Qualifying* norms determine the ultimate aims of a practice. Beneficence (doing well to one's patients) is one of these aims. *Conditioning* norms shape the conditions that should be met so that a certain practice may flourish. Social, economic, and legal rules belong to this conditioning and enabling aspect of a professional practice. *Foundational* rules and principles form the basis of a practice. Without them there would not be such a practice. Scientific and technological standards belong to the foundational side of medicine.

The *regulative* ideal or purpose of a practice is in other words not some distant or abstract goal that stands apart from that practice. It is, instead, the perfect realization (or excellence) of that practice. The regulative dimension of a normative practice embodies the attitudes, motivations, and ideals in virtue of which the practice becomes the practice it is meant to be. In other words, the purposiveness of a practice become manifest in the practice itself, as a fundamental motivation, commitment, or ultimate concern that helps professionals and other stakeholders fulfil their proper roles. The term will be used as overarching term for these motivations, commitments and concerns.

The regulative side of practices refers to their dynamic, to the way they evolve over time, to their tendency to integrate or disintegrate, to develop into one direction or into another, to flourish or to fall into decay. Ethos comes close to what the Greeks meant by character and virtue. It is the spirit that motivates the fundamental attitudes, ideas, and values of a practice. Dooyeweerd used the term "ground-motive" for this

Figure 3. Medicine as normative practice

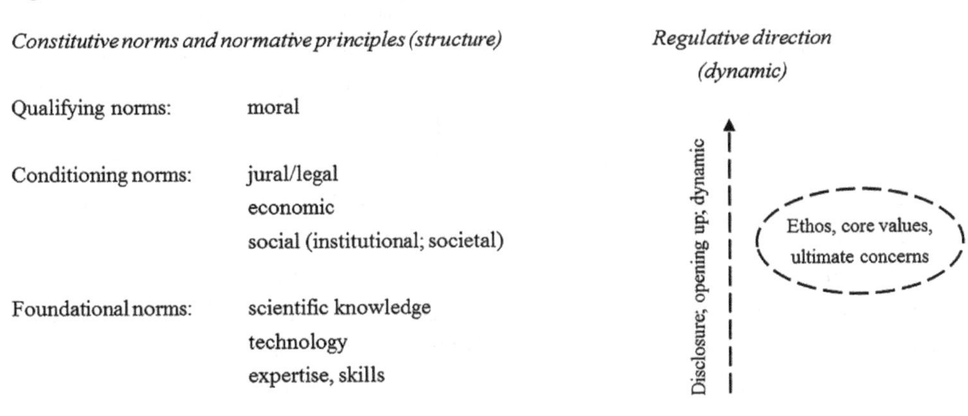

spirit. Ground-motives refer to the regulative dimension at the level of cultures: deep motivating forces in cultures, forces that partially operate behind one's back.

In chapter 1 it was already indicated that the schematic presentation in Figure 3 might be interpreted as suggesting a separation between the two sides of a practice. In reality, however, the two are completely interwoven. The constitutive side is opened up under the guidance of regulative notions (ideas and overarching values), whereas the regulative side can only be brought to life by the constitutive role of certain norms and principle in the formation of a practice. In chapter 1, the terms structure and direction were introduced to simplify the nomenclature somewhat. Structure refers to the constitutive side of a practice, whereas direction refers to the regulative side. Practices evolve over time and develop into a direction that corresponds with or deviates from their (supposed) inner destination. Practices may flourish or fall into decay. Their directedness may be conceived of as a kind of dynamic that pervades the historical development of a practice. This dynamic is more fundamental and precedes every form of objectifying or concrete purposeful action. It is the spirit or ethos or ultimate aim that pervades a practice and gives perspective, meaning, and value to it.

In chapter 1 we gave already a brief example of how the NPA can be put to use in the discussion about the role of professionalism. What was said there holds for medicine in every respect. In medicine there is a crisis in professionalism too. Doctors and nurses are burdened by managerialism, i.e., by the urge to bring their practices under control, not only economically, but also in terms of efficiency, accountability, and transparency. Our brief historical analysis in chapter 1 indicated that lack of professional self-regulation and uncontrollable economic and technological growth formed the basis of this managerialism. The managerialism was in other words interpreted as the societal response to distrust of the public about whether professionals really put all their efforts into the service of others instead of into its own interests. However, we also concluded that overemphasis on bureaucratic control ultimately leads to diminishment of control. In medicine the massive increase of control—administrative, economic, and in terms of accountability, safety, and access —has paradoxically led to an increase in discomfort and distrust, both in (service) users, who are confronted with an increasingly complex system of care/education, and in professionals, who feel more and more alienated from their proper role.

With the help of the NPA, we understood these tensions as the product of a role reversal between conditioning and qualifying norms. The conditioning, economic norm of efficiency is dealt with as if it were a qualifying norm. This role reversal leads to a different definition of professionalism. In healthcare systems in which efficiency norms prevail above other values, a good doctor is an efficient doctor, not primarily a caring doctor. Efficiency, instead of beneficence, becomes the overarching and qualifying norm for a sound and sustainable practice. Advocates of efficiency in medicine claim that there need be no contradiction between efficiency and caring for suffering people. They argue that these aims are complementary. But that is not the issue. The issue is the the specific role the economic norm of efficiency fulfils .... etc. [in the hierarchy of values of medical practice. Efficiency is no longer an auxiliary quality, together with the other necessary conditions. It becomes the most defining (or qualifying) characteristic of good practice. This distorted view on the structure of medical practice erodes the ethos of medical professionalism (Tallis 2004).

Distortions at the structural sides of a profession will ultimately lead to antinomies at the regulative side, i.e., in the 'direction' of that practice. The opposite may occur too: tensions at the regulative side may lead to antinomies at the structural side. The unbounded urge for technocratic control (regulative side; direction; ethos; ground motive) may lead to one-sided emphasis on science, technology, and professional specialization as prerequisites for professionalism (structure). This urge may subsequently jeopardize norms that qualify medical practice, especially the norm of beneficence. What is possible in a technological sense does not (always) coincide with what is good for users or groups of people that are the target of professional efforts. On the other hand, the spirit of managerial control (dynamic, regulative side) that pervades contemporary medicine has an alienating effect on service users and professionals. The system is put central, instead of the professional caring relationship – with effects readers will be familiar with: service users who feel not understood; professionals who complain of being alienated from their core concerns; departments and institutions which, instead of focusing on patient value, steer on competitiveness and market share.

In the next section we will investigate more deeply some of these tensions and ambiguities. This will be done by focusing on the role of the context for the way practices unfold. The role of contexts was already briefly alluded to in Chapter 1. There, it was said, that it is in the interplay between contexts and practices that certain aspects of a practice become more important than others. The next section will explain this with respect to healthcare.

CONTEXTS AND THE DISTINCTION BETWEEN LEVELS AND KINDS

Professionalism evolves today in an increasingly complex societal context, with many partners, different mandates and jurisdictions, and varying responsibilities. In view of this increasing complexity, it is helpful to distinguish between levels and kinds of contexts. The term *levels* refers to micro-, meso-, and macro-levels of interaction. Individual professional encounters are obviously located at the micro-level of interaction. Institutional factors belong typically, but not exclusively, to the meso-level of interaction. Legal changes and other governmental actions take place at the macro-level. The term *kind*, in kinds of contexts, refers to economic, legal, institutional, and administrative forms of interaction and to the distinct responsibilities of actors in these contexts.

It will come as no surprise that today's professionalism is characterized by a much larger impact of meso- and macro-level factors than previous professional arrangements. Rather than discussing a list of all possible contextual factors, I refer to the tentative overview of Table 1. This Figure gives an impression of which kind of stakeholders are aimed at at the meso- and macro-level of historical development of the professions. What the Figure also shows is that the kinds of contextual factors can be connected with distinct responsibilities of the stakeholders.

Let us illustrate the complexity of meso- and macro-level factors with the role of administrative factors within the professions. The new forms of administrative control serve at least three goals: financial control, pursuit of safety, and warrants with respect to the quality of professional services. Note how these different factors refer to different stakeholders in the delivery of these services and how they aim at excellence and sustainability. Financial control refers to the role of the government in maintaining the legal and economic framework for the provision of certain services. It also refers to the role of (insurance) companies, charity funds, and the industry in the financing of the system. Similarly, safety is not only a micro-level social issue but also typically an institutional (meso-level) and public (macro-level) concern. It refers to the role of internal rules within professional facilities as well as to the role of all kinds of supervisory bodies. Quality criteria, finally, are increasingly defined in terms that transcend the individual professional – client relationship. The accessibility of certain facilities is one of the important items in quality assessments. Efficiency and accountability are two other important issues. The supervision and control of these different elements takes place predominantly at the meso- and macro-levels of interaction between stakeholders.

Counterproductive as most of these administrative requirements seem to be for many individual professionals, they seem to be more or less inevitable from a broader perspective. It is at this point that two macro-level developments intersect, namely, the profession's attempt to regain trust, on the one hand, and the need to put an end to the spiraling costs of certain services (health care; education), on the other hand. Both developments reinforce each other in the sense that both lead to an increase of the administrative burden.

The weakening of trust in the professions can at least partially be attributed to individual scandals and improper behavior of individual members of the profession. Professions did no longer succeed in keeping up the image of impeccability and of the unconditional desire to put the client's interests above self-interest. As a result, the prestige of professions has diminished. To regain trust, professions, especially in the health care sector, need to accept additional forms of regulation beyond their own self-regulation. Examples of such new regulations can be found in the sphere of safety (prevention of harm), transparency (standardization, protocolization, digitalization, registration), efficiency (registering of the activities of professionals and matching of these activities with certain protocols), and efficacy (outcome monitoring, measuring of client satisfaction). Despite intentions of governments and other stakeholders to deregulate the professionalism, the new rules have laid the basis for a new bureaucracy.

In medicine, this bureaucracy has in turn strongly increased as a result of changes in the financing of the system. These changes are simultaneous with the increase of bureaucratic control. Rising costs put the system under pressure. In many countries, market incentives have been allowed for the purpose of stimulating efficiency and efficacy. Markets, however, do not instill trust: in fact, they tend to have an eroding effect on trust, especially in non-profitable segments of the market (Polder, Hoogland,

Table 1.

<table>
<tr><th>Level of Influence</th><th>Kind of Influence</th><th colspan="2">Examples</th></tr>
<tr><td rowspan="4">Meso</td><td>Economic</td><td colspan="2">Insurance companies (local arrangements)
Local and regional funding agencies
Local government (communities, provinces, regions)</td></tr>
<tr><td>Legal</td><td colspan="2">Regional regulations</td></tr>
<tr><td>Institutional/social</td><td colspan="2">Hospitals/clinics
Outpatient facilities
Practices</td></tr>
<tr><td>Administrative</td><td colspan="2">Management of institutions
Managerial rules and regulations</td></tr>
<tr><td rowspan="6">Macro</td><td>Economic</td><td colspan="2">National government
Insurance companies (nation-wide arrangements)
National funding agencies
Industry and other third parties</td></tr>
<tr><td>Legal</td><td colspan="2">Laws and regulations with respect to
• financing of the health care system
• jurisdictions of professions</td></tr>
<tr><td>Institutional</td><td colspan="2">Government
Professional organizations
Service user groups</td></tr>
<tr><td rowspan="3">Administrative</td><td>Internal professional</td><td>Certification and accreditation Quality control</td></tr>
<tr><td>Semi-governmental</td><td>Registration of demographic and public health-related variables Different forms of quality control</td></tr>
<tr><td>Governmental</td><td>Authorities for the enforcement of legislation Health Care Inspectorate</td></tr>
</table>

and Jochemsen 1996). As mentioned earlier, these segments need additional safeguards against exploitation, misinformation, and insufficient care. Today, these additional safeguards are abundantly—and disturbingly—present; for instance, in the form of rules aimed at the improvement of accountability, transparency, and quality of care. Such rules came on top of the rules just mentioned, which aimed at the reliability and transparency of the physician's behavior. Because of the new rules, providers of professional services were obliged to monitor and report about the various elements of the new agreements.

The issue—increase of administrative burden—shows that there exists an underlying logic behind these developments. The Table helps us to understand how these various factors intersect. In terms of the NPA, the conditioning aspects play a decisive role in the recent reforms in professional behavior, both at the meso- and the macro-level. There is a lively interaction between the legal, economic, and social kinds of normativity, and between these three and professional practice as a larger societal good.

At this juncture, the question arises how trust with respect to doctors and nurses is related to the (societal and scientific) legitimacy of what they are doing. This will be the topic of the next two sections. I will focus on two issues. In the next section, I will return to the individual professional relationship and discuss the role of expert knowledge in discussions about the legitimacy of medicine. Then, in the following section, I will reflect on larger contexts and discuss the impact of differences in context on the definition of the object, purpose, and legitimacy of medicine.

THE ROLE OF EXPERT KNOWLEDGE

We have seen that the expert role is contested today. It is contested by strands within the service user movement. It is under pressure in commercialized sectors of the profession. And it is threatened by inter- and intra-disciplinary competition, loss of status, and fragmentation of the field of health care. Many of these developments are a byproduct of ongoing specialization and introduction of market incentives.

At a more fundamental level there are other issues influencing the very notion of expert knowledge and skills (Glas 2012). It has, for instance, been suggested that the fortunes of professionalism are part of a more general and subtle change in our relation to knowledge and expertise as such (see Beck and Young [2005], who refer to the work of sociologist Basil Bernstein), which consists in the fact that competence is no longer seen as "owned by" scholars and that professions are no longer conceived as embedded in scholarly contexts and traditions. Knowledge has been reduced to bits of information that are freely available to everyone, and skills are seen as more or less isolated abilities that can be appropriated where and when one wants and can be put to use deliberately. The relation between subject and knowledge and between practitioner and competence has become instrumentalist (or, functionalist). Knowledge and skills do not mean anything in themselves—they acquire meaning depending on their use. So, the best thing for a competence is to be *transferable*—i.e., effortlessly transferable from one context to another. Something similar goes for knowledge: it should be *generic*—i.e., general and suitable for use in as many contexts as possible. As a result, education and professionalism are no longer seen as embedded in practices with different styles, cultures, and implicit understandings of the world.

The ideology behind these suggestions and developments is questionable, however. There are at least two major drawbacks.

First, the instrumentalist approach to specialists' knowledge and skills is too abstract. It is simply not true that competences can be operationalized apart from contexts. The competence of communication, for instance, involves quite different abilities that largely depend on the context. Talking with a severely psychotic and violent patient at a police station requires other communicative skills than psychodynamic psychotherapy. And negotiating with a patient at a closed ward about the level of restraint required for reasons of safety appeals to different collaborative skills than negotiating about treatment options with a fully competent anxiety disorder patient. So, competences such as communication and collaboration refer to a wide variety of skills that are highly context-sensitive.

Secondly, the abstractness of the idea that skills can be separated from the persons who use them forms another drawback. The professional role is more than a set of loosely coupled skills. Professionals relate to their roles, and the manner in which professionals do this becomes part of their professional identity. Trainees need to grow into their future roles, and this growing requires that one is embedded in the relevant environments. These environments should, ideally, allow residents to discover their personal balance between who they are and who they are required to be in terms of knowledge, skills, and attitudes.

I readily admit that the relation of "postmodern" professionals to their knowledge and skills is changing. These changes are not new, or even "postmodern": they are, in fact, predictable on the basis of Weber's idea of an ongoing division of labor and of increasing interlacements between different spheres of life. However, these changes offer insufficient ground for a complete revision of the notion of professionalism, including a separation between the professional role, the context, and the professional as a person. The NPA suggests a different direction, to wit, a reinterpretation of *transferability* as "aiming at context-sensitivity." The increasing complexity of current mental health care, both contextually and qua expert role, should not be addressed with a decontextualized concept of competence, but with a notion of competence that is even more contextually sensitive than it used to be. Transferability should not imply isolation and decontextualization. Ideally, it is accompanied by an increased awareness of the responsibilities of the different stakeholders (medical, legal, social, and administrative) and of the interlacements between micro-, meso-, and macro-processes. This awareness is preferably guided by what one might call the principle of "simultaneous norm realization," or some version of it (Van der Kooy 1964; Goudzwaard 1982; see also chapter 2).

The dominant role of contexts in the shaping of knowledge and skills also influences the assessment of the role of expert knowledge in discussions about the legitimacy of professionalism. What is it in expert knowledge that justifies its special role? And to which extent does the legitimacy of professionalism depend on the expert role?

One obvious position on this issue is that the authority of the professional solely depends on the expert role and, more specifically, on its being based on science and evidence-based interventions. This is what one might call a *scientistic* defense of the legitimacy of medical professionalism. This position is ahistorical in the sense that it disregards the role of the social contract with its idea of a public mandate to serve some greater good in exchange for the relative independence of the profession. One-sided emphasis on the scientific foundation of professionalism, in other words, neglects the role of values (e.g., trustworthiness, honesty, altruism) in the very idea of being a medical professional. These values are not accidental, but they form the basis for the social contract that undergirds professional activities. Moreover, another major drawback of such one-sided emphasis on the expert role is paternalism. If science determines what the "real" problem (or the real disease) is, then it is the professional, as representative of science and guardian of truth, who knows what is the matter and, consequently, who knows what is best for the patient. As a reaction to such paternalism, another extreme has emerged; namely, a devaluation of the expert role.

Both the scientistic adumbration of the expert role and the rejection of it by critical patient movements are related to the same improper valuation of science's limitations and the same neglect of the distinctions between science, clinical practice, and worldview. The NPA helps to provide a proper place for science and technology in medical professionalism. The scientistic defense of the legitimacy of medicine (and psychiatry) expects too much from science; namely, that science is or will be able to eliminate every uncertainty in the consulting room. The critical view assumes that expert knowledge belongs to a system with oppressive and disempowering traits. Both views fail to appreciate sufficiently the inherent limitations in scientific approaches to medical problems—limitations that follow from the abstract mode of observing and thinking of the scientist. Scientists may speak with authority when they respect the limitations of their methods and say no more than can be justified on the basis of their proper use.

That said, doctors as well as patients will always have to deal with what Gorovitz and MacIntyre (1976) have called the "inherent and necessary fallibility" of medical knowledge. Even in the ideal case of having complete knowledge of all the relevant causes and mechanisms, doctors will never be able to predict with 100% certainty what will happen in an individual case. There are therefore already on epistemic grounds good reasons to argue for a basis for medicine's legitimacy that is broader than epistemic. Expert knowledge is important, even crucial—without it, there is no medical professionalism. That is what the NPA means when it attributes a foundational role to scientific knowledge and technology. But science and technology cannot be the only or the ultimate ground for what doctors do.

To summarize:

- Expert knowledge and skills deserve a special status because they are foundational for the practice of medicine.
- The expert role functions in a broader framework of normative relations.
- Contexts are part of this framework of normative relations; public responsibility of professionals (and of other stakeholders) is at the heart of professionalism.
- Knowledge is never "just knowledge" but always part of a practice—a practice of knowing (as in science) or construing (as in technology) or predicting (as in policy making and treatment). All these practices have, as we have seen, normative dimensions.

Expert knowledge itself cannot fully justify the authority of doctors nor undergird the legitimacy of what they are doing. Although expert knowledge is a sine qua non for medical professionalism, for the legitimation of the professional practice other norms are relevant, such as social, economic, and juridical norms. These norms refer to the broader context in which medicine as normative practice is executed. In terms of the NPA, doing justice to social, economic, and juridical (i.e., conditioning) norms is the proper way to let the professional role take shape against the background of the broader contexts discussed above. Ideally, these broader normative dimensions assure that the expert contributes to the patient's good—not only by opening up the clinician's understanding, but also by attuning professional insight to what is good for this particular patient in this particular set of contexts.

CONTEXTS AND THE DEFINITION OF RESPONSIBILITIES AND JURISDICTIONS

I will finish by making some remarks on the role of contexts in the definition of professional authority and jurisdiction. Do the roles and responsibilities of the professional and other actors in the field of health care differ depending on the level of context?

What follows is not an analysis of all the relevant elements for the discussion nor a systematic overview of all kinds of contexts, but a sketch of how the framework we have developed may be worked out. I will, moreover, only discuss *levels* of contexts and how they have an impact on professional responsibilities. Contexts are decisive for the definition of responsibilities.

Ideally, the discussion about duties and jurisdictions of health care professionals and other parties is settled on the basis of a realistic assessment of what can be demanded from the various partners given their competence, their social (contextual) horizon, legal constraints, and their specific role in the delivery of care. In practice the picture is much more messy, ambiguous, and characterized by unresolved tensions. Not only the content of care is negotiated—the "products," so to say—but also the terms under which these products are delivered. These terms co-define the rights, duties, and responsibilities of the relevant stakeholders. There is no blueprint for the definition of these responsibilities. Bloom, Standing, and Lloyd (2008) discuss "new partnerships" between representative bodies within the state, market players, and civil society organizations. Castellani and Hafferty (2006) predict a proliferation of professional styles.

Blueprint or not, it seems obvious that the duties and jurisdictions of physicians at a micro-level differ from duties and jurisdictions of doctors at other social levels. Differences in duties and jurisdictions are based on differences in responsibility; these, in turn, are based on differences in domain (or object) and the type of good that needs to be realized in that domain. For example, a physician in the board of a regional hospital has other responsibilities than a physician in a private practice. Professionals involved in macro-level policy making have duties and responsibilities that substantially differ from the duties and responsibilities of their colleagues in private practices and hospital boards. These differences can be traced back to differences in domain and in types of goods associated with these domains.

The domain of the hospital CEO (meso-level) is twofold and concerns, broadly speaking, (i) the relation between the hospital and the practitioners to whom it provides employment; and (ii) the relation between the hospital as institution and other players in the field, both medical and non-medical, such as the state, the legal system, insurance companies, competing institutions, service users, and the public. Much of what the CEO does aims at the improvement and strengthening of the conditions under which practitioners deliver their services. This part of the job has an internal focus. Another part of it is externally focused and consists in negotiations with all relevant stakeholders about how to face health care needs at a regional level. The institution has as a purpose the creation of stable conditions for the delivery of these services. The duties and jurisdictions of the CEO concern, therefore, the norms, rules, and principles that regulate the "conditioning" aspects of medical practice. But the institution has also an externally focused purpose, namely, to adequately respond to the need for medical care in a given catchment area.

This implies four things. First of all, hospitals are not end in themselves. They exist for a greater good—i.e., the care and treatment of people who suffer from illness and decline. Secondly, the focus on this greater good is not at odds with the idea that the primary responsibility of the hospital representative should be the managerial and economic side of the transactions that take place in order to fulfill health care needs. Thirdly, it also means that what CEOs do is a good in its own right. Current medical practice is unthinkable without the guarantees the institutions offer: housing, administrative support, technical equipment, contracts with insurers, platforms for teaching and education, a living for its employees, and so on. So, the kind of good that is associated with the institutional domain and, more particularly, with the hospital as institution, is that it provides safeguards with respect to the conditions under which health care can be delivered. A fourth, more subtle implication is that conditioning norms are not self-contained but related to and determined by qualifying norms: the promotion of the conditions that make health care possible, takes place with an eye to the main purpose of medical practice, which is to cure, to care, and to console. More technically phrased: the norms and principles of the conditioning aspects are "opened up" in the direction of the qualifying aspect of the constitutive side of medical practice.

Something similar holds for the macro-sphere—that is, for the role of the state, advisory and supervisory boards, professional organizations, patient movements, and the legal system. The domain covered by these agencies is diverse and concerns, for instance,

- The laws and agreements that help determine whose behaviors should be sanctioned as deserving professional attention;
- The raising and framing of public awareness of health problems and of expectations about what health care can do (health education);
- The registering and reporting of illnesses for public health purposes;
- Prevention; and
- The raising of awareness of stigma and social exclusion.

Many of these activities are meant to provide the conditions that make health and health care possible. They can be grouped together and placed under the umbrella of medical practice itself with its own telos of serving the ill. This is another way of saying that doing justice to the conditioning aspects is intrinsically related to the moral meaning and purposes of health care. However, given this overarching telos, the focus of local actors will usually aim at the conditioning spheres themselves. The medical advisor at a ministry of health, for instance, can be convinced of the need for patient empowerment; but she will not undertake action herself (for instance, as campaigner) in this respect. Instead, she will maximally promote the conditions which make empowerment possible. This aim can be promoted by subsidies, legal reform, and additional regulations. Such financial, legal, and administrative measures are enabling: not a form of help in themselves, they enable the good cause of patient empowerment.

This account shows that, at the meso- and macro-level, activities of stakeholders are ideally defined as taking place under the umbrella of healing, diminishing of suffering, and consolation. These activities can, in other words, still be understood from the perspective of the NPA, taken in its broadest sense. However, these activities themselves are determined by non-moral types of norms—i.e., norms that are related to efficiency, sound policy making, and justice (e.g., fair distribution of means in a certain region). At the meso-level of analysis, the emphasis is on adequately dealing with the need for health care services. At the macro-level, the focus is on fair distribution of means and on protection of the general population—from natural disaster, epidemics, and general health risks.

CONCLUSION

The NPA is not a blueprint of how medicine and healthcare in themselves are, nor is it a model prescribing what professionals should do. It serves, ideally, as a heuristic device that helps professionals and administrators to orient themselves, both conceptually and normatively, in the field of health care. We have seen that variations in contexts lead to differences in emphasis in the pattern of normatively relevant aspects. This could eventually lead to new and more complex models. But as we have seen, the complexity of the current health care system can still be addressed with the existing NPA, by taking it as a point of reference; by relating the different normative dimensions to core responsibilities of other employees and stakeholders beside medical professionals; and by relating these core responsibilities to the relevant contexts in which these other employees and stakeholders are working.

REFERENCES

Beck, J., & Young, M. F. D. (2005). The assault on the professions and the restructuring of academic and professional identities: A Bernsteinian analysis. *British Journal of Sociology of Education*, *26*(2), 183–197. doi:10.1080/0142569042000294165

Bloom, G., Standing, H., & Lloyd, R. (2008). Markets, information asymmetry and health care: Towards new social contracts. *Social Science & Medicine*, *66*(10), 2076–2087. doi:10.1016/j.socscimed.2008.01.034 PMID:18316147

Castellani, B., & Hafferty, F. W. (2006). The Complexities of Medical Professionalism: A preliminary investigation. In D. Wear, J.M. Aultman (Eds.), Professionalism in Medicine: Critical Perspectives (pp. 3–24). New York: Springer.

Frank, J. R., Jabbour, M., Fréchette, D., Marks, M., Valk, N., & Bourgeois, G. (Eds.). (2005). *Report of the CanMEDS Phase IV Working Groups*. Ottawa: The Royal College of Physicians and Surgeons of Canada.

Frank, J. R., Jabbour, M., & Tugwell, P. (1996). Skills for the new millenium: Report of the societal needs working group, CanMEDS 2000 Project. *Annals of the Royal College of Physicians and Surgeons of Canada*, *29*, 206–216.

Gabbard, G. O., Roberts, L. W., Crisp-Han, H., Ball, V., Hobday, G., & Rachal, F. (2012). *Professionalism in Psychiatry*. Washington, DC: American Psychiatric Publishing, Inc.

Glas, G. (2012). Competence development as normative practice—Educational reform in medicine as heuristic model to relate worldview and education. *Koers—Bulletin for Christian Scholarship, 77*(1), 70–75. . doi:10.4102/koers.v77i1.411

Glas, G. (2017). Public and Institutional Aspects of Professional Responsibility in Medicine and Psychiatry. *Philosophia Reformata*, *82*(2), 146–166. doi:10.1163/23528230-08202005

Glas, G. (2019). Person-centered Care in Psychiatry. Self-relational, normative, and contextual perspectives. London: Routledge.

Gorovitz, S., & MacIntyre, A. (1976). Toward a theory of medical fallibility. *The Journal of Medicine and Philosophy*, *1*(1), 51–71. doi:10.1093/jmp/1.1.51

Goudzwaard, B. (1982). *Kapitalisme en vooruitgang* (4th ed.). Assen: Van Gorcum.

Hengeveld, M. H., Vleugel, L., van der Gaag, R. J., Stek, M., & Glas, G. (2009). *Herziening Opleiding en Onderwijs Psychiatrie (HOOP)*. Utrecht: De Tijdstroom.

Polder, J. J., Hoogland, J., & Jochemsen, H. (1996). *Professie of profijt?* Amsterdam: Buijten & Schipperheijn.

Royal College of Physicians and Surgeons of Canada. (2015). *CanMEDS Framework 2015*. Retrieved from http://www.royalcollege.ca/rcsite/documents/canmeds/canmeds-full-framework-e.pdf

Tallis, R. (2004). *Hippocratic Oaths. Medicine and its Discontents*. London: Atlantic Books.

Van der Kooy, T.P. (1964). De zin van het economische opnieuw beschouwd. *Koers—maandblad vir calvinistische denke, 32*(1), 2–23.

ENDNOTES

1 Parts of this text have been published in Glas (2017) and will be published in Glas (2019).

2 The Canadian Medical Educational Directives for medical Specialists offers a model for a competency-based training of medical specialists, developed by staff members of the McMaster University in Hamilton (Canada) (Frank et al. 1996). The CanMEDS model forms the basis of the reform of medical specialist residency training programs in a couple of European countries. This author was part of the working group who wrote the new training directives in Holland (Hengeveld et al. 2009).

Chapter 9
Education:
The Right Desire

Roel Kuiper
Kampen Theological University, The Netherlands

ABSTRACT

Present discontents and concerns about schooling and learning call for critical reflection about education as a practice. Education is not to be degraded to instrumentalism. The profession is about the formation of pupils in a process of interaction to bring them to "human flourishing." Learning implies mastery and self-responsibility, guided by the "right desire" to do what is ultimately good. This "right desire" in the Aristotelian and Christian tradition precedes the work of any professional or practitioner. The normative practice approach serves as a valuable help for the reflection that is needed. It presents a given set of norms that are appropriate to understand a professional practice. Reflection on the "right desire" in schooling, learning, and teaching helps to redirect education in our time of discontent.

INTRODUCTION

Critical concerns about our system of schooling and learning are increasing in our late-modern world. Present social, cultural and moral discontents feature in current debates about the meaning and purpose of education. What we have in mind in these debates, and also in this chapter, is the schooling of children and teenagers in crucial stages of their life in a world that is rapidly changing. In this world the role of knowledge and skills changes is becoming more instrumental and specialized, which has an impact on the professional outlook of teachers and educators. However,

DOI: 10.4018/978-1-5225-8006-5.ch009

the direction of these changes and professional role-understanding remains unclear and all considerations together make professionals uncertain and hesitant as to where to go. In the meantime new approaches and innovations present themselves to be tried and tested. It seems as if education has lost its way.

These present discontents and criticism can be analyzed at three levels, roughly corresponding with the macro-, meso- and micro-levels Glas presented in chapter 1 of this book. We need to be more precise about the nature of the current debates and therefore I will discern three complexes of core-problems at those levels.

In the first place – on a macro-level - there is the question how education can contribute to society at large and our ambition to (re-)humanize the world. Jan Amos Comenius described the school in the seventeenth century as a 'humanitas officinae', a workshop of humanity (Habl, 2017, xiii). Pedagogical literature since then has considered humanity as core value of education, aiming at the upbringing of civilized members of society as its purpose. According to the Czech pedagogue Jan Habl, discussing the legacy of Comenius, 'humanization' was one of the key principles in the transformation of the educational systems of the second half of the twentieth century in Europe. At the same time this humanity ran in a deep crisis, a crisis characterized by one-sided techno-scientific revolutions, cultural destruction, economic problems, deepening inequality and social disintegration, alienation and depersonalization. Humanity is not well-kept by its shepherds and therefore there is a call for 'new humanism' among educators. Thus stated, this sounds humanistic and idealistic, however in this call one should not notice an ambition to refurbish an old-fashioned *Bildungsideal*, but a genuine response to a deeply felt pedagogical need. Schools must contribute to the pedagogical education of new generations to let them take their place as responsible citizens in a world art, presenting in everyday life the complexities, ambiguities and effects of a multi-religious, multicultural and globalizing cohabitation. Meanwhile, young people grow up in a technological culture, secular by pretention and at the same time searching for moral and ethical nourishment. What does 'being human' mean after all? How can education contribute to the world as a 'better place'?

Secondly, on a meso-level of schooling itself this cultural crisis translates itself in reflections about *good education*. How can education, in the organized setting of the school, support pupils best in their development to become responsible and well-equipped partakers of civil society? Critical voices have asserted that school education and teaching has become as instrumental as many practices in our technological society. By the end of the day, we want to see well-defined 'results', to be measured and produced by our educational system. This system is held accountable for individual-cognitive achievements of pupils, making a new generation ready for the labor market, fit to navigate on all kinds of 'information'. Among educators there is manifest criticism about education degraded as 'technology'. They warn that education itself is in danger, because pupils are no robots or objects to be drilled or disciplined. Rather, education is a work of human interaction, aiming at the formation of men and women that have learned to be adult members of society (Biesta: 2014).

How can education contribute to pedagogical needs when it is perceived to be instrumental with no bigger purpose for life than to succeed in contemporary circumstances? Hannah Arendt criticized the 'conformity' that is reproduced by modern societies (Arendt: 1958). It is often stated that schools 'make' modern citizens after bureaucratic models. Related criticism adds the point that some children cannot learn at all in those system or are spoiled by schools that are concentrating on results and outcomes. No wonder there is also an anti-school-movement getting stronger, advocating 'unschooling'. However, in schools and among educators the debate is running how the human dimension in education can be rediscovered and strengthened again. This requires an understanding of education which acknowledges the normative character of it. Professionals should have a clear understanding of the nature and normative character of their profession.

Thirdly, there is the micro-level of the teacher, the work of the professional with pupils, - mostly - in the classroom. Glas pointed already at the 'crisis of professionalism' in many areas, also among teachers. How can teachers contribute to the formation of their pupils while they feel hunted by sometimes contradictory official requirements and professional standards defined in prescribed procedures and technical skills? There is a sense of 'alienation' in the profession itself, because teachers cannot always design their work as they think it is best with regard to the personal development of their pupils. In some cases, economic conditions and lack of funds and resources limit the possibilities of teachers to do their job well. Teachers, of course, want to dedicate themselves to the task to educate children in a professional way, with personal attention, through relationships that are meaningful for human flourishing. But without clear set conditions and goals that enable them to do the work of education in a proper way teachers are getting lost in educational systems. In other words, what really is getting lost is education as a professional practice with clear-set normative meaning, in the classroom, at school and in society at large.

Having examined and listed the current concerns about education, we may conclude that the situation is precarious and needs further critical reflection. This reflection cannot start immediately with the micro-level, although the results should be felt there after all, and have to result in professional attitudes in the classroom. At the same time we see that teachers feel entangled in the ambiguities of educational systems and need broader perspectives and tools to overcome their complicated situation. We need to provide for these broader perspectives first. This reflection can neither start with the macro-issues of policymaking on a larger scale. From this perspective education has often been made instrumental for political goals and overrated or distorted by societal or economic interests. Policymaking presupposes a proper understanding of the nature of education and what pertains to that. The critical reflection we envisage should therefore start with the nature and possibilities of education itself, with an understanding of education as a *practice*, disclosing opportunities and perspectives for pupils, teachers and society at large.

In this chapter, we will explore the Normative Practice Approach (NPA) to find clues and solutions for the fundamental questions that we have recognized on the meso-level and micro-level of education. The questions that are central in this chapter present themselves on those levels. What is good education and what are we aiming for in education? How can education as a practice help us to understand what is really meaningful for human flourishing and for (re-)humanizing society. What does this imply for professional standards and attitudes to be applied in class? As I will explain, these fundamental questions call for preliminary clarification: what is the nature of the human 'knowledge' we learn at school? How does that relate to the way we experience and live our life's outside the school? Is knowledge 'theoretical' or 'practical', or both? My point will be that the process of learning at school presupposes an understanding of life as a human enterprise. The process of learning is not entirely built on abstract knowledge, but is practical, contextual, designed to serve in life, pointing at human life and therefore humanizing our understanding of learning and teaching. What does this mean for education understood as *practice*?

In this chapter, I will first try to define what education is. Given the assertion that education of young people serve their existence in society and is about their formation, I want to examine what an understanding of 'praxis' implies for education. From there, it is a small step to think about education as a practice with 'ends' and 'goods' of its own. To elaborate this further, the Normative Practice Approach will be explored, asking ourselves what the nature is of the work of a good teacher and how he or she should respond to professional norms. This NPA reveals the deeper frameworks of educational practices. After I have explained what are the most vital parts of this NPA, we discuss the micro-level of professionalism and return briefly to the macro-level of policymaking in the area of education.

WHAT IS EDUCATION?

Formation as Self-Transcending Movement

All experts agree that *formation* is a key value of education. By formation is meant the upbringing of young people in order to mold their character, intellect, capacities and skills, in short the entire set of talents and gifts of a person. Most definitions of education refer to this work of formation as something central in the teachers' profession. All the other activities of instruction, demonstration, equipping pupils, are components of this bigger work of formation.

Education is a process of human interaction and highly relational. It can take place in all kinds of relations, but the relation between teacher and pupil is a fundamental one. Formation is reciprocal or dialogical; it consists of two-directional interaction. This interaction is asymmetrical. It is the teacher that guides and leads the process of learning, albeit that the pupil learns by its own activity of receiving, understanding and reproduction.

Although it is true that discipline in some cases also involves compulsion, formation follows its proper course when the pupil has room to explore. Education involves freedom, creativity, recognition of individual gifts and talents. Freedom is essential for personal formation, because pupils have to reflect on their own attitudes, choices and possibilities in the learning process. While being guided, people direct themselves. While being educated, they develop themselves in their own way. Education is in a famous German phrase from Theodor Litt, 'führen und wachsen lassen' ('lead and let grow'), and part of this latter is that pupils become aware of their own aspirations, ideas and desires. The ultimate goal of formation is to enable someone to judge, act and think as an independent person, being responsible for his or her own life. To arrive at such a position requires freedom of choice and action, and respect for personalities we work with.

Teachers should therefore respect the dignity of the person in its own 'sovereign' sphere and with 'the sovereign power of personality' (Kuyper, 2009 (1898), 95). This is a strong expression, once used by the Dutch theologian Abraham Kuyper, pointing at another element to be examined. To whom do children and teenagers belong and who is entitled to educate? In ancient Sparta and in totalitarian regimes bad examples of state-education have been set by taking over the authority of parents. But what is the answer in free societies? The answer must be that children do belong to (biological) parents who exercise the primary authority over them. It is not the government or even the school that possess this authority. Their authority is temporarily and given by consent. The lives of children are embedded in a nexus of social relationships, communities and institutions and the right to decide and to say something decisive is usually shared by the different authorities that be, like schools, sports clubs, parents, church, governments.

This implies at the same time that children are not autonomous individuals, as liberal theories perhaps would perceive them. Self-determination in a radical sense cannot be the ultimate goal of education, because self-determination is not the ultimate goal of life. Nevertheless, children and teenagers are taught to become self-responsible. What should be respected is the person in his or her uniqueness with special gifts and abilities and what should be learned is to be self-responsible for all this. The child or teenager we educate is a unique person, progressing towards independence, and therefore educators should respect the dignity of that person and his or her 'sovereign' sphere.

For Abraham Kuyper, there is another meaning involved in this expression. In a deeper sense this person does not even belong to him or herself, he or she is not totally independent, but stands in relationship to God, the creator of all life and also the creator of this unique person. Therefore, self-determination and autonomy are misleading concepts, as they suggest that the person is a self-centered 'monad', cut-off from others and the transcendental Other. Instead of these concepts in education we should promote a lively sense of responsibility. In education we should teach pupils to disclose someone's mind for others and for the world with all its creational dimensions as a responsible human being. Christians would say that this responsibility originates from their responsibility to God, humanist, and certainly 'exclusive humanism' (Taylor, 2007), would say that this responsibilities stem from their understanding of human nature.

It is evident that all education presupposes ideas about human nature. The pedagogical key question in education is: what does it mean to be human? The lives of young people are influenced by ideas about what it means to be human and this makes education itself a normative undertaking. Formation is not just a work of discipline; it is the upbringing of a person towards ends that transcend his or her individual existence. Learning is a self-transcending movement of the person to discover and wonder about unknown things, narratives, situations, ideals, all that may be, and encounter what is new or different, the otherness of others, the otherness of the world. And formation means to bring all this home in the human person, learning to appreciate, understand and interpret, under the guidance of normative ideas.

Formation aims at bigger ideas about what it means to be human, and assists pupils in this self-transcending movement. But what is human and who can decide what is human? Different answers are possible here. We can learn that from life itself by studying what human beings do in their best circumstances. Or we can learn to be human by classical standards, delivered by ancient cultures, the arts and philosophies. We can also answer that our responsibilities to sustain and care for a free world inform us what human is, or we can take religion as starting point to answer this question. In any case we could say that the question always refers somehow to the continuation of the community of mankind. The Dutch philosopher Herman Dooyeweerd states that all our normative social responsibilities are rooted in the 'central spiritual community of mankind' (Dooyeweerd, II: 1953, 200). This is about what we think human education is all about, the humanization of our broader human community. Dooyeweerd approaches this from the spiritual (transcendent) side. Isn't it such a community that we after all want to serve in education?

Praxis as Work of the Professional

Before we can proceed to our reflections on teaching as a practice, we need to consider the question how the work of a teacher can be characterized. If is it true that education is a process of human interaction guided by ideas how people ought to be, based on ideas about human nature, what is the nature of the work of teaching? Rousseau has compared it by breeding or cultivating plants, but the kind of interaction between teacher and pupil is more intense than the example of organic growth suggests. John Locke once compared children with wax and education with writing on an empty sheet of paper, but this suggests as if the child is passive and only needs to be molded in the right form (Locke: 1693). The wax-image is inspired by the wrong suggestion that we can discipline, indoctrinate or even make people as we want them to be. This approach has produced harmful systems of education, as we know, and this is not what teachers consider as good work.

We should approach the work of the teacher as *doing*, as a mode of human action, and not as *making* something. The school is not a workplace where 'products' are manufactured, but indeed a workshop where we learn what it means to be human and live humanely, a 'humanitas officinae', as Comenius explained. Although the work of the teacher is confined to school-activities, learning is a broader activity. We learn for life and the process of learning never stops. Unfinishedness is essential to our human condition, Paulo Freire states correctly, and the same counts for learning, which will always be incomplete (Freire, 2001, 52). School teaching means helping young people to learn by themselves, create possibilities, delivering the tools for ongoing lifelong learning. This implies that the teacher not only works with the abilities and capabilities of youngsters, but with their personalities, their desires, their views, hopes and beliefs. We teach them to be a human being that is able to live and act as a human being, a person that is responsible for his or her actions.

This work of the teacher can neither be characterized as sheer application of some theory about man, anthropology or any knowledge to be transferred. One cannot talk about human affairs, or even the nature of any topic from a theoretical perspective only. Teaching means introducing others in a world of meaning. This implies that teachers have learned the language to discern this meaning by themselves. Would teaching consist of the sheer application of some theory about things and objects, we would admit that education is altogether about making something, and not primarily doing something. Teachers that deliver good work are not producing outcomes, they form human beings.

This distinction between doing and making is for the first time introduced by Aristotle. Questioning himself how to define human activities he uses the term *praxis* (doing), to be discerned from *poesis* (making) and also from *theoria*, the kind of contemplation that philosophers exercise. The distinction between producing something (making) and performing an action (doing) is explained by Aristotle in this way:

What produces a product and what performs an action are not the same. For the productive crafts have some other end apart from the producing: for instance, apart from housebuilding, since that is the craft of producing a house, there is a house as its end apart from the producing of it, and similarly in the case of carpentry and the other productive crafts. But in the practical crafts there is no other end apart from the acting: for instance, apart from playing the harp there is no other end, but the end simply is the activity and the action. Wisdom, then, is concerned with action and with matters of action, but craft with producing and with matters of production;... Wisdom is a virtue, it would seem, not a science... (Magna Moralia, 1197a)

So, teaching is not similar to a productive craft, Aristotle holds. At the end of the day the teacher does not deliver a product, ready for use, like a house or a piece of furniture. At the end of the day the teacher wants the pupil to be able to perform the proper action, be it in gymnastics, harp playing, calculating, analyzing discourse, historical interpretation, drawing, or describing chemical processes. A student can do this well or badly; the goal is *eupraxia*, the well-performed action. The way we do it is by practicing and forming habits. To apply this all well one needs practical wisdom, *phronesis*.

Aristotle relates this *praxis* to all human activities, even life itself. His practical philosophy specifies what action is, but the ultimate goal is living the good life. When writing about education Aristotle always had the good man and the good citizen in mind. The praxis of life cannot be distinguished from all other kinds of actions that could be learned, because also in life there is no end apart from the acting. Living the human life means striving towards certain goals, which results in meaningful action. This makes the difference between school and life relative, as we have already noticed. The 'wisdom' how to perform meaningful action in life is a human virtue and makes us human and school-learning serves that bigger goal.

This distinction between doing (action) and making (production) reappears in Hannah Arendt's important analysis of Western culture in one of her most important books *The Human Condition*. Her analysis touches central problems in education. Arendt views that action nowadays is superseded by the attitude of the 'homo faber'. Modern people have been forced to become productive and useful members of society, rather *making* their lives and what pertains to it than *act* as free individuals guided by normative standards. This turnover occurred since the 18th century, since the industrial revolution, directed by utilitarian and materialistic philosophies of those times. A fabrilistic attitude jeopardizes human values and the true existence of man, which is much more found in action, in honor, in creativity, in starting something new, free initiative, the demonstration of someone's unique talents.

Hannah Arendt touches an important point and explains how instrumentalism in so many areas of life has taken over the floor. But is it really this replacement of *doing* by *making* that determines the situation or is there a deeper problem to be analyzed? After all, we still know in all kinds of human contexts, also in education, what it means to act, being responsible for our own deeds and actions. That is not a forgotten or unknown human capacity. Aristotle never expected that human beings would lose their abilities to act. According to him, choosing the right sort of action is a matter of practical reasoning: wisdom. And wisdom is a virtue of character. This is most decisive for any situation and can still be addressed. That makes the formation of character and motivation a key factor in education and cultural development.

How can we arrive at that point? I think Aristotle gives an important clue. According to him practical reasoning should reflect the 'right desire', the motivation, that expresses itself in what we decide to pursue (Aristotle, *Nic. Ethics,* 1139a). The well-developed character is able to recognize this desire for man's *telos* or 'ultimate end' (Lobkowicz, 1967, 76). This is an important observation of human nature. Human beings are self-transcending in and through their desires. James Smith states that human beings are 'fundamentally desiring animals' (Smith, 2009, 33). Life ideals are presenting themselves in what we strive for and in directing the way we think we can achieve our goals, be it by doing or making. It is this desire, the appreciation and love for truth and the ultimate good, that directs our attitudes and activities and also our actions. Therefore, education is about discovering and pursuing the 'right desire' (Arpaly, Schroeder, 2014).

In Christian pedagogic thinking this element of desire and love, which is missing in Hannah Arendt's account of the *vita activa*, proved to be central in understanding the process of teaching and learning. Augustine already made the connection between practical reasoning, wisdom and the movements of a desiring heart, searching for true loving relations. He considered this to be a new starting point for teaching and learning. Love for God and His creation opens up new ways of understanding. This emphasis implies that the work of formation must get psychological and spiritual depth. Not only the mind and all kinds of human capacities should be trained, also heart, character and the human soul. In Western education, due to Greek and Christian influences, character building and the formation of responsible, caring and loving personalities has never been out of professional attention. It gets new attention in our time. Rekindling the 'right desire' for what is good and to act and live humanely should indeed be in the center of anyone who is concerned about the praxis of education and the need for (re-) humanization of Western culture.

Praxis and Practice

Having considered the work of the teacher as *praxis*, we now turn to the regulated professional environment, the *practice* of education. We move from the work of teachers with pupils on the micro-level to the teachers' professional understanding of the process of teaching on a meso-level. What is a good teacher? What kind of desires have to be accounted for in good education? What set of norms constitute the deeper framework of the profession? Both levels are interrelated, of course, the doing (praxis) needs a larger framework to reflect on its own structure and direction. And the understanding of a professional practice requires the understanding of what professional doing entails: experience, expert knowledge, standards, practical wisdom, consent, and so on. In his well-known definition Alasdair MacIntyre formulates in his now-classic *After Virtue*:

By a practice I am going to mean any coherent and complex form of socially established cooperative human activity through which goods internal to that form of activity are realized in the course of trying to achieve those standards of excellence which are appropriate to, and partially definitive of that form of activity, with the result that human powers to achieve excellence, and human conceptions of the ends and goods involved, are systematically extended. (MacIntyre, 1985, 187)

This is Aristotelian, as we know, and emphasizes in its elements the praxis of the professional, the doing of something meaningful. Let us consider this a bit further.

It is clear that MacIntyre is concerned about Western civilization and its moral qualities. He is looking for communities 'within which civility and the intellectual and moral life can be sustained' (MacIntyre, 1985, 263). The kind of practices he defines live by 'human conceptions' of 'ends and goods involved'. His idea of a practice, not only professional practices of course but all practices, is to maintain and continue moral life. This means that practices contribute to what we have called the humanization of communities and society at large. Practices do have external value. There are external goods, apart from internal ones. Contributing to societal and moral goals is to enhance the external value of a practice. This is especially true for the practice of education, which equips people to function as responsible citizens in all kinds of roles and professions. MacIntyre himself had some doubt whether education was a practice, because of the weight of these external values. But at the same time the internal value of learning in and for itself cannot be denied (De Muynck, 2006, 59-61; Smith & Smith, 2011, 11). And teachers like all practitioners respond to professional standards and norms, the deeper frameworks that constitute their practice and can be studied and extended systematically.

What I want to discuss in order to make connection with the NPA, are the 'standards of excellence' and 'obedience to rules' (MacIntyre, 1985, 190) that are appropriate to a professional practice and somehow relate to the 'human powers to achieve excellence' and the 'human conceptions of the ends and goods involved'. Teaching is a normative activity, as we have seen now. Several kinds of norms or rules are involved, and also requirements, conditions, procedures, and so on. Standards of excellence in this definition do not describe the entire normative framework of a given practice. In MacIntyre's approach the excellent professional sets the standard by showing what excellence is, so these standards result from merit. But these are not the same as predicaments about norms and rules that are also 'appropriate' to the 'form of activity' involved and define a given 'practice'. How can this 'form' and therefore this 'practice' be recognized?

The Normative Practice Approach, built on the philosophy of Herman Dooyeweerd and developed by Glas, Jochemsen, Hoogland and others, offers tools to go further along this path. The connection with MacIntyre's philosophical framework can be made because the Dooyeweerdian school of thinking acknowledges that human activity is performed in response to given 'ends', laws and norms. Together they define our experiences and the way reality expresses itself. All life and human activity is subject to this interplay of laws and norms, disclosing new possibilities and developments all the time. In the realm of human affairs there is freedom – therefore we refer to *norms* here, and not laws– and people respond to these norms in their own way. More than any other school of thought the Dooyeweerdian philosophy tries to be precise in discerning the set of norms involved. They have to be self-evident, irreducible, independent from others, interrelated, an entry for meaningful experience and reflection. They refer to one another and together constitute a coherent – even cosmonomic – order (see Chapter 2). It may be clear that the NPA considers a practice as a social entity of its own, not resulting from an application of some theory. This last approach gained the ground since Kant, but also distorts a proper understanding of human activity. It makes education something technical, constructivist, impersonal, not able to understand the working of a given normativity in all actions involved. The NPA itself is a theoretical model and no more than that, but it helps reflection on different normative threads that are interwoven in the praxis of education. It is important to analyze the appropriate norms, as the NPA suggests, and therefore we will use the scheme of foundational, qualifying and conditioning norms at the 'structural' side and regulatory attitudes and beliefs at the 'directional' side. We consider them as the deeper frames of any professional practice. Finally, we will proceed to the question of how these standards can be analyzed and how they relate to 'human conceptions of ends and goods'.

DEEP FRAMES

The Normative Practice Approach in Education

We start with the set of norms that are constitutive for education. They approach the practice of education from its *structural* side, the normative principles that can be discerned. For Dooyeweerd all normative human activity is 'historic'. It is a work of human formation, directed to future development, dealing with contexts and traditions and overcoming restrictions of the past. Human beings are called and challenged to develop a given culture. This historic calling is also foundational for education. Education is the formation of given talents, the formation of character and capacities. Of course, this work of formation needs a goal or direction (for instance to let the person flourish), but this aspect will be dealt with later. It is important to notice here that the 'telos' of education is already operative in formation. Formation implies the ability to form and that notion is needed in the first place. The teacher must be a good practitioner in a technical sense. He or she needs a set of tools to engage pupils and bring them where he or she wants them to be. This involves expertise, control, mastership over (tacit) knowledge and skills. Education is about formation.

Considering education as practice, we recognize that there are cooperative relations that need to be established in this practice. Education is based on a typical relation between teacher and pupil, Dooyeweerd would call them a subject-subject-relationship of a special kind. These typical relations have to be established and thus formed from the outset. This all belongs to the foundational normativity of the practice of education, which is a part of human action and hence 'historic'.

It has been stated that formation is also the goal (or end) of education, but that conclusion is drawn too quickly (De Muynck, 2006). In the work of formation we recognize a loving and caring attitude that qualifies the nature of formation in this subject-subject-relation. Formation can encompass a broad range of actions, of course, and these by themselves do not qualify educational practices as something specific. Education presupposes a typical relation, embedded in the environment of school teaching, and implies attitudes and habits that are deeply 'moral', giving specific meaning to the activity of formation. Pupils are no pieces of wax, to be formed passively, but are specifically supported in a self-transcending movement, which requires from the side of teachers caring attention and loving attitudes. Dooyeweerd would call this area of normativity 'ethical', defined by the 'moral aspect'. This area corresponds with an attitude of love and care. Of course, this is not love in general; this love takes a typical form, fitting the professional relation between teacher and pupil.

To explore this a bit more one can easily see that love or joy for learning and for teaching colors and deepens the main processes that are involved in education.

Children are gifted with talents for learning and teachers help them by kindling interest, receptivity, wonder and love for what they may or must learn. When we take education as a praxis, we can easily see that the end of learning is also the activity in itself. Going back to a given example: it is the joy for playing the flute that motivates to teach and learn flute-playing. Through this one can see children grow in a self-transcending attitude, really learning something new. Teachers are assigned to open hearts and minds of pupils in order to love the activity of learning for what it gives in itself. What they try to call to life in pupils is the *right desire* for learning and action. This love for the doing of learning produces the 'internal goods' of this practice: the skills, virtues and developed capacities. And in and through all this doing persons grow and show their unique personality. This 'end' of education we call human flourishing. What then is a good teacher? He or she has the ability and capacity to kindle pleasure and joy for what can be learned and shared in the self-transcending movement of formation. Of course, this does not go without love for pupils that have to be taught. A good teacher aims at their well-being and hopes for that each individual may flourish. This result may be seen as a corresponding return for the love the teacher invests in his or her pupils. Not only the pupil but also the teacher will 'reap in joy'.

Dooyeweerd or others never explored the moral (or ethical) aspect in this way. The meaning of this aspect was for him summarized in the biblical commandment to love God above everything and our neighbors as ourselves. This commandment however is to be interpreted as the sum of all our loving relationships, also those that are typical for a professional situation. Therefore, the love for teaching pupils is not to be separated from this love for God and for fellow-humans. Formation can be seen as qualified by the moral aspect, and at the same time this loving attitude to guide the pupil to human flourishing is anchored at the regulatory side. The most important thing to say is that the important work of formation in education will not flourish without a loving attitude.

There is even an inner logic to see the process of education form this angle. Firstly, because teaching that what is meaningful to the teacher can be seen as an act of love. Human flourishing cannot be achieved without this dedication and without personal relationship. Secondly, the process of learning functions best when people learn to love their subject while approaching it. In education we teach pupils to love the world in its different elements and aspects. That is the meaning or destination of all education. And thirdly, learning can indirectly be seen as an act of caring love for others who we serve by our skills and knowledge and for the preservation of the world and the entire human community. So, education can be defined as the process of human formation aiming at human flourishing, performed in a loving attitude for pupils and for the activity and end of learning, under beneficiary conditions.

This loving attitude is anchored at the regulatory side, guiding the direction of all human action.

Each practice has logic of its own, as Bourdieu would state it (Bourdieu, 1990). The logic of the teachers' practice can be approached from the structural side, but is directed from the regulatory side as an act of love. This counts for all the norms that can be discerned, also the norms that *condition* this typical process of human formation, like social and economic preconditions, a public-legal and juridical framework to work in. They need careful arrangement to support what is typical and where it is all about in the doing of the teacher. The notion that norms belong to an integral normative order, prevents at the same time from a one-sided idea of human flourishing, the 'end' of this practice. Human formation involves a range of normative aspects that are to be disclosed as well: the psychic, physic, logic, linguistic, social, economic, esthetic, moral, juridical and spiritual. Human flourishing is an integral concept.

At this stage we have to add a few words more about the 'directional' or 'regulatory' side. It is obvious that practitioners do have beliefs and views of their own. Those are formed by education, cultural environments, informed by faith and established in fundamental beliefs or specific worldviews. These beliefs and views are *regulatory,* which means that they – deliberately or not – direct human action (Hegeman, Edgell, Jochemsen, 2011). What people believe, what they hold for the ultimate truth, what they think is really good, influences thoughts and actions, and that is also the case in education. As convictions of the heart faith and beliefs direct and open up the normative side of the educational practice. They color all the normative aspects, providing for motivation and orientation, the right desire that is needed. Together the regulatory side and the structural side constitute a dynamic whole, guiding human action to what people belief to be good 'ends'. They stand for the religious orientation of the practitioner.

This religious orientation is not an 'extra', something 'subtractional' that can be stripped away some day (Taylor, 2007, 22). It is a framework for the understanding of meaning, a matter of faith and trust in ultimate truths. This religious orientation decides therefore also what we understand by human and being human, because it views human beings in relation to God (or not), to themselves, others and the world. This religious orientation is not specific for Christians, but for all believers, and since all humans do believe, it is an orientation that belongs to human nature. Religious orientation helps to orientate in human affairs and is necessary to understand the world and is also crucial in the process of learning. Education is never morally or religiously neutral. To the contrary, our fundamental understanding of things, our worldviews and beliefs are needed to raise pupils and help them discover what meaning is in reality and what grounds their hope for the future to come.

This religious or world view orientation helps to understand the right desire that we described as vital element in human action. This is the desire to do well, to act and behave as we ought to do, to serve others in a loving attitude. Education aims at awaking this right desire, for the performance of any given action and ultimately for living the good life. Religious motives help us to understand what this good life is. Therefore, good teachers use their beliefs and convictions deliberately in education, not to force their pupils into the frames of their own understanding, but to help them to orient themselves, find their place as human beings, examine their own heart and develop their ability to believe, hope and trust. In forming character and heart of the pupils the teacher needs to bring his or her faith and beliefs into action, because shaping the right desire in the pupils' heart is perhaps the most central part of education.

Therefore, this religious orientation is helps to understand what it means to live the human life and also for education. What does it convey? First of all, it shows us that we are unfinished, incomplete being, in need for horizons and meaning to live a human life. Secondly, a religious conviction helps to find a human position in the world, among others and in relation to what transcends us. Thirdly, it helps us to develop the 'plausibility structures' for our understanding (Berger and Luckman, 1991) and also the moral and cultural capital that informs us about the order in the world and how this should be kept. Finally, it gives us a clue about human flourishing and what that should mean. Charles Taylor has stated that 'life-fulfillment' is a common human ideal. Every human being has ideas about human development and what 'constitutes a fulfilled life' (Taylor, 2007, 16). That fulfillment can be seen in the 'here and now' or in the life hereafter. In both cases it involves an idea about human flourishing as 'end' of education.

Western civilization has been built on such a religious orientation, placing human beings under God as part of creation, acknowledging that man is a 'noble creature' (Comenius) and a 'social being' (Aristotle), responsive and creative, and at the same time morally depraved and in need of help and support of others to learn what it means to serve and flourish in the human community. This is a Christian formulation of what it means to be human and it has always been an important one for education. It gives an answer to questions regarding human nature and the purpose (or 'end') of education. It helps to understand what should be conveyed in a teachers' practice.

It also helps to get an idea about (re-) humanizing Western culture. This can only origin from the right desire to be human and live humanely. It is a genuine task of educators to orient themselves to what this may mean. The right desire is a movement of the soul in Aristotle's account and does not originate in reason itself. Inspiring students is the art of the teacher. Instrumentalizing education, considering it as a world of techniques, tools and things, and seeing pupils primarily as future labor force, means alienating teachers from this task. That is a main source of the present discontents in education. The school should return to its humanizing task and revive the right desire for teaching and learning, guiding the youngest generations to dedicate themselves to a humane world. This desire belongs to the inherent goods of education and need continuous care and attention of practitioners. The excellent teacher succeeds in achieving those goods, guided by right desires. The NPA helps indeed to find the road and the standards for what is essential in the teacher's practice.

Standards of Excellence and Contextual Plurality

As we have seen in MacIntyre's definition of a practice there is a prominent place for what he calls 'standards of excellence' - to be distinguished from 'obedience to rules'. How should these be found and understood? MacIntyre is not very clear about those standards. The history of practices show what the 'best standards realized so far' are (1985, 190). It is the excellent practitioner that decides what this contains. It is the excellence of the best practitioners that set a standard for others. With the NPA we can come to a closer understanding of these standards. The good or excellent professional has the talent and skill to respond competently to the inherent norms that defines a given practice. He or she knows how to realize the internal goods involved, inspired by an understanding of the right desire to deliver good or excellent work. Interestingly, the first internal good for the teacher is a certain kind of life, the life of a dedicated professional. This is the teacher with the desire to show what it means to be a good professional.

Stated in terms of the NPA: a good or excellent teacher knows how to bring the integral norms that are constitutive for the practice of education together with regulatory beliefs, motivations and views into an integral approach. It is the right desire, the love for what the doing of education entails, that elaborates this integrative approach. Excellence grows by knowing how to respond, shaping skills and attitudes so that all professional actions involved are supportive for the ends to be realized in education. This calls for a capable, responsive and competent practitioner that can set standards of good work by doing, showing and reproducing the right actions. These standards reflect professional authority, but they are never absolute or above criticism. In fact, they are fluid and depend on professional and cultural contexts and the practical wisdom of the practitioner.

Cultural sensitivity is needed as well, apart from constitutive and regulative aspects. The understanding of the role of a teacher and the required skills he or she has to have is also contextual. In an information-society the teacher is becoming much more a guide than an expert. The professional has to deal with changing circumstances of schooling and learning. In fact there is a plurality of contexts, cultural and political, and they have to be taken in account as well. Being a good teacher in China or Mexico is not the same as being a good teacher in Europe.

These contexts belong to the macro-level we discerned at the beginning of this chapter. Education as a practice has to deal with expectations and regulations at the larger scale of a nation for instance. Concerns about education at this level can only be responded by creating the right conditions. Excellence itself however, doing the right work in the right way, is a quality connected to the actions of professionals. They, of course, are aware of the challenges of education on their level of competence. The issues concerning the (re-)humanizing of our late-modern culture matter to them. This is a big and critical task for educators and teachers today and they know it. They can feel this as a burden in their circumstances. But the remedy will always be to start again by what can be found at the inside of any practice and where it is all about in good education: the joy of the right desire.

REFERENCES

Arendt, H. (1958). *The Human Condition*. Chicago: The University of Chicago Press.

Aristotle. (2014a). Magna Moralia. In Aristotle's Ethics. Writing form the Complete Works. Princeton, NJ: Princeton University Press.

Aristotle. (2014b). Nicomachean Ethics. In Aristotle's Ethics. Writing form the Complete Works. Princeton, NJ: Princeton University Press.

Arpaly, N., & Schroeder, T. (2018). *In Praise of Desire*. New York: Oxford University Press.

Berger, P., & Luckman, T. (1991). The Social Construction of Reality. A Treatise in the Sociology of Knowledge. London: Penguin Books. (Originally published 1966)

Biesta, G. (2014). *The Beautiful Risk of Education*. Boulder, CO: Paradigm Publishers.

Bourdieu, P. (n.d.). *The Logic of Practice*. Stanford, CA: Stanford University Press.

Castke, E. B. (1961). *Ancient Education and Today*. Baltimore, MD: Penguin Books.

de Muynck, A. (2006). De praktijk van het onderwijs. In Een theorie over praktijken. Normatief Praktijkmodel voor zorg, sociaal werk en onderwijs. Amsterdam: Buijten en Schipperheijn.

Dooyeweerd, H. (1953). *A New Critique of Theoretical Thought* (Vols. 1-3). Amsterdam: H.J. Paris and The Presbyterian and Reformed Publishing Company.

Freire, P. (1993). *Pedagogy of the Oppressed*. Penguin Books.

Freire, P. (2001). *Pedagogy of Freedom. Ethics, Democracy, and Civic Courage.* Oxford, UK: Rowman & Littlefield Publishers.

Habl, J. (2007). *On Being Human(e). Comenius' Pedagogical Humanization as an Anthropological Problem.* Eugene, OR: Pickwick Publications.

Hegeman, J., Edgell, M., & Jochemsen, H. (2011). *Practice and Profile. Christian Formation for Vocation.* Eugene, OR: Wipf & Stock.

Kuyper, A. (2009). Calvinism. New York: Cosimo. (Originally published 1898)

Lobkowicz, N. (1967). *Theory and Practice. History of a Concept from Aristotle to Marx.* Notre Dame, IN: University of Notre Dame Press.

MacIntyre, A. (1985). *After Virtue. A Study in Moral Theory.* London: Gerald Duckworth.

Smith, J. K. A. (2009). *Desiring the Kingdom. Worship, Worldview and Cultural Formation.* Grand Rapids, MI: Baker Academic.

Taylor, C. (2007). *A Secular Age.* The Belknap Press of Harvard University Press.

Section 3

Chapter 10
Management as a Supportive Practice:
The Complexity of Management Unraveled

Maarten J. Verkerk
University Maastricht, The Netherlands.

ABSTRACT

In this chapter, the nature of the management practice is investigated. The scene is sketched by telling a couple of stories from the experience of the author. Then, it is argued that an organizational approach is needed to understand the thinking and behavior of managers. It is shown that practice approaches are very suitable because they take their starting point in the daily activities, do justice to the nature of different activities, and make underlying ideals, values, and basic beliefs explicit. The Triple I model is used to investigate the practice of management in detail. It is shown that practices and management practices are intimately intertwined. The author's conclusion is that management is a supportive practice that is disclosed by the intrinsic values of the specific domain.

INTRODUCTION

I have been a manager for more than forty years. I have managed factories in the Netherlands, Taiwan and Germany. I have managed professional organizations like psychiatric hospitals and innovation networks. The smallest organization that I managed employed about ten people and brought in less than one million Euros

DOI: 10.4018/978-1-5225-8006-5.ch010

per year, the largest one had more than 900 employees and generated three hundred million Euros of revenue per year. I have also managed voluntary organizations like churches, study centers, and reflection networks. These organizations varied in size from about 10 to 300 people and the budget varied from hundred to hundred thousand Euros per year. For all these different organizations and contexts, the words 'manage' and 'management' are often used. The nature of voluntary organizations is quite different of that of professional organizations. Despite that, also in voluntary organizations I used my managerial capabilities for policy discussions, making multi-year plans, evaluations of progress, chairing meetings, and so on. Last but not least, I experienced in voluntary organizations the same type of stress as in professional organizations.

The idea of 'management' raises a lot of questions. One set of question refers to the different contexts. What are the similarities and differences between managing professional organizations like factories and hospitals? What are the similarities and differences between managing voluntary organizations like churches and study centers? What are the similarities and differences between managing professional and voluntary organizations? Another set of questions refers to the nature of the managerial activities. What is management? How to understand the complexity of management? Is management a practice? If yes, what type of practice?

The research question of this chapter is: What is the nature of a management practice? To answer this question we first have to address three sub questions:

1. What type of approach to management is required?
2. What type of philosophical approach is required?
3. How to understand the relationship between a practice and the management of an organization in which this practice is embedded?

This chapter has the following outline. First, we explore the managerial scene by telling stories. Then, we investigate the first, second and third sub question respectively. Finally, we return to the research question: What is the nature of the management practice? We discuss the results and draw some conclusions.

STORIES FROM THE MANAGERIAL PRACTICE

A pitfall in studying management is to focus on theoretical and philosophical ideas and to lose sight of the real practical questions and challenges. This pitfall can only be avoided by taking the daily activities and experiences of managers as a starting point for philosophical reflection. This section is mainly based on Verkerk (2015).

Importance of Stories

We would like to make an initial exploration of the scene by looking into some of my own, real-life management stories. The main reason for this resides in the fact that stories offer us an in-depth insight into the richness and complexity of organizational life and into the ins and outs of management. They open up a window into the inner life of moral leaders, their motives, their hopes, their doubts and their fears. At the same time, they also reveal how managers manage their organizations, how they interpret their profession, and how they understand their moral responsibility. Finally, they help to show how managers are perceived by their employees and colleagues. All things considered, stories are of the utmost importance in the attempt to explore, understand and reflect on the idea of management.

Yiannis Gabriel (2000) emphasizes that stories have to do with meaning and sense making. He writes: 'Stories emerged as the great factories of *meaning*, creating it, transforming it, testing it, sustaining it, fashioning it, and refashioning it. And storytelling, far from being the preserve of old grandmothers during those long Nordic winter nights, became ubiquitous; the craft and the trade of artists and advertisers, the stuff of television talk shows, the preoccupation of lawyers and managers, the unending project of all people trying *to make sense* of their daily lives and experiences' (italics MJV) (Gabriel, 2000, p. 4).

The stories told in this chapter serve not only as illustrations of management but also as an empirical foundation for the analysis of the activities of managers. To borrow an expression from Donald Schön (1983), they are meant to present the perspective of a 'reflective practitioner'.

Five Stories From the Management Practice

The first story, which deals with the field of manufacturing, touches on the issues of the meaning of simple rituals in an organization. This meaning came forward when a new plant manager did not perform one of these rituals. The consequences were very serious.

Story 1: Shaking Hands on the Shop Floor

In 1997, I started my job as a manufacturing manager in the Glass Factory in Aachen (Germany). One important ritual was shaking hands on the shop floor. Every morning, I visited a part of the factory, shook hands with the employees and exchanged some words with them (I speak German fluently). My boss, John Cadier, who was responsible for the whole plant, also visited the shop floor regularly and shook hands with the employees. One year after I took the job, my boss John moved on and was succeeded by Ricardo Fernandez, an expatriate from South America. Several people advised Ricardo to visit the shop floor and to shake hands. However, amongst others because he did not speak the German language, he did not follow this advice. This change in management induced a significant deal of distrust among the factory workers and middle managers. As one department manager observed, 'the employees have no trust in the new plant manager. The former one visited the shop floor regularly. The employees knew him. He talked with them. The new plant manager never visits the shop floor. They don't know him, they don't see him and they don't trust him.' Similarly, the chairman of the workers council made the following remark: 'The employees have no trust in the new plant manager. He does not speak German and he does not visit the people on the shop floor. The employees do not believe that he fights for them and for their future.' Finally, a department manager expressed doubt about the leadership potential of the new plant manager: 'He does not know what happens on the shop floor. Therefore, he cannot control the organization.'

The second story deals with the closure of a factory. It tells the story of an employee whose work was more than earning money. It is a story about the meaning of work.

Story 2: Closing the Factory

In 1990, I was responsible for the manufacturing activities of ceramic multilayer actuators. At the time, it took a lot of effort to develop the dicing process. In this step, a ceramic plate was diced into individual products. An operator, named Peter, had worked from the very beginning in the dicing department. He had assisted in the organization and the improvement of the dicing process. By that point in time, Peter had been with the company for a full twenty-five years, and during a company celebration, I was fortunate enough to have him tell me about his background. As he related to me, he had been raised in a small family together with one brother, who later became a successful captain of a ship. While he had been jealous of his brother's career for many years, this changed dramatically with his own successes in reworking the dicing production process. He was also particularly proud to be the first operator of his shift. Only five years after its opening, however, the factory had to be shut down due to adverse developments in the market. Several days after the announcement, during an evening shift, I had another long talk with Peter. As he told me, he felt very down – indeed, tears even came to his eyes, for the factory, as he said, was his factory, and now it was going to be closed. His job in our factory had clearly meant a great deal to him – much more than a mere means of earning money, it was an integral part of his life's work.

The third story is about a psychiatric hospital. It deals with the issue of developing new clinical pathways for patients with severe mental disorders. This story addresses the question 'What is good care?' and the importance of dialogues with societal stakeholders.

Story 3: Developing Clinical Pathways for Patients Suffering From Severe Mental Disorders

In 2004, I became the director of a psychiatric hospital and held the final responsibility for all of its activities. At the time, there was an intense discussion going on about reworking the care for patients suffering from severe mental disorders. The major point of discussion centered around the question of what good care for such patients should look like. In total, there were two basic options. The first option was to follow the classical approach of long-term care, which covered everything from admission to the hospital to therapy and daily activities. The second option emphasized the rehabilitation and participation of the patient. It focused on the patients' independent living and included the support of a multi-disciplinary team that would take care of all of the patient's activities. Another point of discussion concerned the question of how to involve other societal stakeholders – that is, both the family and friends of the patients, as well as other participants in the broader community, such as the police and judicial authorities. In the end, a great deal of time, conscientious dialogue and leadership was needed in order to arrive at a consensus that didn't lose sight of 'optimal care' and that did justice to 'responsibility' of the various stakeholders involved.

The fourth story is the about an innovation network. It touches on the role of values and ideals in management. It shows that, beyond merely having a vision or being driven by certain ideals, managers and directors also have the capability to translate their vision and ideals into organizational processes and in motivating their employees to work accordingly.

Story 4: Cooperating With Mayo Clinic

Since 2008, I have worked as a board member at VitaValley, an innovation-network in health care. VitaValley has a strategic cooperation with Mayo Clinic, a foundation that is one the best health-care organizations in the United States. The mission of the Mayo Clinic, in its own words, is '[t]o inspire hope and contribute to health and well-being by providing the best care to every patient through integrated clinical practice, education and research' and its motto is '[t]he needs of the patient come first.' Over the course of the past years, I have spoken with countless employees at Mayo Clinic, from the Chief Executive Officer to the hospital's taxi drivers, from doctors to nurses, from managers to secretaries. Regardless of their position or rank in the organization, everyone echoes the same, central message: 'the needs of the patients come first'. This clearly shows how the Clinic's mission and its primary value guide all aspects of each employee's daily work.

The final story is about 'management' in church. It is a story about opposing views and developing support.

Story 5: Buying a Piano

I have been the chairman of the church board for many years. Our church employs only one person: the pastor. All other activities in the community are done by volunteers. In the last decades, the 'power' of the church board is decreasing. More and more, it is important to develop support for policies, year plans, and practical decisions. Easily, discussions about 'small' topics can flare up. Once, we had at a church meeting a discussion about a new music instrument. Music and singing are seen as key activities to experience community and to honor God. The background of this discussion was that the existing organ was not suitable for guiding the community in singing modern revival songs. The question was: Do we buy a piano or a grand piano? An advantage of a grand piano is that it more easily fills the whole church. But, a grand piano is much more expensive. During the meeting it appeared that the differences of opinion were large. Some people choose the piano (lower costs) and others the grand piano (higher quality). At the time, no decision was made. After the meeting, I had a discussion with the church member. He suggested hiring a piano and grand piano to do a try-out. Additionally, he suggested inviting the members of the church to judge the quality of both instruments. Luckily, we could hire at the same time a piano and a grand piano. Additionally, it was agreed that the rent costs would be waived when we would buy one of them. In a three month period, both instruments were tried out with different type of songs. The judgment of the community was: both instruments meet the specifications and the differences in quality between the piano and grand piano were small. One member was decided to purchase the cheaper piano.

Observations

We can make the following observations:

- These stories suggest that some characteristics of management come back in every context, e.g. developing support for policy plans and the execution of these plans (story 3 and 5).
- These stories make it plausible that there are differences in the type of considerations between different contexts. Factories are about controlling

processes (story 2), health care about caring for patients (story 3 and 4), and churches about making music for the glory of God.

- These stories show that values (story 1, 3, and 4) and meaning of life (story 2) play an important role.
- Story 1 is about sense making of daily rituals in relation to the behavior of managers.
- Story 3 addresses the importance of dialogues with stakeholders.
- Finally, the nature of management strongly depends on the nature of the primary process of the organization.

In discussing the nature of the managerial work we have to take into account these observations.

AN ORGANIZATIONAL APPROACH TO MANAGEMENT

How to understand the nature of management? In this section, we would like to argue that an organizational approach is very fruitful to answer the research question.

Different Types of Approaches

Peter Northouse (2013) shows that there are different approaches to understand management. For example, the traits approach focuses on the personal characteristics that make people great managers, the skills approach on the skills and abilities that can be learned and developed, the style approach on what leaders do and how they act, the situational approach on the ability of a manager to adapt his style to the demands of his subordinates, the contingency approach on the match between the style of the manager and the requirements of the context, and the servant leadership approach on the concerns of the employees.

In this section, we will focus on an organizational approach to management (Verkerk, 2004). The reason for that is that the role and function of management is strongly influenced by the design of the organization. In organization science there are two main paradigms for organizing: Taylorism and Participative democracy. Each paradigm is supported by its own values, uses its own principles for organizing, and prescribes its own style of management.

Taylorism

The engineer Frederick Taylor (1856-1915) introduced scientific methods in industry and proposed new concepts of management. His views have formed several generations of engineers and managers and his concepts have been exported from the USA to Europe, Russia and the Far East. In his book *The Principles of Scientific Management* (1911) he proposes four principles. The first principle implies that the production process is divided in elementary steps. For every step the 'one best way' and 'one best implement' have to be developed to run the production as efficient as possible. The second principle involves that the workers are selected with respect to their physical and intellectual qualities. After that they are trained to work according to the one best way by using the one best implement. The third principle requires heartily cooperation between management and workmen. Such cooperation, as he states, implies a 'mental revolution' on both sides. The last principle implies a division of responsibilities. The management has to do 'brain work' and the workers 'hand work'.

The objective of Frederick Taylor was to control the manufacturing process completely. This idea is strongly expressed in *The Principles of Scientific Management* (1911) where he writes that 'In the past man has been first; in the future the system must be first' (p. 7). In other words, managers have to be empowered and employees have to be controlled. Taylor was a controversial person. Many saw him as a maker of the modern world and other viewed him as a modern slave driver. The inhuman aspects of the Taylor system were criticized by many politicians and journalists (Kanigel, 1997). Despite all criticism, Taylor's ideas spread quickly. The principles of Taylor – in combination with the moving assembly line of Henry Ford – have shaped western industry and fueled western prosperity. However, these principles also had a bitter other side: the extreme division of labor and its hierarchical style of management led to fear, mistrust, dehumanization and alienation in industrial organizations (e.g. Blauner, 1964).

Participative Democracy

The most important and well-developed counter movement to Taylorism is the Socio-Technical Systems Design (STSD). Later on this movement was referred to as participative approach, democratic tradition or participative democracy. The basic objective of the Socio-Technical Systems Design (STSD) is to put an end to the extreme division of labor that has dominated industry since the introduction of Taylor's principles. Socio-Technical Systems Design implies a fundamental redesign of the organization. This redesign is focused on the design of the workplace, design of the factory, control of labor, and communication. Van Eijnatten (1993, p. 33) characterizes STSD by the following qualities: (a) it adds a set of democratic values to organization theory, (b) it is a holistic approach that combines both management and workers interests, (c) it adds to the usual technical and economic goals a set of relevant human goals, (d) it propagates both democratic structures and democratic social processes, (e) it is developed as an action research movement, and (f) it includes conceptual and methodological diversity. These six statements express – especially in comparison with Taylorism – a paradigmatic change in organizational theory.

In the democratic tradition a shift has been advocated from representative democracy ('workers council') to participative democracy. In this tradition design models and theories of change have been developed. The kernel of this approach is that every employee needs to have the power to manage their own work; this also holds for (middle) managers. A democratic approach has a positive influence on all aspects of organizing: employee satisfaction, loyalty to the company, trust in management, quality of products or services, and efficiency of the organization (Eijnatten, 1993; Verkerk, 2004).

Organizational Design and Style of Management

Taylorism and Participative democracy reflect two different paradigms about the nature of human being, the organization of labor, and the style of management. Taylorism believes that operators are lazy and balky. They need to be managed hierarchically to keep them under control to keep them under control and to work efficiently. Participative democracy believes that operators are sources of creativity and quality control. They need to be empowered to deliver a good performance.

PRACTICE APPROACHES

Managers and directors perform a lot of activities. It is believed that these activities have to be done in a professional way. The adage is that professional managers and directors use professional techniques and standards. Even in voluntary organizations these techniques and standards seep through. So, it is tempting to describe management as a practice. In this section, we will explore the different practice approaches in view of management.

MacIntyre: Management as Tradition and Community

MacIntyre is one of the fathers of the practice approach (see chapter 2). He interprets practices in terms of tradition and community. In his view practices are shaped in the course of history and are embedded in society. They are characterized by four features: (a) a practice is a 'cooperative human activity': it is not about individuals but about cooperating human beings, (b) a practice is 'socially established': the activities are related to or rooted in a community, (c) the practice realizes 'goods internal to that form of activity': the produced goods are characteristic for that practice, and (d) the practice operates to 'standards of excellence': the activities in this practice meet certain standards of quality (MacIntyre, 1984, p. 187).

Is management a practice? MacIntyre strongly criticizes the attitude and behavior of managers. In his view, managers are 'stock characters' in the 'social drama of the present age' (MacIntyre, 1984, p. 27). He describes managers as rational bureaucrats who judge situations from a 'purely universal and abstract point that is totally detached from all social particularity' (pp. 31-32) and who conceive themselves as 'morally neutral characters whose skills enable them to devise the most efficient means of achieving whatever end is proposed' (p. 74). He blames managers that they serve the 'modern economic order' with 'its individualism, its acquisitiveness and its elevation of the values of the market to a central social place' (p. 254). It goes without saying that MacIntyre reduces the world of management to Taylorist approaches, which are characterized by 'neutral' and 'rational' approaches. This reduction hinders him to investigate the nature of management practices. Brewer (1997), Moore and Beadle (2006), and Beabout (2012), however, argue that MacIntyre's definition of a practice also can be applied to management practices to develop the idea of virtuous organizations.

Jochemsen and Others: Practices as Normative Structures

Jochemsen, Glas and Hoogland (Jochemsen & Glas, 1997; Hoogland & Jochemsen, 2000; Jochemsen, 2006) have developed the so-called normative practice approach for understanding professional practices in healthcare (see chapter 2). The normative practice offers three perspectives to understand professional practices: structure, context and direction. The structure describes the qualitative aspects of a practice, the context the influence of the environment wherein a practice is developed, and the direction the basic beliefs that underlie a practice. Verkerk (2015) has shown that this approach fruitfully can be applied to the world of management and organization. He uses this approach to normative aspects of professional practices in general and the moral responsibility of managers in particular.

Nicolini: Practices as 'Sayings' and 'Doings'

Nicolini (2012, pp. 1-6) believes that practice theories can have a 'distinctive contribution to the study of work and organization'. In his view this type of approaches can offer a 'radically new ways of understanding and explaining social and organizational phenomena'. Especially, because these approaches are inherently relational, leave space for the initiative, creativity, and individual performance of individual agents, and put emphasis on the importance of power, conflict and politics as constitutive elements of our social reality. Nicolini (2012, p. 221) emphasizes that the study of practices always starts in the middle of action: 'Attention should be towards issues such as: what are people doing and saying? What are they trying to do when they speak? What is said and done? How do the patterns of doing and saying flow in time?' In conclusion, the main message of Nicolini is that reflection on management and management practices has to start in the middle of the action: the shop floor and the board room. With that, Nicolini (2012) also legitimizes and stimulates storytelling as a source of knowledge.

Verkerk: Practices as Embedded Structures (Triple I Model)

MacIntyre (1984, p. 194) says that practices needs institutions for their sustenance. He argues that practices focus on internal goods and institutions on external goods like money, power and status. MacIntyre, however, does not present an organizational perspective on the relationship between practices and institutions. In addition, his analysis of the management practice as servants of the 'modern economic order' is too one-sided to be a reliable guide.

Verkerk (2014) and Verkerk, Holtkamp, Wouters, and Van Hoof (2017) have developed an organizational variant of the normative practice approach, the so-called Triple I approach. This variant is inspired by the ideas of MacIntyre, Jochemsen, Glas, Hoogland, Nicolini and others. The development of this variant is motivated by the fact that practices do not function independently but always function in an organizational context. Practices (1) are embedded in organizations, (2) cooperate with other practices in other organizations, and (3) interact with and are influenced by the stakeholders of their own organization.

The Triple I approach offers three perspectives to understand professional practices: 'identity and intrinsic values', 'interests of stakeholders', 'ideals and basic beliefs' (Figure 1). The first 'I' refers to the 'identity and intrinsic values' of a practice. It focuses on the nature of a practice and what is important for that practice. The second 'I' refers to the 'interests of stakeholders' of a practice. It recognizes that practices interact with and are co-shaped by stakeholders. The third 'I' refers to the 'ideals and basic beliefs' that are embedded in the practice (past), that influence the practice (present), and that will change the practice (future). Ideals and basic beliefs co-shape protocols and guidelines, habits and attitudes of the employees, and managerial relationships.

Evaluation

The practice approaches presented in this section offer a variety of ideas and thoughts to investigate the research question of this chapter. Additionally, they function as spotlights to understand the different stories told in a previous section.

Figure 1. The Triple I approach to practices

For example, these stories describe what managers and directors are doing and saying (Nicolini), address topics like creativity, power and conflict (Nicolini), stress quality standards (MacIntyre), emphasize the own nature of a practice (MacIntyre, Jochemsen, Verkerk), underline normative aspects of behavior in practices (MacIntyre, Jochemsen, Verkerk), highlights ideals and basic beliefs (Jochemsen, Verkerk), and considers stakeholders (Verkerk). We conclude that practice approaches are relevant to investigate the nature of management. Especially, we will use the Triple I model because this approach is developed in close cooperation with professionals and is co-shaped by organizational and managerial considerations.

ANALYSIS OF MANAGEMENT PRACTICES

To understand the nature of management practices we will analyze these practices from the perspective of the different I's.

First I: Identity and Intrinsic Values

The organizational concepts discussed in a previous section are universally applicable. They have been used and are still used to organize factories, healthcare institutions, and religious organizations. Many scholars and practitioners believe that management is a discipline that can be applied universally. In other words, they believe that management methods and control techniques are independent of the specific nature of a practice and its context. After all, as the argument goes, management always has to do with the same sorts of activities: satisfying clients (customers, patients, members), managing people (employees, volunteers), and keeping a handle on finances. What this conclusion fails to take into consideration is how the nature of management as such is determined by the identity of the 'primary process' of the organization. The notion of 'primary process' is crucial. In brief, it refers to the operational processes that constitute the core activities of an organization and that generate value for clients, members, citizens and society. In the terminology of MacIntyre: the 'goods internal to that form of activity' are different.

The primary process of a factory is the production of goods, that of a hospital is curing illnesses and caring for people, and that of a church to glorify God and to serve society. In factories, hospitals, and churches there are also a wide variety of subsidiary activities that need to be done, such as administration, finance and human resources. While these sorts of activities are undoubtedly necessary for the operation of a factory, a hospital, and a church, they do not belong to the core activity as such, nor do they – spoken black and white – generate value for customers, patients or members. As I would like to argue, the nature and character of management is (co-)determined by the different sorts of primary processes that are carried out in different organizations.

The relationship between identity and intrinsic values is a reciprocal one. On the one hand, values concretize the identity of the practice, and on the other hand, values constitute the identity. Let us start with the identity. The identity of a factory is intimately bound up with the work of controlling technical processes. As such, a factory's basic challenge consists in managing the manufacturing process in such a way that its products can be delivered to customers by the promised date and according to the agreed standards of quality. All of the different processes that go on in factories – from equipment maintenance to quality control, from personnel training to human resources and management – ultimately have to be focused on the control of the production process. The main intrinsic values of manufacturing processes are controlled production, safety, quality, efficiency, sustainability, and so on. The identity and the intrinsic values clearly illustrate what manufacturing managers 'do' and what they 'talk about'.

The core identity of a healthcare institution is tied up with the activities of caring for and curing the diseases and illnesses of its patients. The primary challenge of a general hospital is to make accurate diagnoses and to cure its patients. In case healing is not possible, than the hospital will support patients to cope with their limitations or offer palliative care. The example of a psychiatric hospital clearly shows that care has a broad meaning. The challenge of a psychiatric institution is to cure its patients, or, at the very least, to ease their mental suffering in some measure. In many cases, however, patients suffer from illnesses and disorders that are chronic (or incurable). As such, another essential component of a hospital's work, or primary process, will need to be focused on care – that is, on enhancing a patient's existing capabilities, on helping patients to cope with limitations, on supporting a broader societal participation and on adapting medication to the patient's needs. All of the different processes involved in healthcare work – from diagnosis and therapy to pharmacy prescription and in-patient admission, and from support to referrals – ultimately have to focus either on the cure of or the care for the patient. The main values in healthcare are empathy, close proximity, care, love, and respect. The identity and the intrinsic values of health care clearly show what managerial excellence is: a hospital that cares in an excellent way for its patients.

The identity of a religious institution is connected to its religious activities. In case of Christianity, the primary process it is about organizing services, spiritual care, preaching the gospel, and diaconal activities. Churches believe that they are not only called to care for their members but also acknowledge that they have a societal responsibility, e.g. prophetic speaking, preaching the gospel, and diaconal activities. Surely, the chairman of the board is also responsible for maintenance of the facilities and the finances. However, its main attention goes out to 'managing' the primary process. The main values in a Christian church are loving God, loving other people, living by grace, and surrender.

As the above analysis clearly shows, the practice of management strongly depends on the nature of the primary process of the organization. Management 'as such' has not an own identity and no own intrinsic values. The nature of management practices is fully determined by the identity and intrinsic values of the organization in question. The importance of this conclusion can be clearly illustrated in cases where managers coming from a financial background take on the role of a factory manager or a health care director. Some of them will use their first few months in the new position to gain a better understanding of the organization's primary process, its identity and its intrinsic values. Afterwards, they may then put their managerial and financial expertise to use in streamlining and further enhancing the organization's operations. Others, however, are liable to persist in the belief that an organization's success ultimately (or exclusively) resides in its financials, and they will act accordingly. Consequently, the primary process will be hollowed out and its intrinsic values will be corrupted to realize financial targets.

One could object, of course, that some activities ('doings') and rhetoric ('sayings') have to be done in every management context and every organization. For example, one of the key responsibilities of a manager or director is to develop a strategic plan for the future. In addition, every manager or director has to meet key performance indicators with respect to its activities, human resources management, and financials. While we will not disagree that managers and directors need to excel in these sorts of activities, we would also want to argue that strategic plans and key performance indicators are not 'abstract' and 'context-free' but also can be understood and gain meaning from the primary process of the organization.

First I: Identity and Intrinsic Values – A Philosophical Account

In the foregoing section, we argued that the nature of management practices is determined by the identity and intrinsic values of the organization in question. We would like to sharpen this statement from a philosophical point of view. The philosopher Herman Dooyeweerd (1969) has developed the so-called theory of individuality structures. He argues that society is not a 'whole' or a 'unity' but is mixture of different human structured. In his view, these structures have a different nature, cannot be reduced to each other, and interact with each other. He claims that every societal structure has an own nature that can be qualified by a certain aspect or dimension (qualifying aspect). Table 1 gives an overview of the qualifying aspect of different societal structures. For example, a shop is characterized by the economic aspect, a court by the juridical aspect and a choir by the aesthetical aspect. Dooyeweerd recognizes that a shop also functions in the juridical and aesthetical aspect: a shop is bound to regulation and an attractive design of the shop stimulates the sales. In essence, however, a shop is not about judging whether customers comply with the law or enjoy the beauty of the shop, but about selling goods and making a profit. The same holds for a court: a court also functions in the economic aspect (a court needs a budget) and in the aesthetical aspect (beauty of the exterior and interior of the building). But the essence of the court is to do justice. Finally, a choir also functions in the economic (a choir makes expenses) and juridical aspect (to prevent noise disturbance). But the essence of a choir is to give an excellent aesthetical performance.

The theory of individuality structures supports us to understand the nature of the practices discussed in this chapter: a factory is technologically qualified (controlled production), a hospital morally (giving care), and a church spiritual (religious activities). In the words of Mouw and Griffioen (1993), all these practices exhibit 'unique pattern' of living together. One such unique pattern is found in the factory, another in the hospital and again another in the church. These unique patterns are co-shaped by managers and directors. It is their responsibility that people act and cooperate in such a way that factories produce excellent products, hospital excellent care, and churches excellent religious activities.

Second I: Inclusion of the Justified Interests of Stakeholders

While it is generally accepted that managers and directors need to manage the interests of stakeholders, a number of questions on what this entails remain open

Table 1. Overview of the qualifying aspect of societal structures

Societal structure	Qualification / qualifying function
Family	moral (caring for each other)
Sports club	social (enjoying to do a sport with others), biological (training the body)
Reading club	social (enjoying to read a book together), lingual (enjoying literature)
Debate club	social (enjoying to debate topics with each other), analytical (logical argumentation)
Grocery store	economic (making profit by offering products)
Car shop	economic (making profit by selling cars)
Factory	technical control, shaping (control of technical processes)
Elderly union	social (enjoying each other's accompany), juridical (improving juridical position of elderly)
Schools and universities	shaping or forming (education, development of capabilities)
Museum of arts	aesthetic (enjoying the beauty of art)
Music hall	aesthetic (enjoying the beauty of music)
Authorities (local, regional, national)	juridical (making and executing laws)
Political party	juridical (influencing societal developments by proposing laws and by critically checking authorities
Churches, mosques	spiritual (relation to God)
New age communities	spiritual (relation to the whole cosmos)

to debate. Who exactly are the stakeholders of a company? When and how are their interests justified? And how should these interests be incorporated into a company's planning and operation?

We would like to start with three comments. Firstly, most organizations have many stakeholders. Easily, five, ten or even more stakeholders can be identified. The nature of these stakeholders can be understood by using the theory of individuality structures of Dooyeweerd as discussed in the foregoing section. In the stakeholder analysis given below, the qualifying aspect will be given between brackets. Secondly, in everyday speech all parties involved in a practice or an organization are named as stakeholder. For example, employees of a factory, patients in hospitals, and members of a church. We do understand the reason behind this use of words: all these groups have a 'stake' in the relevant practice or organization. However, from a systematic point of view we would like to distinguish between people who are part of a practice and shape its activities, and people who are not part of that practice and have a stake in its activities. Finally, in environmental discussions often 'nature' or 'the environment' is indicated as stakeholder. Sometimes, the interests of nature are defended by action groups or nature protection associations.

The most important stakeholders of factories are suppliers of materials, suppliers of equipment and software (economic), customers in the industrial sector (economic), customers in health care (moral), local, regional and national authorities (juridical), local community (economic), unions (economic, juridical), neighbors (social, economic), and so on. The most important stakeholders of a hospital are suppliers of medicine (economic), suppliers of equipment and software (economic), family (moral), associations of doctors and nurses (moral), health care inspection (moral, juridical), neighbors (social, economic), local, regional and national authorities (juridical), local community (moral, economic), unions (economic, juridical), and so on. Finally, the most important stakeholders of churches are the local community in general (spiritual), local community in a diaconal perspective (moral), and authorities (juridical).

We would like to elaborate one of the stories: the issue of stakeholder interests emerged in my attempt to develop clinical pathways for patients suffering from severe mental disorders (story 3). Ultimately, the whole discussion centered on the fundamental question, 'What does good care look like for such patients?' For the classical approach to psychiatric care, the roles and the interests of the different stakeholders were quite clear. In order to address the issues of patient 'rehabilitation' and greater societal 'participation', however, a new and somewhat more complicated model was needed. For instead of simply keeping the patient confined to the hospital 'under lock and key', we now needed to find a way to include the family and the local authorities in such a way that the patients would be able to live, under the guidance of psychiatric professionals, as relatively 'normal', quasi-independent individuals. Instead of simply paying irregular visits to the patient, for example, family members were going to need to be able to actively support their suffering relatives (both materially and emotionally) to a much greater degree. In addition to helping them live relatively independent lives, family relatives were also going to have to function as the 'eyes and ears' of the professionals in case problems like mental breakdowns happened to arise. The new model also needed to take the participation and concerns of the local authorities into consideration. After all, placing patients in relatively independent living situations posed the risk of causing trouble for the patient's new neighbors (for example, in the case of a potentially violent, psychotic episode). In addition, the direct presence of the patients in the community was likely to attract the attention of opportunistic drug dealers. In both cases, then, we were clearly going to need to cooperate with the local authorities. Finally, the new operating model also implied that the psychiatric professionals would be working in teams in different parts of the city. As it turned out, this change was largely positive in nature, for it opened up new opportunities to care for the city's homeless who were suffering from psychiatric problems. By taking each of these different sets of concerns into account, our new working model adapted the primary process of our operations in order to meet the needs of the patients and to address the concerns of a wider set of stakeholders.

The idea of taking the interests of stakeholders into account is based on the stakeholder theory developed by Freeman (2001), which is now widely accepted in the business community and figures prominently in many business textbooks. The idea of interests, however, has to be refined. After all, not every interest is a justified interest. The notion of individuality structures with their own qualifying function helps us to identify the justified interests of a stakeholder. We would like to give some examples. Firstly, the qualifying function of the local government is juridical insofar as its main objective is to ensure that justice is maintained in the public sphere and that the local laws are upheld. As such, its primary justified interest is found in (and limited to) the juridical field, and its normative character serves to differentiate between good laws and bad laws, or between conforming to the law and transgressing it. Secondly, the qualifying function of an enterprise is economical because it relates to the delivery of products and the performance of services at a certain price. Here too, the economic law has an inherent normative character (for example, poor pricing can ruin a company). Thirdly, the qualifying function of psychiatric hospitals is moral, focusing as it does on the delivery of quality care to patients. Our transition from a traditional model of care to a model based on rehabilitation and broader social participation was inspired by the idea that, from a moral point of view, the latter model would excel beyond the former in certain important respects. Finally, we would like to give an example of an interest that is not justified. Once I had a discussion with a professor in architecture about designing a long term home for psychiatric patients. At a certain moment, he remarked that the peers of an architect are an important stakeholder in view of the aesthetic beauty of the building. To his dismay, I commented his suggestion and said that the most important stakeholders with respect to the beauty of the building are patients, care professionals, and the neighbors. In addition, I remarked that colleague architects are no stakeholder of the new long term home and that they have no justified interest.

This analysis learns us a lot about the nature of management. At first, every type of organization has its own 'set' of stakeholders. That means that the stakeholders of a factory differ strongly different from the stakeholders of a hospital. Similarly, the stakeholders of a church differ also from the stakeholders of a hospital or a factory. Second, every stakeholder has its own justified interests. The justified interests are primarily determined by the qualifying aspect of the relevant stakeholder. Finally, managers have to determine whether or not an interest is a justified interest. Also they have to reflect on the question how to do justice to the justified interest of stakeholders without affecting care in a negative way.

Third I: Ideals and Basic Beliefs

At first, we would like to explore the field of ideas and basic beliefs. Then we will return to the different practices. In each of the stories presented above, ideals and basic beliefs play a crucial role. The story 'Shaking hands' touches on certain cultural ideals. The story 'Closing a factory' is about a worker grappling with the meaning, or lived significance, of his work – as well as its loss. The story 'Developing clinical pathways' recounts the dreams of professionals to rehabilitate psychiatric patients and to offer them an opportunity to participate as full citizens in society. The story 'Cooperating with Mayo Clinic' presents the mission and values of a healthcare organization. Finally, the story, 'Buying a piano' shows that 'simple' decisions as buying a piano is triggered by basic beliefs about faith and honoring God.

Ideals and basic beliefs also play a crucial role in designing and managing organizations. We have shown that there are two main paradigms for organizing: Taylorism and Participative democracy. Each paradigm has its own principles for organizing, requires a certain style of management and it driven by different ideals and basic beliefs. Taylorism believes in a separation between hands and brains, between doing and thinking. It believes that employees have to execute only one simple task and need to be managed in a hierarchical to keep them under control and to work efficiently. On the other hand, participative democracy believes in an integration of hands and brains, of doing and thinking. It believes that operators are sources of creativity and quality control. They need to be empowered to deliver a good performance. The relationship between 'ideals and basic beliefs' and 'organization and style of management' is complex. On the one hand, the existing organizational structure, organizational culture and style of management are an expression of the ideals and basic beliefs of the past. On the other hand, present ideals and basic beliefs shape the future development of the organization structure, organization culture, and style of management. Especially in setting up a new organization, there are many degrees of freedom in shaping the organizational structure and developing the culture and style of management.

Now, we return on the role of ideals and basic beliefs on the different practices. On first sight, one could argue that managers and directors are influenced by the same ideals and basic beliefs, i.e. that of western society in the 21st century. From that perspective, one could also argue that managing a factory, hospital or church are not that different. However, a further analysis shows that ideals and basic beliefs do not wipe out the differences between practices. On top of that, we would claim that they articulate the own nature of every practice. There are two reasons for that.

The first reason is that the identity and intrinsic values of a practice are co-shaped by ideals and basic beliefs. The mechanism for co-shaping strongly depends on the nature of the practice. The second reason is ideals and basic beliefs emerge from different 'sources', e.g. culture, discipline, organization and individual. Each source has its own mechanism to co-shape the identity and intrinsic values.

Firstly, culture as a source of ideals and basic beliefs. As we known, Western culture has been shaped by a variety of different traditions: Greek, Christian, modern and postmodern. Each of these traditions is shaped by ideals and basic beliefs about nature, human being, morality, and transcendence (Ferry, 2010). The ideals and basic beliefs of these broader traditions are still present in our society, shaping both the actions and aspirations of individuals and organizations. Secondly, the relevant disciplines are also sources of values. Generally, there are in every discipline different views or schools of thought. For example, the story dealing with patients suffering from severe mental disorders highlighted a conflict between the traditional view of psychiatric care and a newer model, which promoted rehabilitation and broader societal participation. Every discipline and every school has its own ideals and basic beliefs. Thirdly, organizations are also a source of ideals and basic beliefs. Generally, they have worded their ideals and basic beliefs their vision, mission statement, and company values. Mostly, the 'hand' of the founder is still present in this type of documents. Organizations actively evaluate their own histories and intentionally determine where and how to position themselves in relation to their surrounding cultural and natural environment. These processes come to the fore particularly clearly in policies by means of which organizations reinterpret their missions and set about putting their values into action. Finally, individual employees themselves are also sources of ideals and basic beliefs. Generally, the ideals of beliefs of individual employees do not fully coincide with the leading values of the organization. In the best case, there is an overlap in the most important values, in the worst case there is a tension between the different value systems. We would like to emphasize the influence of the discipline on ideals and basic beliefs. Every discipline develops its own view on the nature of a practice. Especially, the development of different schools highlights the discussion within the own discipline to define the nature of its practice. Therefore, these discussions will result in an articulation of the nature of the practice. Similarly, the influence of cultural, organizational and individual sources of ideals and basic beliefs will trigger the discussion about the nature of the practice.

The analysis of the influence of ideals and basic beliefs learns us a lot about management. Firstly, it shows that the practices in which managers and directors work are co-shaped by ideals and beliefs. Second, it makes it plausible that the influence of ideals and beliefs do not wipe out the differences between practices but articulate these differences.

DISCUSSION AND CONCLUSION

The research question of this chapter is: What is the nature of a management practice? To answer this question we first addressed three sub questions:

1. What type of approach to management is required?
2. What type of philosophical approach is required?
3. How to understand the relationship between a practice and the management of an organization in which this practice is embedded?

What Type of Approach to Management Is Required?

In a previous section we have pled for an organizational approach to management, in particular because this approach highlights the relationship between the role and the function of a manager and the design of the organization. In view of the third sub question, the argumentation for this choice can be strengthened: an organizational approach to management is needed to investigate the relationship between a practice and the management of the organization in which a practice is embedded.

The organizational approach for management has two main paradigms for organizing: Taylorism and Participative democracy. MacIntyre (1984) also chooses an organizational approach to management. In his view, all managers fit to the archetype of the scientific manager who follows the principles of Taylor's philosophy. This statement, however, conflicts with its own view on the unpredictability of human behavior as pointed out by Brewer (1997). Additionally, in the 'best case' this statement holds for Taylorist organizations that are managed by bureaucratic managers, but surely do not apply for participative democratic organizations that are managed by people managers. The Triple I analysis clearly shows that both the practice of bureaucratic managers and that of people managers can be characterized as management practice. However, these practices strongly differ in intrinsic values and have been shaped by different ideals and basic beliefs.

The first sub question leads to two conclusions:

1. An organizational approach to management is needed to understand the nature of the management practice.
2. This approach makes it plausible that there are two main types of management practices: a Taylorist management practice and a participative democratic management practice. These types are shaped by different ideals and basic beliefs.

What Type of Philosophical Approach Is Required?

In a previous section we have explored different practice approaches. On the one hand, these approaches build on each other. On the other hand, they all present a specific perspective. Nicolini emphasizes that an investigation to management practices has to start in the middle of an action. In his view, researchers has to focus on 'what is said' and 'what is done'. We would like to add: it is equally important to reflect on 'what is not said' and 'what is not done' (Verkerk, 2004). This chapter recognizes the importance of the action. For that reason, we have presented a couple of stories in the beginning of this chapter.

MacIntyre highlights the idea of 'inner goods' and 'standards of excellence'. This contribution to understanding practices cannot be underestimated. It articulates that each practice has an 'own ethics' that – under normal conditions – that cannot be overruled by another practice. Whatever the relation may be between, for example, a healthcare practice and a management practice, it is not allowed that the healthcare practice is overruled by the management practice or the other way around. Jochemsen, Glas and Hoogland emphasize the normative aspects of professional practices. From this perspective, it is not acceptable that that the normativity of one practice is dominated by another one. Regarding this topic, Verkerk 'sings the same song', although the words differ. He emphasizes the identity and the intrinsic values of every practice.

Jochemsen, Glas, Hoogland, and Verkerk underline the directional component: all practices are co-shaped by certain ideals, values, and basic beliefs. This chapter has shown that this also holds for management practices. From this perspective, management practices are not 'neutral' but always reflect a view on man, organization, society and market.

The Triple I model as proposed by Verkerk is co-shaped by organizational considerations. This model is developed in close cooperation of professionals in different practices. Amongst other, it explicitly addresses the interests of stakeholders.

The second sub question leads to the following conclusions:

3. Practice approaches are very suitable to investigate the nature of the activities of managers. The main reasons are that these approaches take their starting point in the daily activities, do justice to the own nature of different activities, and make underlying ideals, values and basic beliefs explicit.
4. The Triple I model is co-shaped by organizational considerations. This model is very suitable to investigate the nature of management practices.

How to Understand the Relationship Between a Practice and the Management of an Organization in Which This Practice Is Embedded?

MacIntyre makes a clear distinction between a practice and the organization in which a practice is embedded. He believes that practices focus on 'internal goods' and organizations on 'external goods'. He also states that organizations are necessary for the sustenance of practices. MacIntyre (1984, p. 194) writes: 'Institutions are characteristically and necessarily concerned with (...) external goods. They are involved in acquiring money and other material goods; they are structured in terms of power and status, and they distribute money, power and status as rewards (…). For no practices can survive for any length of time unsustained by institutions. Indeed so intimate is the relationship of practices to institutions (…) the ideals and the creativity of the practice are always vulnerable to the acquisitiveness of the institution, in which the cooperative care for common goods of the practice is always vulnerable to the competitiveness of the institution'. The stories told in a previous section, the organizational approach presented above, and the analysis of managerial practices, clearly show that the distinction between 'internal goods' and 'external goods' cannot not be held up. It is widely believed that good managers focus on excellence with respect to 'internal goods' and that good professionals also take 'external goods' in consideration.

MacIntyre (1984, p. 194) addresses the 'corrupting power' of organizations: 'In this context the essential feature of the virtues is clear. Without them, without justice, courage and truthfulness, practices could not resist the corrupting power of institutions.' However accurate this comment may be, MacIntyre goes too short in the turn. First, as pointed out above, MacIntyre has only Taylorist organizations in mind. Due to its hierarchical structure this type of organizations are vulnerable for corruption. However, that does mean that in every hierarchical organization corruption is lurking. For example, many family businesses are known for their focus on 'internal goods' and their values. And, most of these businesses are hierarchically managed. Second, not only the corrupting power of managers and organizations is immense, but also the corrupting power of professionals in practices is enormous. Management literature offers many examples of both corrupting powers, e.g. Verkerk (2004).

We would like to return to the organizational perspective. Corruption can take place at any level of the organization. A key condition to prevent corruption is the development of a 'virtuous organization' (Moore and Beadle, 2006). The development of such an organization requires that the virtues are anchored in the individual employees, in the organizational and managerial culture, and in the relationships with the environment (stakeholders). In general, virtuous organizations only will develop in participative democratic organization, see above. The reason is that in this type of organizations are based on respect for the authority, knowledge and skills of every employee. In the terminology of Moore and Beadly (2006, p. 375), a 'power balanced structure' has to be developed. In hierarchical organizations, however, virtuous behavior will only develop when the values related to the 'internal goods' are internalized by both management and employees.

The third sub question leads to the following conclusion:

5. Practices and management of practices organizations are intimately intertwined. Corruption of such intertwined structures takes place when employees (practice) and managers (organization) do not share the same values with respect to the 'internal goods' and the 'external goods' of the organization. Positively formulated: employees and managers have to respect the identity and intrinsic values of each other's practices and have to honor each other's contribution to the organization. Such a respect has to be founded in the organizational structure and its corresponding management style, e.g. in a participative democratic approach.

What Is the Nature of a Management Practice?

Our stories from the shop floor, our organizational approach, and our analysis of management practices from the perspective of the Triple I model show that activities of managers always have to sprout from and have to be focused on the primary process of the organization. In other words, management is not an 'independent' activity and management practices cannot be 'sold separately'.

Our stories from the shop floor, our organizational approach, and our analysis of management practices from the perspective of the Triple I model also show that managers have an own contribution to practices in organizations. They use their knowledge and skills to realize the conditions so that the practices can flourish (identity, intrinsic values). These knowledge and skills are in the area of strategy, organizing, planning, financials, and so on. That own contribution can be qualified – in a Dooyeweerdian terminology – as shaping, giving form to, exerting influence, and using power. From this point of view, management can be described as a practice with an own identity and intrinsic values.

Now we return to the key question of this chapter: What is the nature of a management practice? We would like to introduce the idea of a supportive practice. This idea combines two notions. The first notion is that management is a practice. It has an own identity and own intrinsic values. We have described this identity as shaping, giving form, exerting influence, and using power. The second notion is that it is a specific type of practice, namely, it supports the functioning of other practices.

As a consequence, the identity (and intrinsic values) of a management practice are 'colored' by the specific nature of the domain. May be, the Dooyeweerdian idea of 'disclosure' describes this coloring in an adequate way: all management techniques and methods are adapted to and used in such a way that the supported practice will flourish.

Beabout (2012, p. 414) characterizes management as a 'domain-relative practice'. Rightly, he identifies two qualities of a management practice: '(1) possess internal standards of excellence identifiable to practitioners, and (2) are always related to another particular domain.' The idea of 'supportive practice' strongly expresses the serviceable character of a management practice: it supports a domain. A manager does not cure patients, does not produce any products and does not give pastoral care. A manager supports all these activities. May be, the best description is that a management practice is a supportive practice that are colored – disclosed in a Dooyeweerdian terminology – a by the intrinsic values of the specific domain. This discussion also sheds light on the intrinsic values of a management practice. One of the key values is integrity: respecting and supporting the intrinsic values of the domain. Another key value is courage: the courage to start dialogues with professionals in case of domain related corruption, the courage to start dialogues with managers in case of management related corruption, and the courage to start dialogues with stakeholders in case of unjustified interests.

6. Our final conclusion is that management is a supportive practice that is disclosed by the intrinsic values of the specific domain.

REFERENCES

Beabout, G. R. (2012). Management as a Domain-Relative Practice That Requires and Develops Practical Wisdom. *Business Ethics Quarterly*, *22*(2), 405–432. doi:10.5840/beq201222214

Blauner, R. (1964). *Alienation and Freedom*. Chicago, IL: University of Chicago Press.

Brewer, K. B. (1997). Management as a Practice: A Response to Alasdair MacIntyre. *Journal of Business Ethics*, *16*(8), 825–833. doi:10.1023/A:1017997200200

Ferry, L. (2010). *Learning to live. A user's manual*. New York, NY: Canongate.

Gabriel, Y. (2000). *Storytelling in Organizations: Facts, fictions and fantasies*. Oxford, UK: Oxford University Press. doi:10.1093/acprof:oso/9780198290957.001.0001

Hoogland, J., & Jochemsen, H. (2000). Professional autonomy and the normative structure of medical practice. *Theoretical Medicine and Bioethics*, *21*(5), 457–475. doi:10.1023/A:1009925423036 PMID:11142442

Jochemsen, H. (2006). Normative practices as an intermediate between theoretical ethics and morality. *Philosophia Reformata*, *71*(1), 96–112. doi:10.1163/22116117-90000377

Jochemsen, H., & Glas, G. (1997). *Verantwoord medisch handelen*. Amsterdam: Buijten & Schipperheijn. (in Dutch)

Kanigel, R. (1997). *The One Best Way. Frederick Winslow Taylor and the Enigma of efficiency*. London: Little, Brown and Company.

MacIntyre, A. (1984). *After Virtue. A Study in Moral Theory* (2nd ed.). Notre Dame, IN: University of Notre Dame Press.

Moore, G., & Beadle, R. (2006). In Search of Organizational Virtue in Business: Agents, Goods, Practices, Institutions and Environments. *Organization Studies*, *27*(3), 369–389. doi:10.1177/0170840606062427

Mouw, R. J., & Griffioen, S. (1993). *Pluralisms and Horizons. An Essay in Christian Public Philosophy*. Grand Rapids, MI: W.B. Eerdmans.

Nicolini, D. (2012). *Practice Theory, Work, & Organisation. An Introduction*. Oxford, UK: Oxford University Press.

Northouse, P. G. (2013). *Leadership: Theory and Practice* (6th ed.). Los Angeles, CA: Sage.

Schön, D. A. (1983). *The Reflective Practitioner: How professionals think in action*. London: Ashgate.

Taylor, F. W. (1947a). Shop Management. In *Scientific Management*. London: Harper & Row. (Original work published 1903)

Taylor, F. W. (1947b). The Principles of Scientific Management. In Scientific Management. London: Harper & Row. (Originally published 1911)

van Eijnatten, F. M. (1993). *The Paradigm that Changed the Work Place*. Assen: Van Gorkum.

Verkerk, M. J. (2004). *Trust and Power on the Shop Floor. An Ethnographical, Ethical and Philosophical Study on Responsible Behaviour in Industrial Organisations* (Thesis). Maastricht University, Maastricht. Delft: Eburon.

Verkerk, M.J. (2014). A philosophy-based "toolbox" for designing technology: The conceptual power of Dooyeweerdian philosophy. *Koers – Bulletin for Christian Scholarship, 79*(3), 1-7.

Verkerk, M. J. (2015). A practitioner's reflections on moral leadership: Towards a philosophical foundation. In P. Nullens & S. van den Heuvel (Eds.), *Challenges of Moral Leadership* (pp. 47–72). Leuven: Peeters.

Verkerk, M. J., Holtkamp, F. C., Wouters, E. J. M., & Van Hoof, J. (2017). Professional Practices and User Practices: An Explorative Study in Health Care. *Philosophia Reformata, 82*(2), 167–191. doi:10.1163/23528230-08202001

Chapter 11
Corporate Communication

Jan van der Stoep
Christian University of Applied Sciences Ede, The Netherlands

Peter Jansen
Christian University of Applied Sciences Ede, The Netherlands

ABSTRACT

In September 2015, it appeared that the Volkswagen Group had circumvented the rules for testing diesel car exhaust gases. Although the organization presents itself as eco-friendly, it used a "default device" for diesel cars to produce less CO_2 during test situations. Due to this kind of scandal, corporate communication is often associated with greenwashing and the manipulation of minds. Using the normative practice approach, the authors introduce some basic distinctions that may help to come to a better understanding of what the specific duty and responsibility of communication professionals is. They argue that corporate communication stands or falls with public trust. Building confidence and public legitimation is the main task of communication professionals. Although communication is about the construction of a communal world, that does not mean that framing and strategic reasoning are not important. In order to bring in a legitimate point of view, one has to present this point of view in an impactful way. Communication professionals have to balance between the interests of the organization and the requirements of public legitimation. They also have to make convincingly clear how their personal biography and the narrative of the organization are interrelated.

DOI: 10.4018/978-1-5225-8006-5.ch011

INTRODUCTION

In its corporate sustainability report of 2014, the Volkswagen Group claimed that aims to be ‘the world’s most environmentally compatible automaker.’ This was not just an isolated statement, but part of a broader communication strategy in which the Volkswagen Group presented itself as an eco-friendly company (Siano, Vollero, Conte and Amabile, 2017). On September 8, 2015, however, it appeared that Volkswagen had circumvented the rules. To ensure that Diesel cars produce less CO_2 emission during tests, the company made use of a ‘default device’, specialized software that detects test situations. On the road the Diesel cars were far more polluting. This obviously caused serious damage to Volkswagen’s reputation. It was difficult to maintain that the Volkswagen company really cared about the environment. The image of the organization as a reliable partner became a topic of discussion. In the USA newspapers journalists spoke about ‘fraud’, ‘scandal’ and ‘cheating’ (Siano et al., 2017, p. 31). From that moment on, a lot of effort has been put in restoring the reputation of the Volkswagen Group (Painter and Martins, 2017).

The Volkswagen case is not unique. Similar stories can be told for example about BP, ExxonMobil or Enron. It is not uncommon that organizations present themselves better than that they actually are, causing a discrepancy between ‘talk’ and ‘action’. Due to scandals like this communication often has a bad name. People associate public relations and corporate communication with propaganda, the deliberate manipulation of the minds of people by means of mass psychology. At the same time organizations expect that communication professionals will position the organization as powerful as possible. The identification of communication with propaganda puts the profession under pressure. It faces a double crisis of trust (Hoffjann and Seidenglanz, 2018). On the one hand the public doubts the trustworthiness of corporate communication. On the other hand communication professionals who ask critical questions are easily framed by organizations as trouble makers.

Stories about greenwashing and misleading reporting raise the question what exactly the role of communication professionals should be. Are they just there to serve the interests of the company or do they have their own professional autonomy and responsibility? What is good communication in the case of the Volkswagen group and in the other cases mentioned? Is communication just a technical skill, or is it a practice that serves a higher public goal? In this chapter we will argue that corporate communication can best be understood as a normative practice, a practice with its own codes of conduct and its own teleological structure. The relevance and credibility of the profession stands or falls with public trust. Therefore, communication professionals have to be sensitive to the concerns of the public and have to tell a story that is credible. If they damage the confidence of the public, they also damage the company for which they are working.

In order to clarify the specific role and duty of communication professionals we use the Normative Practice Approach as it is developed by Jochemsen (2006), Verkerk, Hoogland, Van der Stoep & De Vries (2016) and others. First of all, we ask what the foundational function of communication is. What is a communication professional doing, what exactly is his specific skill? Secondly, the question is raised what the qualifying function of communication is. What is the purpose of communication? What is the ultimate goal? Why is it so important to influence the minds of people? Thirdly we will show that corporate communication has a layered structure. Communication professionals give voice to organizations in the public sphere and at the same time their activities are embedded within these organizations. Although they have their own code of conduct, they also have to serve the interests of the organization. Finally, we ask whether or not communication professionals should take a neutral stance towards the company that they are serving. We will argue that the usual distinction between form and content does not hold. Instead of this we introduce another distinction, the distinction between the constitutive and the regulative side of communication practices.

FOUNDATIONAL FUNCTION: GENERATION OF IMPACT

Communication professionals operate at the interface of organizations and the public sphere. They support companies, governmental organizations and NGOs in telling their story to a wider audience or to specific target groups. Corporate communication is a powerful tool to promote the interests of organizations and companies. It gives legitimation to what organizations are doing, without it being necessary to fall back on the use of force or violence (Castells, 2009, p. 11). It is therefore in the interest of organizations that they succeed in putting their message into the spotlight. They also have to tell their story in such a way that it has an effect in the long run. In terms of the Normative Practice Approach, one may call this the foundational function of corporate communication. More than others, communication professionals know how framing, agenda setting and public legitimation are working. Their authority is based on the fact that they have access to knowledge and skills that are helpful to create shared meaning. The reason why they are hired by organizations is that they are sensitive to what is going on in society and that they know how to deal with issues of public legitimation.

A quite common understanding of communication is that it has to be a matter of free exchange of arguments and ideas. This of course is an idealistic idea of communication. Nobody would seriously hold that in the public sphere power, money and rhetoric play not a single role. The point, however, is that a focus on the effect of words should not have a place in public discourse. What only should count is the force of the better argument. Famous is the distinction made by Jürgen Habermas between strategic and communicative action. In communicative action the other is treated not as an instrument to reach one's goals, but as a dialogue partner. Conversation partners must strive to reach mutual understanding (Habermas, 1996, p. 18). That first of all implies the possibility to disagree with one another. Nobody should be forced to accept an argument that does not convince him. In order to get acceptance for one's point of view, participants have to make validity claims. They have to refer to propositional truth, normative righteousness or personal sincerity (Habermas, 1996, p. 5).

James E. Grunig, the grandfather of contemporary public relations, takes a quite similar position. According to Grunig two-way symmetrical communication is better than other forms of communication. Two-way symmetrical communication is dialogical. It presumes an interaction between conversation partners, and it balances the interests of the organization and its public. As a result, it 'produces better long-term relationships with publics than do the other models of public relations' (J.E. Grunig, L.A. Grunig, Dozier, 2006, p. 47). By arguing that two-way symmetrical communication is the most excellent form of communication, Grunig makes a sharp distinction between propaganda and public relations (Moloney, 2006). Propaganda is about the manipulation of human minds. Public relations on the other hand is about dialogue and balancing of interests. It does not use force or manipulation. It is dialogical in nature and more ethical than other forms of communication.

According to Habermas, public relations work, propaganda and advertising contaminate the public sphere by strategic reasoning. They use money and power to get influence (Habermas, 1996, pp. 367, 376-377). That certainly would not be the position of Grunig. According to him, public relations is not wrong in itself. It has to be done, however, in the proper way, according to the rules of two-way symmetrical communication. Most codes of conduct for communication professionals are based on this idea. The approaches of Habermas and Grunig provide us with important insights of what communication actually should be. What they expect from good communication, however, puts a heavy burden upon the shoulders of communication professionals (Fawkes, 2015, p. 95). Whichever way you look at it, persuasion plays an important role in the activity of communication professionals. Clients expect from communication professionals that they serve the interests of the organization and influence public opinion. Simone Chambers (1996) makes a distinction between persuasion and coercion that may be helpful in this regard. According to her persuasion is not wrong; it is coercion that is problematic. The question, however, is where persuasion ends and coercion begins. Is persuasion just about the force of the best argument, or may it also involve an appeal to emotions or the use of communication tactics and psychological insights?

Both Habermas and Grunig hold that dialogue and mutual understanding are the starting point of a good communication practice. One may question, however, if agonistic models of communication do not give a more workable and realistic account of what is going on when it comes to public legitimation. According to Moloney (2006, p. 75), for example, the public sphere is an arena where political parties, governments and other participants sell their opinion to voters and mobilize sufficient support for their ideas. It is not the search for mutual understanding that drives the public debate, but the competition for the most convincing view in the eyes of the public. This also explains the omnipresence of communication professionals in our media-saturated society. Political parties, NGOs and corporations have to make themselves visible and have to position themselves in relation to their competitors, in order to get public awareness and public recognition.

Moloney's understanding of the public sphere closely resembles the ideas of Pierre Bourdieu about the political field and political representation. Bourdieu (1991) describes the public debate as a struggle for recognition. Status, skills, money and social position are indispensable in order to make oneself heard. Not every citizen has the opportunity and means to get a recognized position in the public debate. At the same time, however, the public sphere is organized in such a way that spokesmen and opinion makers have to justify their position by referring to the general interest. Only those voices that represent a common good are counted as legitimate voices. This means that actors in the political field or public sphere have to speak on behalf of the people. They have to present themselves as the voice of a specific group or interest in order to get recognition. This only works, however, if people give them credit and credence. People have to allow them to act as representative of their concerns.

Bourdieu's theory of political representation can easily be interpreted in a cynical way. In serving the common good or the general interest journalists, politicians and opinion makers first of all serve their own interest. It gives them status, authority or just a source of income. Bourdieu would not deny that this is part of the game. At the same time, however, he holds that such a behavior does not necessarily leads to a situation in which everything is possible. The other side of the coin is that actors in the public sphere have an interest in presenting themselves as advocates of the common good. That stimulates them to appeal to universal values like truth, justice and equality and to put into question the good intentions of themselves or others (Bourdieu, 2000). Only those voices are legitimized that can stand the test of criticism. It is exactly the interest in disinterestedness, the particular interest in the universal, which leads to a further autonomization of the public field. Thus, according to Bourdieu, an agonistic point of view does not necessary imply a relativist position. Precisely because the public discourse is a struggle for the most disinterested point of view, people are stimulated to take the general interest as serious as possible.

Moloney and Bourdieu show us that strategic reasoning in public opinion making is not necessarily wrong. It is an integral part of public communication. In many situations, and also in the public sphere, one has to compete with others in order to make oneself heard. One must communicate as effectively as possible, using the resources and insights that are available. In order to promote a point of view that deserves public attention, one has to position oneself. One has to make one's story as attractive and convincing as possible. And one must gather allies and engage ambassadors to reach one's goal. It is not without reason that ratings, circulation figures and page views are so important in the communication business. Communication that has no impact, that does not reach an audience or does not mobilize people, cannot count as good communication.

Strategic reasoning is unavoidable in communication. Sometimes, especially in situations in which a certain truth is not so self-evident for people as it should be, a lot of effort and strength is needed in order to make one's point clear. That does not mean, however, that Habermas and Grunig are wrong when they emphasize the importance of voluntary consent or the balancing of interests. Corporate communication or public relations turns out to become propagandistic if the control of the minds of people is the main purpose. Cheating, spinning and covering up troublesome facts may work for a time, but on the long run they often will turn out to be counterproductive. If they come to light, they undermine the credibility of the participants. The viewpoints that are brought in must be suitable to receive general approval. Also, the use of instruments must be appropriate, in accordance with the situation and the goal that is pursued. It is truth, trustworthiness and credibility that count in the public sphere and nothing else. Communication skills and impact are important, but they do not have the last word. That brings us to the qualifying function of corporate communication, the reason why people communicate and what they want to achieve with it.

QUALIFYING FUNCTION: ARTICULATION OF MEANING

Communication, as we have seen, is more than just the shaping of minds. It is founded on the use of technical skills, but it is not qualified by it. The creation of shared meaning, the exchange of ideas that deserve public consent, is what qualifies corporate communication. In order to get a more precise understanding of what communication is, it is helpful to refer to a distinction made by Carey (2009, pp. 11-18) between a transmission view on communication and a ritual view. In the transmission view communication is understood as informing others, the sending and receiving of messages. The ritual view of communication, on the other hand, has to do with the building of a community, the representation of shared beliefs, the negotiation and exchange of meaning. Think about what is happening in an organization when employees celebrate an important anniversary, when representatives of an organization sign a contract with a client or when a supervisor is asking a supervisee to complete a specific task (Cooren, 2015, p. 1). People celebrate events, commit themselves to others and give directions. They exchange meaning and try to make sense of what is going on. In this way they constitute a new reality, they build up a communal world.

Communication as creation of a shared meaning does not necessarily exclude a transmission way of thinking. It is still useful, sometimes, to think in terms of sender and receiver, or of communication as conveying messages to others (Carey, 1999, p. 127). But that is not the main purpose of communication. Communication has to do with how people orientate themselves in the world, with how people are doing things together and how they participate in a larger whole (Aula & Mantere, 2008, p. 169). When people make sense of the world they not just give an interpretation or representation of a current state of affairs, but also construct together a new reality, a meaningful perspective that creates a common purpose and gives direction to their actions (Weick, 1995). Following Benedict Anderson, Charles Taylor speaks in this respect about social imaginaries. The idea of social imaginaries is related to what Lakoff calls 'frames'. Frames may function on a surface level, as slogans, images and metaphors, but also on a deep level, the level of convictions, moral orientations and worldviews (Lakoff, 2006, p. 28). According to Taylor a social imaginary is a common understanding of how the world looks like, a shared sense of legitimacy. A social imaginary incorporates 'a sense of how things usually go, but this is interwoven with an idea of how they ought to go, of what missteps would invalidate the practice' (Taylor, 2007, p. 172). Mostly social imaginaries are not expressed in theoretical terms, but are carried in images, stories, legends etc. (Taylor, 2007, p. 172).

In order to give direction to organizational behavior, it is helpful to pay attention to the 'why' of the organization, its telos or ultimate goal. The book 'Start with why' of Simon Sinek (2011) has been a milestone in this regard. The attention for the why of the organization is indeed important. By articulating the reason of existence of an organization, one defines a common purpose and gives the organization a license to operate. An organization has to tell a coherent and consistent story about itself, a story that both strengthens the bonds that bind employees to the company and positions the company in relation to rivals (Van Riel, 2012, p. 160). What communication professionals are doing is shaping the social imaginary of organizations. They make sense of what an organization is doing. By articulating the essence of the organization or company they explain why an organization is acting in a certain way. They strive to obtain sympathy for its behavior. This may also imply that sometimes communication professionals have to admit that an organization does not behave as it should do. Putting public legitimation at the center of the attention helps us to develop a perspective that surpasses the opposition between agonistic models of communication and models that are more dialogical (Van Ruler and Verĉiĉ, 2005). It acknowledges the importance of framing and strategic reasoning and at the same time holds on that credibility and trustworthiness are the central concern.

Generally speaking it is not easy to give an unequivocal answer to the question why an organization exists. Interpretations may differ and often organizations change over time. Dependent upon the circumstances the meaning or essence of an organization may be articulated in a different way. There is not one definite definition about its essential core that meets the expectations once and for all. That does not mean, however, that the core identity of an organization is just a matter of contingence. Very helpful in this regard is the distinction that Nicholas H. Smith (1997) makes between the weak hermeneutics of Friedrich Nietzsche, Richard Rorty and Postmodernism and the strong hermeneutics of Hans-Georg Gadamer, Paul Ricoeur and Charles Taylor. According to weak hermeneutics every interpretation of reality is just a social construction. There is no single statement that may claim to be in accordance with a reality beyond interpretation. Strong hermeneutics in this regard is different. It acknowledges the existence of competing ideas about how the world should look like, but at the same time it holds that human beings are able to differentiate between more or less convincing points of view. According to strong hermeneutics we learn to know reality through experience and interpretation. That is part of our human condition, our being in the world. Articulations of meaning, however, make more or less sense to the extent that they make our world more intelligible and deepen our understanding of reality.

Social imaginaries, the stories, images and metaphors people use to give meaning to the world are intrinsically moral in nature. They not only describe how the world looks like, but also how the world should be. That is an important insight that strong hermeneutics brings. It is an insight that is also very relevant for the business of corporate communication. Following Balmer & Greyser (2003) communication professionals often make a distinction between actual identity, communicated identity, conceived identity, ideal identity and desired identity. How useful such a distinction may be, what disappears from the eye is the moral nature of organizational identity. More helpful in this regard is it to differentiate between two types of evaluations. Weak evaluations are evaluations based on desire, on the longing for certain material or immaterial goods. Strong evaluations, on the other hand, have to be articulated in terms of value: good or wrong, just or unjust, profound or superficial, etc. (Taylor, 1985). They do not depend upon contingent situations, but have to do with the kind of person we want to be, our core identity. The identity of an organization, the answer to the question why an organization exists, is not just a matter of weak evaluations or preferences. It is a matter of moral agency. What that means can nicely be illustrated on the basis of the Volkswagen case. The Volkswagen Group wants to present itself as an ecofriendly automaker and is known by the general public as a reliable partner ("Made in Germany"). Those are moral qualifications. The emissions scandal, however, raises the question whether the Volkswagen company is not primarily a cunning merchant or a cynical manipulator. The company is blamed for a lack of character.

Moral character is important. But that is not enough. In order to convince people NGO's governmental organizations and companies also have to tell a story about themselves that both is in accordance with their past history and opens up new horizons for future action. That is a second lesson we may learn from strong hermeneutics. The narrative that an organization tells about itself has to be coherent and reliable (Fisher, 1989). Without a certain level of predictability there will be no trust. At the same time, however, organizations must also have openness to the future. They have to develop a sense of direction and must show that they are future-proof. By bringing in a novel perspective one may change the game and attract the attention of the public (Barry and Elmer, 1997). An innovative story makes new challenges visible and helps to distinguish oneself from competitors. Instructive in this regard is Ricoeur's notion of emplotment. Emplotment, according to Ricoeur (1984), is the way in which a narrative brings together dispersed facts and events into a new meaningful whole. Such a reconfiguration of the world invites us to see the world with different eyes. We see things and discover things that we did not see before. Emplotment is based, however, on a delicate balance. If the story of an organization is not innovative enough it will not surprise us and will only be considered as a repetition of what we already knew. If it is insufficiently in line with what we experienced in the past, however, it lacks plausibility and will be rejected as unrealistic or too bold.

Corporate communication is a matter of articulating the why of the organization and making sense about what an organization is doing. In this way it contributes to the development of a communal world. The close connection between corporate identity and the articulation of meaning encourages us to characterize communication as a lingual practice. Communication first of all has to do with collective sense-making and the exchange of meaning (Jansen, Van der Stoep and Jochemsen 2017). What lingual practices are, however, should not be taken too narrowly. It is important to say this expressly because people quite often are not aware of the full potential of the lingual capacity of human beings. They assume that language is just a means to describe reality in an accurate way. Although it is important that human beings express themselves in a clear and distinct way, that is not the only way that language works. The words, images and metaphors that people are using also have an evocative character. They open up new perspectives for action and help us to approach the world in a new way (Rorty, 1999). In the case of corporate communication, the use of words and the articulation of meaning are especially meant to constitute contexts in which people organize things together and participate into a larger whole. This building of common realities and a shared meaning, however, may fail. Communication is intrinsically normative in nature. It can be done in a more or less convincing way. Coherence, plausibility and accurateness are not just standards imposed on communication from a distant ethical framework. These criteria help us to differentiate between good and bad communication, communication that deserves public attention and communication that does not deserve it (Van der Stoep, 2018).

A LAYERED STRUCTURE: SERVING TWO MASTERS

Communication is about the articulation of meaning, the creation of social imaginaries that are plausible and generate public support (qualifying function). Also, effectiveness is important. Organizations want to communicate in an impactful way (foundational function). In this section we will bring in a new complexity in order to better understand the specific task and duty of communication professionals. We will put the issue on the table what the adjective 'corporate' means, when people speak about corporate communication. Usually communication professionals work for companies or other organizations. Even if communication professionals are not employed by an organization, they are at least paid by it. They have to relate to the concerns and interests of the organization that they serve. In the case of companies like the Volkswagen Group these interests are primarily economic in nature. At the same time, however, communication professionals have their own rules of conduct. They know how public legitimation works and how to obey the rules of good communication. The moment they construct fake stories or distort facts, it will backfire upon their credibility and also upon the faith people put into the company for which they are working. They have to serve two masters: the demands of the organization with its interests on the one hand and the rules of public legitimation on the other. These two interests do not necessarily have to be at odds with each other, but usually there is a tension between them.

The complexity and tension we are talking about here, arise because corporate communication is a practice with a layered structure. Communication professionals have to balance in a proper way the interest of public legitimation and the interest of the organization. Helpful in this regard is the notion of enkaptic interlacements as introduced by Herman Dooyeweerd (1969). In an enkaptic interlacement two practices are intertwined, without losing their own functionality. The communication practice, integrally interwoven with the public sphere, becomes part of another practice, the practice of the organization, be it a company, a government organization, or an NGO (Jansen, Van der Stoep and Jochemsen, 2017). Communication professionals should highlight the central purpose of the organization as sharply as possible, if they want to ensure that organizations get the attention they deserve. In this way they make true what their profession stands for. Vice versa, organizations have to respect the intrinsic nature of the communication practice, in order to make proper use of it. If companies want to sell enough products, not only today but also in the long run, they do well to build a good reputation, based upon a solid communication strategy.

As a communication professional, one serves the interests of organizations the best, if one sticks to the primary task of one's profession: the articulation of meaning. That implies that one must have a sharp focus on the added value that an organization or company delivers. A communication professional has to be committed to the central purpose of the organization and must make every effort to express this purpose as sharply and convincingly as possible. He must be very conscious, however, that he has just a supporting role. He facilitates organizations in formulating their reason for existence. Communication professionals do not control the story of the organization. They have to focus on what management and employees want to communicate to others. As a supporting practice, however, communication also has a critical role. Communication professionals have to keep organizations focused on their primary goal and on what is publicly acceptable. They must not restrict themselves to the presentation afterwards of the strategy formulated by the organization, but also have to be supportive in defining and redefining what this strategy is (Van Ruler, 2018). That requires an independent attitude. If it goes as it should, communication professionals function as the moral compass of organizations. Directors and managers must take care that they give communication professionals enough room to fulfill their critical role and that they do not override them.

The practice of communication has a layered structure. That may be interpreted as a weakness, but it may also be seen as a force. Communication professionals know what is going on in society and may hold a mirror to organizations. First of all, communication professionals are especially sensitive to issues that have to do with aspiration and the degree to which organizations fulfill their pretensions. If communication professionals can handle the forces in the boardroom, they can be good allies in giving direction to the future of the organization. As we have noticed in the introduction, there is often a discrepancy between 'talk' and 'action', between what organizations say that they are doing and what they actually do. If the gap between what the organization promises and what it actually does is too big, it puts the credibility of the organization at risk. An organization must do what it promises. If you want to be trusted, you should be trustworthy (Meijboom, Visak and Brom, 2006). A good reputation depends upon the deeds of the organization (Aula and Mantere, 2008, p. 18). Corporate communication, however, is also aspirational in nature. The social imaginaries produced by the organization not only describe what the organization actually is, but also how it would look like (Christensen, Morsing, Thyssen, 2013). By imagining a desired future, this future may be brought closer.

But caution is in order here. If ambitions are not anchored in reality, they easily put too much pressure upon people, which ultimately leads to window dressing and deceptive behavior (Siano et al., 2017).

Secondly, the layered structure of corporate communication may help to bridge the gap between the board room and the shop floor and between the organization and external parties. Because of their intermediary role, communication professionals hear things from people that the management does not hear. They are trained to switch between different circuits and to speak different languages. Listening is important for organizations because the official story is just one of the stories that are told (Boje, 2008). On the shop floor other stories about the organization are circulating. And clients also have their own communication circuits. Most of the time, the stories that are told are incomplete, fragmented and fluid. They are narratives without a beginning, middle and end, that are meant to bring new meanings into the game (Boje, 2001, pp. 1-2). Many organizations have a culture in which 'telling' and 'doing' are more appreciated than 'listing' and taking time to talk with each other. Especially in messy and complex situations this may be problematic because executives depend in their decision making on the information they get from others (Schein, 2013, pp. 53-67). If employees and other stakeholders do not trust the management, they will not tell them when something is going wrong. Or they will tell it to them, when it is already too late. Communication professionals may bring to the attention of the board the concerns of others, thereby supporting organizations to become more responsive. They only are effective in listening, however, if they have a sharp focus on the goal of the organization. Listing itself is not enough. Only with a clear sense of direction one may differentiate between what is important and what is not (Van Woerkum and Aarts, 2011, p. 177).

CONSTITUTIVE AND REGULATIVE SIDE: PROFESSIONAL RESPONSIBILITY

Corporate communication is intrinsically normative in nature. Organizations may communicate in a good way, sincerely building public trust, but they may also behave as 'cheaters' or as 'cunning merchants'. That raises the question what the own responsibility of communication professionals is in relation to the organizations that they are serving. An answer that seems obvious at first sight is that one has to make a distinction between form and content. Communication professionals are specialists in the form. They know how to convey messages and how to change the perceptions of people. What exactly the content of the message is, does not have to be their concern. It is the responsibility of the organizations that they are serving.

What we have discovered so far, however, shows that this argument is not correct. Communication is more than just a transmission of messages; it has to do with the constructing of communal worlds, the building of a shared meaning. The framing of collective narratives is in itself already a matter of content. A communication professional cannot ignore the need for 'narrative engagement' (Goodall 2010, 27). He is accountable for the way he deals with misleading stories, incorrect claims and lies for good. That is more particularly the case because, more than others, he is an expert in how the framing of narratives works.

More helpful in this regard is a distinction made in the Normative Practice Approach between the constitutive and regulative side of professional practices. That distinction is based on Searle (2010), who differentiates between different types of rules. Constitutive rules, according to Searle, are rules that make a certain practice possible. In order to play chess, for example, certain rules are required. Without these rules the chess game as such cannot exist. Regulative rules, on the other hand, are rules that relate to the style or way of life of the players. Even if you master the rules of the game, you can play the game in different ways. You can choose an aggressive game mode or, for example, go for 'fair play'. If we apply the distinction, introduced by Searle, on the practice of corporate communication, it makes sense to argue that communication professionals know better than others how the rules that constituted the game work and what the pitfalls are. They know how to improve public trust and how to cope with objections and counter-narratives. The constitutive side of communication, however, cannot be disconnected from the regulative side. They are two sides of the same coin. One cannot separate the playing of the game, according to its rules, from the particular way the game is actualized. One may communicate for example in a more or less compelling way, take more or less risks, or choose a defensive or just an offensive style. That depends on how one assesses the situation and on the preferences and convictions that one has.

Because people differ in worldview, they also have a different understanding of the rules that constitute communication. At the same time, however, there is a common sense about what counts as good communication. People often refer to the same intuitions and share a common ground. Without that, a dialogue about what is right or wrong would be rather meaningless. Almost everyone will agree that coherence, plausibility and reliability count when it comes to public legitimation. How these values are articulated and actualized by people, however, may differ. What counts as good communication inescapably is a subject of struggle between competing convictions and worldviews, no matter how much consensus sometimes there may be. It is important to realize that the communication profession itself is a site of cultural production (Edwards, 2011). Professionals are often trained in an environment in which especially technical skills are highly valued. Besides that, working for a large multinational is often better valued than working for a small company, government agency or an NGO. These kinds of mechanisms easily contribute to a situation in which a neoliberalist ideology is promoted. What is forgotten is that neoliberalism itself is a story that is highly debatable, no matter how many people consider it to be inevitable and convincing (Michaels, 2011; Raworth, 2017). For the good of society we are in need of professionals who understand this situation, who take their responsibility, make choices that are not obvious at first sight and are capable of developing counter-narratives.

That, of course, is a huge task. In order not to make expectations too high, and to overcharge individual agency, we must be aware of the fact that professional responsibility is always embedded within a network of relations. The contribution that communication professionals bring, cannot be isolated from the contribution of other relevant players in the organization. In ambiguous domains like corporate communication, 'pure' professionalism does not exist. One has to establish meaningful relationships in dialogue with others (Noordegraaf, 2007). The communication professional is not an autonomous actor, who can take the world by himself alone. He participates in a complex network of relationships in which he constrains and is constrained by others, and in which he enables and is enabled by others (Stacey, 2009, p. 299). An appeal to professional distance does not work in such situations (Schein, 2016, p. 15). One has to build relationships of trust in order to become effective. Communication professionals must not overestimate themselves. When it comes to the influence and responsibility that communication professionals can have, much depends upon the room of maneuver that is granted to them. Experienced professionals with a lot of seniority get more things done than others. Newcomers, on the other hand, have to fight for a position.

Communication professionals have to deal with conflicting styles of behavior and conflicting views of what good communication is. A communication professional does not need to endorse the views and convictions of their employers or clients in detail, in order to be able to deliver good work. But there must at least be a plausible connection between the biography of the professional and how the organization behaves and presents itself. If you work for the Volkswagen Group, or for another organization, you have to tell at least a coherent narrative about why this appointment fits with your personal story and beliefs. The gap between the personal narrative and the organizational narrative cannot be stretched too far. Sometimes, it may be appropriate to point to mitigating circumstances or to compromises that have to be made. If communication professionals do not agree with their employer or client, they still may have good reasons to continue to do their job, and to seek for themselves a margin of freedom. That does not relieve communication professionals from their own specific responsibility, however. They can be held responsible if they do not do the right thing. There is a thin line between participating in a questionable organization in order to perform a corrective function on the one hand

and collaborating in activities that cannot stand the light of day on the other. It is a delicate balance that requires much of the personality of the people involved. Time and again, one has to ask the question what permissible behavior is and what is not. The goal does not always sanctify the means and also one cannot just hide behind the limited influence that one has.

CONCLUSION

Rightly or wrongly, communication professionals are often blamed for greenwashing or for spreading misleading messages. They are portrayed as lackeys that just serve the interests of organizations. Even communication professionals themselves sometimes adopt such a view and behave accordingly. In this chapter we have argued that these images are based on a limited account of what communication actually is. Corporate communication stands or falls with public trust. In order to come to a better understanding of what good communication is, we introduced some important distinctions based on the Normative Practice Approach. First of all, we introduced the distinction between the foundational function and the qualifying function of corporate communication. Good communication, it is true, has to be effective and impactful (foundational function). But primarily, it has to do with reliability and the creation of a communal world (qualifying function). The purpose of communication is to win confidence and public recognition. Secondly, we differentiated between organizational goals and the requirements of public legitimation. Communication professionals have to deal with tensions between ambition and reality. They also have to be sensitive of what is going on in society, without losing out if sight the purpose of the organization. Lastly, a distinction is made between the constitutive and the regulative side of communication. That helps us to better deal with the discrepancies between personal and organizational narratives. With the introduction of this framework, based on the Normative Practice Approach, not all questions and problems encountered by communication professionals in their daily work are solved. However, the framework does help to identify tensions and dilemmas and to find a common language. Above all, it shows that communication is more than just a technical skill. It is a profession with its own intrinsic normativity that requires practical wisdom.

REFERENCES

Aula, P., & Mantere, S. (2008). *Strategic Reputation Management. Towards a Company of the Good*. New York: Routledge.

Balmer, J. M. T., & Greyser, S. A. (2003). Managing the Multiple Identities of the Corporation. In J. M. T. Balmer & S. A. Greyser (Eds.), *Revealing the Cooperation. Perspectives on Identity, Image, Reputation, Corporate Branding and Corporate-Level Marketing* (pp. 15–29). New York: Routledge. doi:10.4324/9780203422786

Barry, D., & Elmes, M. (1997). Strategy retold. Towards a narrative view of strategic discourse. *Academy of Management Review*, *22*(2), 429–452. doi:10.5465/amr.1997.9707154065

Boje, D. M. (2001). *Narrative methods for organizational and communication research*. London: Sage. doi:10.4135/9781849209496

Boje, D. M. (2008). *Storytelling organizations*. London: Sage.

Bourdieu, P. (1991). *Language and symbolic power*. Cambridge, UK: Polity Press.

Bourdieu, P. (2000). *Pascalian meditations*. Cambridge, UK: Polity Press.

Carey, J. W. (2009). *Communication as culture. Essays on media and society* (revised edition). New York: Routledge.

Castells, M. (2009). *Communication power*. Oxford, UK: Oxford University Press.

Chambers, S. (1996). *Reasonable democracy. Jürgen Habermas and the politics of discourse*. Ithaca, NY: Cornell University Press.

Christensen, L. T., Morsing, M., & Thyssen, O. (2013). CSR as aspirational talk. *Organization*, *20*(3), 372–393. doi:10.1177/1350508413478310

Cooren, F. (2015). *Organizational discourse. Communication and constitution*. Cambridge, UK: Polity Press.

Craig, R. T. (1999). Communication theory as a field. *Communication Theory*, *9*(2), 119–161. doi:10.1111/j.1468-2885.1999.tb00355.x

Dooyeweerd, H. (1969). *A new critique of theoretical thought. Philipsburg*. Presbyterian and Reformed Publishing Company.

Edwards, L. (2011). Public relations and society. A Bourdieuvian perspective. In *Public relations, society and culture. Theoretical and empirical explorations* (pp. 61–74). London: Routledge. doi:10.4324/9780203832134

Fawkes, J. (2015). *Public relations ethics and professionalism. The shadow of excellence*. London: Routledge.

Fisher, W. R. (1989). *Human communication as narration. Towards a philosophy of reason, value, and action*. University of South Carolina Press.

Goodall, H. L. (2010). *Counter-narrative. How progressive academics can challenge extremists and promote social justice*. Walnut Creek, CA: Left Coast Press.

Grunig, J. E., Grunig, L. A., & Dozier, D. M. (2006). The excellence theory. In C. H. Botan & V. Hazleton (Eds.), *Public Relations Theory II* (pp. 21–62). New York: Lawrence Erlbaum Associates.

Habermas, J. (1996). *Between facts and norms. Contributions to a discourse theory of law and democracy*. Cambridge, UK: Polity Press. doi:10.7551/mitpress/1564.001.0001

Hoffjann, O., & Seidenglanz, R. (2018). Allmächtige PR, ohnmächtige PR. Die doppelte Vertrauenskrise der PR. In O. Hoffjann & R. Seidenglanz (Eds.), *Allmächtige PR, ohnmächtige PR. Die doppelte Vertrauenskrise der PR* (pp. 1–14). Wiesbaden: Springer VS. doi:10.1007/978-3-658-18455-1_1

Jansen, P., Van der Stoep, J., & Jochemsen, H. (2017). Government communication as a normative practice. *Philosophia Reformata*, *82*(2), 121–145. doi:10.1163/23528230-08202004

Jochemsen, H. (2006). Normative practices as an intermediate between theoretical ethics and morality. *Philosophia Reformata*, *71*(1), 96–112. doi:10.1163/22116117-90000377

Lakoff, G. (2006). *Thinking points. Communicating our American values and vision*. New York: Farrar, Strauss & Giroux.

Meijboom, F. L. B., Visak, T., & Brom, F. W. A. (2006). Trust to trustworthiness. Why information is not enough in the food sector. *Journal of Agricultural & Environmental Ethics*, *19*(5), 427–442. doi:10.100710806-006-9000-2

Michaels, F. S. (2011). *Monoculture. How one story is changing everything*. Red Clover Press.

Moloney, K. (2006). *Rethinking public relations. PR propaganda and democracy* (2nd ed.). New York: Routledge. doi:10.4324/9780203030592

Noordegraaf, M. (2007). From 'pure' to 'hybrid' professionalism. Present-day professionalism in ambiguous public domains. *Administration & Society*, *39*(6), 761–785. doi:10.1177/0095399707304434

Painter, Ch., & Martins, J. T. (2017). Organizational communication management during the Volkswagen diesel emissions scandal. A hermeneutic study in attribution, crisis management and information orientation. *Knowledge and Process Management*, *24*(3), 204–218. doi:10.1002/kpm.1544

Raworth, K. (2017). *Doughnut economics. Seven ways to think like a 21th-century economist*. London: Penguin.

Ricoeur, P. (1984). *Time and narrative* (Vol. 1). Chicago: The University of Chicago Press.

Rorty, R. (1999). Truth without correspondence to reality. In *Philosophy and social hope* (pp. 23–46). London: Penguin Books.

Schein, E. H. (2013). *Humble inquiry. The gentle art of asking instead of telling*. San Francisco: Berrett-Koehler Publishers.

Schein, E. H. (2016). *Humble consulting. How to provide real help faster*. San Francisco: Berrett-Koehler Publishers.

Searle, J. R. (2010). *Making the social world. The structure of human civilization*. Oxford, UK: Oxford University Press. doi:10.1093/acprof:oso bl/9780195396171.001.0001

Siano, A., Vollero, A., Conte, F., & Amabile, S. (2017). 'More than words'. Expanding the taxonomy of greenwashing after the Volkswagen scandal. *Journal of Business Research*, *71*, 27–37. doi:10.1016/j.jbusres.2016.11.002

Sinek, S. (2011). *Start with why. How great leaders inspire everyone tot take action*. New York: Penguin.

Smith, N. H. (1995). *Strong hermeneutics. Contingency and moral identity*. London: Routledge.

Stacey, R. (2007). The challenge of human interdependence. Consequences for thinking about the day-to-day practice of management in organizations. *European Business Review*, *19*(4), 292–302. doi:10.1108/09555340710760125

Taylor, Ch. (1985). What is human agency. In Ch. Taylor (Ed.), *Human agency and language* (pp. 15–44). Cambridge, UK: Cambridge University Press. doi:10.1017/CBO9781139173483.002

Taylor, Ch. (2007). *A secular age*. Cambridge, MA: The Belknap Press of Harvard University Press.

Van der Stoep, J. (2018). Normative dimensions of corporate communication. In G.J. Buijs & A.K. Mosher (Eds.), The future of creation order: Vol. 2. Order among humans; humanities, social science and normative practices. New York: Springer.

Van Riel, C. B. M. (2012). *The alignment factor. Leveraging the power of total stakeholder support*. New York: Routledge. doi:10.4324/9780203124536

Van Ruler, B. (2018). Communication theory. An underrated pillar on which strategic communication rests. *International Journal of Strategic Communication*, *12*(4), 367–381. doi:10.1080/1553118X.2018.1452240

Van Ruler, B., & Verĉiĉ, D. (2005). Reflective communication management. Future ways for public relations research. *Communication Yearbook*, *29*, 239–274. doi:10.120715567419cy2901_8

Van Woerkum, C., & Aarts, N. (2011). Organizing by projective hearing. The active use of a passive sense. *International Journal of Strategic Communication*, *5*(3), 171–182. doi:10.1080/1553118X.2011.566902

Verkerk, M. J., Hoogland, J., Van der Stoep, J., & De Vries, M. J. (2016). *Philosophy of technology. An introduction for technology and business students*. London: Routledge.

Weick, K. E. (1995). *Sensemaking in organizations*. Thousand Oaks, CA: Sage.

Chapter 12
International Cooperation in Development:
The Need for a Multidimensional Normative Approach

Henk Jochemsen
Wageningen University & Research, The Netherlands

Corné J. Rademaker
Wageningen University & Research, The Netherlands

ABSTRACT

The development aid of affluent to poor countries is currently much debated. Though in the decades of aid many people have been helped to survive and improve their living conditions, the problem of severe poverty and injustice is far from solved. Three types of critique explain this failure to a large extent: first, the way in which the development assistance is provided, or not; second, the observation that motivational and informational problems frustrate the collective-actions that should lead to "development"; third, ideological critique that the cooperation is too much an extension of the predominant modernist, neoliberal economic, and financial system of our time. Analyzing development cooperation and assistance with the NPA leads to the identification of normative characteristics of this practice. If the actual realization of development cooperation and the larger institutional context of this professional practice would respect that normativity, the effectiveness and justice of the cooperation could significantly be improved.

DOI: 10.4018/978-1-5225-8006-5.ch012

INTRODUCTION

Development aid of wealthy to poor countries continues to be a matter of debate and political controversy. In recent years several traditional donor countries (mainly Western Europe and North America) have moved to some combination of aid and trade (EC, 2016; OECD & WTO, 2015).

The criticism of spending money on development cooperation is not new. Especially since the 90s, scholars have presented thorough critiques on the (mainstream) practice of aid or cooperation in development. We will summarize and discuss their main arguments in the next section.

Before doing so, we want to point out that the aid and cooperation given in recent decades have had positive results at the level of the quality of life of many people (Crosswell, 2009). The report of the Dutch Scientific Council for Government Policy (Van Lieshout, Went, and Kremer, 2010) makes clear that in social sectors advancements have been realized, like decreased infant mortality and an increased rate of children that go to school. At a global level, we can note that the outcomes of the former Millennium Development Goals can certainly be seen in many of the areas that the goals addressed, including halving extreme poverty and global under-five mortality while literacy rates, gender equality and environmental sustainability increased more or less substantially (UN, 2015).

Yet these achievements are not the whole story. In spite of relative improvements many of the poorest countries have actually seen their real per capita incomes decline since the 1970s and more than one billion people still live on less than $1.25 a day (Ovaska, 2015, p.175; World Bank, 2015). Overall however, the percentage of extremely poor has declined in many countries. At the same time the economic and financial inequality has increased (Oxfam International, 2015). The critique of some scholars is not that aid has not helped many people directly, but that the structures that maintain poverty have not been changed. One scholar for Africa summarized the situation as follows (Tesfaye, 2010).

The continuing failure of official international aid to encourage the emergence of a self-sustaining growth in agricultural and industrial sectors, geared to local needs, has led many to question the appropriateness of aid per se. [....]

Development has to come from within and not without, if it is to be sustainable. Aid creates aid dependency and aid addiction that undermines Africa's capacity to help itself. A situation where aid becomes the biggest component of the annual budget of a country's recurrent expenditure and almost all of its capital expenditure undermines democracy and accountability to citizens.

We conclude that in spite of achievements at the level of people's needs, during the last 7 decades development cooperation has not resulted in an eradication of severe poverty for substantial groups of the population and in the establishment of strong, just institutions and in significant endogenous economic development in 'developing countries', even though in some countries progress can be seen on some of these goals. This raises the question what factors could explain this situation and how improvements could be realized. In this chapter we will begin answering these questions, realizing that a full treatment of the complex issue of international cooperation in development is beyond this contribution. After this introduction we will present some of the main critiques of the character of development aid as given form during those decades. This will lead to identify essential elements in the explanation of the lack of satisfactory results so far. Subsequently, we will indicate how the normative approach for development cooperation would look like and how its use could lead to improvements, realizing that there is no 'silver bullet' here.

CRITIQUES OF DEVELOPMENT COOPERATION

Critiques of development cooperation can be ordered according to the level at which it is directed. Some criticism regards the actual performance of the development cooperation, without addressing the institutional architecture of the cooperation, e.g. that many donor countries (OECD countries) do not fulfil their promise of allocating 0.7% of their GNI to ODA (official development assistance). Other critiques do regard that institutional architecture of the cooperation and of the dispense of the aid. This criticism concerns the practices involved in development cooperation at different levels, from the level of international agencies like UN and EU organizations, to the practice of cooperation on the ground, as well as the values they inhere. The third type of criticism has a philosophical and often ideological character. Its main spokespersons are postmodern and (post-)structuralist philosophers that in this field are sometimes indicated as post-developmentalists. We will briefly present these criticisms.

Operational Critique

The first type comes from scholars and professionals in the field who come up with the diagnosis rendered in the introduction. For example, Tesfaye whom we just quoted, also mentions a number of factors in the way development cooperation is realized that (at least partly) explain the lack of results. These factors are:

1. Since some of the aid is in the form of loans rather than direct grants, poorer countries may find themselves getting into increasing debt;
2. A considerable proportion of any aid package is swallowed up in payments to technical experts, the field-staff of the donor countries, or on the costly housing, transport, and diet arrangements made for them in the host country. In this way a lot of the aid is in fact spent on behalf of the donor country (see also Shah, 2012).
3. An important form of assistance to Third World countries is food aid. In the long term, food aid can have serious social and economic consequences. Economically it tends to undermine the Third World agricultural sector by depressing local markets and so discouraging local production.
4. Aid often increases dependency by being loaned to a country on condition that it is used to purchase goods from the donor country: this is known as aid tying. Almost 70 per cent of British aid is loaned on these terms, which means in effect that aid provides an important market for British manufacturers.
5. Aid beneficiaries in the Third Word tend to be urban-centered—the bureaucrats, entrepreneurs, politicians, and industrial workers. The poorest in the rural sectors, those that one might think are supposed to benefit most from aid, particularly food aid, usually end up seeing very little of it.

Though these factors do play a role, the degree to which they explain the problem of structural results is open for debate. A complicating factor here is that Tesfaye seems to address both emergence aid and structural development cooperation, without distinguishing the two. In our view those factors can only explain part of the problematic that is identified more profoundly by others.

Institutional Critique

Two groups of authors that dig deeper are Giri and Van Ufford (2004) and Ostrom et al. (2001).

Giri and Van Ufford suggest an interpretative framework of development cooperation consisting three interrelated historical processes, also to be seen as perspectives on development cooperation. The three perspectives are thematic rather than chronological: 1) works of hope; 2) practices of politics and administration; and 3) critical understanding. Very briefly: (1) Hope for a better world has been one of the motives for development cooperation, especially for the NGOs; (2) However, for a diversity of reasons, according to Giri and Van Ufford, moral motivations are marginalized by professionalization and an emphasis on funding in the performance of 'development'. As a consequence the standard mode of action emphasizes a managerial approach to projects while trying to improve the situation of the intended beneficiaries; (3) Critical reflection, however, has led to deconstructive critiques of the 'development industry', dismantling the underlying tendencies that, in general, are not recognized by the managers, or they are unable to deal with them due to institutional interests. In essence, the arguments of these critics undermine the main beliefs and values that are rooted in the modernization paradigm (e.g., human rights discourses, including the right to decent labor and income) on which many of the large development institutions were founded and that upholds them (we will come back to the modernization paradigm as root of 'development').

The problems of a top-down bureaucratic implementation of development cooperation put forward by Giri and Van Ufford are elaborated and elucidated by Elinor Ostrom (Noble price laureate for economy) and colleagues. The latter's view is well-presented in a report commissioned by and in collaboration with Swedish International Development Cooperation Agency (Sida). An elaboration of the theoretical background is given in Ostrom (2010). Ostrom et al. argue that development cooperation can be seen as forms of *collective action* and that collective-action problems must be seen as a major obstacle to sustainable development outcomes. This concept of collective-action is a core concept in their institutional theory.

They explain: "A collective-action situation occurs whenever two or more individuals associate to produce something of value together when it would be difficult to produce it alone." And "collective-action problems occur when a lack of motivation and/or missing or asymmetric information generates incentives that prevent individuals from satisfactory resolving a collective-action situation". This means in their view "that a successful approach to the problem of development must focus on how to generate appropriate incentives so that the time, skill, knowledge and genuine effort of multiple individuals are channeled in ways that produce jointly valued outcomes." (Ostrom et al., 2001, pp. xiii and 10-12)

Motivation and information problems exist at the operational, collective choice, and constitutional levels. [...] Problems of motivation include those involved with public goods (risk of free-riding behavior), common-pool resources, and the Samaritan's dilemma. The problem concerning common-pool resources (e.g. natural resources) is that without effective institutions too many users overharvest; cf. the tragedy of commons. The Samaritan's dilemma occurs in situations of a good-willing donor and a calculating recipient. For the donor the effect of a subsidy is largest when the recipient puts in a lot of effort. However, for the recipient it may be beneficial to put in little effort and receive more subsidies from the donor without contributing much. This dilemma is relevant to development cooperation especially in the maintenance of infrastructures (Ostrom et al, 2001, pp. xvii and 25-32). However, in fact all forms of long-term development assistance may become a Samaritan's Dilemma.

The other type of major problems Ostrom et al. identified in collective-action situations is missing or asymmetric information. Missing information may occur when local knowledge is insufficiently included in the design and implementation of the program. Asymmetric information manifests itself in three problems that involve poor incentives for collective-action that leads to 'development'. These are principal-agent problems, moral hazard problems (related to motivational problems) and adverse selection problems. We explain them very briefly,

First, principal-agent problems occur where subordinates in an organization know more about what they do than their superiors and the goals of the subordinates and the superior differ. Such situations lead to inefficient outcomes that increase with the number of layers in the hierarchy.

Second, moral hazard problems occur in situations where individuals are guaranteed a benefit or protected against loss once a contract has been entered, regardless of whether their actions are professionally appropriate. For example, the availability of aid creates a moral hazard since the aid helps to protect incompetent governments against the results of their actions, viz., aid undermines governments' accountability toward the population.

Third, adverse selection problems occur when information is hidden, leading to the selection of incompetent individuals or bad means or measures in a program (Ostrom 2001, pp. xviii and 37-41). All these situations and problems are discussed extensively in the report. One of the conclusions of the theoretical underpinning of their approach is that reputation and trust among the participants of a collective action, as well as the acceptance of reciprocity, are crucial factors for the action's success (Ostrom, 2010, p. 104).

Improvement of the situation requires a well-crafted institutional context in the recipient countries that generate the productive incentives, and a strengthening of ownership of people in the recipient community, that can help solve the information problems. Ostrom et al formulate four criteria for the kind of ownership that is at least a condition for overcoming the collective-action problems described. These are (Ostrom et al 2001, pp. xx and 15):

1. Beneficiary owners need to enunciate a demand for aid;
2. Beneficiary owners need to exercise some control over the resources made available;
3. Beneficiary owners need to allocate at least some of their own assets to the project or program so that they have a real stake in the way their own and other actors' assets are used;
4. Beneficiary owners need to have clear assignments of responsibility and be able to participate in decisions regarding continuance or non-continuance of a project.

To support this analysis, we mention one other study. Williamson also argues that problems with respect to incentives and information, and especially the combination of these two, are responsible for the lack of (structural) results in development cooperation (in which large sums of money are transferred). These problems occur both at the side of the donor (countries) and the recipient countries. Williamson argues that several of these problems are related to the top-down bureaucratic realization of development aid. Giving more space to competition on a market place would lead to better results. (We will come back to this suggestion).

Ideological Critique

We now turn to the third level of criticism of current development cooperation, that addresses its philosophical and ideological roots. Goudzwaard and colleagues have argued that development cooperation and its problems should be understood as a manifestation of modernity and its problems. A very important aspect of the legacy of modernism, that is especially relevant for development cooperation, constitutes the quest for rational goal-oriented thinking also in the field of economy. This has culminated in the concept of '*homo economicus*', the rational, self-interested individual on which much of economic theory continues to be based in spite of increasing criticisms (Goudszwaard et al., 2007, pp. 85-98). This has led to quantitative thinking and results-oriented development practices, often without considering processes and the real impact on people's lives. Evidently, this rationalization of evaluating complex social practices in which the actual practice is lost out of sight has deeper and wider consequences than in the realm of economics alone. In the context of the 'development industry', the anthropologist Roderick L. Stirrat speaks of a "culture of modernity," by which he means "a formal commitment to a particular view of reality and a faith in 'rationality'" (Stirrat 2000, p. 35; for a broader discussion see Rademaker & Jochemsen, 2018, p. 11). Central in this culture of modernity is the opposition of rational objectivity—which is what the "modernizers" have—to irrational, non-objective culture—what most other people have. That is, modernizers present themselves as a-cultural. In turn, the assumed irrationality to be found with other people takes different forms: "it may be economic—not following the logic of market principles; it can be technical—following what appear to be irrational agricultural practices or whatever; it may be social—the seclusion of women or their exclusion from education" (Stirrat 2000, p. 38). Goudzwaard et al. even go further, arguing that, in relation to global poverty, it is often neglected what goes on at the deepest level in people's hearts and minds, what engages and moves them, what captures their imaginations, fills their hearts, and satisfies their expectations. Thus, they argue that the spiritual and religious dimension is still not acknowledged while, in fact, this underlies every decision that is made and project that is implemented, also in the development sector. This is in line with the critique that not taking into account cultural differences, that are strongly related to religious differences, has been a major reason why development assistance has not had the desired effect of overcoming severe inequality and poverty and building a flourishing society (VanderWalt, 2006, pp. 55ff).

In recent decades, critiques directed at the ideological roots of the modern development project and the way they manifest themselves in global development practices of states and multilateral institutions have received academic support from the so-called post-development school of thought. (For a more extensive treatise see Jochemsen & Van Dijke, 2018, pp. 17-47). Philosophically, this thinking is postmodern in spirit and ranging from structuralist to poststructuralist in its approach. Especially the work of Foucault is an important inspirational source for those authors. These thinkers, though diverse, attack the modern development system set up 70 years ago and (also) argue that the current malfunctioning of development cooperation has deep roots. In essence, the arguments of these critics undermine the just mentioned modernist beliefs and values, on which many of the large development institutions were founded. Furthermore, as expressed in the term *post*-development, these scholars believe that current 'development' should be left behind. One of the scholars in this very critical stream of thinking is James Ferguson, who argues that the sector denies the inherently political nature of development and the hegemonic tendencies of the Western worldview that are deeply ingrained and strongly connected to the whole development apparatus (Ferguson, 1994). Ferguson and other post-development scholars often refer to the concept of neoliberal hegemony and point to the overarching power structures that govern and regulate development processes (Thomas, 2000). Arturo Escobar, criticizing cultural globalization and development, also strongly warns for such a Western neoliberal hegemony and the universalization of western thinking (Escobar, 1995). Gilbert Rist even calls for abandoning the whole term 'development'. He argues that the concept is too vague and, moreover, does not alleviate but deepens the crises of poverty, security, and environmental degradation. He describes development as a buzzword, being stripped of all intrinsic meaning, becoming nothing more than an empty shell to which virtually any meaning can be connected (Rist, 2007). As a final example of critique from post-development thinkers, we mention Tanya Murray Li. She follows Ferguson in his critique of the de-politicization of development cooperation, but goes even deeper in that she explicitly critiques the 'will to improve' that is constitutive for development cooperation. The link to Nietzsche's will to power resonates clearly in the background and the abyss between "critic and programmer" is complete (Li, 2007, p. 2). Li, as a critic, has no suggestions for improvement, as that would only amount to an exercise of power over other people.

In weighing these criticisms, we should keep in mind the characteristics and limitations of the post-development school of thought in which it roots. Acknowledging the value of this criticism we disagree with its approach. We agree with Giri and Van Ufford that many post-development critics remain so suspicious to the practice of development cooperation that little room is left to more reconstructive thinking and activity to detect and value the opportunities within the system, also as long as a major system change is not within reach (Giri & VanUfford, 2004, pp. 7-9).

How are we going to address these criticisms? As mentioned already we do not believe in some magic trick that would at once solve the major problems briefly presented above. However, we do believe that the normative practice approach can be valuable in trying to overcome some of the major problems identified by the different types of critiques we discussed. The problematic ideological background in the modernity paradigm relates to beliefs and motives of the regulative side of the Normative Practice Approach (NPA). The negative consequences of the bureaucratic top-down (often donor-driven) organization of development cooperation and related motivational and informational problems can be best approached from the structural side of the NPA, also taking into account the context in which the development cooperation practices should be positioned.

In the remainder of our contribution we will present a normative view of development cooperation using the NPA, and indicate in what way this could help in working towards positive change of the work. This will involve a change in incentives that require and promote the desired institutional adaptations. The latter topic can only be touched upon briefly.

A NORMATIVE PRACTICE APPROACH TO DEVELOPMENT COOPERATION

Regulative Side

We begin this presentation of the NPA for development cooperation with a discussion of the directional (or regulative) side, dealing with its ideological background. We open this with a few remarks on the meaning of this side (cf. chapter 1).

Characteristic for mankind is that the human being actively relates to himself and his physical and social environment. In these relationships human beings interpret their existence and situation and try to find meaning and coherence in their life. This interpretative activity necessarily departs from fundamental ideas, motivations, images a person has about himself and his situation and the good life (Clouser, 2005). The directional side of practices refers to the control beliefs, motivations, normative convictions that form part of one's worldview and constitute that person's interpretative meaning-giving framework. As that worldview and interpretative frame work are largely shared among (groups of) the population and more specifically among groups of professionals, these control beliefs and normative convictions often are not immediately apparent, yet they function strongly in the form of unwritten, sometimes even unspoken codes of conduct and customs, convictions on what is decent and indecent. How does this apply to development cooperation?

The ideological background of development cooperation as a sector of society is characterized by modernization, globalization, and the pursuit of wealth by economic growth as already explained and criticized above. In our philosophical approach we hold a different view on mankind and human life. We summarize our position as follows:

1. In view of human dignity severe poverty is ethically unacceptable and must be seen as a serious form of injustice (Stok, 2018). This is a fundamental belief behind the very existence of development cooperation as we know it. Poverty, is to be seen as a multidimensional phenomenon (OECD, 2015)
2. We reject an attitude of goal-rational control of human (social) life and our environment. Science-based technology harbors a reductive view of reality that on the one hand gives it its effectiveness. On the other hand it required that applications of modern technology, certainly when they are used at large scale, do need a normative framework within which they are implemented (Wigboldus et al, 2016). At the same time we affirm that normative applications of technology provide important opportunities to support and safeguard human life and society.
3. Human beings should be seen as responsible subjects, not just objects of help by others, let alone victims of the situation, though after a calamity this may be a strong element of the situation. This is why it is important to distinguish between emergency aid and cooperation in structural development, without separating the two (cf. Van Wessel et al., 2018). Therefore, ownership of assistance, rehabilitation and development should be with the intended beneficiaries as much as possible.
4. Development should not be understood as basically economic development that in its slipstream would take care of the other aspects of development. We understand development as multiple value realization in practices and institutions, that together work towards a flourishing society (see below). This is based on our philosophical approach in which we distinguish in reality multiple normative dimensions. As a consequence we reject the absolutization of anything in created reality, whether it is economic growth, total control of life and health or happiness. Valuable as these things are in their correct context, their absolutization would imply that the fundamental values of justice,

stewardship, care for people and nature would be made subservient to those absolutized values. This is precisely one of the backgrounds of today's crises (cf. Goudzwaard et al., 2007).

5. Cooperation with people presupposes taking people seriously. And taking people seriously, involves taking seriously their worldview, which may consist in an explicit and institutionalized religion. This does not mean that one agrees with every element of other people's worldview but it requires a serious dialogue in which this dimension of life is addressed in the cooperation.

In this context it is very interesting that on the basis of her analysis, Ostrom (2010, p. 156) argues that "[n]one of these structural variables [presumed to affect the likelihood of individuals achieving collective action to overcome social dilemmas], however, should really make any difference in the probability of successful collective action if we continue to treat the model of rationality that has proved successful in explaining behavior and outcomes in competitive market settings as a universal theory of human behavior". In other words, the model of the rational *homo economicus,* that is a central element of the ideology behind mainstream 'development' and that we criticized above, can be useful for specific societal settings but hinders a fruitful understanding of human behavior in other settings. This undergirds points a) and b) of our view presented above.

In the second place, Ostrom et al. (2001, pp. xx, 15) also argue that leaving ownership for the intended beneficiaries is crucial for successful collective actions, supporting our philosophical view rendered in point d) above.

These findings demonstrate that worldview and normative beliefs, which in our approach form the regulative side of practices, do influence the way practitioners perform their practice. The modernist (neo)liberal approach to mankind, to society and to de understanding of 'development' have given the practices that constitute the 'development sector' characteristics that in many situations would prevent development projects from contributing to sustainable development of which the ownership rests with the local population. This raises the question: What does a fruitful and effective development practice looks like? What specific principles and norms should it embody?

This brings us to the structural side of practices of development cooperation.

Structural Side

The first step in identifying the normative structure of a certain practice is the identification of its telos. What would be the telos of development cooperation? To answer this question it is helpful to first discuss the concept of development (cf. Jochemsen, 2016, pp. 135, 136).What do we mean by it? Is development the same as modernization and economic growth? This idea is still strongly present among governments and international institutions (mainly the UN institutions like World Bank, IMF, UNHDP, FAO; see McNeil and St Clair, 2009) even though one would argue that such growth should be sustainable in economic, social and ecological respect; this is the broadly accepted, but not always practiced, triple P concept. From the criticism we presented above, it will be clear that we reject a one-sided emphasis on modernization, focusing on economic growth in which ecological and social values are just boundary conditions. What does it mean for the practice of development cooperation?

Development and Development Cooperation

As argued before (Jochemsen, 2016; Rademaker and Jochemsen, 2018), development can best be seen as essentially value-realization. People in general pursue values in a variety of practices and institutions (MacIntyre, 1984, pp. 181-203). Each of the practices and institutions – the latter being seen as the broader formal societal structures that (should) facilitate practices as described above – provides the environment in which people pursue the realization of important values, viz. the telos of the respective practice. We are referring here to practices in which people live and pursue the good life, like running the household, private economic sector, work to gain a living or produce food (forms of agriculture), educating the young generation, excising justice, caring for people who are dependent on care, fulfilling an office in political structures, providing financial services, etcetera. Hence, development can be understood as the process that is the fruit of human action aiming at the realization of values in the variety of society's practices and institutions, like those mentioned. Development is not so much the product of goal-oriented rational human action but rather the fruit that grows when people realize a diversity of practices according to their normativity.

Telos of Development Cooperation Practice

The telos of a practice is realized best when a constellation of 'standards of excellence is observed' – the normative practice approach explained in chapters 1 and 2.

The next question in this treatise of development *cooperation* is: what does our approach mean for the practice of development cooperation? (The question whether development cooperation can be seen as a practice was answered affirmatively in Rademaker & Jochemsen, 2018; in this treatise we build on that view). What are development professionals doing? Let us give a few examples and then try to identify the common denominator. Development professionals train local groups of people like farmers, nurses, school teachers, or they train the local trainers/teachers who then train people from the local population. They help people organize themselves in organizations and institutions like famers' cooperatives, a (local) school, a health care institution, a business, a value chain, an institution to regulate land tenure, etcetera. To realize this they bring together the relevant stakeholders in a certain field, including (institutional) donors and facilitate the process of realizing together the establishment of the desired institution and the practices involved. In more technical terms, they facilitate multi-stakeholder processes to support the population in realizing the values people want to pursue in the relevant practices. More generally, development cooperation aims at the promotion of the well-functioning of the practices and institutions that people consider valuable in a certain setting. The development professional facilitates processes, including training local people in performing their practices, in order to realize 'development' in the sense explained above. Of course, the reality of development cooperation is not as smooth and as this description suggests. There are all kinds of obstacles, like lack of trust among stakeholders, misunderstandings in communication, stakeholders, or intended beneficiaries going for a short-term self-interest etc. However, reading programs and evaluations of development cooperation these are the kind of activities that development professionals pursue. All these activities are rooted in the background belief that severe poverty, as multidimensional concept, is unacceptable (see above).

We therefore conclude that the telos of development cooperation practice consists in the facilitation of practitioners in pursuing the goods of their practices to alleviate the various forms of (severe) poverty, which in this context can be understood as lack of realization of fundamental values in the life of people. In this process, linkages with other stakeholders and practices often need to be made as well. In order to be really facilitatory, this will require a cooperative effort by development professionals and those facilitated to disclose meaning

In the facilitated practices, in which technique, in the broadest sense of the word, plays a pivotal role. Technically phrased, development cooperation is qualified by "meaning-oriented shaping" (Jochemsen 2016, p.138; Rademaker & Jochemsen, 2018, p. 23) corresponding with the so-called formative aspect in Reformational philosophy. Development cooperation is thus the meaningful shaping of practices (in which the meaning refers to the telos), including organizational practices, through cooperation with the people in those practices (ibid., 33). As such, it aims at the realization of values, i.e. development.

So we see that the qualifying aspect of the development professional practice is the formative aspect with meaning-oriented shaping as its telos, which in this context gets the meaning of training and facilitation.

Other Normative Aspects

But in addition to the qualifying aspect the structural side also pertains to the other modal aspects. For our purposes in this chapter we restrict ourselves to the aspects beyond the biotic (Cf. chapter 2). Just one remark on the *biotic aspect*. It pertains to life in its diversity; this implies it relates to biodiversity and to biological health of plants, animals and human beings; obviously an important prerequisite for a 'healthy' development of people and society!

The *psychic aspect* concerns the perceptions and experiences of people. For development professionals this means they should be aware of the influence of their behavior and work on the target population to make sure that people feel they are taken seriously. They can relate confidently to the professional and the view and information he presents. In other words, the observational and psychological functions of the professionals should function properly.

The *formative aspect* is qualifying as we saw. However, in our view it is also the major foundational aspect; the social, organizational and communication techniques and didactical methods used in the facilitation process are to be seen as formative methods pertaining to the formative aspect. Developmental professionals should therefore be equipped with state of the art methods and knowledge of facilitating multi-stakeholder processes and of training people.

Next comes the *lingual aspect*; observing its core value and related norms implies using clear and understandable language. In the transcultural setting that at some social-organizational level is inherent in development cooperation, this requires specific training and a cultural sensitivity and literacy. Clear and honest language in communication, which strongly relates to the *social aspect*, is crucial to make collective-action processes a success. Here we can easily identify ethical notions that should guide the social interaction and communication in the actual developmental work of facilitation. Values like reciprocity in the sense of a balance between peoples efforts in a certain collective-action (project) and the benefits they may obtain from it, is a social value with clear ethical and juridical overtones. It is very close to a kind of fairness. Other values in this context are trust, also among the participants of the collective-action, and reputation, that is related to trust (e.g. people with a bad reputation will not be trusted and they will not be allowed to participate).

These aspects and their related core values obviously strongly relate to what Ostrom et al. (2002) consider to be major factors in realizing successful collective action, i.e. developmental projects, namely informational and motivational problems. These problems concern questions like: do those who decide at the governance level of states, of institutional donors and of (international) NGOs really have the relevant information about the real situation of the target population, their values, their feelings about the plans, the level of trust of the implementing organizations and professionals, the possible 'strategic' behavior of some in the target population in the interest of themselves or their 'in-group'? Professionals 'on the ground', whether expats or locals, often realize that the internationally sponsored programs do not fit well the local situation and they tend to maneuver between the formal leaders and the local people which they try to involve in a fruitful way, if only to maintain their job (see Rademaker and Jochemsen, 2018, pp. 12 -14, dealing with agricultural development and referring among others to the work of Norman Long).

Other problems mentioned by Ostrom et al. (2002) are asymmetric power relations and asymmetric information; above we already mentioned the 'Samaritan's dilemma'. Here we see that a performance of development practice that observes the normativity related to the various modal aspects is required to realize fruitful collective actions. What that normativity exactly entails can be elucidated by research as done by authors like Ostrom et al. (2001) and others mentioned above. In this context a more general observation about the NPA is in place. The NPA gives a formal structure for considering the diversity of normative perspectives and the core values as guiding principles, but the specific rules to be observed in practices requires empirical research.

We continue the discussion of the different normative aspects. After the social comes the *economic aspect.* Above we warned against an absolutization of economic growth as the essence of development. This is far too narrow. Yet the economic aspect is an irreducible aspect of all practices and is qualifying for those practices commonly indicate with the term business. In another chapter of this book we dedicated a section to our understanding of this aspect. Here we just repeat what we consider to be the core value of that aspect. "We see as typical for the economic aspect human activity aiming at providing people (the household) with goods and services through production and trade. Those activities encompass efficient management of resources (production factors and means of trade). As the core value we propose 'efficient provision'". Even if one would prefer a different wording for the core value, it is clear that economic activities aiming at providing people with things they value (not least basic needs like food, clothing and housing) is a dimension of development. It is, therefore, to be applauded that more NGOs are dedicating themselves to furthering just and sustainable economic activities in 'developing countries', aiming at independency from financial donations by other states or NGOs. In this context an important challenge is to prevent those economic activities (businesses and markets) becoming fully subservient to the neoliberal economic system that appears to embody a tendency to accumulate wealth into the hands of a few (Shah, 2011; see also Jochemsen, 2018, pp. 47, 316).

The economic aspect also pertains to efficient management of resources in practices and institutions that are not economically qualified like education and health care. Also financial incentives in practices, be it in the form of salaries or benefits from participating in a development program (collective-action) pertain to this aspect underlining even more its importance. Financial incentives related to informational and motivational problems mentioned above can easily form an obstacle to fruitful and effective collective actions. Empirical research (cf. above) should elucidate what organizational arrangements and financial incentives are furthering development practices that lead to fruitful and effective collective-action.

The aesthetic aspect refers to values like harmony, enjoyment, expressiveness. In development practices it would resist littering the natural environment or spoiling the landscape by ugly buildings or constructions, and preventing cities that due to their structure and constructions are sometimes alienating for their inhabitants and contributing to violence and criminality (cf. Van Steden et al. this volume; Hummel-Verhoef and Hooglander, 2018).

The importance of the *juridical aspect*, with justice,[1] what is due to people and things, as its core values, does not need a long argument. We could even argue that in a sense the overall guiding principle for international relationships and policy should be righteousness, in a broad sense of seeing to it that all people and groups of people get their due as a precondition for their individual and communal flourishing (Jochemsen, 2018, p. 144-146). In this sense it is not just a juridical normative principle but also an ethical principle. Referring to our section on the regulative side of practices and the section on the telos of development cooperation, *we could say that this ethical and juridical principle and value of justice are leading elements of the regulative side of development practices* as they aim at the realization of values and thus alleviate poverty. They form part of the motivation of many to be involved in these activities at all, if just as a small private donor or one of the NGOs in this field. At the same time, it is the core value of the juridical aspect of all (development) practices. This requires that in these practices people and things (e.g. social structures, natural environment) get their due, justice is being done to them. This has significance for the internal functioning of the development practice but also for its functioning in the broader macro structures of society. We will briefly comment on both levels, beginning with the macro-level of state and multilateral structures.

At the macro level justice should be promoted by the state in its own activities in international relationships and diplomacy and in its policy regarding defense and economic relations and treaties, and secondly in its support to multilateral organizations like WHO, UNICEF, FAO, UNHCR and IMF. These organizations initiate activities at a global level and fulfil an important coordinating role, but in the context of development as understood here they certainly are not beyond serious criticism (McNeil and St Clair, 2009).

It will be obvious that national and international policies and governance structures will significantly influence the practices involved in the developmental process at the meso- and micro-level. In our view, macrostructures, like states, multilateral organizations, international financial markets and value chains should facilitate and further the meso- and micro-level practices in which people pursue the values that give their lives substance and meaning (see above). Unfortunately we have to note that to a significant extent the reverse is true. The international trade arrangements and monetary structures often are disadvantageous for poor countries (Pogge, 2001). In particular the neoliberal economic ideology that in recent decades has been prevalent in the affluent Western world, has generated cycles of inclusion of those groups that had already achieved a certain level of modernization and of exclusion of the really poor. An elaboration of this issue is beyond the scope of this contribution (See Goudzwaard et al, 2007, pp.162-166). We give just one example. In March 2011 the European Parliament adopted a resolution on 'Tax and Development -Cooperating with Developing Countries on Promoting Good Governance in Tax Matters' (European Parliament, 2011). In this resolution the EP "26. Notes with concern that billions of dollars per year left the African continent between 1991 and 2004; in particular, underlines that these outflows are estimated at 7,6% of the annual GDP of the region, which makes African countries net creditors of donor countries;" and "55. Highlights that as much as EUR 800 billion is lost each year from developing countries to tax havens and illicit financial flows". A report produced by Eurodad gives a more detailed confirmation of this pattern (Griffiths, 2017). Clearly the international financial-economic power structures contain gross injustices that prevent an effective handling of the sever poverty of around a billion people in the world. This situation of global injustice is ethically intolerable and it suggests a kind of ideological support for a focus on financial self-interests that already lasts for several decades.

At the meso- and micro-level, many industrial states are involved in development cooperation in the context of bilateral relations with other states and by financing development NGOs and private companies. Just a few remarks on each of these approaches. Bilateral development cooperation generally forms part of the foreign policy of a state and should therefore be guided by the principle of public justice, both in the donor and the receiver countries (the juridical aspect being qualifying for the state). This type of support almost always contains a mixture of true support of the receiving country and self-interests of the donor country. Which of these two prevails, varies from one country to another and from one government to another in the same country through the years. This may be acceptable (expecting long-term pure altruism from states is probably not realistic) as long as it is transparent what are the goals and ambitions of the partners and there is a true win-win. This latter requires that the actual practices in the receiving country that are being facilitated and supported by development practices observe the constellation of principles and norms that according to the NPA should be observed.

For development assistance in the form of subsidizing the private companies the balance between self-interests and the developmental interest is even more fragile. On the one hand, the establishment and development of private economic activities is an essential part for societal development and private investors from other countries can play a role. On the other hand, the results of financial support by states to private companies in view of development cooperation, is at best contested (Kwakkenbos, 2012; Jamali, 2004).

Many European and North American countries have a tradition of also subsidizing development NGOs that are involved in some form of development cooperation. This may vary from direct poverty alleviation to institution building, strengthening lobby capacity of national NGOs in the receiving countries, to human rights activism. In this context of the actual development practices at both micro- (e.g. facilitating the establishment a farmers' cooperation) and meso-level (e.g. linking an agricultural value chain to international markets), the juridical aspect often gets the form of a 'rights-based approach'; in this approach to developmental, work human rights are central (Jochemsen, 2016, pp. 144-145). This approach can be fruitfully applied in development practices, as long as it is not made into an absolute, considering that the juridical represents just one of the normative aspects.

However, the activities at the meso- and micro-level will only be effective, fruitful and sustainable if there is an enabling environment at the macro level, mentioned above. Here the influence of notions that in the NPA belong to the regulative side becomes clear. For it is on the basis of these regulative notions that a view of a just and sustainable international economic and political order can be formulated. In order to remediate injustices at an international level indicated above, in our view it is necessary that the predominant neoliberal model of modernization be replaced by more integral views of 'development' and 'progress'. In these integral views, social and ecological justice and the well-fare of all people must be given at least the same weight as growth of the GNP of countries. Again this is a field on which there is a lot of literature that cannot be reviewed here. Here we just indicate how the NPA serves as heuristic to get a clear view on the issues in this complex field and provides a constellation of normative principles that can inspire the work in this field at various levels.

Ethical Aspect

In the list of modal aspects, the ethical aspect comes after the juridical. With respect to this aspect, it is helpful to distinguish two levels of abstraction. Firstly, the level of ethics as reflection on the good life in a broad sense. We already referred to it when we called justice also an ethical principle that can have a *regulative function* for practices. A fundamental conviction at this level is also the acceptance of the normativity that applies to one's practice; in our approach this is the normativity as laid out in the structural side of the NPA. Other ethical notions that in development practices can and in our view should pay a role, are e.g. the inalienable dignity of human beings independent of their condition or stage of life, and stewardship as a guiding principle for our dealings with the natural environment. These principles reject a full instrumentalization of people as labor force or nature as a stock of materials. Also a view on the importance of human relations and social structures as not just contractual agreements, but as an irreducible dimension of the very life of people (Chaplin, 2011) in development cooperation, should be part of the discussion on cooperation and of forming consortia. It is very important that the donor NGO and the implementing partners and representatives of the target population come to a mutual understanding of the ethical positions from which each is involved in the cooperation.

The second level at which the ethical aspect should function and ethical principles be observed, is as one of the aspects of the *structural side* of practices. In all the relations in which practitioners function, their behavior should be ethically correct. For coming to ethically justifiable decisions in concrete situations in life, the ethical reflection is often guided by one of three normative ethical theories, or a combination of them. These are deontology or duty ethics, consequentialism in one form or another, of which at present utilitarianism is most popular; and finally virtue ethics (Fieser, undated).

In these theories the ethically correct action is respectively, the action that observes the valid duties/principles/commands in a certain situation; the action that in that situation leads to the best results for those involved; the action that embodies the virtues relevant in that situation. These ethical theories are certainly helpful in reaching a justified ethical decision in difficult situations. We refer to ethics handbooks for elaborations of the use of these theories in ethical dilemmas. However, in the context of this treatise of the NPA for development cooperation we like to indicate how these theories relate to the NPA and can be seen as supporting tools to achieve an optimal functioning of the NPA.

Duty ethics can help to operationalize the normative principles of the different aspects of the structural side. It should be reminded that in Dooyeweerdian philosophy the later modal aspects guide the positivization of the earlier aspects. In other words, the disclosure of the earlier aspects requires the guidance of the ethical aspect. For example, how should the social principle of human interaction be implemented in different relations? What rules can be derived from that principle, possibly combined with the lingual principle of clear meaning? In other words what does the ethical principle of respect for individuals tell about the way we communicate to others? Idem for the other aspects and their normative principles.

The consequentialist approach can be related to the telos of the practice.[2] The ethically desirable result then is interpreted as the realization of the telos of the practice, which requires the simultaneous realization of the normative principles of all aspects. The telos of the practice is as we saw, the facilitation of cooperation processes leading to the realization of values in practices and institutions of the 'developing' society and thus alleviate poverty in a broad sense. However, what ethical rules should be observed in the facilitation process to optimize the outcome? Consequentialist rules like proportionality and subsidiarity can help here.

Thirdly, virtue ethics can be related to the practitioner who should observe habitually the normative principles of all the aspects; this means those principles should be embodied in his or her behavior as a virtue. Virtue ethics can tell a lot about the various virtues like sensitivity for people's experience (psychic aspect), making clear and correct distinctions (analytic aspect), meaning-orientedness in intervening in natural or social processes (formative aspect), etcetera.

The final aspect is the faith or pistic or fiduciary aspect. It pertains to the observation that people's actions are necessarily rooted in a fundamental commitment, e.g. a commitment to trusting one's senses and one's reasoning in navigating through life. The acceptance of the true reality of bodily life of humans, or to the view that matter, including the body, ultimately is illusionary (like in Buddhism). And so on. Only in choosing a position can people really get knowledge. In the NPA these fundamental commitments belong to the regulative side of practices.

Sharing Commitments

After this brief exposition of the different elements of NPA for development practice we want to come back to one element that in our view is crucial in these practices. This is the importance of devolving ownership to the target population. This is also stressed by Ostrom et al. (2001). We like to present a method that could help in doing this, not just at the level of actual decision power but also at the level of normative convictions functioning in the regulative side as well as in the structural side as explained above. This method is a variant of triple loop learning as used in professional education, often in the form of supervision and intervision.

Above we commented that true cooperation on an equal footing requires the sharing and discussion of normative views about the work that the partners are envisioning to execute together. The method proposed here intends to elucidate the core values and views of Southern partners is the so-called triple loop learning that is also called deep learning (see Figure 1). This form of reflection digs deeper than the ordinary reflection in intervision in professional practices. For that reason it has also been called deep learning (Hegeman et al., 2011, pp. 196-203, 249-263; see also Jochemsen, 2018, p.72).

Figure 1. The two loops of deep reflection

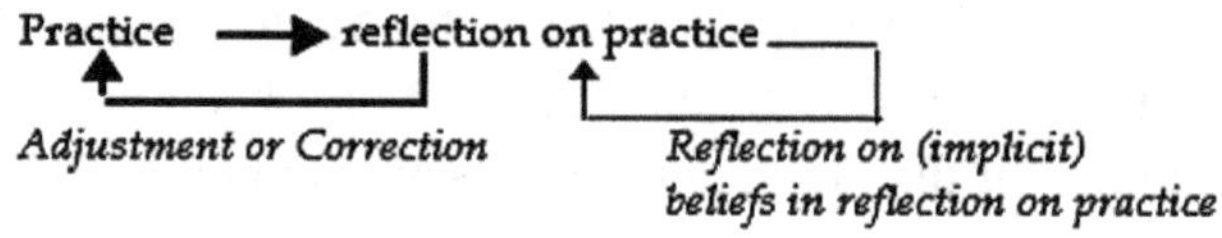

The first loop is the common reflection on the question: did I perform my practice according to the professional standard, or were there good (ethical) reasons to deviate from it (The arrow to the right in Fig. 2)? This reflection underlines the importance of (applied) ethics. Deep reflection contains two more types of reflection. The second loop concentrates on the question: did I do the right things? Did I use my practice to achieve the true purpose of the practice? At this point the understanding of 'development' and the practice of development cooperation will be topics of reflection and discussion. In answering this question, the practitioners somehow draw on normative beliefs and stances that are, however, in common practice seldom made explicit. This is what the third loop of deep reflection does, making it deep reflection. Deep reflection calls for reflection on the normative beliefs and stances that are often taken for granted during the first and second type of reflection. It reflects on the view of the practice and its telos and normative principles in light of the practitioner's or the organization's own normative views and convictions. In this way, workers in development cooperation and professionals of (implementing) partner organizations are trained in relating one's professional practice to one's more personal spiritual beliefs and how these can be expressed and discussed with respect to the consequences for their integration in the cooperation in development. This does not mean that the participants in this type of reflection would have to be willing beforehand to give up one's beliefs and faith – certainly not. But, one should be willing and able to explain them and to relate them to one's practice. If in this process the views of the target population are taken seriously and integrated in the programming and implementation, the ownership of the target population can be strengthened. A precondition for making this happen is to leave a considerable discretionary power to the professionals in the field, so that they can adapt to the actual situation and positioning of the people they are working with. Doing so at the same time can help in dealing with the informational problems Ostrom et al. identify as one of the major problems in development cooperation (see above).

CONCLUDING REMARKS

- Development cooperation in today's sense can be seen as a project of modernization of the rich industrialized countries to tag along poor countries in a similar process of 'development', directed at (material) economic growth through industrialization with the aid of science and technology. Justified moral motives and well-understood self-interest formed the background of this project.
- As a result of the self-interests of the wealthy countries the international financial, economic and political constellation allowing rich countries to enrich themselves and their own industries more than local people and companies.
- Developmental work as performed during the latest seven decades departed from an overestimation of one's own modern culture that prevented taking into account sufficiently the culture and the ownership of the target populations. The way in which development assistance and cooperation was programmed and implemented has resulted in helping many people with basic needs, but at the same time contained arrangements that entailed informational and motivational problems that frustrated a true endogenous development that would make those populations and countries independent from external support.
- At the same time it has to be acknowledged that the wealthy countries had established an economy with a level of production and consumption that already has brought our present world in a number of related crises that seriously threaten the future of billions of people. The development model of the industrialized countries and of the emergent economies has reached its limits and constitutes a threat. At the same time the continuation of the often appalling poverty is morally unacceptable.
- In this contribution an attempt is made to present a normative view of development and development cooperation that could be the beginning of a normative framework for a more just and sustainable development, both in the rich and in the poor countries. In this view, development is seen as the fruit of a society in which people realize values that are important for them by living and working in a diversity of practices and institutions that exist precisely in view of the realization of their core value. Respect for the intrinsic normativity of those practices and institutions, forms a precondition for such a more just and sustainable society.

REFERENCES

Basden, A. (2000). *Dooyeweerd pages*. Retrieved from http://www.dooy.salford.ac.uk/juridical.html

Blokhuis, P. (2003). Book Review of Kees Boersma, Jan van der Stoep, Maarten Verkerk, Ad Vlot (eds.), Aan Babels stromen. Een bevrijdend perspectief op ethiek en techniek. Amsterdam 2002: Buijten en Schipperheijn. 312 pagina's. ISBN 9058810682. Philosophia Reformata, 68(1), 86–88. doi:10.1163/22116117-90000277

Chaplin, J. (2011). *Herman Dooyeweerd: Christian Philosopher of State and Society*. Notre Dame, IN: University of Notre Dame Press.

Clouser, R. A. (2005). *The myth of religious neutrality* (rev. ed.). Notre Dame, IN: Notre Dame University Press.

Crosswell, M. (2009). The development record and the effectiveness of foreign aid. *PRAXIS The Fletcher Journal of Development Studies, 15*. Retrieved from http://fletcher.tufts.edu/Praxis/Archives/~/media/Fletcher/Micro-sites/praxis/xv/Crosswell.pdf

Escobar, A. (1995). *Encountering Development: the making and unmaking of the third world*. Princeton University Press.

European Commission. (2016). *Development*. Retrieved from http://ec.europa.eu/trade/policy/countries-and-regions/development/

European Parliament. (2011). Cooperating with developing countries on promoting good governance in tax Matters. *European Parliament resolution of 8 March 2011 on Tax and Development Cooperation with Developing Countries on Promoting Good Governance in Tax Matters* (2010/2102(INI)). Retrieved from http://www.europarl.europa.eu/sides/getDoc.do?pubRef=-//EP//NONSGML+TA+P7-TA-2011-0082+0+DOC+PDF+V0//EN

Ferguson, J. (1994). The anti-politics machine; Development, Depoliticization, and Bureaucratic Power in Lesotho. *The Ecologist, 24*(5), 176–181.

Fieser, J. (n.d.). *Ethics*. Retrieved from https://www.iep.utm.edu/ethics/

Giri, A. K., & Van Ufford, P. Q. (2004). *A Moral Critique of Development: Ethics, Aesthetics and Responsibility*. Aalborg, Denmark: Institut for Historie, Internationale Studier og Samfundsforhold, Aalborg Universitet.

Goudzwaard, B., VanderVennen, M., & David Van Heemst, D. (2007). *Hope in Troubled Times: A New Vision for Confronting Global Crises*. Grand Rapids, MI: Baker Academic.

Griffiths, J. (2017). *Is the global financial and economic system fit to deliver the Sustainable Development Goals?* Eurodad. Retrieved from https://eurodad.org/files/pdf/1546835-is-the-global-financial-and-economic-system-fit-to-deliver-the-sustainable-development-goals--1509613918.pdf

Hegeman, J. J., Edgell, M., & Jochemsen, H. (2011). *Practice and profile. Christian formation for vocation*. Eugene, OR: Wipf&Stock.

Hummel-Verhoef, R., & Hooglander, K.-J. (2018). Development and aid in urban contexts. In H. Jochemsen (Ed.), *For the twig to blossom…* (pp. 165–185). Maastricht: Shaker Publishing.

Jamali, D. (2004). Success and failure mechanisms of public private partnerships (PPPs) in developing countries. Insights from the Lebanese context. *International Journal of Public Sector Management, 17*(5), 414–430. doi:10.1108/09513550410546598

Jochemsen, H., & VanDijke, J. (2018). Hope, action and reflection as perspectives on development cooperation and its future. In H. Jochemsen (Ed.), *For the twig to blossom…*. Maastricht: Shaker.

Kwakkenbos, J. (2012). *Private profit for public good? Can investing in private companies deliver for the poor?* Eurodad. Retrieved from https://eurodad.org/files/pdf/1543000-private-profit-for-public-good-can-investing-in-private-companies-deliver-for-the-poor-.pdf

Li, T. M. (2007). *The Will to Improve: Governmentality, Development, and the Practice of Politics*. Durham, NC: Duke University Press. doi:10.1215/9780822389781

MacIntyre, A. (1984). *After virtue*. Notre Dame, IN: University of Notre Dame Press.

McNeil, D., & St Clair, A. L. (2009). *Global poverty, ethics and human rights. The role of multilateral organisations*. London: Routledge. doi:10.4324/9780203881309

OECD. (2015). *Keeping the multiple dimensions of poverty at the heart of development*. OECD and Post 2015 reflections, element 1, paper 1. Retrieved from https://www.oecd.org/dac/POST-2015%20multidimensional%20poverty.pdf

OECD & WTO. (2015). *Aid for Trade at a Glance 2015*. Reducing Trade Costs for Inclusive, Sustainable Growth. doi:10.1787/aid_glance-2015-

Ostrom, E. (2010). Analyzing collective action. *Agricultural Economics. International Association of Agricultural Economists*, *41*(s1), 155–166. doi:10.1111/j.1574-0862.2010.00497.x

Ostrom, E., Gibson, C., Shivakumar, S., & Andersson, K. (2002). *Aid, Incentives, and Sustainability. An Institutional Analysis of Development Cooperation*. Sida Studies in Evaluation 02/01. Retrieved from https://www.sida.se/contentassets/34b423c6b93e41798038c901e30cd4d1/12924.pdf

Ovaska, T. (2003). The failure of development aid. *The Cato Journal*, *23*(2), 175–188.

Oxfam International. (2015). Wealth: having it all and wanting more. *Oxfam issue briefing*. Retrieved from http://www.oxfam.org/en/research/wealth-having-it-all-and-wanting-more

Pogge, T. (2001). Priorities of global justice. *Metaphilosophy*, *32*(1-2), 6–24. doi:10.1111/1467-9973.00172

Rademaker, C. J., & Jochemsen, H. (2018). Beyond Modernization: Development Cooperation as Normative Practice. *Philosophia Reformata*, *83*(1), 1–32. doi:10.1163/23528230-08301007

Rist, G. (2007). Development as a buzzword. *Development in Practice*, *17*(4-5), 485–491. doi:10.1080/09614520701469328

Shah, A. (2011). *Poverty around the world. Global Issues. Social, political, economic and environmental issues that affect us all.* Retrieved from http://www.globalissues.org/article/4/poverty-around-the-world#TheWealthyandthePoor

Stirrat, R. L. (2000). Cultures of Consultancy. *Critique of Anthropology*, *20*(1), 31–46. doi:10.1177/0308275X0002000103

Stok, L. (2018). Reaching and involving the poorest of the poor. In H. Jochemsen (Ed.), *For the twig to blossom....* (pp. 187-208). Maastricht: Shaker.

Tesfaye, H. (2010). *Africa and the Failure of Development Aid: Time for Designing an Exit Strategy*. Retrieved from http://aigaforum.com/articles/Africa_and_the_Failure.htm

Thomas, A. (2000). Development as practice in a liberal capitalist world. *Journal of International Development*, *12*(6), 773–787. doi:10.1002/1099-1328(200008)12:6<773::AID-JID716>3.0.CO;2-7

UN. (2015). *The Millennium Development Goals Report 2015*. New York: United Nations. Retrieved from http://www.un.org/millenniumgoals/2015_MDG_Report/pdf/MDG%202015%20rev%20(July%201).pdf

Van der Walt, B. (2006). *When African and Western cultures meet*. Potchefstroom: Institute of Contemporary Christianity in Africa.

Van Lieshout, P., Went, R., & Kremer, M. (2010). *Less Pretention, More Ambition. Development Policy in Times of Globalization*. Amsterdam: Amsterdam University Press. doi:10.5117/9789089642950

Van Wessel, A., Bennema, M., Hoogland, L.-M., Mulder, C., & Jochemsen, H. (2018). Developments in Humanitarian Aid. In H. Jochemsen (Ed.), *For the twig to blossom…* (pp. 143–164). Maastricht: Shaker.

Wigboldus, S., Klerkx, L., Leeuwis, C., Schut, M., Muilerman, S., & Jochemsen, H. (2016). Systemic perspectives on scaling agricultural innovations. A review. *Agronomy for Sustainable Development*, *36*(3), 46. doi:10.100713593-016-0380-z

World Bank. (2015). *Data*. Retrieved from https://data.worldbank.org/

ENDNOTES

1 Sometimes also indicated as 'retribution', or 'due to all', 'appropriateness', 'rightfulness'; see Andrew Basden, "The juridical aspect", Andrew Basden, *Dooyeweerd pages,* 2000, http://www.dooy.salford.ac.uk/juridical.html, accessed January 30, 2015.

2 We do realize that duty ethics and consequentialism as they are commonly employed, are at several points fundamentally opposed to each other. However, the problem in such polemics is that the significance of respectively the rule (duty ethics) and the goal (consequentialism) are absolutized. This absolutization results from a more fundamental worldview, or what we called a vision of the good life (cf. Blokhuis, 2003).

APPENDIX

Abbreviations

CSO: Civil Society Organiation(s).
EC: European Commission.
EP: European Parliament.
FAO: Food and Agriculture Organisation, of the United Nations.
GNI: Gross National Income.
GNP: Gross National Product (see https://www.economicshelp.org/blog/3491/economics/difference-between-gnp-gdp-and-gni/).
IMF: International Monetary Fund.
ODA: Official Development assistance.
OECD: Organization for Economic Co-operation and Development.
UNDP: United Nations Development Programme.
WTO: World Trade Organization.

Chapter 13
Security Networks:
Applying the Normative Practice Approach to Nodal Governance Theory

Ronald van Steden
VU University Amsterdam, The Netherlands

Robert van Putten
VU University Amsterdam, The Netherlands

Jan Hoogland
VU University Amsterdam, The Netherlands

ABSTRACT

Studies into organizational networks and governance tend to analyze professional behavior through the lens of rational (self)interest, resources, conflict, and power relations. However legitimate, this viewpoint overlooks the normative dimensions of networks. Therefore, in studying nodal security governance, the authors introduce the concept of "social practice," which highlights the intrinsic normativity of what networked actors do. Social practices, they argue, deepen the theory of nodal governance by focusing more precise attention on the mentalities and value-laden characteristics of actors in highly complex settings. Drawing on this insight, the chapter presents a theoretical framework for analyzing social practices in nodal security governance, after which an empirical example concretizes our rather abstract line of reasoning.

DOI: 10.4018/978-1-5225-8006-5.ch013

THE NEGLECT OF NORMATIVITY IN NETWORK GOVERNANCE

In criminology and political science, it is common knowledge that the police are increasingly surrounded by a host of organizations on local, regional, national, and international levels. We think of (multinational) private security firms and municipal law enforcement agencies, for example, but schools, businesses, housing associations, health care services, civil society initiatives, NGOs, and active (groups of) citizens are also important. These "nodal" actors, defined as "sites of governance" (Buris et al., 2004), ideally make up security networks: "a set of institutional, organizational, communal, or individual agents or nodes that are interconnected in order to authorize and/or provide security to the benefit of internal or external stakeholders" (Dupont, 2004, p. 78). Nodal actors themselves may consist of smaller nodes, with single people as the ultimate units of analysis: "firms, for instance, can be seen as a product of networks within the firm" (Burris et al., 2005, pp. 38-39). Different providers of security on multiple levels try to relate to another if they feel they have a common goal to reach.

There is widespread acceptance among scholars that the complexity arising from security networks can legitimately be captured by the concept of "governance" as a means of managing "the course of events in a social system" (Burris et al., 2005, p. 30). Political science and public administration literature lead the way in theorizing the contours of governance – that is, the ways nodal actors and their institutional structures interchange within the context of tight interconnectedness, mutual power relations, and financial, political, and juridical constraints on what can and cannot be achieved (e.g. Burris et al., 2008; Provan & Kenis, 2008; Klein & Koppenjan, 2012). A major challenge is how exactly nodal actors can achieve good cooperation and collaboration in volatile and agile network settings. Depending on the problem at hand, the police, private security firms, government bodies, and numerous others constantly struggle with who should take which position and be responsible for what.

Wood and Shearing make clear that "nodal" actors are not always "networked" actors. Nodal actors do not necessarily have many links: they may have a few or "may not come together to form 'networks' at all" (2007, p. 27). As such, the term "nodal" only refers to a radical dispersal of power relations—of Foucauldian "governmentality" (Rose et al., 2006)—among assorted actors. Where nodes constitute network intersects, the actors involved can be said to display a type of "team play" (van Steden et al., 2016), but networks do not automatically flourish. Also, either public or private actors might take the lead when governing networks in an improvised fashion. For this reason, the nodal school provides a conceptual lens that is neutral about the nature of governance: it "is equally comfortable with the idea that governance can be contested and uncoordinated as it is with the idea that it can be cooperative and coordinated" (Wood & Shearing, 2007, p. 28). Empirical research should provide answers about what is happening when nodal actors meet up to tackle social problems, including insecurity, crime, and disorder.

So far, academic publications explaining why nodal actors do or do not collaborate mostly adopt a one-dimensional approach that centers primarily on interests, conflicts, resources, and uncertainties in the course of tackling "wicked" problems (e.g. Crawford, 2006; Klein & Koppenjan, 2012). Wicked problems such as crime, disorder, terrorism, and other security issues are difficult, if not impossible, to solve because of contradictory requirements, enduring disagreement about the nature of the problem itself, and byzantine interdependencies between the actors involved (Rittel & Webber, 1973). Governing security, it seems, means "muddling through" (Lindblom, 1959) a vast number of barriers, obstacles, and setbacks. Yet, in order to genuinely understand why "team play" does or doesn't flourish, we should also be aware of the *normative* elements implied in nodal security governance. People, as much as institutions, host a set of norms and values that guide their (professional) behavior and are implicated in "ways of thinking (*mentalities*) about the matters that the node has emerged to govern" (Burris et al., 2004, p. 341; italics in the original). It is to be hoped that nodal mentalities make governance a joint undertaking, though this collaborative element is certainly not always present.

The question now arising is how a better understanding of "normativity" can help to enhance team play within security networks. In our view, the nodal governance school as developed by Clifford Shearing and colleagues—see Holley and Shearing (2017) for an overview—offers a promising route for exploring this question in more depth as it seeks to bring more clarity to "the internal characteristics of nodes" (Burris, 2004, p. 341). Instead of taking governance as an overarching program, nodal scholars outline the technologies, logics, resources, capacities, and—indeed—mentalities of individual actors (see Johnston & Shearing, 2003, chapter 2). Consistent with Stenning, it is precisely these "mentalities" (or "mental frameworks") of nodal actors that embody

> *the most significant dimension of governance [...] that shapes the way we think about the world and, as a result, the way we react to the situations and circumstances we encounter in our daily lives. It sets the terms within which our perceptions and thoughts are constructed and translated into action. (Stenning in Johnston & Shearing, 2003, p. 29)*

Building on Stenning's important claim, our aim here is to devote explicit attention to the normative dimensions—the "value-laden" basis—of security governance. We will explore this topic more fully by interpreting the activities of nodal actors as social practices.

Our chapter is structured as follows. First, we discuss the importance of normativity in a secular age and where it can be found. Second, we delve into the idea of "social practice" and its significance for appreciating intrinsic normativity. We then argue how the "normative practice approach" provides a more detailed understanding of the multiple normative dimensions of social practices. Drawing on this, we analyze how the normative practice approach can be applied to the theory of nodal security governance. We illustrate our argument with an empirical example from The Netherlands, followed by a discussion how to conceptually understand the relationship between social practices and nodal security governance. We close our chapter with some remarks on the further use of the social practice approach for understanding cooperation and governance in organizational networks.

NORMATIVITY IN A SECULAR AGE

Along with interests and conflicts—often identified as crucial elements of organizational networks and governance structure—normative dimensions of life are also meaningful in everyday human behavior and interaction. In very general terms, there are always norms and values in play when people do things together. Those norms and values may be voiced through explicit ideological, philosophical, or religious convictions, but when it comes to professional settings they are normally implicit and are not strongly articulated (Taylor, 1989). In any case, value-free human behavior does not exist. As yet, many criminological and public administration studies are oriented towards positivist scientific methods. Such studies pay little attention to normativity, as can be seen in the mainstream governance discourse. In a sense, this omission is the fate of an instrumental rationality that haunts contemporary social science and philosophy (Raz, 2005). Consequently, the meaning of a value-laden rationality has been pushed to the margins of academic curricula and research programs. In studying governance systems, it is quite difficult to find a place for normativity – for normative beliefs and reason.

At first glance, the influential positivist—rational and instrumental—perspective seems to be right. Indeed, values and normative inspiration are peculiar themes in a late-modern (or postmodern) society. We live in a "secular age" (Taylor, 2007) where religion and values have been demystified as historical constructs. Whereas five hundred years ago it was impossible not to believe in God, today the situation is reversed. Believing in God and, more broadly, in a normative Idea (or Ideal) has become one option among many others, just as the State and the Police have lost their sacred status in Western societies (Reiner, 1992). Although governments and police forces are still there, we now recognize a "diversity of entities, what we term 'nodes', that function as auspices or providers of security" (Wood & Shearing, 2007,

p. 34). Think of private security companies, for example. In this context, security governance is typically seen as a post-ideological and therefore pragmatic endeavor. To quote Boutellier:

The pursuit of common convictions and ties is something we might [...] leave undone, since every effort is sure to be in vain and even more so since it keeps us from our own self-creation, the endless rewriting of our life history and strivings. The only thing that counts in a secular, liberal society is that people are vulnerable to humiliation and cruelty, pain and suffering; the extent to which we show ourselves to be sensitive to other people's experiences of this kind determines the morality of our culture. Our solidarity is not a value in itself, but is based on the recognition and acknowledgement of each other's possible suffering. (2000, p. 15)

Bauman's analysis of a "liquid modernity" (2000)—that is, the vanishing of physical and normative boundaries in today's society—is significant in problematizing the notion of moral clarity as a vital aspect of (professional) normativity. Since the "grand narratives" of history have lost momentum, a rational and control-oriented policy orientation sets the tone. Practitioners and citizens alike want to prevent "the worst" at all costs, hence their preoccupation with a negative moral valence. Nevertheless, attitudes, values, and beliefs about "the good life" have not disappeared fully from the public sphere. We may, rather, speak of "moral embarrassment": literally and figuratively, "valuable" humanistic and religious sources from which people draw their normative orientations have become obsolete or hard to reach (Taylor, 1989). Many late-modern people have difficulty in clearly founding their values and normative standards.

However, this is not a reason to abort completely the search for normativity in professional actions. Values and beliefs continue to exist and have a social function in guiding people's behavior. Luckily, in the absence of God or of a shared normativity, Western societies have not fallen into chaos and disorder. In fact, Europe, North America, and Australia are the most stable continents of our world. Yet, "complexity without direction" is the hallmark of a globally networked society that has emerged over the last decades. Networks lack a value-laden anchoring and this fuels a simmering unease about "who we are" and "where to go" (Boutellier, 2013). Some sort of normative orientation is thus needed.

It is therefore not surprising that sociologists and philosophers display renewed interest in the existential depths of living together (see Habermas, 2006). These depths involve humanistic sentiments "from within" (van den Brink, 2016) as well as spiritual or religious values "from outside", from God, or from any other heavenly Order (Houston et al., 2008). Furthermore, scholars study the presence of various values associated with professional organizations (e.g. van der Wal et al.,

2008), or point to the value-laden calling of "best persons" whose work contributes to successful policy outcomes (van Hulst et al., 2012). In line with this, research into "normative professionalism" lays emphasis on the quality and lived values of practitioners. As Kunneman says, "normative professionalization is based [...] on the development of reflexive connections between cognitive insights, organizational norms and existential values on the level of practical work processes" (2005, p. 195)—processes that are decisive in the effective implementation of, *inter alia*, security policies.

Perhaps precisely due to the lack of moral sensitivity in explaining human motives and decision making, values, normativity, and spirituality are again objects of study. One point that remains in doubt is where exactly normativity can be located when, in a secularized society, values do not necessarily sprout from a traditional religious world view. For this reason, we speak of "intrinsic normativity" that is immanent in individual and organizational professionalism. We do so from the realization that, for many, seeking normativity "from outside" is problematic. Nevertheless, the concept of intrinsic normativity stresses that there is yet another realm for norms and values—for beliefs about right and wrong—than merely scattered personal tastes and individual consciousness. Intrinsic normativity transcends atomistic positions as they are integrated in the larger whole of histories, communities, and traditions. On this note, we join a broad sociological movement that is gaining popularity and can best be located under the banner of "social practice" (Schatzki, 1996; Reckwitz, 2002; Nicolini, 2012). Theories of social practice locate normativity within routine human activities. We will explore this below.

NORMATIVITY IN SOCIAL PRACTICES

Our journey into the normative characteristics—i.e. the value-laden destinations—of actors starts from the premise that security governance is rooted in all kinds of social practices. So understood, both the definition and production of nodal security policies are being shaped by interplay between social practices that clusters activities, including policing, caring, guarding, teaching, housing, and sheltering. Social practices do not exemplify something completely arbitrary; quite the contrary. Those practices stem from "a coherent form of human activity and related competences [...] grounded in rules [...] of intuitive awareness" (Hoogland & Jochemsen, 2000, p. 463) that cannot be learned by the book, but must be lived through. In addition, those practices have a "teleo-affective structure": they have a specific purpose or *telos* (Schatzki, 1996). Without such a purpose, social practices become meaningless; their activities thus always inhibit a certain goal or sense. Relatedly, MacIntyre (1981) distinguishes between "internal" and "goods" goods, the first being inherently linked to the "logic" or "core values" of a practice that guide proper, not to say virtuous, behavior.

The basic argument that practice scholars sets forth can also be found in the broader social sciences that attempt to articulate the importance of practices and their normativity from various angles. As outlined above, Kunneman's publications on normative professionalism search for the "normative structure" of a practice (or a profession). He is particularly interested in unravelling what is specific about, for example, social work, and what drives professionals to take care of others (Kunneman, 2005). This "specificity"—the "core values"—of a practice refers to its "destination" or "intention" (*telos*). In the case of social work, professionals show deep emotional involvement with vulnerable people; their motive is to help and assist people because of their inalienable dignity. A different clue can be found in Overeem and Tholen's criticism of New Public Management (NPM): the idea that government can be run like a business (cf. Osborne & Gaebler, 1992). They believe that the *telos*—the goal, destination, or intention—of public administration is to strive for the "general interest" or the "common good" (the *bonum commune*). "The realization of the good itself", Overeem and Tholen (2011, pp. 741-742) stress, "involves some participation of members of the community". Such a political community is not formed by "clients" (NPM-newspeak) who defend their rational preferences through deliberations and referenda, but by "social, excellence-seeking" people who sail on their normative compass and like to contribute positively to society.

A normative understanding of social practices can be further analyzed along the lines of the "normative practice" approach (Hoogland & Jochemsen, 2000; also see Chapter 1 in this book). Characteristic for this approach is its more detailed understanding of the normative structure of social practices and the presence of several forms of normativity within such practices. As outlined before, this approach distinguishes two dimensions regarding the 'normative structure of social practices': the *constitutive* side (which includes rules and norms for action) of a social practice together with its *regulative* (or "direction-oriented") side.

On the first level, the constitutive side of a social practice distinguishes into founding, qualifying, and conditioning principles. Founding principles "are the rules that prescribe the activities characteristic of a specific practice" (Jochemsen, 2008, p. 6). Next, the qualifying principles of a practice cover its normative depth: they embody "something we value, something we consider as an important good" (Glas, 2012, p. 287). Finally, conditions such as laws, economic realities, and social norms facilitate the realization of the qualifying function (the core values) of a practice. They guide a competent performance of any social practice.

On the second level, social practices are regulated by mentalities, which give a specific interpretation of rules from which the direction (*telos*) of practitioners' activities and performances stems. As Jochemsen (2008, pp. 7-8) writes, "regulative ideas […] about […] the good life […] will influence the way in which the constitutive rules are applied". The concept of "social practice" thus delves into the normative dimensions of what practitioners do, and why they do it, in both their own organizations and in the nodal environments they work in.

NETWORKED COLLABORATION THROUGH A SOCIAL PRACTICE-LENS

To this point, we have analyzed the relevance of intrinsic normativity, which can be found in social practices, for a secularized society. A social practice inhabits a normative orientation and structure that underlies its irreducible identity. Previous publications on the importance of normativity in social practices concentrated on single practices such as health care and education (e.g., Hoogland & Jochemsen, 2000; Kunneman, 2005). However, in this chapter, we are primarily interested in a *collection* of social practices— that is, of security practices in nodal settings that seek to work together. Here we deal with several actors, professionals, and organizations. As already mentioned before, the field of security governance is a messy business because the enormous diversity of public, commercial, and non-profit actors in networked settings creates ambiguity and conflict about "who is responsible for what" and "how to arrive at a satisfying outcome." Therefore, our question is how a better understanding of the normative structure of social practices can improve collaboration between different nodal actors in the governance of security.

Our claim is that for a better determination of those actors in nodal networks it is necessary to go deeper into the normative layers and destinations that can be found in their routine social practices. Indeed, the intrinsic normativity of nodal actors conflates with the core function they perform in a security network. If that core function is unclear or fuzzy, cooperation within a network does not flourish easily—if it flourishes at all. As Boutellier observes:

> *Occasionally it seems as though professionals 'forget' that their positions are based (or should be based) on a meaning that inheres in the practice itself. […] If there is a lack of shared 'sense' in a practice then it loses its meaning. Giving direction in a practice begins with the practice itself, that is to say, the manner in which its core function has developed historically. (2013, pp. 149-151)*

A vital point here is that each nodal actor in a network represents not only its own resources and interests, but also its own relative independence and normativity with regard to other partners. This intrinsic normativity explains the actor's mentality or *raison d'être*. It helps professionals to grasp what their core function and matching destination is within a nodal governance setting. Put differently, nodal actors and their institutions inhabit a unique identity from which they try to create complementary bonds and social matrices. Without some sort of stable, value-laden basis, it is hard to decide where one's own tasks and responsibilities end and where other nodal actors may take over.

NORMATIVITY IN SECURITY GOVERNANCE

We illustrate the application of the social practice approach to nodal governance theory by sketching an empirical case of security governance in IJburg, a relatively young borough of Amsterdam, the capital city of the Netherlands (see van Marissing et al., 2010). In the course of 2002, the new residents of this borough received the keys to their houses. They displayed a strong pioneering spirit: IJburg, an artificially created island on the eastern side of the city, aimed to be brighter, cleaner, and safer than the other boroughs. However, over the years, it has become clear that residents have been unable to create a fortress strong enough to resist urban problems such as youth nuisance. People regularly complain that youth are littering, loitering, and creating loud noise, complaints that are focused in a few "hot spots:" squares that slowly turn into breeding grounds for serious criminal behavior. Some problem youth are dragged into drug trafficking, prostitution, holdups, and theft.

This problem is interlinked with the presence of dysfunctional and "anti-social" families in the borough of IJburg. Several "criminogenic" factors may be influential here: for instance, unemployment, poverty, divorce, cramped living conditions, substance abuse, and truancy (van Steden et al., 2013). Within the Dutch welfare state, troubled families and individuals are supported by a system of professionals who design intervention strategies to reduce disorderly and criminal conduct. The immediate question is whether professionals are doing the right thing in setting up a security network in IJburg. Professionals in a nodal security network, such as the one in IJburg, should address a comprehensive mapping of both the players and of the "wicked" problems. What is the diagnosis? Are we talking about serious—organized—crime, about petty theft, or about social disorganization and disorder? Our social practice approach is especially instructive for unraveling this kind of complexity in nodal governance. Depending on the answers given, a local security network, which is normally composed of professional actors, can be set up systematically.

Analysis of the case shows that there are at least three types of social practices active in IJburg. First, there are street police officers who exercise their mandate in light of founding principles (their organization, skills, methods, and technologies) and have a certain qualifying mandate (maintaining the public order and using violence if necessary) within conditioning economic, judicial, and administrative boundaries that ensure effective and efficient performance. Subsequently, social workers want to offer trust and guidance to, in their eyes, vulnerable problem youth (the qualifying side of their practice) by applying welfare-oriented interventions and techniques – again, within established conditioning rules and restrictions. Similar understanding can be offered of the final social practice of schools and education: teachers like their pupils to learn something (foundation) and try to shape their character and education (qualification) by following a prescribed program of lessons (condition). They do this from a substantive world view (direction) about raising children and guiding them on the road to maturity.

If we apply the theory of normative practices to IJburg, it appears that social workers are best suited to intervene when youth problems are fairly minor: when young people are roaming the borough's streets and behaving uncivilly. Nevertheless, in the case of illegal activities, police officers should take the lead in firmly restoring public order. Conversely, police officers may not need to spend too much time on bored youngsters who are simply annoying people. Social workers presumably have better ideas about running sports and recreational activities that help to reduce disorder, for example, thereby establishing natural links with schools that try to educate their pupils about "good citizenship". At the same time, the mapping exercise in IJburg pointed at juveniles who are members of anti-social and even criminal families. This is obviously a police matter which should not be left to teachers, family support, and youth care alone. If security problems become more severe, schools and social services are no longer capable of coping with them. From this we can see that networked social practices are hard to align, as a result of conflicting constitutive and regulative factors: street police officers take a short-term security-oriented attitude towards deviant youth, while social workers habitually emphasize the devastating long-term effects of poverty, unemployment, and divorce on how youngsters behave.

Taking this practice-lens shows that security and security governance is much more than policing. In addition to protecting people against crime and disorder, as the police usually do, civic institutions such as social work and schools are busy building communities that deliver security through social attachment, trust, and care. Thereby a much broader idea of security is created; it transcends a pragmatic avoidance of loss, danger, and damage. Security is, on an ontological level, also a performative undertaking that is formed by day-to-day experiences and interactions with others. This dimension of security has no primacy in the dominant judicial-political discourse but is vital for establishing nodal initiatives (Schuilenburg et al., 2013). In order to "team up" with others, actors thus need to respect their core function: policing concerns law enforcement, doctoring relates to the promotion of health, education has to do with the transfer of knowledge, and so on (see Schwartz, 2011; Boutellier, 2013). *What lends coherence to nodal security governance is congregating assorted views of the "common good" that are derived from a substantial normative understanding of one's own and others' social practices.*

Although our empirical illustration of security governance in IJburg does not immediately lead to problem-solving performance, providing insights in the normative structure of the nodal actors' own position within the network is relevant for improving their mutual collaboration. Analyzing the respective normative structure of each actor creates a sharper insight into the (potential) conflicts and possibilities for collaboration in a nodal setting. It shows what to expect from each actor when providing security—whether in the form of law enforcement, support or care—and deepens our understanding of the multi-dimensionality of security governance. As such, the normative practice approach has the ability to improve (the foundations for) collaboration among nodal actors in a security network.

THE RELATION BETWEEN SOCIAL PRACTICES IN SECURITY NETWORKS

The previous section has discussed how paying attention to the normative structure of multiple actors in a nodal security network and highlights their mentalities and core functions. A not yet mentioned issue related to this concerns the way multiple actors may relate to each other in a network. As we have seen, in the reality of nodal security governance, the police are not alone; they are surrounded by heterogeneous and sometimes interrelated public and private actors. Accordingly, the challenge is to interpret how nodal actors, as an embodiment of social practices, may or may not work together. Building on van Burken and de Vries' (2012) typology based on the work of Herman Dooyeweerd, there are three possibilities.

First, at one extreme, social practices are an integral part of an overarching system without which the system and its practices can no longer survive. The lungs, liver, and heart keep human beings alive, but all cease to function when taken out of the body. Second, at the other extreme, practices operate "next to each other without any strict ties" (van Burken & de Vries, 2012, p. 143); nodes show indifference towards each other and, at worst, adopt (mutual) hostilities—they don't form a network at all. Third, somewhere in the middle, there is (loose) collaboration and coordination among social practices in settings where "the part contributes to the functioning of the whole, but [...] does not lose its sense outside that whole" (van Burken & de

Vries, 2012, p. 144). Referring to Dooyeweerd's vocabulary, van Burken and de Vries call this latter position "enkaptic interlacements".

From the perspective of nodal governance theory, the first position is inherently problematic as, for this theory, governance is not solely a hierarchical ("top down") undertaking, but as a process of enrollment and alignment. Police forces and other government bodies are no longer, if they ever were, the sole or principal actors in a complex and multilevel security field. Put differently, power is not something to be owned by a dominant actor trying to enforce his will on others but comes from all directions. It is simply more dispersed, diffused, and limited because of an increasingly multifaceted network of actors (Wood & Shearing, 2007, pp. 33-34). The social practice approach underscores this line of thought. Nodal actors all have irreducible identities that should be respected by the state and to which the state must guarantee plurality. Consequently, nodes cannot be simply converged, or allowed to rule over one another, and cannot be seen as part of a bigger whole: Society or the State. There is no such thing as "universalism" with potential totalitarian consequences, although nodes can certainly be (closely) related.

The nodal governance theory recognizes the second position of indifference between public and/or private actors, but this position is also problematic because it neglects the whole idea of interconnectedness and of working (closely) together as the practical goal of security governance. To be genuinely productive actors need to form networked teams consisting of nodal players whose semi-autonomous status must not be confused with negative liberty or with non-interference. Relationships are as important as individuality since security governance is ultimately about building relationships. Therefore, the third position of (loose) collaboration and coordination among nodal actors seems the most viable one. We can describe this kind of collaboration as "network enkapsis" (Verkerk et al., 2018); actors can dynamically hop in and hop out of networks without shedding their own identity and they might operate in a plurality of (overlapping) networks at the same time. Community police officers, for example, simultaneously engage with multiple "chess boards" where health care services, municipal department, housing associations, private security companies, and many others position themselves.

Understanding security governance as "network enkapsis" instead of "part-whole-structure" implies not that collaboration between nodal actors in a security network takes place on a purely horizontal basis. Although nodal actors cannot be hierarchized in the bureaucratic body of a state, public authorities retain the right to interfere if nodes break the law or express hostility towards others. Indeed, as Burris et al. acknowledge, "all nodes are not created equal" (2005, p. 39). Governments, as a sort of "meta" or "superstructual" nodes, set the legal boundaries of plural networks, exercise symbolic authority, and may stimulate security as a constitutive good through which citizens feel part of a larger community (cf. Loader & Walker,

2007). In so doing, they own more financial, political, and cultural resources than others, making them "the command centers of networked governance" (Burris et al., 2005, p. 38). The central nodes in Dutch security networks are normally police and (local) government authorities (Boutellier & van Steden 2011), although they may have a limited capacity to genuinely manage or coordinate security networks: "in some cases the coordination may be fragmented among several of the participants or may be shifted from one to another" (Terpstra, 2008, p. 220).

Therefore, a new sort of professional has emerged: integrally operating case-coordinators vested with the task of making a network flourish. This signals a shift from a "task-based" to a "goal-based" approach towards crime and disorder – that is: there is a shift of focus from isolated incidents and aspects of someone's life to a broader view of "criminogenic" factors (van Steden et al., 2013) that underlie delinquent behavior. As touched upon above, local authorities bear a vital and growing responsibility for facilitating and directing networked partners to intervene in problem situations: "the definition of 'integral security' by various national administrations has been sufficiently broad to grant municipal authorities a significant degree of discretion in setting local policy agendas" (Devroe, 2013, p. 318). Mayors are becoming specifically important in governing local security in the Netherland. However, they lack any special training or tools to make the management of urban networks happen, which currently leads to various policy experiments, including the deployment of case-coordinators who stimulate "network enkapsis" between actors aiming at a similar goal (enhancing public safety and security), but without shedding off their own identity and direction. Yet, in years to come, this tightening of nodal collaboration may lead to a "higher order enkapsis": the development of networked practices guided by their own core values (cf. Verkerk et al., 2018). Networks, after all, are not neutral structures, as they co-shape and are co-shaped by the basic ideals and beliefs of those involved in the team play.

FINAL REMARKS

In this paper, we have discussed the links between nodal governance theory and the intrinsic normativity of social practices. Our main goal was to shed more light on the importance of normativity in security networks and to increase good collaboration. To sum up, scholarship on the management of organizational networks has been preoccupied with the resources, interests, power relations, and conflict that shape interactions between actors. While this might be a valid point of view, the value-laden dimensions of security governance must not be ignored. We have argued that (a lack of) collaboration within nodal security settings goes beyond (conflicting) interests and the instrumental logics of professionals. Intrinsic normativity also deserves a place in the analysis of such settings. Sensitivity to this theme is key to good governance through the enrollment and alignment of nodal actors according to their historically-rooted core functions and intrinsic motivations.

The normative practice approach provides a framework to better understand (the lack of) collaboration within assorted networks. Nodal actors have an intrinsic normative structure—one may say: they have a particular "destination"—that both determines their own functioning and their interaction with others. The idea of social practices thus advances nodal governance theory by highlighting the unique quality of each node, without denying the importance of "state-anchored pluralism" (Loader & Walker, 2007) to the day-to-day functioning of security networks. We might here distinguish between "unorganized" and "organized" associations (Stafleu, 2004), the latter having a kind of "facilitators" or "coordinators" exerting political-administrative authority over nodal actors, without subsuming them.

This, in turn, raises novel theoretical questions about the moral character of security governance. Can the work of central case-coordinators, whose task is to "govern" organizational networks, be regarded as a new social practice in itself? Is the governance of security an irreducible normative good? Can security networks, as a whole, be interpreted as overarching social practices inhabiting a unique normative structure? Or are such networks nothing more than relatively loose "enkapsis" bound together by assorted social practices? In other words: future research is needed to further develop our understanding of intrinsic normativity involved in networked security governance (and in other fields of networked governance) beyond that of individual nodal actors.

REFERENCES

Bauman, Z. (2000). *Liquid modernity*. Cambridge, UK: Polity Press.

Boutellier, H. (2000). *Crime and morality: the significance of criminal justice in postmodern culture*. Dordrecht: Kluwer Acadamic Publishers. doi:10.1007/978-94-009-0013-4

Boutellier, H. (2013). *The improvising society: social order in a boundless world*. The Hague: Eleven.

Boutellier, H., & van Steden, R. (2011). Governing nodal governance: the "anchoring" of local security networks. In A. Crawford (Ed.), *International and comparative criminal justice and urban governance: Convergences and divergences in global, national and local settings* (pp. 461–482). Cambridge, UK: Cambridge University Press. doi:10.1017/CBO9780511974953.018

Burris, S. (2004). 'Governance, microgovernance and health'. *Temple Law Review*, *77*, 335–362.

Burris, S., Drahos, P., & Shearing, C. (2005). Nodal governance. *Australian Journal of Legal Philosophy*, *30*, 30–58.

Burris, S., Kempa, M., & Shearing, C. (2008). Changes in governance: A cross-disciplinary review of current scholarship. *Akron Law Review*, *1*, 1–66.

Crawford, A. (2006). Networked governance and the post-regulatory state? Steering, rowing and anchoring the provision of policing and security. *Theoretical Criminology*, *10*(4), 449–479. doi:10.1177/1362480606068874

Devroe, E. (2013). Local political leadership and the governance of urban security in Belgium and the Netherlands. *European Journal of Criminology*, *10*(3), 314–325. doi:10.1177/1477370812473544

Dupont, B. (2004). Security in the age of networks. *Policing and Society*, *14*(1), 76–91. doi:10.1080/1043946042000181575

Glas, G. (2012). Medicine is a science *and* a normative practice. *Philosophy, Psychiatry, & Psychology*, *19*(4), 285–289.

Habermas, J. (2006). Religion in the public sphere. *European Journal of Philosophy*, *14*(1), 1–25. doi:10.1111/j.1468-0378.2006.00241.x

Holley, C., & Shearing, C. (2017). A nodal perspective of governance: advances in nodal governance thinking. In P. Drahos (Ed.), *Regulatory theory: foundations and applications* (pp. 163–180). Canberra: Australian National University Press. doi:10.22459/RT.02.2017.10

Hoogland, J., & Jochemsen, H. (2000). Professional autonomy and the normative structure of medical practice. *Theoretical Medicine and Bioethics*, *21*(5), 457–475. doi:10.1023/A:1009925423036 PMID:11142442

Houston, D., Freeman, P., & Feldman, D. (2008). How naked is the public square? Religion, public service, and implications for public administration. *Public Administration Review*, *68*(3), 428–444. doi:10.1111/j.1540-6210.2008.00880.x

Jochemsen, H. (2008). Medical practice as the primary context for medical ethics. In N. Weisstub & G. Díaz Pintos (Eds.), *Autonomy and human rights in health care: an international perspective* (pp. 189–204). Dordrecht: Springer. doi:10.1007/978-1-4020-5841-7_14

Johnston, L., & Shearing, C. (2003). *Governing security: explorations in policing and justice*. London: Routledge.

Klijn, E. H., & Koppenjan, J. (2012). Governance network theory: Past, present and future. *Policy and Politics*, *40*(4), 587–606. doi:10.1332/030557312X655431

Kunneman, H. (2005). Social work as laboratory for normative professionalisation. *Social Work & Society*, *3*(2), 191–200.

Lindblom, C. (1959). The science of "muddling through". *Public Administration Review*, *19*(2), 79–88. doi:10.2307/973677

Loader, I., & Walker, N. (2007). *Civilizing security*. Cambridge, UK: Cambridge University Press. doi:10.1017/CBO9780511611117

MacIntyre, A. (1981). *After virtue: a study in moral theory*. Notre Dame, IN: Notre Dame University Press.

Nicolini, D. (2012). *Practice theory, work and organization: an introduction*. Oxford, UK: Oxford University Press.

Osborne, D., & Gaebler, T. (1992). *Reinventing government: how the entrepreneurial spirit is transforming the public sector*. Reading, MA: Addison-Wesley.

Overeem, P., & Tholen, B. (2011). After managerialism: MacIntyre's lessons for the study of public administration. *Administration & Society*, *43*(7), 722–748. doi:10.1177/0095399711413728

Provan, K., & Kenis, P. (2008). Modes of network governance: Structure, management and effectiveness. *Journal of Public Administration and Theory*, *18*(2), 229–252. doi:10.1093/jopart/mum015

Raz, J. (2005). The myth of instrumental rationality. *Journal of Ethics and Social Philosophy*, *1*(1), 2–28.

Reckwitz, A. (2002). Towards a theory of social practices: A development in cultural theorizing. *European Journal of Social Theory*, *5*(2), 243–263. doi:10.1177/13684310222225432

Reiner, R. (1992). Policing a postmodern society. *The Modern Law Review*, *55*(6), 761–781. doi:10.1111/j.1468-2230.1992.tb00940.x

Rittel, H., & Webber, M. (1973). Dilemmas in a general theory of planning. *Policy Sciences*, *4*(2), 155–169. doi:10.1007/BF01405730

Rose, N., O'Malley, P., & Valverde, M. (2006). Governmentality. *Annual Review of Law and Social Science*, *2*(1), 83–104. doi:10.1146/annurev.lawsocsci.2.081805.105900

Schatzki, T. (1996). *Social practices: a Wittgensteinian approach to human activity and the social*. Cambridge, UK: Cambridge University Press. doi:10.1017/CBO9780511527470

Schuilenburg, M., van Steden, R., & Oude Breuil, B. (Eds.). (2014). Positive criminology: reflections on care, belonging and security. The Hague: Eleven.

Shearing, C. (2008). *The nexus policing toolkit*. Canberra: The Australian National University.

Stafleu, M. (2004). On the character of social communities, the state and the public domain. *Philosophia Reformata*, *69*(2), 125–139. doi:10.1163/22116117-90000321

Taylor, C. (1989). *Sources of the self: the making of the modern identity*. Cambridge, UK: Cambridge University Press.

Taylor, C. (2007). A secular age. Cambridge, MA: The Belknap press of Harvard University Press.

Terpstra, J. (2008). Police, local government, and citizens as participants in local security networks. *Police Practice and Research*, *9*(3), 213–225. doi:10.1080/15614260701797520

van Burken, C. G., & de Vries, M. J. (2012). Extending the theory of normative practices: An application to two cases of networked military operation. *Philosophia Reformata*, *77*(2), 135–154. doi:10.1163/22116117-90000530

van den Brink, G. (Ed.). (2016). *Moral sentiments in modern society: a new answer to classical questions*. Amsterdam: Amsterdam University Press. doi:10.2307/j.ctv8pzcx4

van der Wal, Z., de Graaf, G., & Lasthuizen, K. (2008). What's valued most? Similarities and differences between organizational values of the public and private sector. *Public Administration*, *86*(2), 465–482. doi:10.1111/j.1467-9299.2008.00719.x

van Hulst, M., de Graaf, L., & van den Brink, G. (2012). The work of exemplary practitioners in neighborhood governance. *Critical Policy Studies*, *6*(4), 434–451. doi:10.1080/19460171.2012.730763 van Marissing, E., Tan, S., & Boutellier, H. (2010). *Het is hier net Amsterdam: een veiligheidsarrangement voor IJburg* [It is just like Amsterdam: a community safety arrangement for IJburg]. Utrecht: Verwey-Jonker Institute.

van Steden, R., Boutellier, H., Scholte, R., & Heijnen, M. (2013). 'Beyond crime statistics: The construction and application of a criminogenity monitor in Amsterdam'. *European Journal on Criminal Policy and Research, 19*(1), 47–62. doi:10.100710610-012-9179-x

van Steden, R., Wood, J., Shearing, C., & Boutellier, H. (2016). The many faces of nodal policing: Team play and improvisation in Dutch community safety. *Security Journal, 29*(3), 327–339. doi:10.1057j.2013.30

Verkerk, M., Ribeiro, P., Badsen, A., & Hoogland, J. (2018). An explorative philosophical study of envisaging the electrical energy infrastructure of the future. *Philosophia Reformata, 83*(1), 90–110. doi:10.1163/23528230-08301006

Wood, J., & Shearing, C. (2007). *Imagining security*. Cullompton: Willan.

Conclusion

INTRODUCTION

This book started with a serious concern about professional practices. As Glas showed in Chapter 1, professionals can feel a loss of meaning and pleasure in their work due to tendencies towards instrumentalization, bureaucracy and anonymity and as a result they feel alienated from the original intentions with which they entered the professional practice. In the book the Normative Practice Approach is proposed as an answer to this concern. This approach focuses on norms and values that shape professional practices. Problems and tensions in such practices are related to these norms. The Normative Practice Approach serves two purposes. In the first place it can be used as an analytical instrument to identify where these tensions arise due to norm-related issues. These can be conflicts between norms or the presence of norms that do not fit well with the nature and purposes of the professional practice. In the second place, the Normative Practice Approach can serve as a source of inspiration for finding alternatives in those cases where professionals suffer from alienation and tensions between their idealistic reasons to become part of the practice and the way the 'practice of the practice' conflicts with those ideals. In Chapter 2 Glas has elaborated on this alternative approach by pointing out the need to do justice to the complexity of reality and the value of taking the 'heart' of humans as a basis for the way humans function, privately and professionally. Chapter 3 by Hoogland argues for 'meaning' as the basis for a good practice. Meaning is the why and how humans exist. Meaning is not something that is only present when we ascribe it to reality; it is given with reality. In this claim a worldview is visible that sees reality as deliberate creation, not as the outcome of a random process. This seems to seriously limit the attraction of the Normative Practice Approach as it suggests that a religious worldview is needed to embrace it. Although such a worldview is indeed the most 'natural' embedding for the Normative Practice Approach, the outcomes and analysis and proposed 'therapy' for professional practices can also comply with other worldview, be it not with all of those. It will almost by definition be in conflict with a worldview in which reality can be completely controlled by our human actions and can be shaped entirely according to our human intentions. As Hoogland wrote, a scientifically based or inspired approach with a technical-instrumental view on professional activities will never fit well with the Normative Practice Approach. Even stronger: it is this very approach that the Normative Practice approach seeks to identify as the course of the uneasiness that professionals experience, as described by Glas.

In the following chapters these general ideas have been used to investigate a variety of professional practices. A distinction has been made into two categories of practices: those practice that have a definite purpose that has a value of its own right, and those practices that function as a support of other practices. In the first category we find such practices as industry, engineering, military operations, education, care, and food supply. In the second category, we find practices like governance, communication, management and international cooperation in development. In this chapter some 'red threads' running through the consecutive 'application' chapters will be discussed and finally some general conclusions will be drawn as to what would characterize flourishing practices in which professionals feel that their ideals can be 'lived out' for the better of other people. The chapter has a practical rather than a theoretical nature. This book is primarily intended to help practitioners who are interested in a better understanding in their own practice get hints and suggestions as to how to deal with frustrations they experience in their practice, as far as they are the effect of the sort of instrumentalist approach that was identified in the beginning of the book. The 'harvest' in this chapter seeks to bring together insights from the more theoretical chapters for the sake of improving practices based on a meaning-oriented normative practice approach.

THE DANGER OF SUPPRESSING VALUES

Several of the chapters in the second, application-oriented part of this book, contain the notion of values being suppressed in the current situation of a particular professional practice. Particularly in the chapters on engineering, food, education, industry, management and international cooperation in development we find such remarks.

The chapter on engineering describes the case of a sustainable practice in which water management in Iran was executed in a harmonious cooperation between farmers and a the Mirab as a representative body of the local users of water by using natural underground water supplies or qanats. This practice was replaced by a modernist and reductionist approach in which the Mirab became a commercial company that was only interested in using each and every drop of water to make profit, which resulted in an environmental disaster. Values of sustainability and local democracy were suppressed by economic interests and efficiency norms. A similar modernist approach was identified in the chapter on food production in which again sustainability values, based on the wisdom of local farmers, were replaced by economic norms in the practice of agriculture. The result of this reductionist, over-industrialized and homogenizing approach was a decline in soil fertility and a loss of biodiversity. The chapter on education identifies the suppression of the ideal to make young people grow personally and acquire not just knowledge and skills but also wisdom and responsibility. Instead of these values, norms of economic and organizational efficiency became more and more important and teachers feel they are forced to sacrifice their pedagogical ideals for the sake of norms that they consider to be in conflict with the human nature of the educational process as a personal interaction between teachers and learners.

In two of the chapters concerning supporting practices we also find these findings. The three types of critique expressed in the chapter on international cooperation in development (operational, institutional and ideological) are all related to suppressed values. International values dominate over local values, economic values dominate over justice values. The four case stories in the chapter on management also reflect how neglecting personal values in management can lead to frustrations with the professionals working in the practice that is to be managed.

Dealing with all values that are held by different professionals in a practice is not easy. In most cases it will not be possible to do justice to all values. But the systematic suppression of values that professionals see as the core of their motivation to be involved in the practice leads to serious problems, both for the professionals themselves, but also for the practice as a whole.

We have seen that the tensions in professional practices occur both in practices that have an aim in themselves and 'supporting' practices that serve those practices. Problems in the supporting practices can come on top of problems in the practices they support and thus they can add to frustrations that are already experienced in the supported practice. Even if the situation in the practice-to-be-supported is fine in itself, tensions in the supporting practice can have a negative effect on that practice and thus spoil rather than support that practice. This can be a reason to be extra alert for tensions in the supporting practices

THE IMPORTANCE OF DOING JUSTICE TO COMPLEXITY

Several of the chapters in this book emphasize the complexity of professional practices. This is due to the fact that in most professional practices many different actors are involved. In the chapter on care, Glas mentions one of the consequences of this complexity when it is combined with a modernist control-oriented approach, namely that it leads to distrust rather than trust. The many actors involved in the professional practice of care, not only doctors and nurses, but also insurance companies and governments, all have to be taken seriously as experts in their own discipline and a well-functioning practice requires interaction between actors in which each of them can bring in their own values. The chapters on engineering, industry, development cooperation, and military operations also mention complexity as important characteristics of the practice they describe. Developing new technologies is process in which engineers are involved, but also users, buyers (not always the same as users), legislators, managers, interest groups, etcetera. In the military operations, the use of technology is embedded in a complex situation in which decisions are made by pilots, sergeants, governments and even the media can play a role. The chapter on industrial practices pointed out the role of different stakeholders and Verkerk proposed to do justice to their norms and values by using a Triple I (Identity and intrinsic values, Interests of stakeholders, and Ideals and basic beliefs) approach as a variation of the normative practice approach. In the engineering chapter, it was suggested to combine the normative practice approach with an actor-network analysis to map out the complexity of the practice, and thus to enable a more precise analysis of what norms and values are at stake.

In a modernist, control-focused approach, complexity is seen as a barrier. The complexity makes it difficult to keep a grip on the whole process. In the normative practice approach, this aspect is recognized, but at the same time, this complexity is seen as part of the 'richness' of reality and therefore is to be appreciated as an opportunity. Engineers, for instance, realize that the different aspects of reality all contribute to a long and complex list of requirements. But at the same time, all these aspects are, as it were, variables that can be manipulated to optimize the design. One can 'play' with combinations of better safety and higher price, less spilling of resources and lower price, and many more scenario's that provide a rich variety of possible solutions. In the same way, the complexity of the variety of actors involved in a practice can be appreciated as something that enriches the possibilities of the practiced for its well-functioning. Values that are emphasized by one actor may have been overlooked by another actor. Complexity is an 'asset' also, not only a problem.

AVOIDING CONFLICTS OF NORMS BETWEEN AND WITHIN PRACTICES

The complexity would not even be a problem when the practice would consist of actors that do not interact but all independently play their own role. That is mostly not the case. A practice consists of what in the book is called sub-practices that interact in different ways. Sometimes a sub-practice derives its meaning from the practice in which it is embedded (the pilots with their jets can only function in a military context). Sometimes a sub-practice could easily well function in the content of a different context (the canteen in a military base could just as well be the canteen in a university or a business company). Sometimes sub-practice stand next to each other and one is not part of the other but they are both part of the larger whole. Dealing with values becomes more of a challenge when different sub-practices with different values become entangled with each other in these different ways.

Norms can already be in conflict within one sub-practice. If a company has as one of its strategic (direction) norms to prioritize environmental concerns, but in the structural norms there is no clarity about whom or what department is responsible for complying with environmental concerns, this practice is inherently contradictory in its norms. The result will be that environmental care cannot be practiced properly, which will probably lead to frustrations within the company. Conflicts can also arise between intertwined practices. The canteen can have as its directional policy to make the best coffee for the price it is worth. But if that canteen has to function in the context of a company that underpays their workers so that they have little money to spend on coffee, this will not work. The chapter on military operations showed what can happen when norms clash between sub-practices in which one sub-practice is dependent on the other for having its meaning. The pilot was forced to perform against his own sub-practice norms and the result was a disaster. In a similar way a conflict between two practices on equal level was identified in the chapter on security: street police officers take a short-term security-oriented attitude towards deviant youth, while social workers habitually emphasize the devastating long-term effects of poverty, unemployment, and divorce on how youngsters behave.

As stated earlier, complexity can be richness, but that can only be the case when there are no conflicts within and between norms in the totality of the cooperating sub-practices. Here the normative practice approach comes in as a valuable tool to identify where possible clashes between norms will occur. This can be an important step towards resolving conflicts between norms and improving the functioning of the practice.

CELEBRATING VALUES AND WORLDVIEWS

In the normative practice approach the worldviews of the people who are involved in the practice plays an important role. The worldview of the modernist approach is one that is based on mastery and control, and in such an approach there is no room for worldviews with other values. In the previous sections it was argued that it is very difficult to make a practice work on the basis of such an approach, as it is unavoidable that there will be conflicting values due to the complexity of practices. People do not easily allow the values that are close to their heart to be suppressed and that is why there are tensions in the practices that were discussed in the various chapters. Good practices will enable for non-modernist values and worldviews to be held and lived out.

In the chapter on education such worldviews refer to how we see humans: learners and teachers. In a reductionist view they are no more than numbers, marks, fte's, drop-out rates, and etcetera. In a Christian worldview they will be creatures that were brought forth by God with the purpose to live for Him and their fellow creatures (Goheen and Bartholomew, 2008). Such a worldview yields very different norms and values for the educational practice. Teachers, learners and schools will then be evaluated in a quite different way, not just by quantifying inputs and outputs. Numerical data are a reduction of people more so than qualitative data. More and more we see education being evaluated on the basis of quantitative data. An important reason for that is the suggestion of control that comes along with numbers, a suggestion that in hard to substantiate yet has a strong appeal. The role of worldviews was also thematized in the chapter on communication. Different worldviews produce different views on what proper communication is, even though there are agreements between different worldviews on some basic notions. This will be taken into account in a proper communication practice. In the chapter on care the view on humans – doctors and patients for instance – was also identified as a matter of great importance for that practice and again this view depends on the worldview one holds.

Empirical research has shown how much worldviews drive practitioners (Goldberg, 2009). Janet Clark wrote about 'an increased professional interest in spiritually-sensitive social work practice' (Clark, 2017). This entailed that social workers ought to understand the worldview of their clients. But this interest can easily be extended to understanding one's own worldview and using that understanding to develop the practice in a direction that does more justice to that worldview. After all, what is good for dealing with the client is probably also good for dealing with one's own identify as partaker in the professional practice.

CLOSING REMARKS

This book offered an alternative view on professional practices in which normativity plays a key role. The normative practice approach seeks to avoid the frustration experiences by professionals in a reductionist view on practices that is inherent to all modernist views on social practices that assume that complete control over reality is an ideal that should be pursued. This apparent utopia mostly turns out to be a dystopia in which the values that are held by professionals are largely ignored and forces the professionals to ignore the original deeper motives for taking part in the professional practice. The authors of this book believe that the Normative Practice

Approach is sufficiently matured to be presented and proposed to practitioners for reflection on their own practices. As Donald Schön has shown, it is the reflective practitioners using creativity to deal with situations that are puzzling, troubling and uncertain, that feel most comfortable in their practice. Reflection on norms and values should be an essential component in that. This book aims to contribute to that reflection.

Marc J. de Vries
Delft University of Technology, The Netherlands

REFERENCES

Clark, J. L. (2017). Listening for Meaning: A Research-Based Model for Attending to Spirituality, Culture and Worldview in Social Work Practice. *Critical Social Work: An Interdisciplinary Journal Dedicated to Social Justice*, *7*(1).

Goheen, M. W., & Bartholomew, C. G. (2008). *Living at the Crossroads. An Introduction to Christian Worldview*. Grand Rapids, MI: Baker Academic.

Goldberg, R. M. (2009). How Our Worldviews Shape Our Practice. *Conflict Resolution Quarterly*, *26*(4), 405–341. doi:10.1002/crq.241

Schon, D. (1983). *The reflective practitioner: How professionals think in action*. New York: Basic Books.

Compilation of References

Abbott, A. D. (1988). *The System of Professions: An Essay on the Division of Expert Labor*. Chicago: University of Chicago Press. doi:10.7208/chicago/9780226189666.001.0001

Action plan Process Intensification. (n.d.). Retrieved August 31 2018 from https://www.rvo.nl/sites/default/files/bijlagen/Action_Plan_Process_Intensification.pdf

Adorno, Th. W., & Horkheimer, M. (1947). *Dialektik der Aufklärung*. Amsterdam: Querido.

Aftalion, F. (1991). *History of the International Chemical Industry: From the Early Days to 2000*. Philadelphia: University of Pennsylvania Press.

Agricola, G. (1556). *De re metallica*. Basil: Hieronymus Froben & Nicolaus Episcopius.

Alberts, D. S. (2007). Agility, Focus, and Convergence: The Future of Command and Control. *The International C2 Journal, 1*(1), 1-30.

Alberts, D. S., Garstka, J. J., Hayes, R. E., & Signori, D. A. (2002). *Understanding Information Age Warfare*. Washington, DC: CCRP Publication Series.

Alberts, D. S., & Hayes, R. E. (2006). *Understanding Command and Control, The Future of Command and Control*. Washington, DC: CCRP Publication Series.

Al-Salem, S. M., Lettieri, P., & Baeyens, J. (2009). Recycling and recovery routes of plastic solid waste (PSW): A review. *Waste Management (New York, N.Y.), 29*(10), 2625–2643. doi:10.1016/j.wasman.2009.06.004 PMID:19577459

Andrady, A. L. (2011). Microplastics in the marine environment. *Marine Pollution Bulletin, 62*(8), 1596–1605. doi:10.1016/j.marpolbul.2011.05.030 PMID:21742351

Arendt, H. (1958). *The Human Condition*. Chicago: The University of Chicago Press.

Aristotle. (2014a). Magna Moralia. In Aristotle's Ethics. Writing form the Complete Works. Princeton, NJ: Princeton University Press.

Aristotle. (2014b). Nicomachean Ethics. In Aristotle's Ethics. Writing form the Complete Works. Princeton, NJ: Princeton University Press.

Arpaly, N., & Schroeder, T. (2018). *In Praise of Desire*. New York: Oxford University Press.

Atabaki, T. (2013). The Comintern, the Soviet Union and labour militancy in interwar Iran. In Iranian-Russian Encounters: Empires and Revolutions Since 1800 (Vol. 14). Routledge.

Aula, P., & Mantere, S. (2008). *Strategic Reputation Management. Towards a Company of the Good*. New York: Routledge.

Balali, M. R., Keulartz, J., & Korthals, M. (2011). Reflexive land and water management in Iran: Linking Technology, Governance and Culture, Part 1: Land and Water Management Paradigms. *Iranian Journal of Water research in Agriculture, 24*(2), 73–97.

Balmer, J. M. T., & Greyser, S. A. (2003). Managing the Multiple Identities of the Corporation. In J. M. T. Balmer & S. A. Greyser (Eds.), *Revealing the Cooperation. Perspectives on Identity, Image, Reputation, Corporate Branding and Corporate-Level Marketing* (pp. 15–29). New York: Routledge. doi:10.4324/9780203422786

Barrientos, S., & Dolan, C. (Eds.). (2006). *Ethical Sourcing in the Global Food System*. Earthscan.

Barry, D., & Elmes, M. (1997). Strategy retold. Towards a narrative view of strategic discourse. *Academy of Management Review*, *22*(2), 429–452. doi:10.5465/amr.1997.9707154065

Basden, A. (2000). *Dooyeweerd pages*. Retrieved from http://www.dooy.salford.ac.uk/juridical.html

Basden, A. (n.d.). *The economic aspect*. Retrieved October 11, 2018, from http://dooy.info/economic.html

Bauman, Z. (2000). *Liquid modernity*. Cambridge, UK: Polity Press.

Beabout, G. R. (2012). Management as a Domain-Relative Practice That Requires and Develops Practical Wisdom. *Business Ethics Quarterly*, *22*(2), 405–432. doi:10.5840/beq201222214

Beaumont, P. (1974). Water resource development in Iran. *The Geographical Journal, 140*(3), 418–431. doi:10.2307/1796535

Beck, J., & Young, M. F. D. (2005). The assault on the professions and the restructuring of academic and professional identities: A Bernsteinian analysis. *British Journal of Sociology of Education*, *26*(2), 183–197. doi:10.1080/0142569042000294165

Berger, P., & Luckman, T. (1991). The Social Construction of Reality. A Treatise in the Sociology of Knowledge. London: Penguin Books. (Originally published 1966)

Besselink, L. F. M. (2008). Geweldsmonopolie, Grondwet en krijgsmacht. *Publikaties van de Staatsrechtkring*, *26*, 67–124.

Bezooijen, B. V., & Kramer, E.-H. (2015). Mission Command in the Information Age: A Normal Accidents Perspective on Networked Military Operations. *The Journal of Strategic Studies*, *38*(4), 445–466. doi:10.1080/01402390.2013.844127

Biesta, G. (2014). *The Beautiful Risk of Education*. Boulder, CO: Paradigm Publishers.

Billib, M., Bardowicks, K., & Arumí, J. L. (2009). Integrated water resources management for sustainable irrigation at the basin scale. *Chilean Journal of Agricultural Research*, *69*(Suppl 1), 69–80.

Bin2Barrel. (n.d.). Retrieved August 6 2018 from Http://bin2barrel.com/

Björnberg, K. E. (2013). Rational Goals in Engineering Design: The Venice Dams. In *Norms in Technology, Philosophy of Engineering and Technology* (pp. 83–99). Springer Netherlands. doi:10.1007/978-94-007-5243-6_6

Blackbourn, D. (2006). *The Conquest of Nature. Water, Landscape and the Making of Modern Germany*. London: Jonathan Cape.

Blauner, R. (1964). *Alienation and Freedom*. Chicago, IL: University of Chicago Press.

Blokhuis, P. (2003). Book Review of Kees Boersma, Jan van der Stoep, Maarten Verkerk, Ad Vlot (eds.), Aan Babels stromen. Een bevrijdend perspectief op ethiek en techniek. Amsterdam 2002: Buijten en Schipperheijn. 312 pagina's. ISBN 9058810682. Philosophia Reformata, 68(1), 86–88. doi:10.1163/22116117-90000277

Bloom, G., Standing, H., & Lloyd, R. (2008). Markets, information asymmetry and health care: Towards new social contracts. *Social Science & Medicine*, *66*(10), 2076–2087. doi:10.1016/j.socscimed.2008.01.034 PMID:18316147

Boje, D. M. (2001). *Narrative methods for organizational and communication research*. London: Sage. doi:10.4135/9781849209496

Boje, D. M. (2008). *Storytelling organizations*. London: Sage.

Borgmann, A. (1984). *Technology and the Character of Contemporary Life*. Chicago: University of Chicago Press.

Bourdieu, P. (n.d.). *The Logic of Practice*. Stanford, CA: Stanford University Press.

Bourdieu, P. (1991). *Language and symbolic power*. Cambridge, UK: Polity Press.

Bourdieu, P. (2000). *Pascalian meditations*. Cambridge, UK: Polity Press.

Boutellier, H. (2000). *Crime and morality: the significance of criminal justice in postmodern culture*. Dordrecht: Kluwer Acadamic Publishers. doi:10.1007/978-94-009-0013-4

Boutellier, H. (2013). *The improvising society – Social order in a boundless world*. The Hague: Eleven International Publishers.

Boutellier, H., & van Steden, R. (2011). Governing nodal governance: the "anchoring" of local security networks. In A. Crawford (Ed.), *International and comparative criminal justice and urban governance: Convergences and divergences in global, national and local settings* (pp. 461–482). Cambridge, UK: Cambridge University Press. doi:10.1017/CBO9780511974953.018

Bozorgmehr, N. (2014). *Iran: Dried out*. Retrieved from http://www.ft.com/cms/s/0/5a5579c6-0205-11e4-ab5b-00144feab7de.html#ixzz3HjOF1vfm

Brelet, C. (2004). *Some examples of best ethical practice in water use*. Retrieved from http://portal.unesco.org/shs/fr/files/4382/10796934191water_use.pdf/water_use.pdf

Brewer, K. B. (1997). Management as a Practice: A Response to Alasdair MacIntyre. *Journal of Business Ethics*, *16*(8), 825–833. doi:10.1023/A:1017997200200

Brint, S. (2015). Professional Responsibility in an Age of Experts and Large Organizations. In D. E. Mitchell & R. K. Ream (Eds.), *Professional Responsibility. The Fundamental Issue in Education and Health Care Reform* (Vol. 4, pp. 89–107). New York: Springer. doi:10.1007/978-3-319-02603-9_6

Broadbent, J., Dietrich, M., & Roberts, J. (Eds.). (1997). *The End of the Professions? The Restructuring of Professional Work*. London: Routledge.

Burris, S. (2004). 'Governance, microgovernance and health'. *Temple Law Review*, *77*, 335–362.

Burris, S., Drahos, P., & Shearing, C. (2005). Nodal governance. *Australian Journal of Legal Philosophy*, *30*, 30–58.

Burris, S., Kempa, M., & Shearing, C. (2008). Changes in governance: A cross-disciplinary review of current scholarship. *Akron Law Review*, *1*, 1–66.

Byman, D. (2006). Remaking Alliances for the War on Terrorism. *The Journal of Strategic Studies*, *29*(5), 767–811. doi:10.1080/01402390600900887

Capone, R., Bilali, H. E., Debs, P., Cardone, G., & Driouech, N. (2014). Food System Sustainability and Food Security: Connecting the Dots. *Journal of Food Security*, *2*(1), 13–22. doi:10.12691/jfs-2-1-2

Cardeli, L. (2017). *Loren Cardeli: "Agriculture got us here, and agriculture can also save us."* Retrieved from https://foodtank.com/news/2017/09/loren-cardeli-summit-interview/

Carey, J. W. (2009). *Communication as culture. Essays on media and society* (revised edition). New York: Routledge.

Casebeer, W. D., & Churchland, P. S. (2003). The Neural Mechanisms of Moral Cognition: A Multiple-Aspect Approach to Moral Judgment and Decision-Making. *Biology & Philosophy*, *18*(1), 169–194. doi:10.1023/A:1023380907603

Castellani, B., & Hafferty, F. W. (2006). The Complexities of Medical Professionalism: A preliminary investigation. In D. Wear, J.M. Aultman (Eds.), Professionalism in Medicine: Critical Perspectives (pp. 3–24). New York: Springer.

Castells, M. (2009). *Communication power*. Oxford, UK: Oxford University Press.

Castke, E. B. (1961). *Ancient Education and Today*. Baltimore, MD: Penguin Books.

CEFIC. (2018). *Facts & Figures 2017 of the European chemical industry*. Retrieved August 6 2018 from Http://www.cefic.org/Facts-and-Figures/

Chambers, S. (1996). *Reasonable democracy. Jürgen Habermas and the politics of discourse*. Ithaca, NY: Cornell University Press.

Chang, H.-J. (2008). *Bad Samaritans: The Guilty Secrets of Rich Nations and the Threat to Global Prosperity*. London: Random House.

Chaplin, J. (2011). *Herman Dooyeweerd: Christian Philosopher of State and Civil Society*. Notre Dame, IN: Notre Dame University Press.

Chemelot. (n.d.a). *Staatsmijn Maurits: kolen (1926-1967)*. Retrieved May 24 2018 from https://www.chemelot.nl/chemelot/historie/staatsmijn-maurits

Chemelot. (n.d.b). *See the synergy, feel the energy*. Retrieved August 24 2018 from https://www.chemelot.nl/chemelot/feiten-cijfers

Christensen, L. T., Morsing, M., & Thyssen, O. (2013). CSR as aspirational talk. *Organization*, *20*(3), 372–393. doi:10.1177/1350508413478310

Christensen, S. H., Mitcham, C., Li, B., & An, Y. (2012). *Engineering, development and philosophy: American, Chinese and European perspectives* (Vol. 11). Berlin: Springer. doi:10.1007/978-94-007-5282-5

CIAT. (2017, June). *CIAT Strategic Initiative on Sustainable Food Systems*. International Center for Tropical Agriculture (CIAT). Retrieved from https://cgspace.cgiar.org/bitstream/handle/10568/79795/SUSTAINABLE_FOOD_SYSTEMS_CIAT_STRATEGY_DOCUMENT.pdf

Clapp, J. (2014). Financialization, distance and global food politics. *The Journal of Peasant Studies*, *41*(5), 797–814. doi:10.1080/03066150.2013.875536

Clark, J. L. (2017). Listening for Meaning: A Research-Based Model for Attending to Spirituality, Culture and Worldview in Social Work Practice. *Critical Social Work: An Interdisciplinary Journal Dedicated to Social Justice*, *7*(1).

Clouser, R. A. (2005). *The myth of religious neutrality* (rev. ed.). Notre Dame, IN: Notre Dame University Press.

Cochrane, W. (1979). *The Development of American Agriculture: A Historical Analysis*. Minneapolis, MN: University of Minnesota Press.

Cooren, F. (2015). *Organizational discourse. Communication and constitution*. Cambridge, UK: Polity Press.

Craig, R. T. (1999). Communication theory as a field. *Communication Theory*, *9*(2), 119–161. doi:10.1111/j.1468-2885.1999.tb00355.x

Crawford, A. (2006). Networked governance and the post-regulatory state? Steering, rowing and anchoring the provision of policing and security. *Theoretical Criminology*, *10*(4), 449–479. doi:10.1177/1362480606068874

Crosswell, M. (2009). The development record and the effectiveness of foreign aid. *PRAXIS The Fletcher Journal of Development Studies, 15*. Retrieved from http://fletcher.tufts.edu/Praxis/Archives/~/media/Fletcher/Micro-sites/praxis/xv/Crosswell.pdf

D'Souza, S. M. (2008). 'Unity of Effort': The Missing Link in the Afghan Counter-Insurgency Campaign. *Strategic Analysis*, *32*(5), 855–878. doi:10.1080/09700160802309225 de Muynck, A. (2006). De praktijk van het onderwijs. In Een theorie over praktijken. Normatief Praktijkmodel voor zorg, sociaal werk en onderwijs. Amsterdam: Buijten en Schipperheijn.

De Nevers, R. (2007). NATO's International Security Role in the Terrorist Era. *International Security*, *31*(4), 34–66. doi:10.1162/isec.2007.31.4.34

de Rooij, S. J. G., de Lauwere, C. C., & van der Ploeg, J. D. (2010). Entrapped in Group Solidarity? Animal Welfare, the Ethical Positions of Farmers and the Difficult Search for Alternatives. *Journal of Environmental Policy and Planning*, *12*(4), 341–361. doi:10.1080/1523908X.2010.528882

De Schutter, O. (2014). *Final report: The transformative potential of the right to food. Report of the Special Rapporteur on the right to food, Olivier De Schutter (No. A/HRC/25/57)*. United Nations General Assembly.

De Vries, G., De Hoog, J., & Dijstelbloem, H. (2016). *Towards a Food Policy* (WRR report No. 93). The Hague: The Netherlands Scientific Council for Government Policy (WRR). Retrieved from https://english.wrr.nl/publications/reports/2016/12/13/towards-a-food-policy

De Vries, M. J., Hansson, S. O., & Meijers, A. W. (2012). *Norms in technology* (Vol. 9). Springer Science & Business Media.

Dekker, A. (2005). A taxonomy of network centric warfare architectures. *Proceedings of the Systems Engineering / Test and Evaluation Conference*.

Devroe, E. (2013). Local political leadership and the governance of urban security in Belgium and the Netherlands. *European Journal of Criminology*, *10*(3), 314–325. doi:10.1177/1477370812473544

Dooyeweerd, H. (1953-1957). *A New Critique of Theoretical Thought* (3 Vols.). Philadelphia: The Presbyterian and Reformed Publishing Company.

Dooyeweerd, H. (1953–1958). *A New Critique of Theoretical Thought, Vol. I–IV*. Amsterdam: Presbyterian and Reformed Publishing Company.

Dooyeweerd, H. (1984). A New Critique of Theoretical Thought. The General Theory of the Modal Spheres (3rd ed.; Vol. 2). Jordan Station, Ontario: Paideia Press Ltd.

Dooyeweerd, H. (1953). *A New Critique of Theoretical Thought* (Vols. 1-3). Amsterdam: H.J. Paris and The Presbyterian and Reformed Publishing Company.

Dooyeweerd, H. (1969). *A new critique of theoretical thought*. Philadelphia: The Presbyterian and Reformed Publishing Company.

Dooyeweerd, H. (1969). *A new critique of theoretical thought. Philipsburg*. Presbyterian and Reformed Publishing Company.

DSM. (n.d.). Vision Chemelot, 2025. *DSM*.

Duffey, T. (2000). Cultural Issues in Contemporary Peacekeeping. *International Peacekeeping*, *7*(1), 142–168. doi:10.1080/13533310008413823

Duintjer, O. D. (1977). *Rondom regels: Wijsgerige gedachten omtrent regel-geleid gedrag [Around Rules – Philosophical Thoughts about Rule-following Behavior]*. Boom.

Dupont, B. (2004). Security in the age of networks. *Policing and Society*, *14*(1), 76–91. doi:10.1080/1043946042000181575

EC (European Commission). (2011). *'Plastic Waste: Ecological and Human Health Impacts', Science for Environment Policy, In-depth Reports*. EC.

EC (European Commission). (2017). *Circular Economy research and innovation - Connecting economic & environmental gains*. Retrieved October 31 2018 from Https://ec.europa.eu/programmes/horizon2020/sites/horizon2020/files/ce_booklet.pdf

EC (European Commission). (2018). *A European Strategy for Plastics in a Circular Economy*. Retrieved October 31 2018 from Http://ec.europa.eu/environment/circular-economy/pdf/plastics-strategy-brochure.pdf

EcoNexus. (2013). *AGROPOLY - A handful of corporations control world food production*. Berne Declaration (DB) & EcoNexus. Retrieved from http://www.econexus.info/publication/agropoly-handful-corporations-control-world-food-production

Edwards, L. (2011). Public relations and society. A Bourdieuvian perspective. In *Public relations, society and culture. Theoretical and empirical explorations* (pp. 61–74). London: Routledge. doi:10.4324/9780203832134

EFCE. (n.d.). *European Roadmap for Process identification*. Retrieved August 31 2018 from http://efce.info/efce_media/Downloads/wppi/European_Roadmap_PI.pdf

Eikeland, O. (2006). Phrónêsis, Aristotle, and action research. *International Journal of Action Research*, *2*(1), 5–53.

Elron, E., Shamir, B., & Ben-Ari, E. (1999). Why Don'T they Fight each Other? Cultural Diversity and Operational Unity in Multinational Forces. *Armed Forces and Society*, *26*(1), 73–97. doi:10.1177/0095327X9902600105

Escobar, A. (1995). *Encountering Development: the making and unmaking of the third world*. Princeton University Press.

Eslami, M. (2010). *Zayandehrud, the Past, Now and Future*. Paper presented at the A conference on reviewing crisis of the Zayandehrud River, Isfahan, Iran. Retrieved from http://www.isfahan.ir/Dorsapax/userfiles/file/shora/pazhuhesh/zayanderood.pdf. (in Persian)

Essens, P. (2008). Cultural Challenges in Joint and Combined Command: A Military Leader's Perspective. *Proceedings of the NATO RTO 'Adaptability in Coalition Teamwork.*

Euro Chlor. (2016). Retrieved October 31 2018 from Http://www.eurochlor.org/media/110998/capacities_1-1-2016-for_information_sheet.pdf

European Commission. (2016). *Development.* Retrieved from http://ec.europa.eu/trade/policy/countries-and-regions/development/

European Parliament. (2011). Cooperating with developing countries on promoting good governance in tax Matters. *European Parliament resolution of 8 March 2011 on Tax and Development Cooperation with Developing Countries on Promoting Good Governance in Tax Matters* (2010/2102(INI)). Retrieved from http://www.europarl.europa.eu/sides/getDoc.do?pubRef=-//EP//NONSGML+TA+P7-TA-2011-0082+0+DOC+PDF+V0//EN

Evetts, J. (2003). The Sociological Analysis of Professionalism. Occupational Change in the Modern World. *International Sociology*, *18*(2), 395–415. doi:10.1177/0268580903018002005

FAO. (2017). The future of food and agriculture - Trends and challenges. Rome: FAO (Food and Agriculture Organization of the United Nations).

Fawkes, J. (2015). *Public relations ethics and professionalism. The shadow of excellence.* London: Routledge.

Ferguson, J. (1994). The anti-politics machine; Development, Depoliticization, and Bureaucratic Power in Lesotho. *The Ecologist*, *24*(5), 176–181.

Ferry, L. (2010). *Learning to live. A user's manual.* New York, NY: Canongate.

FIDIC (International Federation of Consulting Engineers). (2014). *Code of Ethics.* Retrieved from http//fidic.org/about-fidic/fidic-code-ethics#sthash.GUfmvN9W.dpuf

Fieser, J. (n.d.). *Ethics.* Retrieved from https://www.iep.utm.edu/ethics/

Fisher, W. R. (1989). *Human communication as narration. Towards a philosophy of reason, value, and action.* University of South Carolina Press.

Floridi, L. (2014). *The Fourth Revolution: How the Infosphere is Reshaping Human Reality.* Oxford University Press.

FLOWID. (2016). Retrieved October 31 2018 from https://www.flowid.nl/akzonobel-making-a-big-effort-on-breakthrough-technology/

Fox, T., & Vorley, B. (2006). Small Producers: Constraints and Challenges in the Global Food System. In S. Barrientos & C. Dolan (Eds.), *Ethical Sourcing in the Global Food System* (pp. 163–177). London: Earthscan. Retrieved from http://eureka.sbs.ox.ac.uk/1343/

Frank, J. R., Jabbour, M., Fréchette, D., Marks, M., Valk, N., & Bourgeois, G. (Eds.). (2005). *Report of the CanMEDS Phase IV Working Groups*. Ottawa: The Royal College of Physicians and Surgeons of Canada.

Frank, J. R., Jabbour, M., & Tugwell, P. (1996). Skills for the new millenium: Report of the societal needs working group, CanMEDS 2000 Project. *Annals of the Royal College of Physicians and Surgeons of Canada*, *29*, 206–216.

Freeman, R. E. (2001). The Stakeholder Theory of the Modern Corporation. In Ethical Theory and Business (6th ed.; pp. 56-65). Prentice Hall.

Freidson, E. (2001). *Professionalism. The Third Logic*. Chicago: University of Chicago Press.

Freire, P. (1993). *Pedagogy of the Oppressed*. Penguin Books.

Freire, P. (2001). *Pedagogy of Freedom. Ethics, Democracy, and Civic Courage*. Oxford, UK: Rowman & Littlefield Publishers.

Friedman, M. (1962). *Capitalism and Freedom*. Chicago: The University of Chicago Press.

Gabbard, G. O., Roberts, L. W., Crisp-Han, H., Ball, V., Hobday, G., & Rachal, F. (2012). *Professionalism in Psychiatry*. Washington, DC: American Psychiatric Publishing, Inc.

Gabriel, Y. (2000). *Storytelling in Organizations: Facts, fictions and fantasies*. Oxford, UK: Oxford University Press. doi:10.1093/acprof:oso/9780198290957.001.0001

Geels, F. W. (2004). From sectoral systems of innovation to socio-technical systems: Insights about dynamics and change from sociology and institutional theory. *Research Policy*, *33*(6), 897–920. doi:10.1016/j.respol.2004.01.015

Giddens, A. (1984). *The Constitution of Society. Outline of the Theory of Structuration*. Berkeley, CA: University of California Press.

Giri, A. K., & Van Ufford, P. Q. (2004). *A Moral Critique of Development: Ethics, Aesthetics and Responsibility*. Aalborg, Denmark: Institut for Historie, Internationale Studier og Samfundsforhold, Aalborg Universitet.

Glas, G. (2012). Competence development as normative practice—Educational reform in medicine as heuristic model to relate worldview and education. *Koers—Bulletin for Christian Scholarship, 77*(1), 70–75. . doi:10.4102/koers.v77i1.411

Glas, G. (2019). Person-centered care in psychiatry. self-relational, normative, and contextual perspectives. London: Routledge.

Glas, G. (2009). Modellen Van 'Integratie' in De Psychologie En Psychiatrie (II) - Het Normatieve Praktijk Model. *Psyche en Geloof, 20*(3/4), 165–177.

Glas, G. (2012). Medicine is a science *and* a normative practice. *Philosophy, Psychiatry, & Psychology, 19*(4), 285–289.

Glas, G. (2017). Public and institutional aspects of professional responsibility in medicine and psychiatry. *Philosophia Reformata, 82*(2), 146–166.

Glas, G. (2019forthcoming). *Person-centered care in psychiatry: Self-relational, normative, and contextual perspectives*. London: Routledge.

Glas, G. (accepted). Psychiatry as normative practice. *Philosophy, Psychiatry, & Psychology.*

Glas, G., & de Ridder, J. (Eds.). (2018). The Future of Creation Order: Vol. I. *Philosophical, scientific, and religious perspectives on order and creation.* Dordrecht: Springer.

Godfray, H. C. J., Beddington, J. R., Crute, I. R., Haddad, L., Lawrence, D., Muir, J. F., ... Toulmin, C. (2010). Food Security: The Challenge of Feeding 9 Billion People. *Science, 327*(5967), 812–818. doi:10.1126cience.1185383 PMID:20110467

Godfray, H. C. J., Crute, I. R., Haddad, L., Lawrence, D., Muir, J. F., Nisbett, N., ... Whiteley, R. (2010). The future of the global food system. *Philosophical Transactions of the Royal Society of London. Series B, Biological Sciences, 365*(1554), 2769–2777. doi:10.1098/rstb.2010.0180 PMID:20713383

Gohari, A., Eslamian, S., Mirchi, A., Abedi-Koupaei, J., Massah Bavani, A., & Madani, K. (2013). Water transfer as a solution to water shortage: A fix that can Backfire. *Journal of Hydrology (Amsterdam), 491*, 23–39. doi:10.1016/j.jhydrol.2013.03.021

Goheen, M. W., & Bartholomew, C. G. (2008). *Living at the Crossroads. An Introduction to Christian Worldview*. Grand Rapids, MI: Baker Academic.

Goldberg, R. M. (2009). How Our Worldviews Shape Our Practice. *Conflict Resolution Quarterly, 26*(4), 405–341. doi:10.1002/crq.241

Goodall, H. L. (2010). *Counter-narrative. How progressive academics can challenge extremists and promote social justice*. Walnut Creek, CA: Left Coast Press.

Gorovitz, S., & MacIntyre, A. (1976). Toward a theory of medical fallibility. *The Journal of Medicine and Philosophy*, *1*(1), 51–71. doi:10.1093/jmp/1.1.51

Goudzwaard, B. (1982). *Kapitalisme en vooruitgang* (4th ed.). Assen: Van Gorcum.

Goudzwaard, B., VanderVennen, M., & David Van Heemst, D. (2007). *Hope in Troubled Times: A New Vision for Confronting Global Crises*. Grand Rapids, MI: Baker Academic.

Goudzwaard, B., & Verweij, M. (2001). Kleine autonomie van het ontwikkelingsbegrip. In G. J. Buijs (Ed.), *Als de olifanten vechten... Denken over ontwikkelingssamenwerking vanuit christelijk perspectief* (pp. 138–154). Amsterdam: Buijten & Schipperheijn.

Granados-Mendoza, P. (2016). *Intensification of the chlor-alkali process using a rotor-stator spinning disc membrane electrochemical reactor* (PhD thesis). Eindhoven University of Technology.

Gray, A. (2016, December 7). *Which countries spend the most on food? This map will show you.* Retrieved October 26, 2018, from https://www.weforum.org/agenda/2016/12/this-map-shows-how-much-each-country-spends-on-food/

Griffiths, J. (2017). *Is the global financial and economic system fit to deliver the Sustainable Development Goals?* Eurodad. Retrieved from https://eurodad.org/files/pdf/1546835-is-the-global-financial-and-economic-system-fit-to-deliver-the-sustainable-development-goals--1509613918.pdf

Grunig, J. E., Grunig, L. A., & Dozier, D. M. (2006). The excellence theory. In C. H. Botan & V. Hazleton (Eds.), *Public Relations Theory II* (pp. 21–62). New York: Lawrence Erlbaum Associates.

Habermas, J. (1984). The Theory of Communicative Action. (2 Vols.; T. A. MacCarthy, Trans.). Boston: Beacon.

Habermas, J. (1996). *Between facts and norms. Contributions to a discourse theory of law and democracy*. Cambridge, UK: Polity Press. doi:10.7551/mitpress/1564.001.0001

Habermas, J. (2006). Religion in the public sphere. *European Journal of Philosophy*, *14*(1), 1–25. doi:10.1111/j.1468-0378.2006.00241.x

Habl, J. (2007). *On Being Human(e). Comenius' Pedagogical Humanization as an Anthropological Problem*. Eugene, OR: Pickwick Publications.

Hafferty, F. W. (2006b). Professionalism—The Next Wave. *The New England Journal of Medicine*, *355*(20), 2151–2152. doi:10.1056/NEJMe068217 PMID:17065632

Harandi, M. F., Yarahmadian, S., Sepehrifar, M., & Van Gelder, P. (2014). The dichotomous Markov process with nonparametric test application; a decision support method in long-term river behavioural analysis: the *Zayandehrud* River; a case study from central Iran. *Stochastic Environmental Research and Risk Assessment*, *28*(7), 1889-1896. doi:10.100700477-014-0854-y

Harandi, M. F., & De Vries, M. J. (2014). An Appraisal of Qualifying Role of Hydraulic Heritage Systems; A Case Study of Qanat in the Central Iran. Journal of Water Science and Technology: *IWA Water Science and Technology. Water Supply Journal*, *14*(6), 1124–1132. doi:10.2166/ws.2014.074

Harandi, M. F., Nia, M. G., & De Vries, M. J. (2015). Water Management: Sacrificing Normative Practice Subverting the Traditions of Water Apportionment—'Whose Justice? Which Rationality?'. *Science and Engineering Ethics*, *21*(5), 1241–1269. doi:10.100711948-014-9593-1 PMID:25300408

Hardeman, E., & Jochemsen, H. (2012). Are There Ideological Aspects to the Modernization of Agriculture? *Journal of Agricultural & Environmental Ethics*, *25*(5), 657–674. doi:10.100710806-011-9331-5

Harmsen, J. (2010). Process intensification in the petrochemicals industry: Drivers and hurdles for commercial implementation. *Chemical Engineering and Processing*, *49*(1), 70–73.

Head, B. W. (2009). From government to governance: explaining and assessing new approaches to NRM. In Contested country: local and regional natural resources management in Australia. Academic Press.

Heidegger, M. (1954). The question concerning technology and Other Essays. In C. Hanks (Ed.), *Technology and values: Essential readings* (pp. 99–113). Singapore: John Wiley & Sons.

Hengeveld, M. H., Vleugel, L., van der Gaag, R. J., Stek, M., & Glas, G. (2009). *Herziening Opleiding en Onderwijs Psychiatrie (HOOP)*. Utrecht: De Tijdstroom.

Hermans, L. (2005). *Actor analysis for water resources management: putting the promise into practice* (PhD thesis). Delft University of Technology, Delft, The Netherlands.

Hermans, L. M., Naber, A. C., & Enserink, B. (2012). An approach to design long-term monitoring and evaluation frameworks in multi-actor systems--a case in water management. *Evaluation and Program Planning*, *35*(4), 427–438. doi:10.1016/j.evalprogplan.2012.01.006 PMID:22391616

Heschel, A. J. (1965). *Who is Man?* Stanford, CA: Stanford University Press.

Hoffjann, O., & Seidenglanz, R. (2018). Allmächtige PR, ohnmächtige PR. Die doppelte Vertrauenskrise der PR. In O. Hoffjann & R. Seidenglanz (Eds.), *Allmächtige PR, ohnmächtige PR. Die doppelte Vertrauenskrise der PR* (pp. 1–14). Wiesbaden: Springer VS. doi:10.1007/978-3-658-18455-1_1

Hoksbergen, R. (1986). Approaches to evaluation of development interventions: The importance of world and life views. *World Development*, *14*(2), 283–300. doi:10.1016/0305-750X(86)90060-4

Holley, C., & Shearing, C. (2017). A nodal perspective of governance: advances in nodal governance thinking. In P. Drahos (Ed.), *Regulatory theory: foundations and applications* (pp. 163–180). Canberra: Australian National University Press. doi:10.22459/RT.02.2017.10

Holt-Giménez, E., & Shattuck, A. (2011). Food crises, food regimes and food movements: Rumblings of reform or tides of transformation? *The Journal of Peasant Studies*, *38*(1), 109–144. doi:10.1080/03066150.2010.538578 PMID:21284237

Hoogland, J., Polder, J.J., Jochemsen, H., & Strijbos, S. (1995). *Professioneel beheerst - Professionele autonomie van de arts in relatie tot instrumenten voor beheersing van kosten en kwaliteit van de gezondheidszorg* [Professional autonomy of the physician in relation to instruments for controlling costs and quality of health care]. Ede, The Netherlands: Prof. dr. G.A. Lindeboom Instituut.

Hoogland, J., & Jochemsen, H. (2000). Professional autonomy and the normative structure of medical practise. *Theoretical Medicine and Bioethics*, *21*(5), 457–475. doi:10.1023/A:1009925423036 PMID:11142442

Hortinext. (2018). *Haalbaarheid CO2-transport Limburg via NAVO-pijpleiding opnieuw onder de loep*. Retrieved August 24 2018 from https://hortinext.nl/haalbaarheid-co2-transport-limburg/

Hossaini, S. (2006). Water use and social organisation in the desert border of Iran. In *Environment agriculture and poverty in developing countries* (pp. 17–32). New Delhi, India: Concept Publishing Company.

Houston, D., Freeman, P., & Feldman, D. (2008). How naked is the public square? Religion, public service, and implications for public administration. *Public Administration Review*, *68*(3), 428–444. doi:10.1111/j.1540-6210.2008.00880.x

Howard, P. H. (2016). *Concentration and Power in the Food System: Who Controls What We Eat?* London: Bloomsbury Publishing.

Hummel-Verhoef, R., & Hooglander, K.-J. (2018). Development and aid in urban contexts. In H. Jochemsen (Ed.), *For the twig to blossom…* (pp. 165–185). Maastricht: Shaker Publishing.

Hu, X. J., Xiong, Y. C., Li, Y. J., Wang, J. X., Li, F. M., Wang, H. Y., & Li, L. L. (2014). Integrated water resources management and water users' associations in the arid region of northwest China: A case study of farmers' perceptions. *Journal of Environmental Management*, *145*, 162–169. doi:10.1016/j.jenvman.2014.06.018 PMID:25026372

Ingram, J. (2011). A food systems approach to researching food security and its interactions with global environmental change. *Food Security*, *3*(4), 417–431. doi:10.100712571-011-0149-9

Irvine, D. (2001). Doctors in the UK: Their new professionalism and its regulatory framework. *Lancet*, *38*(9295), 1807–1810. doi:10.1016/S0140-6736(01)06800-3 PMID:11734261

Irvine, D. (2003). *The Doctors' Tale. Professionalism and Public Trust*. Abingdon, UK: Radcliffe Medical Press.

Jamali, D. (2004). Success and failure mechanisms of public private partnerships (PPPs) in developing countries. Insights from the Lebanese context. *International Journal of Public Sector Management*, *17*(5), 414–430. doi:10.1108/09513550410546598

Jansen, P., Van der Stoep, J., & Jochemsen, H. (2017). Government communication as a normative practice. *Philosophia Reformata*, *82*(2), 121–145. doi:10.1163/23528230-08202004

Jensen, K. M. (2013). Viewpoint–swimming against the Current: Questioning development policy and practice. *Water Alternatives*, *6*(2), 276–283.

Jochemsen, H. (2006). Normative practices as an intermediate between theoretical ethics and morality. *Philosophia Reformata*, *71*(1), 96–112. doi:10.1163/22116117-90000377

Jochemsen, H. (2006b). Voedselethiek vraagt om landbouwethiek. *DenkWijzer. Studieblad van Het Wetenschappelijk Instituut En de Bestuurdersvereniging van de ChristenUnie. Thema Voedsel.*, *6*(3), 8–11.

Jochemsen, H. (2008). Medical practice as the primary context for medical ethics. In N. Weisstub & G. Díaz Pintos (Eds.), *Autonomy and human rights in health care: an international perspective* (pp. 189–204). Dordrecht: Springer. doi:10.1007/978-1-4020-5841-7_14

Jochemsen, H. (2012). Towards sustainable food production: a normative analysis of agrarian practice. In L. Botes, R. Jongeneel, & S. Strijbos (Eds.), *Reintregrating technology and economy in human life and society* (pp. 121–136). Bloemfontein: IIDE/Rozenberg.

Jochemsen, H., & Glas, G. (1997). *Verantwoord medisch handelen*. Amsterdam: Buijten & Schipperheijn.

Jochemsen, H., & Glas, G. (1997). *Verantwoord medisch handelen. Proeve van een christelijke medische ethiek*. Amsterdam: Buijten & Schipperheijn.

Jochemsen, H., & Glas, G. (1997). *Verantwoord medisch handelen: Proeve van een christelijke medische ethiek* [Responsible Medical Action. A Preliminary Draft of Christian Medical Ethics]. Amsterdam: Buijten & Schipperheijn.

Jochemsen, H., & Hoogland, J. (1997). 'De Normatieve Structuur Van De Medische Praktijk. In H. Jochemsen & G. Glas (Eds.), *Verantwoord Medisch Handelen. Proeve Van Een Christelijke Medische Ethiek, Vol.Lindeboomreeks, deel 10* (pp. 64–99). Amsterdam: Buijten and Schipperheijn.

Jochemsen, H., & VanDijke, J. (2018). Hope, action and reflection as perspectives on development cooperation and its future. In H. Jochemsen (Ed.), *For the twig to blossom…*. Maastricht: Shaker.

Johnston, L., & Shearing, C. (2003). *Governing security: explorations in policing and justice*. London: Routledge.

Jones, T. M., & Wicks, A. C. (1999). Convergent stakeholder theory. *Academy of Management Review*, *24*(2), 206–221. doi:10.5465/amr.1999.1893929

Kanes, C. (2010). Challenging professionalism. In C. Kanes (Ed.), *Elaborating Professionalism, Studies in Practice and Theory 5* (pp. 1–16). Dordrecht: Springer.

Kanigel, R. (1997). *The One Best Way. Frederick Winslow Taylor and the Enigma of efficiency*. London: Little, Brown and Company.

Kaul, A. J. (1986). The proletarian journalist: A critique on professionalism. *Journal of Mass Media Ethics*, *1*(2), 47–55. doi:10.1080/08900528609358266

Klein, G. A. (1993). A recognition-primed decision (RPD) model of rapid decision making. In G. A. Kein, J. Orasanu, R. Calderwood, & C. E. Zsambok (Eds.), Decision Making in Action: Models and Methods (Vol. 1, pp. 138–147). Norwood, NJ: Ablex.

Klijn, E. H., & Koppenjan, J. (2012). Governance network theory: Past, present and future. *Policy and Politics*, *40*(4), 587–606. doi:10.1332/030557312X655431

Koppenjan, J. F. M., & Klijn, E. (2004). *Managing Uncertainties in Networks a Network Approach to Problem Solving and Decision Making*. London: Routledge.

Krause, E. A. (1996). *Death of the Guilds: Professions, States and the Advance of Capitalism, 1930 to the Present*. New Haven, CT: Yale University Press.

Kroes, P. A., & Meijers, A. W. M. (2006). Introduction. The dual nature of technical artifacts. *Studies in History and Philosophy of Science*, *37*(1), 1–4. doi:10.1016/j.shpsa.2005.12.001 PMID:16473265

Kunneman, H. (2005). Social work as laboratory for normative professionalisation. *Social Work & Society*, *3*(2), 191–200.

Kuyper, A. (2009). Calvinism. New York: Cosimo. (Originally published 1898)

Kwakkenbos, J. (2012). *Private profit for public good? Can investing in private companies deliver for the poor?* Eurodad. Retrieved from https://eurodad.org/files/pdf/1543000-private-profit-for-public-good-can-investing-in-private-companies-deliver-for-the-poor-.pdf

Lakoff, G. (2006). *Thinking points. Communicating our American values and vision*. New York: Farrar, Strauss & Giroux.

Lambert, D. A., & Scholz, J. B. (2005). *A Dialectic for Network Centric Warfare*. DSTO.

Larson, M. S. (2013). The Rise of Professionalism. Monopolies of Competence and Sheltered Markets. New Brunswick, NJ: Transaction Publishers. (Originally published 1977)

Larson, M. (2003). Professionalism: The third logic. *Perspectives in Biology and Medicine*, *46*(3), 458–462. doi:10.1353/pbm.2003.0037

Laster, J. & Iannotta, B. (2012). Learning from Fratricide-US Deaths in Sangin Valley Bring Long-Sought Tactical Intel Changes. *C4ISR-Journal of Net-Centric Warfare, 11*(2), 24-27.

Latour, B. (1996). *Aramis or the love of technology*. Cambridge, MA: Harvard University Press.

LEO. (2015). *A Framework for a Push/Pull Approach: To Inclusive Market Systems Development*. Washington, DC: United States Agency for International Development (USAID). Retrieved from https://www.marketlinks.org/library/framework-pushpull-approach-inclusive-market-systems-development

Levinson, W., Ginsburg, S., Hafferty, F. W., & Lucey, C. R. (2014). *Understanding Medical Professionalism*. New York: McGraw Hill.

Lindblom, C. (1959). The science of "muddling through". *Public Administration Review*, *19*(2), 79–88. doi:10.2307/973677

Li, T. M. (2007). *The Will to Improve: Governmentality, Development, and the Practice of Politics*. Durham, NC: Duke University Press. doi:10.1215/9780822389781

Loader, I., & Walker, N. (2007). *Civilizing security*. Cambridge, UK: Cambridge University Press. doi:10.1017/CBO9780511611117

Lobkowicz, N. (1967). *Theory and Practice. History of a Concept from Aristotle to Marx*. Notre Dame, IN: University of Notre Dame Press.

Long, N., & Van der Ploeg, J. D. (1989). Demythologizing Planned Intervention: An Actor Perspective. *Sociologia Ruralis*, *29*(3–4), 226–249. doi:10.1111/j.1467-9523.1989.tb00368.x

MacIntyre, A. (1981). *After Virtue: A Study in Moral Theory*. London: Duckworth.

Mahmoudian, M. (1969). *Zayandehrud of Isfahan*. Isfahan, Iran: Isfahan University press. (in Persian)

March, J. G., & Olsen, J. P. (1989). *Rediscovering institutions : The organizational basis of politics*. New York: Free Press.

Marmor, T. R., & Gordon, R. W. (2014). Commercial Pressures on Professionalism in American Medical Care: From Medicare to the Affordable Care Act. *The Journal of Law, Medicine & Ethics*, *42*(4), 412–419. doi:10.1111/jlme.12164 PMID:25565609

McAllister, J., van Praag, E., & van Soest, J. P. (2010). *Earth Fever. Living consciously with climate change*. New York: Cosmo Books.

McMichael, P. (2009). A food regime analysis of the 'world food crisis.'. *Agriculture and Human Values*, *26*(4), 281–295. doi:10.100710460-009-9218-5

McNeil, D., & St Clair, A. L. (2009). *Global poverty, ethics and human rights. The role of multilateral organisations.* London: Routledge. doi:10.4324/9780203881309

Meijboom, F. L. B., Visak, T., & Brom, F. W. A. (2006). Trust to trustworthiness. Why information is not enough in the food sector. *Journal of Agricultural & Environmental Ethics*, *19*(5), 427–442. doi:10.100710806-006-9000-2

Michaels, F. S. (2011). *Monoculture. How one story is changing everything*. Red Clover Press.

Minoia, P. (2012). Mega-Irrigation and Neoliberalism in Postcolonial States: Evolution and Crisis in the Gharb Plain, Morocco. *Geografiska Annaler. Series B, Human Geography*, *94*(3), 269–286. doi:10.1111/j.1468-0467.2012.00414.x

Minten, B., Randrianarison, L., & Swinnen, J. F. M. (2009). Global Retail Chains and Poor Farmers: Evidence from Madagascar. *World Development*, *37*(11), 1728–1741. doi:10.1016/j.worlddev.2008.08.024

Molle, F. (2008). Why enough is never enough: The societal determinants of river basin closure. *International Journal of Water Resources Development*, *24*(2), 217–226. doi:10.1080/07900620701723646

Molle, F., & Mamanpoush, A. (2012). Scale, governance and the management of river basins: A case study from Central Iran. *Geoforum*, *43*(2), 285–294. doi:10.1016/j.geoforum.2011.08.004

Molle, F., Mollinga, P. P., & Wester, P. (2009). Hydraulic bureaucracies and the hydraulic mission: Flows of water, flows of power. *Water Alternatives*, *2*(3), 328–349.

Moloney, K. (2006). *Rethinking public relations. PR propaganda and democracy* (2nd ed.). New York: Routledge. doi:10.4324/9780203030592

Moore, G., & Beadle, R. (2006). In Search of Organizational Virtue in Business: Agents, Goods, Practices, Institutions and Environments. *Organization Studies*, *27*(3), 369–389. doi:10.1177/0170840606062427

Moore, W. E. (1970). *The Professions: Roles and Rules*. New York: The Russell Sage Foundation.

Mottet, A., de Haan, C., Falcucci, A., Tempio, G., Opio, C., & Gerber, P. (2017). Livestock: On our plates or eating at our table? A new analysis of the feed/food debate. *Global Food Security-Agriculture Policy Economics and Environment*, *14*, 1–8. doi:10.1016/j.gfs.2017.01.001

Mouw, R. J., & Griffioen, S. (1993). *Pluralisms and Horizons. An Essay in Christian Public Philosophy*. Grand Rapids, MI: W.B. Eerdmans.

Nair, C. (2014). *Tackling a Drought in Iran*. Retrieved from http://www.nytimes.com/2014/11/10/opinion/tackling-a-drought-in-iran.html?_r=0

Nicolini, D. (2012). *Practice theory, work and organization: an introduction*. Oxford, UK: Oxford University Press.

Noordegraaf, M. (2007). From 'pure' to 'hybrid' professionalism. Present-day professionalism in ambiguous public domains. *Administration & Society*, *39*(6), 761–785. doi:10.1177/0095399707304434

Northouse, P. G. (2013). *Leadership: Theory and Practice* (6th ed.). Los Angeles, CA: Sage.

NRC Handelsblad. (2006). *Laatste chloortrein Akzo is vertrokken* [Last chlorine train Akzo has left]. Author.

OECD & WTO. (2015). *Aid for Trade at a Glance 2015*. Reducing Trade Costs for Inclusive, Sustainable Growth. doi:10.1787/aid_glance-2015-

OECD. (2015). *Keeping the multiple dimensions of poverty at the heart of development*. OECD and Post 2015 reflections, element 1, paper 1. Retrieved from https://www.oecd.org/dac/POST-2015%20multidimensional%20poverty.pdf

Oliver, C. (1990). Determinants of Interorganizational Relationships: Integration and Future Directions. *Academy of Management Review*, *15*(2), 241–265. doi:10.5465/amr.1990.4308156

Osborne, D., & Gaebler, T. (1992). *Reinventing government: how the entrepreneurial spirit is transforming the public sector*. Reading, MA: Addison-Wesley.

Ostrom, E., Gibson, C., Shivakumar, S., & Andersson, K. (2002). *Aid, Incentives, and Sustainability. An Institutional Analysis of Development Cooperation*. Sida Studies in Evaluation 02/01. Retrieved from https://www.sida.se/contentassets/34b423c6b93e41798038c901e30cd4d1/12924.pdf

Ostrom, E. (2010). Analyzing collective action. *Agricultural Economics. International Association of Agricultural Economists*, *41*(s1), 155–166. doi:10.1111/j.1574-0862.2010.00497.x

Ovaska, T. (2003). The failure of development aid. *The Cato Journal*, *23*(2), 175–188.

Overeem, P., & Tholen, B. (2011). After managerialism: MacIntyre's lessons for the study of public administration. *Administration & Society*, *43*(7), 722–748. doi:10.1177/0095399711413728

Oxfam International. (2015). Wealth: having it all and wanting more. *Oxfam issue briefing*. Retrieved from http://www.oxfam.org/en/research/wealth-having-it-all-and-wanting-more

Painter, Ch., & Martins, J. T. (2017). Organizational communication management during the Volkswagen diesel emissions scandal. A hermeneutic study in attribution, crisis management and information orientation. *Knowledge and Process Management*, *24*(3), 204–218. doi:10.1002/kpm.1544

Parsons, T. (1964). The Professions and Social Structure. In T. Parsons (Ed.), Essays in Sociological Theory (rev. ed.; pp. 34-49). New York: Free Press. (Originally published 1939)

Peralta, A. (2017). *Food and Finance. Toward Life-Enhancing Agriculture.* Geneva: World Council of Churches Publications.

Perry, C. (2013). ABCDE+ F: A framework for thinking about water resources management. *Water International*, *38*(1), 95–107. doi:10.1080/02508060.2013.754618

Petit, J. R., Jouzel, J., Raynaud, D., Barkov, N. I., Barnola, J.-M., Basile, I., ... Stievenard, M. (1999). Climate and atmospheric history of the past 420,000 years from the Vostok ice core, Antarctica. *Nature*, *399*(6735), 429–436. doi:10.1038/20859

Petraeus, D. (2011, July 27). *Memorandum for Record - Sangin friendly fire incident.* DoD. Retrieved from https://archive.org/details/295339-new-redacted-roi

Plumecocq, G., Debril, T., Duru, M., Magrini, M.-B., Sarthou, J. P., & Therond, O. (2018). The plurality of values in sustainable agriculture models: Diverse lock-in and coevolution patterns. *Ecology and Society*, *23*(1), art21. doi:10.5751/ES-09881-230121

Pogge, T. (2001). Priorities of global justice. *Metaphilosophy*, *32*(1-2), 6–24. doi:10.1111/1467-9973.00172

Polder, J. J., Hoogland, J., & Jochemsen, H. (1996). *Professie of profijt?* Amsterdam: Buijten & Schipperheijn.

Provan, K., & Kenis, P. (2008). Modes of network governance: Structure, management and effectiveness. *Journal of Public Administration and Theory*, *18*(2), 229–252. doi:10.1093/jopart/mum015

Rademaker, C. J., Glas, G., & Jochemsen, H. (2017). Sustainable livestock farming as normative practice. *Philosophia Reformata*, *82*(2), 216–240. doi:10.1163/23528230-08202002

Rademaker, C. J., & Jochemsen, H. (2018). Beyond Modernization: Development Cooperation as Normative Practice. *Philosophia Reformata*, *83*(1), 1–32. doi:10.1163/23528230-08301007

Rademaker, C. J., & van den Hee, J. (2018). Agribusiness development within the bounds of life-enhancing food systems. In H. Jochemsen (Ed.), *For the twig to blossom... Cooperation in development from a Christian perspective* (Vol. 5, pp. 209–230). Maastricht: Shaker Publishing.

Raworth, K. (2017). *Doughnut Economics. Seven Ways to Think Like a 21st-Century Economist.* New York: Random House Business Books.

Raz, J. (2005). The myth of instrumental rationality. *Journal of Ethics and Social Philosophy*, *1*(1), 2–28.

Reckwitz, A. (2002). Toward a Theory of Social Practices. A Development in Culturalist Theorizing. *European Journal of Social Theory*, *5*(2), 243–263. doi:10.1177/13684310222225432

Reiner, R. (1992). Policing a postmodern society. *The Modern Law Review*, *55*(6), 761–781. doi:10.1111/j.1468-2230.1992.tb00940.x

Ricoeur, P. (1984). *Time and narrative* (Vol. 1). Chicago: The University of Chicago Press.

Rist, G. (2007). Development as a buzzword. *Development in Practice*, *17*(4-5), 485–491. doi:10.1080/09614520701469328

Rittel, H., & Webber, M. (1973). Dilemmas in a general theory of planning. *Policy Sciences*, *4*(2), 155–169. doi:10.1007/BF01405730

Rockström, J., Williams, J., Daily, G., Noble, A., Matthews, N., Gordon, L., ... Smith, J. (2017). Sustainable intensification of agriculture for human prosperity and global sustainability. *Ambio*, *46*(1), 4–17. doi:10.100713280-016-0793-6 PMID:27405653

Röling, N. (2016). Innovation Systems, Douglas, Douglass and Beyond: Using Cultural Theory to understand Approaches to Smallholder Development in Sub-Saharan Africa. In J. Francis, L. Mytelka, A. van Huis, & N. Röling (Eds.), *Innovation systems: Towards effective strategies in support of smallholder farmers* (pp. 202–238). CTA and Wageningen University and Research Centre. Retrieved from https://cgspace.cgiar.org/handle/10568/79166

Rorty, R. (1999). Truth without correspondence to reality. In *Philosophy and social hope* (pp. 23–46). London: Penguin Books.

Rose, N., O'Malley, P., & Valverde, M. (2006). Governmentality. *Annual Review of Law and Social Science*, *2*(1), 83–104. doi:10.1146/annurev.lawsocsci.2.081805.105900

Royal College of Physicians and Surgeons of Canada. (2015). *CanMEDS Framework 2015.* Retrieved from http://www.royalcollege.ca/rcsite/documents/canmeds/canmeds-full-framework-e.pdf

Rueschemeyer, D. (1983). Professional Autonomy and the Social Control of Expertise. In R. Dingwall & P. Lewis (Eds.), *The Sociology of the Professions: Lawyers, Doctors and Others* (pp. 38–53). London: Macmillan. doi:10.1007/978-1-349-16979-5_3

SABIC. (2018). *SABIC demonstrates commitment to sustainable development.* Retrieved August 24 2018 from https://www.sabic.com/en/news/10040-sabic-demonstrates-commitment-to-sustainable-development-at-wef-with-iconic-structure-icehouse

Safaei, M., Safavi, H. R., Loucks, D. P., Ahmadi, A., & van der Krogt, W. (2013). Integrated river basin planning and management: A case study of the *Zayandehrud* River basin, Iran. *Water International*, *38*(6), 724–743. doi:10.1080/02508060.2013.823815

Schatzki, T. R. (2008). Social Practices – A Wittgensteinian Approach to Human Activity and Social Practices. Cambridge, UK: Cambridge University Press. (Originally published 1996)

Schatzki, T. (1996). *Social practices: a Wittgensteinian approach to human activity and the social*. Cambridge, UK: Cambridge University Press. doi:10.1017/CBO9780511527470

Schatzki, T. R., Knorr Cetina, K., & von Savigny, E. (Eds.). (2001). *The Practice Turn in Contemporary Theory*. London: Routledge.

Schein, E. H. (2013). *Humble inquiry. The gentle art of asking instead of telling*. San Francisco: Berrett-Koehler Publishers.

Schein, E. H. (2016). *Humble consulting. How to provide real help faster*. San Francisco: Berrett-Koehler Publishers.

Schmidt, J. J., & Peppard, C. Z. (2014). Water ethics on a human-dominated planet: Rationality, context and values in global governance. *Wiley Interdisciplinary Reviews: Water*, *1*(6), 533–547. doi:10.1002/wat2.1043

Schon, D. (1983). *The reflective practitioner: How professionals think in action*. New York: Basic Books.

Schuilenburg, M., van Steden, R., & Oude Breuil, B. (Eds.). (2014). Positive criminology: reflections on care, belonging and security. The Hague: Eleven.

Schuurman, E. (2003). *Faith and Hope in Technology*. Toronto: Clements Publishing.

Sciulli, D. (2005). Continental Sociology of Professions Today: Conceptual Contributions. *Current Sociology*, *53*(6), 915–942. doi:10.1177/0011392105057155

Scott, J. C. (1998). *Seeing Like a State: How Certain Schemes to Improve the Human Condition Have Failed.* New Haven, CT: Yale University Press.

Searle, J. (1969). *Speech acts: An essay in the philosophy of language*. Cambridge, UK: Cambridge University Press. doi:10.1017/CBO9781139173438

Searle, J. R. (2010). *Making the social world. The structure of human civilization.* Oxford, UK: Oxford University Press. doi:10.1093/acprof:osobl/9780195396171.001.0001

Shah, A. (2011). *Poverty around the world. Global Issues. Social, political, economic and environmental issues that affect us all.* Retrieved from http://www.globalissues.org/article/4/poverty-around-the-world#TheWealthyandthePoor

Shearing, C. (2008). *The nexus policing toolkit.* Canberra: The Australian National University.

Siano, A., Vollero, A., Conte, F., & Amabile, S. (2017). 'More than words'. Expanding the taxonomy of greenwashing after the Volkswagen scandal. *Journal of Business Research, 71*, 27–37. doi:10.1016/j.jbusres.2016.11.002

Sinek, S. (2011). *Start with why. How great leaders inspire everyone tot take action.* New York: Penguin.

Smith, E. A. (2006). *Complexity, Networking and Effects Based Approaches to Operations.* Washington, DC: CCRP Publication Series. doi:10.21236/ADA457293

Smith, J. K. A. (2009). *Desiring the Kingdom. Worship, Worldview and Cultural Formation.* Grand Rapids, MI: Baker Academic.

Smith, N. H. (1995). *Strong hermeneutics. Contingency and moral identity.* London: Routledge.

Sodano, V. (2012). Food Policy Beyond Neo-Liberalism. In D. Erasga (Ed.), *Sociological Landscape: Theories, Realities and Trends* (pp. 375–402). InTech. doi:10.5772/37175

Soeters, J. (2017). Information Sharing in Military and Security Operations. In I. Goldenberg, J. Soeters, & W. H. Dean (Eds.), *Information Sharing in Military Operations* (pp. 1–15). Cham: Springer International Publishing; doi:10.1007/978-3-319-42819-2_1

Soeters, J., & Tresch, T. S. (2010). Towards Cultural Integration in Multinational Peace Operations. *Defence Studies, 10*(1), 272–287. doi:10.1080/14702430903155175

SPIRE. (n.d.). *SPIRE roadmap, A-spire.* Retrieved May 24 2018 via https://www.spire2030.eu/sites/default/files/pressoffice/spire-roadmap.pdf

Stacey, R. (2007). The challenge of human interdependence. Consequences for thinking about the day-to-day practice of management in organizations. *European Business Review, 19*(4), 292–302. doi:10.1108/09555340710760125

Stafleu, M. (2004). On the character of social communities, the state and the public domain. *Philosophia Reformata, 69*(2), 125–139. doi:10.1163/22116117-90000321

Stankiewicz, A., & Moulijn, J. (2000). Process intensification transforming chemical engineering. *Chemical Engineering Progress, 96*(1), 22–34.

Stirrat, R. L. (2000). Cultures of Consultancy. *Critique of Anthropology*, *20*(1), 31–46. doi:10.1177/0308275X0002000103

Stok, L. (2018). Reaching and involving the poorest of the poor. In H. Jochemsen (Ed.), *For the twig to blossom….* (pp. 187-208). Maastricht: Shaker.

Sukhdev, P., May, P., & Müller, A. (2016). Fix food metrics. *NATNews*, *540*(7631), 33. doi:10.1038/540033a PMID:27905460

Sullivan, W. M. (2004). Can professionalism still be a viable ethic? *The Good Society - PEGS*, *13*(1), 15–20. doi:10.1353/gso.2004.0032

Swyngedouw, E. (1999). Modernity and hybridity-The production of nature: Water and modernisation in Spain. *Annals of the Association of American Geographers*, *89*(3), 443–465. doi:10.1111/0004-5608.00157

Tallis, R. (2004). *Hippocratic Oaths. Medicine and its Discontents.* London: Atlantic Books.

Taylor, C. (2007). A secular age. Cambridge, MA: The Belknap press of Harvard University Press.

Taylor, F. W. (1947b). The Principles of Scientific Management. In Scientific Management. London: Harper & Row. (Originally published 1911)

Taylor, C. (1985). *Philosophical papers. Philosophy and the Human Sciences* (Vol. 2). Cambridge, UK: Cambridge University Press. doi:10.1017/CBO9781139173490

Taylor, C. (1989). *Sources of the self: the making of the modern identity.* Cambridge, UK: Cambridge University Press.

Taylor, C. (2007). *A Secular Age.* The Belknap Press of Harvard University Press.

Taylor, F. W. (1947a). Shop Management. In *Scientific Management.* London: Harper & Row. (Original work published 1903)

TEEB. (2018). *The Econonomics of Ecosystems and Biodiversity (TEEB) for Agriculture & Food. Scientific and Economic Foundations Report.* Geneva: UN Environment. Retrieved from http://teebweb.org/agrifood/scientific-and-economic-foundations-report/

Terpstra, J. (2008). Police, local government, and citizens as participants in local security networks. *Police Practice and Research*, *9*(3), 213–225. doi:10.1080/15614260701797520

Tesfaye, H. (2010). *Africa and the Failure of Development Aid: Time for Designing an Exit Strategy.* Retrieved from http://aigaforum.com/articles/Africa_and_the_Failure.htm

Thomas, A. (2000). Development as practice in a liberal capitalist world. *Journal of International Development*, *12*(6), 773–787. doi:10.1002/1099-1328(200008)12:6<773::AID-JID716>3.0.CO;2-7

Thompson, P. B. (2015). *From Field to Fork: Food Ethics for Everyone*. Oxford, UK: Oxford University Press. doi:10.1093/acprof:oso/9780199391684.001.0001

TNO. (n.d.). *TNO roadmap 'Sustainable chemical industry: reducing cost & time to market'*. Retrieved May 24 2018 via https://www.tno.nl/en/focus-areas/industry/roadmaps/sustainable-chemical-industry/

Toner, C. (2006). Military Service as a Practice: Integrating the Sword and Shield Approaches to Military Ethics. *Journal of Military Ethics*, *5*(3), 183–200. doi:10.1080/15027570600911993

UN. (2015). *Sustainable Development Knowledge Platform*. Retrieved August 24 2018 from Https://sustainabledevelopment.un.org/topics/sustainabledevelopmentgoals

UN. (2015). *The Millennium Development Goals Report 2015*. New York: United Nations. Retrieved from http://www.un.org/millenniumgoals/2015_MDG_Report/pdf/MDG%202015%20rev%20(July%201).pdf

van Burken, C. G., & de Vries, M. J. (2012). Extending the theory of normative practices: An application to two cases of networked military operation. *Philosophia Reformata*, *77*(2), 135–154. doi:10.1163/22116117-90000530

van de Lagemaat, D. (1986). *Onderwijzen in ondernemen. Een studie betreffende de didactische voorwaarden en uitwerking van de beginselen van de structuurleer en het exemplarisch leren in relatie tot het middelbaar agrarisch onderwijs* (PhD thesis). Landbouwhogeschool Wageningen, Wageningen.

van de Poel, I., Fahlquist, J. N., Doorn, N., Zwart, S., & Royakkers, L. (2012). The problem of many hands: Climate change as an example. *Science and Engineering Ethics*, *18*(1), 49–67. doi:10.100711948-011-9276-0 PMID:21533835

van den Brink, G. (Ed.). (2016). *Moral sentiments in modern society: a new answer to classical questions*. Amsterdam: Amsterdam University Press. doi:10.2307/j.ctv8pzcx4

Van der Kooy, T.P. (1964). De zin van het economische opnieuw beschouwd. *Koers—maandblad vir calvinistische denke, 32*(1), 2–23.

Van der Stoep, J. (2018). Normative dimensions of corporate communication. In G.J. Buijs & A.K. Mosher (Eds.), The future of creation order: Vol. 2. Order among humans; humanities, social science and normative practices. New York: Springer.

Van der Walt, B. (2006). *When African and Western cultures meet*. Potchefstroom: Institute of Contemporary Christianity in Africa.

van der Wal, Z., de Graaf, G., & Lasthuizen, K. (2008). What's valued most? Similarities and differences between organizational values of the public and private sector. *Public Administration*, *86*(2), 465–482. doi:10.1111/j.1467-9299.2008.00719.x

Van Dunné, J. M., Boeles, P., & Heerma van Voss, A. J. (1977). *Acht civilisten in burger*. Zwolle: Tjeerd Willink.

van Eijnatten, F. M. (1993). *The Paradigm that Changed the Work Place*. Assen: Van Gorkum.

van Hulst, M., de Graaf, L., & van den Brink, G. (2012). The work of exemplary practitioners in neighborhood governance. *Critical Policy Studies*, *6*(4), 434–451. doi:10.1080/19460171.2012.730763

Van Lieshout, P., Went, R., & Kremer, M. (2010). *Less Pretention, More Ambition. Development Policy in Times of Globalization.* Amsterdam: Amsterdam University Press. doi:10.5117/9789089642950

van Marissing, E., Tan, S., & Boutellier, H. (2010). *Het is hier net Amsterdam: een veiligheidsarrangement voor IJburg* [It is just like Amsterdam: a community safety arrangement for IJburg]. Utrecht: Verwey-Jonker Institute.

Van Riel, C. B. M. (2012). *The alignment factor. Leveraging the power of total stakeholder support.* New York: Routledge. doi:10.4324/9780203124536

Van Ruler, B. (2018). Communication theory. An underrated pillar on which strategic communication rests. *International Journal of Strategic Communication*, *12*(4), 367–381. doi:10.1080/1553118X.2018.1452240

Van Ruler, B., & Verĉiĉ, D. (2005). Reflective communication management. Future ways for public relations research. *Communication Yearbook*, *29*, 239–274. doi:10.120715567419cy2901_8

van Steden, R., Boutellier, H., Scholte, R., & Heijnen, M. (2013). 'Beyond crime statistics: The construction and application of a criminogenity monitor in Amsterdam'. *European Journal on Criminal Policy and Research*, *19*(1), 47–62. doi:10.100710610-012-9179-x

van Steden, R., Wood, J., Shearing, C., & Boutellier, H. (2016). The many faces of nodal policing: Team play and improvisation in Dutch community safety. *Security Journal*, *29*(3), 327–339. doi:10.1057j.2013.30

Van Wessel, A., Bennema, M., Hoogland, L.-M., Mulder, C., & Jochemsen, H. (2018). Developments in Humanitarian Aid. In H. Jochemsen (Ed.), *For the twig to blossom...* (pp. 143–164). Maastricht: Shaker.

Van Woerkum, C., & Aarts, N. (2011). Organizing by projective hearing. The active use of a passive sense. *International Journal of Strategic Communication*, *5*(3), 171–182. doi:10.1080/1553118X.2011.566902

Vanlauwe, B., & Giller, K. E. (2006). Popular myths around soil fertility management in sub-Saharan Africa. *Agriculture, Ecosystems & Environment*, *116*(1), 34–46. doi:10.1016/j.agee.2006.03.016

Varinsky, D. (2018, May 29). *The $66 billion Bayer-Monsanto merger just got a major green light — but farmers are terrified.* Retrieved October 26, 2018, from http://www.businessinsider.com/bayer-monsanto-merger-has-farmers-worried-2018-4

Verkerk, M. (2004). *Trust and Power on the Shop Floor. An Ethnographical, Ethical, and Philosophical Study on Responsible Behavior in Industrial Organisations* (Dissertation). Delft: Eburon Academic Publishers.

Verkerk, M.J. (2014). A philosophy-based "toolbox" for designing technology: The conceptual power of Dooyeweerdian philosophy. *Koers – Bulletin for Christian Scholarship, 79*(3), 1-7.

Verkerk, M. J. (2015). A practitioner's reflections on moral leadership: Towards a philosophical foundation. In P. Nullens & S. van de Heuvel (Eds.), *Challenges of Moral Leadership* (pp. 47–72). Leuven: Peeters.

Verkerk, M. J., Holtkamp, F. C., Wouters, E. J. M., & Van Hoof, J. (2017). Professional Practices and User Practices: An Explorative Study in Health Care. *Philosophia Reformata, 82*(2), 167–191. doi:10.1163/23528230-08202001

Verkerk, M. J., Hoogland, J., Stoep, J., & Vries, M. J. (2015). *Philosophy of Technology: an introduction for technology and business students.* Abingdon, UK: Routledge. doi:10.4324/9781315696362

Verkerk, M. J., & Zijlstra, A. (2003). Philosophical analysis of industrial organisations. *Philosophia Reformata, 68*(2), 101–122. doi:10.1163/22116117-90000286

Verkerk, M., Ribeiro, P., Badsen, A., & Hoogland, J. (2018). An explorative philosophical study of envisaging the electrical energy infrastructure of the future. *Philosophia Reformata, 83*(1), 90–110. doi:10.1163/23528230-08301006

Visser, J. (2010). *Down to earth. A historical-sociological analysis of the rise and fall of "industrial" agriculture and of the prospects for the re-rooting of agriculture from the factory to the local farmer and ecology.* Wageningen: Wageningen University. Retrieved from http://edepot.wur.nl/135447

WCED (World Commission on Environment and Development). (1987). *Our Common Future.* United Nations. Retrieved October 31 2018 via http://www.un-documents.net/our-common-future.pdf

Weber, M. (1978). *Economy and Society.* Berkeley, CA: University of Calefornia Press.

Weick, K. E. (1995). *Sensemaking in organizations.* Thousand Oaks, CA: Sage.

Wester, P., Vargas-Velázquez, S., Mollard, E., & Silva-Ochoa, P. (2008). Negotiating surface water allocations to achieve a soft landing in the closed Lerma-Chapala Basin, Mexico. *International Journal of Water Resources Development, 24*(2), 283–296. doi:10.1080/07900620701723778

WFP. (2018). *Zero Hunger*. Retrieved October 26, 2018, from http://www1.wfp.org/zero-hunger

WHO. (2018, February 16). *Obesity and overweight*. Retrieved October 26, 2018, from http://www.who.int/news-room/fact-sheets/detail/obesity-and-overweight

Wigboldus, S., Klerkx, L., Leeuwis, C., Schut, M., Muilerman, S., & Jochemsen, H. (2016). Systemic perspectives on scaling agricultural innovations. A review. *Agronomy for Sustainable Development*, *36*(3), 46. doi:10.100713593-016-0380-z

Winch, P. (1958). *The idea of a social science and its relation to philosophy (Studies in philosophical psychology)*. London: Routledge & Kegan Paul.

Wittgenstein, L. (1968). *Philosophical investigations*. Oxford, UK: Basil Blackwell.

Wolters, A. (1984). *Creation regained*. Grand Rapids, MI: Eerdmans.

Wood, J., & Shearing, C. (2007). *Imagining security*. Cullompton: Willan.

World Bank. (2007). *World Development Report 2008: Agriculture for Development*. Washington, DC: The World Bank.

World Bank. (2015). *Data*. Retrieved from https://data.worldbank.org/

Zhang, Z. (2012). Dam Construction Ethics in China. In S. H. Christensen, C. Mitcham, B. Li, & Y. An (Eds.), *Engineering, development and philosophy: American, Chinese and European perspectives* (Vol. 11). Berlin: Springer. doi:10.1007/978-94-007-5282-5_19

About the Contributors

Marc J. de Vries, Delft University of Technology, the Netherlands, is Professor of Philosophy of Technology and professor of Science and Technology Education. He is the editor-in-chief of the International Journal of Technology Education (Springer) and author of the book Teaching About Technology. An Introduction to Philosophy of Technology for Non-philosophers (Springer, 2016, 2nd edition) as well as co-author of the book Philosophy of Technology: An Introduction for Technology and Business Students (Routledge, 2016).

Henk Jochemsen got his PhD in molecular biology at Leiden University in 1979. He worked in bioethics in a private institute in The Netherlands and held a special chair of Christian medical ethics at the VU University medical centre from 1998- 2009. Subsequently, from 2008 -2018 he held the (part time) special chair of Christian Philosophy at Wageningen University and Research. That same period he was the director of Prisma, association of Christian organizations in development cooperation. He published and lectured widely in the fields of (medical) ethics and also in development studies and sustainable agriculture. He was one of the scholars that in the nineties of last century developed the first version of the Normative Practice Approach.

***

Christine Boshuijzen-van Burken works as postdoctoral researcher at the Eindhoven University of Technology. Her research focuses on technology and ethics. She has a BSc in Human Kinetic Technology (The Hague University of Technology, 2002), a BSc in Mechanical Engineering (Eindhoven, Fontys University of Professional Education, 2004), a MA at the Vrije Universiteit Amsterdam, Faculty of Philosophy (2006) and a PhD at Eindhoven University of Technology (2014). Her dissertation was about ethics and military technology. She worked as postdoctoral researcher at Linnaeus University until 2017, where she analyzed the role of ethics and technology in the sharing economy. Currently she is working on improving humanitarian logistics for refugees on a project called "The Refugee Crisis in Europe: Modeling Humanitarian Logistics". She uses insights from reformational philosophy to clarify normative issues related to technology in different contexts. Christine is also Assistant Director of the OZSW (Dutch Research School for Philosophy) and reserve soldier at the National Reserve Corps. She worked for several years as a mechanical engineer prior to her doctoral studies. Christine is married to Richard and they have two sons.

Gerrit Glas is psychiatrist and philosopher. He did his PhD in Utrecht on 'Concepts of anxiety and anxiety disorders. A clinical and philosophical study' (Lisse/Amsterdam, 1991). Apart from his clinical work as psychiatrist and director of a residency training program (Dimence Groep, Zwolle), he has two chairs, one in philosophy of neuroscience (Amsterdam UMC) and one in Christian philosophy (Dooyeweerd Chair, VU, Amsterdam). His main areas of interest are conceptual and normative issues at the interface between philosophy, psychiatry, neuroscience, and society. Together with Henk Jochemsen and Jan Hoogland he developed the so-called 'normative practice approach' to professional practices, which was further developed in the fields of medicine, nursing, education, communication studies, psychotherapy and agriculture.

Peter Jansen earned a PhD at Wageningen University and is Senior Lecturer at the Department for Journalism and Communication Studies at Ede Christian University of Applied Sciences in the Netherlands.

Corné J. Rademaker studied Animal Sciences (BSc cum laude; MSc cum laude) at Wageningen University and Research (WUR), and Philosophy (MA) at VU University Amsterdam. Currently, he is affiliated with WUR as an external PhD student in Philosophy, working on a thesis on the ethics of agricultural development interventions, with special reference to sub-Saharan Africa.

J. (Jan) van der Stoep is Professor of Journalism and Communication at the Ede Christian University of Applied Sciences in The Netherlands.

Robert J. van Putten, MA, MSc, is PhD-researcher in the Department of Public Administration and Political Science at the Vrije Universiteit Amsterdam. He took degrees in public administration and philosophy.

Ronald van Steden is Associate Professor in Public Administration and Political Science in the Faculty of Social Sciences at the Vrije Universiteit Amsterdam, the Netherlands. His research interests include: public policing, private and plural policing, policing and public health, professional practices, the governance of security, security and citizenship, security and volunteering, and the religious, moral and philosophical dimensions of security.

Maarten Johannes Verkerk (1953) studied chemistry, theoretical physics and philosophy at the University of Utrecht. In 1982 he got his PhD in Material Science at the Technical University Twente in Enschede with the thesis Electrical Conductivity and Interface Properties of Oxygen Ion Conducting Materials. In 2004 he defended a second thesis on the crossing point of organization science, technology and philosophy: Trust and Power on the Shop Floor. An Ethnographical, Ethical and Philosophical Study on Responsible Behaviour in Industrial Organisations. After his PhD he worked as a senior researcher at the Nat. Lab. of Philips in Eindhoven. After that he worked for more than fifteen years in a number of management functions in the industrial sector of Philips in The Netherlands, Germany, and Taiwan. Later on he worked for five years as a director of a psychiatric hospital in Maastricht, The Netherlands. From 2008 to 2017 he was chairman of the board of VitaValley, an innovation network in health care. He is now an independent consultant. Since 2004 he is an extraordinary professor reformational philosophy at the Technical University of Eindhoven and since July 2008 he has a comparable chair at the University of Maastricht. He has published hundreds of articles in national and international journals about materials science, organisation science, movies, innovation, philosophy of technology, ethics of technology, end-of-life, women & church, and sustainability. He is author and co-author of a number of books.

Index

V

W

Z

www.ingramcontent.com/pod-product-compliance
Lightning Source LLC
LaVergne TN
LVHW081343300926
849161LV00008B/2053
* 9 7 8 1 5 2 2 5 8 0 0 6 5 *